THE
UNCONSCIOUS
ABYSS

SUNY SERIES IN HEGELIAN STUDIES

WILLIAM DESMOND, EDITOR

JON MILLS

THE
UNCONSCIOUS
ABYSS

HEGEL'S ANTICIPATION OF
PSYCHOANALYSIS

STATE UNIVERSITY OF NEW YORK PRESS

Published by
STATE UNIVERSITY OF NEW YORK PRESS
ALBANY

© 2002 State University of New York

All rights reserved

Printed in the United States of America

For more information, address
State University of New York Press
90 State Street, Suite 700, Albany, NY 12207

Production and book design, Laurie Searl
Marketing, Fran Keneston

Library of Congress Cataloging-in-Publication Data

Mills, Jon, 1964–
    The unconscious abyss : Hegel's anticipation of psychoanalysis / Jon Mills.
    p. cm. — (SUNY series in Hegelian studies)
    Includes bibliographical references and indexes.
    ISBN 0-7914-5475-4 (alk. paper) — ISBN 0-7914-5476-2 (pbk. : alk paper)
    1. Psychoanalysis and philosophy.   2. Hegel, Georg Wilhem Friedrich, 1770–1831.
    I. Title.   II. Series.

BF175.4.P45 M55   2002
127'.092—dc21   2002017728

10   9   8   7   6   5   4   3   2   1

To my parents

—ab imo pectore

CONTENTS

PREFACE

This book attempts to excavate an element of Hegel's work that has remained virtually buried from visibility within contemporary Hegel scholarship. There has been no extended treatment of Hegel's theory of the unconscious, and apart from a few passing references, what commentary that does exist is in relation to Hegel's rather concise remarks about madness or *Verrücktheit* revealed mainly in the *Zusätze* or Additions to his *Encyclopaedia of the Philosophical Sciences*. It is rather ironic that the subject matter itself has eluded philosophical attention especially since it plays such a vital role in Hegel's philosophy of subjective spirit. The absence of any detailed treatment on the topic is no doubt due to the fact that Hegel himself does not directly address the nature of the unconscious with any precision. What few remarks he does make leave the commentator with the challenge of determining just how the role of the unconscious fits into his theory of mind and to what extent it may be applied to his overall philosophical system.

There seems to be a continued fascination if not a fixation with the *Phenomenology of Spirit* despite the fact that Hegel never considered it to be a central part of his mature philosophy. I should inform the reader up front that this work is not about the *Phenomenology*, but rather about Hegel's contribution to understanding the psychodynamics of the mind. As a philosopher and practicing clinical psychologist trained in the psychoanalytic tradition, I find myself faced with a dual task informed by competing loyalties: namely, to expound with philosophical clarity Hegel's notion of the unconscious abyss while bringing it into contemporary discourse with the discipline most commonly associated with the advancement of psychodynamic thought. By today's standards, Hegel's treatment of subjective spirit constitutes a treatise on psychodynamic psychology, one that merits our serious attention. This is particularly germane given that both philosophy and psychoanalysis remain largely unaware of Hegel's insights on the dynamic unconscious.

Hegel's theory of the abyss has profound implications for understanding his philosophy of mind. One aim of this project is to spark more general interest in

Hegel's *Philosophy of Spirit*, and particularly on what I wish to refer to as his metapsychology—mainly represented by his anthropological and psychological treatment of subjective spirit, a subject area that still remains underappreciated by mainstream Hegel audiences. A secondary goal is to bring Hegel into dialogue with Freud and show that what Hegel has to say is of relevance for psychoanalysis today. One hope is to appeal to the psychoanalytic community to see the value of Hegel and how he enriches our theoretical conception of the nature and status of the unconscious. For both Hegel and Freud, the unconscious is responsible for the generative activity that makes rational self-conscious thought possible. When juxtaposed to contemporary views on the nature and structure of the psyche, Hegel's ideas on the unconscious share many compatibilities with psychoanalysis. While I do not stress a complete convergence between their respective systems, which is neither possible nor desirable, I will attempt to show points of intersection between Hegel's theory of the abyss and Freud's metapsychology. Not only will I argue that Hegel's notion of the unconscious is an indispensable and necessary feature of his entire philosophy, but he anticipates much of what psychoanalysis claims to be its own unique discovery. By bringing Hegel into dialogue with Freud, new vistas emerge that deepen our understanding of psychic reality.

Because I am attempting to appeal to academic philosophers and psychoanalytic theoreticians, as well as professional clinicians, I am not likely to satisfy all readers. Purists will heckle at reading Freud into Hegel and Hegel into Freud, and those unfamiliar with the jargon from each discipline will likely become annoyed when concepts appear either murky or watered down due to pragmatic considerations governing the need to provide intelligible translations. One thing about Hegel's writing style that is generally uncontested is that it is simply deplorable. His use of rhetoric is outdated by modern standards and his choice of certain words—such as "concept" (*Begriff*)—bring forth different meanings. But because I am mainly concerned with illuminating a much neglected area of Hegel scholarship, I find it necessary to retain certain technical language familiar to such audiences while still attempting to provide general accounts of his terms and ideas in contemporary language in order to make his theories more comprehensible. I will consider myself successful if I can reach some kind of middle ground.

Some readers may also object to my interpretation of the development of the ego in Hegel's system, claiming I go too far in importing a psychoanalytic account into his unconscious ontology. Because Hegel says very little about the nature of ego development in relation to the abyss, I feel I must venture into speculative waters and give voice to what can be said about the unconscious ego inferred from the implications of Hegel's actual words. With this speculative confession—to which Hegel's philosophy itself belongs, I ask the reader to keep an open mind with regard to its viability for advancing contemporary modes of thought. With respect, I must extend my apologies to the purist: I hope you will forgive me.

This work stems from an article, "Hegel on the Unconscious Abyss: Implications for Psychoanalysis," *Owl of Minerva*, 1996, 28(1), 59–75, which is largely the basis of the introduction. I have also produced revised portions from various articles that appeared in previous forms: "Theosophic and Neo-Platonic Influences on Hegel's Theory of the Unconscious Abyss," *Colloquia Manilana: Interdisciplinary Journal of the Philippine Dominican Center of Institutional Studies*, 1998, VI, 25–44; "Hegel on the Unconscious Soul," *Science et Esprit*, 2000, 52(3), 321–340; "Hegel on Projective Identification: Implications for Klein, Bion, and Beyond," *The Psychoanalytic Review*, 2000, 87(6), 841–874; "Hegel and Freud on Psychic Reality," *Journal of the Society for Existential Analysis*, 2000, 12(1), 159–183; and "Dialectical Psychoanalysis: Toward Process Psychology," *Psychoanalysis and Contemporary Thought*, 2000, 23(3), 20–54.

I wish to extend my greatest appreciation to the J. William Fulbright Board of Foreign Scholarships and The Foundation for Educational Exchange Between Canada and the United States of America for awarding me a full research scholarship and travel grant for the 1996–1997 academic year which allowed me to conduct invaluable research at the University of Toronto and York University. I am especially indebted to Les Green and the Department of Philosophy at York University for continuing to provide me with staff and research privileges necessary to complete this book. I am also grateful to Andrew MacRae and The Research Institute at Lakeridge Health for providing me a research grant with regard to this project.

I owe a debt of thanks to many people which these words cannot adequately convey. I wish to give my deepest gratitude to John Lachs for his unwavering commitment and personal care as a mentor and friend whose dedication helped bring this project to fruition. I also wish to thank Daniel Berthold-Bond for his receptivity and detailed comments and suggestions while preparing this book for publication. I am further beholden to John Burbidge for his consultation, correspondence, and receiving my personal visits to discuss crucial aspects of Hegel's texts, to John Russon for his detailed critical feedback and suggestions, and to Errol Harris and Jay Bernstein for their availability, correspondence, and direction regarding significant portions of the manuscript. The staff at the State University of New York Press have been a fabulous team to work with: I am deeply grateful to Jane Bunker, Senior Acquisitions Editor, and Laurie Searl, Production Manager, for their openness and enthusiasm in using my painting on the front cover. I also want to thank Fran Keneston for her marketing ideas and effort, and Alan Hewat, Copy Editor, for not butchering my manuscript. Finally, I wish to thank most of all my wife Nadine for her love, encouragement, and support during my times of intense preoccupation with this project.

A NOTE ON THE TEXTS

From the *Encyclopaedia*, M. J. Petry (Ed.) outlines Section 1 of Hegel's Philosophy of Spirit in *Hegel's Philosophy of Subjective Spirit*, Vol.1: Introductions; Vol.2: Anthropology; and Vol.3: Phenomenology and Psychology (Dordrecht, Holland: D. Reidel Publishing Company, 1978). Petry's edition provides a photographic reproduction of Hegel's original text published in 1830 along with the *Zusätze* added by Boumann when the material was republished in 1845. Petry's edition also indicates variations between the 1927 and 1830 editions of the *Encyclopaedia*. His edition has several decisive advantages over A. V. Miller's edition of the *Philosophie des Geistes* translated as the *Philosophy of Mind*. In addition to having the original German text and his notations of the variations between the 1827 and 1830 editions, Petry also provides notes from the *Griesheim* and *Kehler* manuscripts. He further provides an accurate translation of the word *unconscious* (*bewußtlos*) whereas Miller refers to the "subconscious." For these reasons Petry's edition is a superior text to the Miller translation. For comparison, I have also examined Hegel's 1827–1828 lectures on the Philosophy of Spirit: *Vorlesungen über die Philosophie des Geistes* (Hamburg: Felix Meiner, 1994). I have mainly relied on Petry's translation but provide my own in places that warrant changes. References to the Philosophy of Spirit (*Die Philosophie des Geistes*), which is the third part of Hegel's *Enzyklopädia*, will refer to *EG* followed by the section number. References to the *Zusätze* are identified as such.

I have taken some liberties in translating the German noun *Schacht* as *abyss*. Hegel clearly seems to prefer the word *Schacht* (shaft, pit, mine) to *Abgrund* (abyss, chasm) to stress the wealth of content contained in the unconscious soul. Yet Hegel does refer to an unconscious *Abgrund* in the Anthropology while principally relying on the use of *Schacht* in the Psychology. There is a difference between these terms and their connotations in standard, everyday German; for example, in mining a *Schacht* is a manhole. Perhaps translating them by a common word is at best a convenience forced by the fact that it is hard to find two words similar enough in English to convey their respective differences. However, to use the word *Schacht*, as Hegel does, to stress the abundance of images and content deposited in the pit of the soul, is highly unusual. *Schacht* is and was practically never used figuratively or symbolically in this context, not even in past centuries, thus Hegel himself takes much idiosyncratic, poetic liberty when using the term in this way.

Furthermore, *Schacht* and *Abgrund* overlap in their meanings in a number of relevant ways. A blurring of their distinctions is especially apparent when referring to the unplumbed depths of the human soul (*die Abgründe der menschlichen Seele*). The word *Abgrund* is also used in other contexts: *Abgrundtiefer Jammer*, for instance, signifies a miserable sorrow as deep as an abyss. *Abgrund* or *Abgründe* also has a frightening, uncanny connotation which indicates something cryptic, mysterious, or that which cannot be entirely known. *Die Abgründe der Hoelle* (the abyss of hell) is a frequently used expression implying the presence of uncontrollable or dangerous forces, such as demons or dragons. In other words, Freud's *id*, the pressure of the drives, as well as depression or madness reside in the *Abgrund*, and any soul would desire to emerge from it.

For Hegel, the abyss is the materiality of Nature from which the soul struggles to free itself, intimately tied to a sentient unconscious activity. I believe the significance of the term *abyss* captures a broader range of meanings associated with unconscious processes and contents, which Hegel clearly specifies in both the Anthropology and the Psychology. Furthermore, he uses the term *unconscious* (*bewußtlos*) when referring to both the abyss of the soul and the ego. Finally, we must consider the impact of Hegel's historical predecessors on the formation of his thought, a subject matter I carefully consider in chapter 1. What is especially significant is Jacob Boehme's use of the term *Ungrund* to explain the Godhead's dialectical manifestation from its original undifferentiated non-being, a process similar to Hegel's treatment of the soul. From Boehme to Schelling—who makes multiple references to an unconscious *Abgrund*—along with many neo-Platonic thinkers to which Hegel was exposed, Hegel's use of *Schacht* presupposes multiple meanings. For these reasons I believe I am justified in using the term *abyss* to capture the myriad processes that dynamically inform the unconscious mind.

Attempts have been made to use gender neutral referents; however, for the sake of euphony, and to avoid awkward locutions such as "s/he," I have used the traditional masculine form to signify both sexes. Most references cited in the text refer to the following abbreviations followed by their volume, section, and/or page numbers. For complete details, see the Bibliography:

CPR   *Critique of Pure Reason*

EG   *Philosophie des Geistes*, trans. *The Philosophy of Spirit*, Part 3 of the *Encyclopaedia of the Philosophical Sciences*

EL   *Encyclopaedia Logic*, Vol. 1 of the *Encyclopaedia of the Philosophical Sciences*

HP   *Lectures on the History of Philosophy*, 3 Vols.

PH   *Philosophy of History*, 3 Vols.

PM   *Philosophy of Mind*, Vol. 3 of the *Encyclopaedia of the Philosophical Sciences*

PN   *Philosophy of Nature*, Vol. 2 of the *Encyclopaedia of the Philosophical Sciences*

PR   *Philosophy of Right*

PS   *Phenomenology of Spirit*

RH   *Reason in History*, the Introduction to the *Lectures on the Philosophy of History*

SE   *Standard Edition of the Complete Psychological Works of Sigmund Freud*, 24 Vols.

SL   *Science of Logic*

STI   *System of Transcendental Idealism*

W   *Wissenschaftslehre*, trans. *The Science of Knowledge*

Come now therefore, and let us slay him,
and cast him into some pit, and we will say,
Some evil beast hath devoured him: and we
shall see what will become of his dreams.

Genesis, 37: 20

abyss (ə-bĭ́s) *n.* **1. a.** The primeval chaos. **b.** The bottom-less pit; hell. **2.** An unfathomable chasm; a yawning gulf. **3.** An immeasurably profound depth or void. **4.** Night, space, darkness. **5. a.** An underground. **b.** A mine. **6.** Nether-regions; the Underworld. [LLat. *abyssus* < Gk. *abussos*, bottomless: *a-*, without + *bussos*, bottom.]

INTRODUCTION

HEGEL MAKES VERY FEW references to the unconscious. In fact, his account is limited to only a few passages in the *Phenomenology of Spirit* and the *Encyclopaedia of the Philosophical Sciences*. While Hegel did not explicitly develop a formal theory of the unconscious, nor include it as a central element of his Anthropology or Psychology, he certainly did not ignore the notion. From the *Encyclopaedia*, Hegel talks of the unconscious processes of intelligence as a "nightlike abyss." For reasons I will soon detail, it is important to understand what Hegel means by this nocturnal abyss and how it figures so prominently in his philosophy of subjective spirit. Despite a few noteworthy exceptions that focus on Hegel's theory of mental illness,[1] Hegel's treatment of the unconscious has been largely overlooked.[2] It will be the overall focus of this present work to give systematic voice to Hegel's rather terse view of the unconscious abyss, and through extrapolation, show how it is an indispensable aspect of his entire philosophy. Juxtaposed to psychoanalytic theory, the ontology of the abyss promises to offer significant advances in psychodynamic thought, which may further pave the way for a new movement in psychoanalysis I will call "process psychology," or "dialectical psychoanalysis."

UNCONSCIOUSNESS AND THE UNCONSCIOUS

There are three primary ways of understanding and interpreting any thinker and the philosophical implications of his or her thought. Understanding Hegel, or any other philosopher for that matter, may be facilitated by examining (*a*) the historical precursors that influenced his thinking, (*b*) what he actually says in his texts, and (*c*) the philosophical ideas that grew out of his thought. These three elements inform the purpose and overall structure of this project, showing how Hegel's notion of the unconscious draws on a number of historical figures, is revealed with depth and consistency in his own writings, and may be interpreted

1

from the standpoint of contemporary theories of mind continuous with his postulations on unconscious mental life. Within this context, it becomes important to understand how Hegel's conceptual treatment of the unconscious was informed by his historical predecessors, including the influence of neo-Platonism, theosophic Christianity, early German Idealism, and Natural Philosophy, and how he theoretically appropriated this knowledge and made it part of his own philosophical system. Examining his likely precursors, and the similarities and differences that exist between their respective philosophies, prepares us to engage Hegel's texts with careful precision.

Our understanding of Hegel's position and its implications becomes even broader if we interpret him through the psychoanalytic theories of Freud. While giving meticulous attention to Hegel's texts, I wish to show that the set of ideas among Hegel's successors increase our appreciation of the depth of his contributions to understanding the dynamic processes of the psyche.

In providing a systematic and coherent account of Hegel's theory of the unconscious, I will argue throughout this book that he anticipated much of what psychoanalysis was later to make more intelligible. Because psychoanalysis comes out of the intellectual milieu that was prepared by Hegel, using Freud to read Hegel aids in our appreciation of how revolutionary both of these thinkers were in impacting the way in which we have come to understand the mind. It is in this manner that we can see how Hegel's ideas transcend his time, and how easily we can read Hegel informed by psychoanalytic perspectives. What becomes particularly germane to the question of applied Hegelian theory is whether or not it is able to withstand the scrutiny of contemporary interrogation and prove its relevance to our current understanding of human nature. For Hegel, as for psychoanalysis, the unconscious is a pivotal concept in our comprehension of *Geist*.

The word *Geist* is customarily translated as spirit or mind,[3] but the English equivalents do not capture the full meaning of the term in German. A person's *Geist* signifies the complex integration of his or her intellectual capacity, insight, depth, and personal maturity, and it is a term that always implies a measure of respect for its superiority. Hegel, for instance, and Freud, are *grosse Geister*, literally, "big spirits." To say of someone that he has *einen grossen Geist* is a great compliment and praise for his personality as a whole. A child or average person has *einen kleinen Geist* (a small spirit), meaning he is unable to have a deep insight into the complexities of life, is probably not very intelligent, and will likely fall prey to his petty desires and flaws. While all human beings are primarily equal in terms of their soul (*Seele*), individuals are very unequal in terms of the development and quality of their *Geist*. The term is used for God as well—*der heilige Geist* (the holy ghost)—and thus carries with it a further sense of exaltation. The English word *mind* is much more reductionistic in scope and pertains more to intellectual capacities and biological functioning. There is no corresponding term in German. *Geist*, however, truly combines mind and spirit and always implies a high level of awareness or self-consciousness. This is why for Hegel, Spirit is the process and culmination of pure subjectivity, the coming into being of pure self-consciousness.

Hegel employs the term *unconscious* (*bewußtlos*) in a few limited contexts, in which it carries a variety of meanings. In modern, ordinary German, *bewußtlos* is used principally as a medical term, such as when a person is in a coma, while "unconscious" in Hegel's sense would be translated by today's standards as *unbewußt*, a usage adopted by the time of Freud. While not formally distinguished by Hegel, we may say there are six distinct usages of unconsciousness: (1) that which lacks consciousness, such as the Idea outside of itself instantiated in nature, thus, an unconsciousness that in principle cannot be made conscious; (2) a state or condition of spirit as non or *un*self-consciousness; (3) a realm that is other-than or dialectically opposed to consciousness; (4) that which is outside of or beyond spirit in its current moment, which we may either attribute to (*a*) the realm of pure potentiality not yet actualized by spirit (which would correspond to the second definition), or (*b*) that which is negativity itself and thus a central feature in spirit's development; (5) that which was once conscious but became concealed from self-awareness (as in repression); and (6) a pre-rational unconscious ground or abyss (*Schacht, Abgrund,* or *Ungrund*) that serves as the foundation for all forms of spirit to manifest themselves. This last definition will concern us the most, because Spirit emanates from and is the logical completion of an unconscious ontology.

While Hegel acknowledges the unconscious dimension of world spirit,[4] he largely limits the scope of the unconscious to individual psychology. Hegel tells us that the "*concrete existence*" of spirit as "the *I* or pure self-consciousness" resides in the domain of "*individual personality*" (*SL*, 583). Always in a state of turbulent activity, the ego (*Ich*) as pure self-consciousness is individual personality in the form of Self (*Selbst*). For Hegel, the self as a process of becoming is a complex whole whose "own restless nature impels it to actualize itself, to unfold into actuality . . . that whole, of which to begin with it contained only the possibility" (*EG* § 398, *Zusatz*). In its conceptual totality, the self is the Absolute as the Concept or complex whole.[5]

In common language, spirit is a developmental process of self-actualization realized individually and collectively through reflective, contemplative thought and action. The notion of spirit encompasses a principle of complex holism whereby higher stages of development are attained through dynamic, laborious dialectical mediation. At its apex, subject and object, mind and matter, the particular and the universal, the finite and the infinite—are mutually implicative yet subsumed within the Absolute or Whole process under consideration. This is what Hegel refers to as the "Concept" (*Begriff*), or what we may more appropriately translate as "comprehension." *Begriff* is the noun to the verb *begreifen*, literally, "to grasp with one's hands." *Begreifen* implies a depth of understanding, an ability to fully comprehend all aspects of a subject matter or thing under question. Therefore, *Begriff* is a concise one-word description that captures the essence of something, namely spirit, what we aim to comprehend.

Hegel's account of the concrete actuality of the Concept as individual personality may be said to present a theory of human psychology with unconscious elements always prefiguring intrapsychic and logical operations of thought. In fact, the unconscious makes thought possible. Yet for Hegel, individuality is ultimately explained within the larger context of a collective historical anthropology that informs human relations and the coming to presence of pure self-consciousness. In this sense, we may say that the unconscious is not only non self-consciousness, which is much of world history until spirit returns to itself and comes to understand its process, but is furthermore the competing and antithetical organizations of "impulses" (*Triebe*) that are "instinctively active," whose "basis is the soul [*Seele*] itself" (*SL*, 37), which informs spirit's burgeoning process.

Hegel is concerned not only about explaining individual psychology, but also about providing a universal, anthropological account of humankind. For Hegel, individuality is ultimately subordinated to higher social orders constituted in society by participating in the ethical life (*Sittlichkeit*) of a collective community. This participation rests on the development of a continuous psychosocial matrix of relations that has its origin in the family. The communal spirit and the ethical law embodied within the family of communal consciousness arises from "the power of the nether world" (*PS* § 462)—what one might not inappropriately call the collective unconscious. For Hegel, collective spirit "binds all into one, solely in the mute unconscious substance of all" (*PS* § 474). This "unconscious universality" contains the ethical order as divine law as well as the "pathos" of humanity, the "darkness" of the "underworld" (*PS* § 474). Hegel states:

> [H]uman law proceeds in its living process from the divine, the law valid on earth from that of the nether world, the conscious from the unconscious, mediation from immediacy—and equally returns whence it came. The power of the nether world, on the other hand, has its actual existence on earth; through consciousness, it becomes existence and activity. (*PS* § 460)

Almost a full century before the emergence of depth psychology, Hegel's psychological insights are profound. In this passage, he clearly recognizes that the personal and collective unconscious developmentally and logically precedes consciousness and further sees that each domain maintains its dialectical relation with the other.[6]

Universal self-conscious Spirit "becomes, through the individuality of man, united with its other extreme, its force and element, *unconscious* Spirit" (*PS* § 463). Yet as Hegel points out, there is always a fundamental tension between the drive toward individuality and subordination to the collective:

> The Family, as the *unconscious*, still inner Concept [of the ethical order], stands opposed to its actual, self-conscious existence; as the *element* of the nation's actual existence, it stands opposed to the nation itself; as the *immediate* being of the ethical order, it stands over against that order which shapes and maintains itself by working for the universal. (*PS* § 450)

The family is the locus of identification and the determinant stimulus for the internalization of value—the Ideal. As a result, it becomes the matrix affecting the deep structures of the unconscious and the organization of social life. Yet for Hegel, the dialectical tensions organized within the unconscious of the individual and the collective unconscious of the community will always ensure "a conflict of self-conscious Spirit with what is unconscious" (*PS* § 474).

The universalization or actualization of the unconscious becomes important for Hegel in the depiction of spirit as a dynamically informed, self-articulated totality or complex whole. Thus, he not only focuses on human psychology and collective unconscious forces that determine individual and social relations, but also points to the generic structural operations of the mind that have their origins in the unconscious, which make human consciousness and thought possible. It is this latter point that we will be concerned with here. In the Second Preface to the *Science of Logic*, Hegel states:

> The activity of thought which is at work in all our ideas, purposes, interests and actions is, as we have said, *unconsciously* busy. . . . [E]ach individual animal is such individual primarily because it is an animal: if this is true, then it would be impossible to say what such an individual could still be if this foundation were removed. (*SL*, 36–37, italics added)

Hegel is clear that unconscious activity underlies all dimensions of human subjectivity, from the determinate negativity of death and desire to the emergence of thought and higher forms of reason. He further underscores the point that the unconscious is tied to our natural constitution or animal evolutionary past. The notion of the unconscious as determinate negativity is the dynamic foundation or ground of spirit and is therefore at least partly responsible for its dialectical ascendence toward the Absolute, or what we may call absolute conceiving. In the night of the mind, desire and reason coexist in dialectical tumult as spirit attempts to develop a unity from its unconscious beginnings. For the purpose of giving systematic structure to Hegel's theory of unconscious spirit, it becomes important to explore this fundamental relation between desire and reason first instantiated as a primal ground or *abyss*. By way of a preliminary introduction to Hegel's views on the abyss, let us turn our attention to a succinct overview of his specific treatment of the unconscious within the domain of subjective spirit and the feeling soul.

UNCONSCIOUS SPIRIT AND THE FEELING SOUL

In order to understand Hegel's position on the unconscious modes of subjective spirit, we must focus repeatedly on the dialectical organizations, operations, contents, and intrapsychic structures that are developed in the evolutionary process of the unconscious. I will show that Hegel's account of the contents and operations of the mind as *aufgehoben* is also the structural foundation of the unconscious. On this point, the role of subjectivity in Hegel's philosophy, as this applies to the unconscious mind, is especially important. Throughout his philosophy,

Hegel insists that a subjective ground is the necessary precondition for any cognition that experiences something as objective.[7] Despite the drive toward the Concept (*Begriff*) as authentic reason progressively seeks objective truth, subjectivity as such is never abandoned for a new truth; it is, however, preserved within its new forms and coexists with universality. Therefore, at various levels of the phenomenology, the subjective components of the dialectic will have greater unconscious influence on the vicissitudes of the self in its ascendance toward the Absolute. For Hegel, the abyss is the ultimate ground from which consciousness emerges, and is pure determinate negation which is present throughout the development of spirit. By virtue of its unconscious ontology, the realm of the abyss is a central principle in the phenomenology of spirit.

Hegel gives most of his attention to the unconscious within the stage of presentation (*Vorstellung*), which belongs to the development of theoretical spirit. He refers to a "nightlike abyss within which a world of infinitely numerous images and presentations is preserved without being in consciousness" (*EG* § 453). Hegel offers no explanation of the nature of this nocturnal abyss; he says only that it is a necessary presupposition for imagination and for higher forms of intelligence.[8] These more complex forms of the psychological would not be possible without the preservation of presentations and images in the abyss. Prior to this stage in the development of theoretical spirit, Hegel makes no specific reference to the unconscious abyss in the Psychology. But even if it is not explicitly mentioned, the occurrence of the abyss is already prepared, its existence already implicit in the most archaic forms of the individual, that of the feeling soul and the nascent ego of consciousness.

> [S]pirit attains to absolute being-for-self, to the form which is completely adequate to it. Through this alone it rouses itself from the somnolent state in which it finds itself as soul, since in this state difference is still shrouded in the form of lack of difference and hence unconsciousness. (*EG* § 389, *Zusatz*)

In the *Phenomenology*, Hegel initially defines consciousness as the manifestation of the being of the world to a subject who is not self-conscious or reflectively aware of itself as self. "[C]onsciousness is '*I*', nothing more, a pure 'This'; the singular consciousness knows a pure 'This', or the single item" (*PS* § 91). In the *Encyclopaedia* Phenomenology, he says the same thing: "Initially, consciousness is immediate, and its relation to the general object is therefore the simple unmediated certainty it has of it" (*EG* § 418). The presence of subjective spirit, particularly in its initial unfolding as soul and then as ego, is what I shall refer to as the primal domain of *Unconscious Spirit*. The movement of subjective spirit has its genesis in the unconscious, that is, spirit originally manifests itself as the unconscious. Without equivocation, the abyss is the birthplace of spirit.

> Spirit has determined itself into the truth of the simple immediate totality of the soul and of consciousness. . . . The beginning of spirit is therefore nothing but its own being, and it therefore relates itself only to its own determinations. (*EG* § 440)

As the natural soul, the unconscious is spirit's initial being, "the immediacy of spirit" (*EG* § 412).

For Hegel, the unconscious is merely the immediate determinateness of spirit which manifests itself in two primary modes, namely, as soul and then as the ego of consciousness. Initially, spirit remains hidden to itself, an enigma, asleep within the abyss of its own inwardness, and thus the unconscious is its presupposition.[9] As incarnate, the soul is the core totality of the nascent self as the permeation of spirit, making itself known as consciousness, which is spirit's presence as such. Hegel says, "As soul, spirit has the form of substantial universality" (*EG* § 414), which then assumes its next shape as consciousness. The soul therefore developmentally comes before consciousness. However, consciousness as ego is spirit's ability to make itself an object or reify itself within its own being. Hegel explains:

> As ego, spirit is essence, but since reality is posited in the sphere of essence as immediate being, . . . spirit as consciousness is only the appearance of spirit. (*EG* § 414)

Sensuous consciousness only knows itself as being, a "singular," an "existing thing" (*EG* § 418). Hegel refers here to the subjective existence of the self as a personal, singular "I," with the character of "self-identity" (*EG* §§ 414, 415). From this standpoint, spirit in its initial shape as *I* takes its form as "mine," in the mode of personal identity. Within this context, the unconscious is the subjective ground of the most primitive levels of individuality. This pure or original consciousness, the formal "I," resides within the realm of the abyss, outside our immediate self-conscious awareness of such activity.[10] The soul becomes the formal paradigm for the ego of consciousness because "the soul is already *implicitly ego* in so far as it is subjectivity or selfhood" (*EG* § 412, *Zusatz*). Although this immediate form of consciousness is not yet elevated to perceptive or understanding consciousness, it contains the primal content of feelings, which is the "material of consciousness" and "what the soul is and finds in itself in the anthropological sphere" (*EG* § 418). Hence, within the realm of the subject, unconscious spirit resonates within the soul as feeling and ego. The feeling soul becomes the primary domain of the abyss. Not yet explicit or developed, lacking in articulation and structure, what remains is for it to become explicit in theoretical spirit.

Hegel considers feeling in relation to three different stages in the evolution of subjective spirit. First, feeling belongs to the soul awakening from its self-enclosed natural life to discover within itself the "content-determinations of its sleeping nature" (*EG* § 446, *Zusatz*). The soul comes to feel the totality of its self and awakens into consciousness as ego. Second, in consciousness, feeling becomes the material content of consciousness, distinct from the soul and appearing as an independent object. Third, feeling becomes the "initial form assumed by *spirit as such*," which is the truth and unity of the soul and consciousness (*EG* § 446, *Zusatz*). Before spirit's final transition from feeling to reason, every content of consciousness originally exists and is preserved within the mode of feeling. Thus, for Hegel, the life of feeling is inextricably associated with the domain of the unconscious abyss in all its archaical shapes.

On Hegel's account, the feeling soul unfolding dialectically is tantamount to the nascent self as unconscious spirit unified in the soul and expressed as consciousness. Therefore, the natural soul is the heart of unconscious spirit, intuiting itself as such, and feeling its own being. The unconscious awakening of spirit within its own internal slumbers, and thus the feeling of its totality as its essence in consciousness, unites the soul and spirit in the abyss of their own determinations.

THE INTELLIGENCE OF THE ABYSS

Subjective spirit, in its theoretical modes, expresses itself as cognition actively concerned with finding reason within itself (*EG* § 445). As the stages of the forms of theoretical spirit unfold, the unconscious abyss appears to be the primary domain of this activity. Hegel points out that intelligence follows a formal course of development to cognition beginning with knowledge as (*a*) intuition of an immediate object, to (*b*) presentation, as a withdrawal into itself from the relationship to the singularity of the object and thus relating such object to a universal, leading to (*c*) thought in which intelligence grasps the concrete universals of thinking and being as objectivity. In the stage of intuition as immediate cognizing, intelligence begins with the sensation of the immediate object, then alters itself into attention by fixing on the object while differentiating itself from it, and then posits the material as external to itself, or as "self-external," which becomes intuition proper. The second main stage of intelligence as presentation is concerned with recollection, imagination, and memory, while the final stage in the unfolding of intelligence is thought, which has its content in understanding, judgment, and reason.

As the dialectical forms of intelligence progress, unconscious spirit posits intuition as its own inwardness, recollects itself within it, becomes present to itself, and thus by passing into itself raises itself to the stage of presentation (*EG* § 450). From the standpoint of presentation (*EG* § 451), the various forms of spirit manifest themselves as "singularized and mutually independent powers or faculties" (*EG* § 451, *Zusatz*). Within recollection, the unconscious content is "involuntarily" called forth. The presented content is that of intuition, not only intuited as being, but also recollected and posited as "mine." This unconscious content of intuition is what Hegel calls "image" (*Bild*). In the sphere of imagination, the presented content enters into opposition with the intuited content, in which "imagination works to gain for itself a content which is peculiar to it" and thus seeks to universalize it. As presentation enters into the stage of memory, the unification of the subjective and the objective constitutes the transition to thought (*EG* § 451, *Zusatz*).

Within its initial recollection, however, the "image" that becomes the focal point of intelligence is posited as feeling the inwardness of its own space and time (*EG* § 452). This is spirit taking up what has been put forth by intuition and positing it as spirit's own content.

> Intelligence is not, however, only the consciousness and the determinate being, but as such the subject and implicitness of its own determinations; recollected within it, the image is no longer existent, but is preserved unconsciously. (*EG* § 453)

Here, Hegel points to the Concept of intelligence as the being-for-self, capable of presenting itself to itself as a determined object, and preserving such image within the most remote regions of the abyss. "In another respect therefore, . . . intelligence [is] this unconscious abyss" (*EG* § 453). Unconscious spirit first becomes aware of its existence as feeling; it feels its very life and senses itself as such united in the most rudimentary forms of its intelligibility. Hegel continues:

> The image is mine, it belongs to me: initially however, this is the full extent of its homogeneity with me, for it is still not *thought*, not raised to the *form* of *rationality*, . . . and being not free but a relationship according to which I am merely the *internality*, while the image is something external to me. Initially, therefore, I still have an imperfect control of the images slumbering within the abyss of my inwardness, for I am unable to recall them *at will*. No one knows what an infinite host of images of the past slumbers within him. Although they certainly awaken by chance on various occasions, one cannot,—as it is said,—call them to mind. They are therefore only *ours* in a *formal* manner. (*EG* § 453, *Zusatz*)

Hegel's characterization of the unconscious life within the subject points to the activity of the unconscious which becomes unified in consciousness as the "internality" of the self, and yet is a distinct form of consciousness in which the subject does not control. More precisely, it is consciousness that is a modified form of unconscious structure, whereas the degree, content, and context of awareness become the critical factor that distinguishes the two. Hegel acknowledges the activity of the unconscious abyss, as limitless, infinite, and inaccessible to the conscious will. This conceptualization is similar to psychoanalytic accounts of the unconscious in which drives or impulses (*Triebe*) in the form of wishes as "image" simultaneously press for expression, yet remain repressed within one's "internality" as the abyss of "inwardness," unavailable to immediate introspective self-reflection.

When theoretical spirit continues on its journey from intuition to thought, the role of imagination within presentation becomes important for understanding the influence of the abyss. For Hegel, as for Kant, imagination mediates between intuition and thought. Therefore, imagination belongs to spirit. More precisely, imagination has its place almost exclusively within psychological spirit. Within presentation, imagination is an intermediate faculty of spirit, surfacing between recollection and memory. As Hegel noted in recollection, the content of intuition in its new form as image is "preserved" as "unconsciousness" (*EG* § 453). Therefore, images sleeping in the depths of the abyss can be called forth, related to an intuition, yet separated from both the abyss and intuition. Thereby, the birth of the image for-us becomes the contents of imagination. From this standpoint, imagination determines images, first in reproductive imagination (§ 455), as reproducing images called forth by intuition, second, in associative imagination (§ 456), by elevating images as presentations to the level of universality, and third, in phantasy (§ 457), as a determinant being in the forms of symbols and signs. Hegel ultimately sees imagination through to its end. Following a dialectical course, the image becomes surpassed and integrated into higher shapes of theoretical spirit.

Hegel's account of spirit's movement within presentation ultimately ends with spirit discovering and sublating itself within "phantasy as reason." Thus, for Hegel, imagination is subordinated to cognition as spirit recovers itself in the image. However, the transition from phantasy to reason poses a problem for spirit. Because imagination mediates between intuition and thought, it is susceptible to the powers of the unconscious. Due to the autonomy of unconscious forces and organizations, it is conceivable that the abyss resists the dialectical sublation of its own becoming. John Sallis raises the question: "Does phantasy exceed reason? Or, more generally, is imagination in excess of spirit?"[11] This question leads one to envision imagination as being out of the realm of the dialectic, on the periphery of spirit, not susceptible to its movement, transcending spirit's powers to determine the activity and content of the abyss. This has greater implications for understanding the potential faculties of the abyss, independent from spirit. This becomes a theme that will occupy us throughout this project. Is it possible that the nocturnal pit of images is beyond the call of spirit? Is it possible that the unconscious abyss can influence the very course of imagination and resist integration into spirit? And even if the abyss were to become subordinated to spirit, would not the pit bring with it its own material, its nightness that would be absorbed in spirit's universalization? Is not the pit bound to leave its residue? And what would this residue be? Could it perhaps be fragments of inclinations and passions that coexist with spirit in its transcendence toward reason? Is the host of images drawn from the pit susceptible to the sway of desire that seeks life and fulfillment of its own? To what degree is spirit itself influenced by the psychological?

As unconscious spirit dialectically proceeds from consciousness to self-consciousness, desire (*Begierde*) becomes its new shape as drive (*Trieb*). Hegel states, "desire still has no further determination than that of a drive, in so far as this drive, without being determined by thought, is directed toward an external object in which it seeks satisfaction" (*EG* § 426, *Zusatz*). For Hegel, as for Nietzsche and Freud, the subjective nature of the unconscious, as unconscious spirit, is indissolubly linked to the body, nature, or instinct.[12] Hegel anticipates Freud when he alludes to the instinctual motivations of the unconscious.

Feeling subjectivity is the totality of all content and the identity of the soul with its content. Although it is not free, neither is it bound, what is present being merely a limitation of it. What we called genius is instinctive [*instink-tartig*], active in an unconscious [*bewußtlose*] manner, in opposition to particular determinations. Other oppositions fall within reflection, within consciousness.—What we have before us here is feeling subjectivity, which realizes itself, is active, proceeds forth from simple unity to liveliness. This activity belongs to the determination of the liveliness, and although it awakens opposition within itself, it also preserves itself by sublating it and so endowing itself with a determinate being, with *self-awareness*. This activity is the expression of drive, of desire, its determination or content being drive, inclination, passion, or whatever form this content is given. (*EG* § 407, *Zusatz*)

In this passage, Hegel points to the dialectical activity of the unconscious whereby it generates its own oppositions and transcends itself within itself as *sublation*, or what we might not inappropriately call sublimation. For Hegel, sublation (*Aufhebung*) is the driving process behind the elevation of spirit. His dialectic is structurally differentiated in that it preforms three distinct yet simultaneous tasks: namely, canceling, annulling, or destroying, retaining or preserving, and surpassing, heightening, or transcending. As Errol Harris reminds us, sublation "does not obliterate when it supercedes, but also retains and transmogrifies."[13] Hegel also suggests that self-awareness is born out of such unconscious dialectical activity—an *unconscious self-consciousness*, thus giving the unconscious a primary role in psychic organization and conscious motivation. When Hegel says that the feeling soul "realizes itself" and has "*self-awareness*," he is saying that implicit spirit within the soul is self-conscious of its self, hence possessing an unconscious self-consciousness. He further attributes this process to "intro-reflection" or "self-reflection" (*Reflexion-in-sich*) that is performed inwardly within the unconscious soul before conscious reflection is achieved (*EG* §§ 412, 414). Furthermore, Hegel states that the nature of unconscious content is itself the activity, as drive or desire. This points to the primacy of psychic (unconscious) determination providing the structural organization and the content of its own determinateness which transcends itself in conscious choice. Hegel has paved the way to understanding more precisely the organization, structural integrity, and telic operations of the unconscious.

THE DIALECTICAL STRUCTURE
OF THE UNCONSCIOUS

It should be clear by now that unconscious spirit is the structural foundation of the self, as pure activity always in flux and in a state of psychic turbulence. "It is just this unrest that is the self" (*PS* § 22). Hegel refers here to the unrest of *Aufhebung*, as dialectical process continuously annulled, preserved, and transmuted. As Hegel would contend, the dialectic is both the inner organization and the content of unconscious spirit. It is the dialectic that provides the self with intrapsychic structures and operations that can never be reduced or localized, only conceptualized as pure activity. This pure activity of the dialectic as self is constantly evolving and redefining itself through such movement. The unconscious forms of spirit (initially as feeling soul then as ego) are thereby necessarily organized around such dialectical activity of the abyss. These structural operations, however, are not mechanistic, reductionistic, or physical as in the natural science framework often attributed to traditional psychoanalysis.[14] They are mental, telic, and transcendental, always reshaping spirit's inner contours and the internalized representational world within the night of the mind. Therefore, as a general structure, the unconscious is *aufgehoben*.

For Hegel, the unconscious is pure *process*, a changing, flexible, and purposeful activity of becoming. As the very foundation, structure, and organizing principles of the unconscious are informed by the movement of the dialectic, the architecture of the abyss is continually being reshaped and exalted as each dialectical conflict is sublated by passing into a new form, that in turn restructures, reorganizes, and refurbishes the interior contours of the core self. Therefore, the structural foundations of the self are never static or inert, but always in dialectical movement that has its origin and source in the unconscious, revamping the framework in which spirit emanates. This self-generating dialectical movement of the unconscious is the evoking, responding, sustaining, and transcending matrix that is itself the very internal system of subjective spirit.

The concept of the self as subject in Hegel is of particular importance in understanding the unconscious nature of spirit. Essentially, the stage-by-stage progression of the dialectic is expressed as an epigenetic theory of self-development. As *aufgehoben*, Hegel's notion of the self encompasses a movement in which the subject is opposed to an object and comes to find itself in the object. During the dialectical movement of spirit, the subject recognizes or discovers itself in the object. This entails the mediation of its becoming other to itself, with the reflection into otherness returning back to itself. The process of the development of the self is, therefore, a process of differentiation and integration. For Hegel, Being is characterized by an undifferentiated matrix that undergoes differentiation in the dialectical process of becoming that in turn integrates into its being that which it differentiated through its projection, reclaiming it and making it part of its internal structure.[15] The outcome of the integration is once again differentiated then reintegrated; unification is always reunification. Therefore, it comes to be what it already is: it is the process of its own becoming.[16]

As the darker side of spirit, the unconscious educates itself as it passes through its various dialectical configurations. Parallel to the path of natural consciousness that ascends toward the Absolute, the unconscious also comes to a unity constituted by the bifurcation and rigid opposition that it generates from within itself. Furthermore, it is precisely through such opposition that the unconscious becomes and brings itself into reunification. Thus, the abyss in its evolution undergoes a violence at its own hands. By entering into opposition with itself, it raises this opposition to a higher unity and thus sublates to a new structure. As each unconscious shape or content is confronted with radical opposition, each shape is made to collapse when its non-absolute form is exposed. Indeed, it is always driving the movement on from one shape to the next. Thus, the character of the unconscious is that of negativity and conflict: it is tempestuous, feral, powerful, and dynamic. As such, the unconscious is the source of its own negativity as inversion and destruction pave the way of its progression forward.

There is a necessity in the dialectic that informs the internal structures of the abyss; that is, there is a certain determination to negation. The operation of such determinant negativity comes about through the collapse of each shape. As the negation of a certain content takes place within the realm of the abyss, it derives a certain content from the negation. Therefore, it links shapes into a necessary progression as each form turns into a new one. However, as each form is surpassed, the experience of its alteration is that of death, its end. But for Hegel, death always leads to rebirth. The dialectic is therefore the oscillation between life and death, never separate from one another. Hegel elucidates this point:

> [W]hat is bound and is actual only in its context with others, should attain an existence of its own and a separate freedom—this is the tremendous power of the negative; it is the energy of thought, of the pure 'I'. Death, if that is what we want to call this non-actuality, is of all things the most dreadful, and to hold fast what is dead requires the greatest strength. . . . But the life of Spirit is not the life that shrinks from death and keeps itself untouched by devastation, but rather the life that endures it and maintains itself in it. It wins its truth only when, in utter dismemberment, it finds itself. (*PS* § 32)

As determinate negativity, the unconscious vanquishes itself as it destroys itself. It kills itself as it gives itself life. As each shape alters, however, one assumes that the most primal region of unconscious spirit, that of the feeling soul, experiences, retains, and preserves such destruction. It would follow that the abyss itself undergoes a loss of self, and as feeling soul it enters into despair over its death, a suffering it must endure and preserve, a mourning it perpetually encounters. Indeed, it destroys itself in the service of raising itself, albeit it remembers and feels its suffering. Yet, it is precisely through such negativity that there is progression. Perhaps it needs to hold onto its suffering, its death, in order to advance or take pleasure in its elevation.

From this standpoint, we might say that the unconscious is masochistic; it must suffer in order to gain. Perhaps the double edge of the dialectic, (as negativity resulting in higher unity), poses a dilemma even for spirit itself. Does spirit fight within itself such a process, thereby leading spirit to retreat back into the nocturnal pit, to withdraw itself from its suffering and return to the warm blanket of the abyss? Is this dilemma a natural inclination of spirit or is it merely the result of disease, that of madness?

HEGEL'S THEORY OF PSYCHOPATHOLOGY

Perhaps the implicitness of the abyss has been made most clear in its relation to mental illness. In reference to the role of the unconscious, Hegel's theory of mental illness has received the most attention in the literature.[17] For Hegel, the unconscious plays a central role in the development of insanity (*Wahnsinn*), or more broadly conceived, mental derangement (*Zerstreutheit*). Hegel explains:

> [T]he spiritually deranged person himself has a lively feeling of the contradiction between his merely subjective presentation and objectivity. He is however unable to rid himself of this presentation, and is fully intent either on actualizing it or demolishing what is actual. (*EG* § 408, *Zusatz*)

Hegel explains madness in terms that modern psychiatry and psychology would label as thought disorder: the inability to distinguish between inner subjective states of psychic conflict and the objective reality of the external world. In madness, the person attempts to cling to the belief that his or her subjective presentation is objectively valid despite the evidence against it. Thus, the person is delusional. Hegel continues:

> The Concept of madness just given implies that it need not stem from a *vacant imagination*, but that if an individual dwells so continually upon the *past* that he becomes incapable of adjusting to the *present*, feeling it to be both repulsive and restraining, it can easily be brought about by a stroke of great misfortune, by the *derangement* of a person's individual world, or by a *violent upheaval* which puts the world in general out of joint. (*EG* § 408, *Zusatz*)

Hegel comes remarkably close to Freud's general theory of neurosis as the unconscious fixation of conflicted id impulses, feelings, and experiences from the past that are transferred onto the present. This projected conflict, therefore, ultimately attenuates ego capacities and precludes one from effectively adapting to one's objective environment. Hegel's notion of madness hinges on the dialectical tumult that ensues between desire and reason, emphasizing the struggle to gain mastery over the mind's experience of pain and suffering. Ironically, insanity is a regressive withdrawal back into the abyss; rational consciousness reverted to the life of feeling as a therapeutic effort to ameliorate the "wounds of spirit."[18]

For Hegel, the phenomenon of mental illness is primarily associated to the domains of the feeling soul, as the result of irreconcilable oppositions between the subjective and the objective.[19] In the face of perpetual contradiction and disunity, unconscious spirit engages in a retrogressive withdrawal to the primordial tranquility of the abyss, and thus projects a sense of unity from within itself. Berthold-Bond has labeled this phenomenon the "second face of desire," which constitutes a regression to an earlier nostalgia, a yearning calling consciousness back to the most archaic depths of its peacefulness. In madness, the archaic world of the unconscious draws the mind back to its original shape; subjective spirit is once again an undifferentiated oneness, as a return to the primitive merger within the symbiosis of its blissful inwardness. No longer driven by rational consciousness in its search for unity within the external world, spirit resorts back to its earlier form projecting its desires within phantasy. Perhaps on the most primitive level, spirit seeks to go to sleep once again, to return to a tensionless state and recover its lost unity with the Absolute. Therefore, the fundamental striving for unity leading to the movement of withdrawal back into the abyss, is the basic structural dynamic of madness. From the abyss spirit emanates, and from the abyss madness is informed. Thus, the unconscious becomes the playing field in both mental health and psychopathology.

ANTICIPATING THE ABYSS

Throughout this book, I will be primarily concerned with the ground, scope, and range of the unconscious abyss and its manifestations in subjective spirit. Hegel focuses his attention primarily on the role of the abyss in the recollection stage of theoretical spirit. But by showing how it is anticipated in other parts of his philosophy, we will see that the unconscious plays a central role in his overall system. Throughout the evolution of spirit, there is unconscious spirit asleep within its nocturnal world only to be awakened from its internal slumbers to discover itself as soul, the life of feeling, an "*immediate, unconscious totality*" (*EG* § 440, *Zusatz*), and then it takes yet another shape as consciousness. As consciousness ascends toward the Absolute, every content of consciousness originally exists and is preserved unconsciously within the mode of feeling. Thus, the life of feeling is primordially associated with the domain of the abyss in all its archaic shapes. In its beginning, spirit originally manifests itself as the unconscious.

As a general structure, the unconscious is *aufgehoben*, continually being annulled, preserved, and elevated. The unrest of the dialectic perennially provides and re-provides the intrapsychic structures, operations, and contents of the unconscious as it redefines and reconfigures itself through such movement. As a telic structure, "intelligence as this unconscious abyss," unconscious spirit is grounded in the subject. Thereby, the subjective ground of the abyss continually informs the dialectic throughout spirit's unfolding, transforming into new shapes in its drive toward unity and truth, preserving old ones within the domain of the psychological.

Over the course of these proceeding chapters, I will argue for several key theses:

1. Hegel provides a coherent and surprisingly well articulated theory of the unconscious which becomes a pivotal concept in his entire philosophy of spirit;
2. The unconscious is the foundation for conscious spiritual life, that
3. plays a role in both mental health and illness;

4. Because all mental life has its genesis in unconscious processes, the abyss maintains an ontological and logical priority in the very constitution of spirit;

5. Conscious ego development is the modification of unconscious structure;

6. Having its origins in the unconscious soul, reason is the exalted dialectical outgrowth of desire;

7. Although the unconscious undergoes dialectical evolution, it is never fully sublated, remaining a repository where failed or diseased shapes of spirit return; and

8. Hegel's theory of the unconscious anticipates and parallels Freud's discoveries in many remarkable ways; thus his theory is of significance for psychoanalysis today.

In chapter 1, I examine the concept of original ground (*Grund*) and show how Hegel was profoundly influenced by several historical sources that in all likelihood contributed to his conceptualizations of the unconscious abyss. Jacob Boehme's theosophic Christianity made a favorable impression on Hegel, and we may suspect Boehme has special significance for Hegel's thought. Boehme offered an elementary dialectic and advanced the notion of the mystical being of the deity as the *Ungrund* ("unground"), or the ground without a ground. Boehme was above all interested in the soul, the first subject matter of Hegel's Philosophy of Spirit. Emerging from an inner darkness through internal division and external projection, the *Ungrund* serves as a prototype for the abyss of the feeling soul, thus giving rise to a negative dialectic. Boehme's *Ungrund*, like spirit, is the being whose essence is to reveal itself through orderly stages of progression as it ascends toward self-consciousness, a subject who desires pure self-recognition.

But Hegel's understanding of the *Ungrund* derives from several other sources in addition to Boehme, including neo-Platonism, Fichte, and Schelling. Hegel owes much to Proclus (through Creuzer), Plotinus, Erigena, and Schelling. He was familiar with several neo-Platonic texts, which were a likely source for his ideas. Furthermore, Hegel was deeply engaged with Fichte's *Wissenschaftslehre* and with Schelling's philosophy of identity (*Identitätsphilosophie*) and philosophy of nature (*Naturphilosophie*). His own philosophical thought developed out of their respective philosophies. Boehme had a profound impact on Schelling who was one of the first philosophers to emphasize the importance of irrationality. Schelling's revision of Kant's and Fichte's transcendental idealisms led him to develop a systematic conceptualization of the unconscious.

Hegel's views on the unconscious abyss may be said to have partially derived from these different conceptualizations of the *Ungrund*. He was no doubt influenced by his historical predecessors, but as an independent thinker, his treatment of the abyss shows its own theoretical novelty.

After examining the historical precursors that set the stage for understanding Hegel's unique position on the unconscious, we turn our attention to a careful exegesis of Hegel's texts. Chapter 2 details Hegel's theory of unconscious spirit and the soul. Specific attention is given to key passages in the Anthropology section of the *Encyclopaedia* outlining his references to the abyss and the unconscious processes of the soul's epigenetic development. Through a series of internal tensions, divisions, externalizations, and reincorporations, the dialectic becomes the logical model for the unconscious awakening and flourishing of the soul. The soul awakens to find itself immersed in nature and the life of desire and feeling, which it must overcome through a series of mediated dynamics resulting in the ego of consciousness. I will repeatedly argue that the soul attains for itself a prereflective, nonpropositional self-awareness or unconscious self-consciousness which becomes the template for consciousness and self-conscious spirit. Due to his views on the dialectical operations of the unconscious soul and the primitive presence of the ego, we can engage Hegel in a theoretical dialogue with Freud.

Chapter 3 addresses Hegel's philosophical psychology and the operations of intuition, recollection, and thought within theoretical spirit, with a specific focus on the role of the abyss during the stages of presentation, imagination, and phantasy. Before the formal psychological operations of spirit are examined, however, I give a complete account of Hegel's model of the mind and how it developmentally unfolds as sublation through internal division, differentiation, and modification beginning with the natural soul and progressing to sentience, feeling, ego, consciousness, and self-consciousness as a self-articulated complex totality. By understanding Hegel's developmental stage progression of the soul, we are able to see how the burgeoning ego becomes the central agency for both unconscious and conscious activity and is the ontological force behind the appearance of consciousness that makes the psychological operations of spirit possible.

Spirit essentially is the actualization of a progressive ego expansion that culminates in pure self-consciousness. Hegel's relation to and anticipation of key psychoanalytic concepts are further explored by juxtaposing his notions on the splitting of the ego and the internal modifications of the unconscious to Freud's tripartite model of the mind. Here we are able to see remarkable resemblances between their respective theories on the nature of unconscious drive and desire, ego organization, the primacy of conflict and destruction, and the structure and processes of consciousness.

Chapter 4 looks more closely at the dialectic of desire. The presence of desire is often attributed to the appearance of self-consciousness, but by way of our anthropological treatment of the soul, desire has its foundation in the unconscious. This brings us to address a criticism that has been launched against Hegel's theory of intersubjectivity and self-recognition, namely, that his model of self-consciousness is circular. By readdressing Fichte's argument against the reflection thesis of self-consciousness, and Hegel's treatment of the coming into being of unconscious spirit, I show that this criticism is unwarranted. The feeling soul attains an initial self-certainty of itself as an unconscious self-consciousness, which becomes the logical and developmental model for consciousness and self-consciousness to arise.

This reassessment of Hegel's position on self-consciousness allows us to reinterpret the struggle for recognition represented in the master-slave dialectic. I show that Hegel's account of self-consciousness outlined in the *Encyclopaedia* and the *Berlin Phenomenology* changes significantly from the *Phenomenology* of his Jena period. However, his Jena work proves useful for understanding a general theory of neurosis. By focusing on the alienation, anxiety, and despair of neurotic spirit typified in stoicism, skepticism, and unhappy consciousness, we are able to see the universal and initial dimensions of madness.

Hegel's theory of abnormal psychology is the topic of chapter 5. Rather than offer an extensive taxonomy on the phenomenology of mental illness, Hegel is interested in understanding the ontology or underlying conditions that inform psychopathology. For Hegel, the ontology of madness has its structural form in the symbiotic and undifferentiated universality of the feeling soul. This self-enclosed womb of the soul is the state or condition that all forms of psychopathology assume, ranging from the more severe forms of thought disorder and psychosis that Hegel mentions when he discusses mental derangement and insanity to milder types of symptoms and conditions such as folly or absentmindedness.

The question of madness brings us to confront the issue of whether spirit fights within itself the progressive and elevating thrust of the dialectic for the regressive withdrawal back into the pit of its earlier being. Spirit struggles to achieve absolute unity, but in times of illness it is drawn back to its primitive unity, which it had previously surpassed. This withdrawal, fixation, and regression back to its original undifferentiated being suggests that the unconscious abyss exceeds the elevating process of the dialectic. In the sick soul, as in absolute knowing, spirit strives to sustain a universal merger with an all-encompassing unity, though such unity is vastly different in the diseased mind.

Our final chapter discusses Hegel's contributions to metapsychology and its implications for contemporary psychoanalysis. It is my hope throughout this project to show the remarkable similarity between Hegel's and Freud's ideas on the unconscious as the indispensable psychic foundation of the mind. Hegel is a proper precursor of Freud, and although largely unknown to psychoanalytic discourse, Hegel's philosophy contributes to psychoanalytic thought. There is a preponderance of evidence in traditional and contemporary psychoanalytic theory to conclude that the unconscious is dialectical both in its structural organization and its internal content.[20] In general, psychoanalysis would contend that the dialectical modes of spirit are themselves differentiated and modified forms of primordial mental processes maintained through ego activity, such as the continuity between desire and reason, mechanisms of defense, compromise formation, ethical development and the pursuit of valuation, aesthetic sublimation, and the higher intellectual operations of cognition.[21] For example, the process of the self returning to itself due to its own self-estrangement is what in psychoanalysis is called, "projective identification."[22] This defensive maneuver of the ego or self is generated by the projection of a certain aspect of the self onto the object world, which is then identified with and finally re-introjected back into the subject. In effect, the self rediscovers itself in the product of its own projection and then reintegrates itself within itself as reunification. This is the generic structural movement of the Hegelian dialectic, whereby internal division, external projection, and reincorporation function as a mediating and sublating dynamic. Furthermore, the unconscious is overshadowed by negativity and conflict in both Hegel and psychoanalysis, a point that will be continually reinforced. For Hegel, however, the tempestuousness of the nocturnal abyss as the dialectic is in the service of elevating spirit to higher forms, while in classical psychoanalysis, the dialectical maneuvers of the ego are partially in the service of defending itself from an austere reality, such as the tumultuous forces within. Furthermore, the dialectical patterns in psychoanalysis mainly operate on—but are not limited to—the personal, psychological level, while in Hegel the dialectic extends to the history of the human race.

Despite differences in theory and method, Hegelian and psychoanalytic conceptualizations of the unconscious share many similarities, particularly in reference to the nature of desire and drive, ego development, madness and neurosis, and the role of the dialectic. While Freud's metapsychology has incurred criticism due to its problematic epistemology and natural science framework— a framework vilified by analytic philosophers as not being a science at all,[23] there is much room for a reinterpretation of the unconscious that preserves the integrity of the self, (and that of spirit), as a telic agent without resulting in a conceptual scheme of the unconscious that is lost in biological reductionism.[24] Perhaps Hegelian and psychoanalytic theory can offer something to one another. While Hegel emphasizes the role of the universal, Freud emphasizes the particular, each having its respective truths in our understanding of what it means to be human. Hegel's philosophy, however, may be especially significant for the future of psychoanalysis. If we are to espouse Hegel's great insight that reality—including every intellectual discipline—is about *process*, evolution, transmogrification, and change, then his implications for psychoanalysis may bring about a new relation between wisdom and science.

ONE

RETRACING THE *UNGRUND*

Not "I think," but "it thinks in me."

—*Nietzsche*

THOUGHT LIVES UNDERGROUND. What is the ground (*Grund*) of human consciousness—of subjectivity—the very essence that makes thought, hence spirit, possible? Does such a ground exist, and if so, to whom does it belong—to the *I*, or to an *it* as Nietzsche suggests; or perhaps to nothing at all? If it is necessary to posit a sufficient reason—a ground—for every mental event, then it must be the case that such a ground exists for every determination of thought—for every choice—perhaps even its own ground. For Hegel, "Ground is first, *absolute ground*, in which essence is" (*SL*, 445); thought—spirit itself—grounds its own ground. As the grounding of its own ground, thought determines itself as the "*absolute* foundation," a foundation it has forged by its own hands. If pure thinking is self-determining "*Essence* [that] *determines itself as ground*" (*SL*, 444), then what is the ground of ground? Before thought, before consciousness, before the appearance of essence as ground, there is the *unthought*—unconsciousness—an *Ungrund*. Before thought appears, it lives *underground*.

For Hegel, as for psychoanalysis, the unconscious is the primordial ground of consciousness—an underground *abyss* that inhabits the psychic space between reason and desire, intuition and thought, between the *I* and the *it*. And it is such that this abyss within psychic space is itself a space, a pit that divides consciousness from what it is not, the known from the unknown. It is precisely this pit, this unknown that organizes thought and defines its operations, and yet it is itself beyond thought—perhaps simply the *un*thought. But the unthought that dwells underground hibernates in its pit, an eternal slumber. Such hibernation, however, is not the passive peacefulness of sleep, rather, it is an activity, an unrest

21

of the soul. In Hegel's words, this activity of thought, as well as every intention, idea, desire, and action is "unconsciously busy."[1] Thus, the activity of thought—that which is unthought—taking place "behind the back of consciousness," becomes the primordial ground of Spirit. The abyss, the *Ungrund*—as unthought thought thinking and feeling itself—may be said to even be a "riddle to itself." For how can one think the unthought?

From the *Encyclopaedia*, Hegel talks of the unconscious processes of intelligence as a "nocturnal abyss" (*EG* § 453). Of all of Hegel's philosophical contributions to the understanding of human existence, his ideas on the unconscious abyss remain an underrecognized achievement. While largely overlooked even by himself, Hegel's notion of the abyss becomes a pivotal concept in his entire philosophical enterprise, for the abyss is the womb of spirit. The abyss, what we may compare to the *Ungrund*, not only performs an indispensable function in the dialectical organization and production of spirit, it provides the logical foundation for his philosophical system, a system that is itself foundational. Hegel's system is both architectonic and developmental; that is, spirit grounds its own being in the process of its own becoming. Hence, spirit is a teleological, developmental accomplishment. Yet from the telic and more primordial nether-regions of spirit, ground is always redefined underground, under the world of appearances. As the dialectic paves a progressive unity toward more mature shapes of consciousness, the abyss is never abandoned as such; for it always remains in the shadows, making its presence known as drive and desire, fueling the dialectic itself. As the appearance of unconscious essence, desire reveals the abyss, because for Hegel, "Essence must *appear*" (*EL* § 131): whatever exists within must be made actual. And it is precisely within this underworld that spirit is born—thus consciousness becomes its spawn.

The presence of the abyss is not only developmentally prior to the rational self-conscious subject, it maintains an ontological *priority* in the very constitution of spirit itself. In order to fully appreciate the role and priority of such unconscious activity that underlies the self-grounding nature of spirit, we will need to carefully examine the scope and range of the abyss in Hegel's system. Before we undertake a textual analysis of Hegel's position on the unconscious, however, it will be necessary to address his historical predecessors in order to determine who influenced his thought on the subject. Retracing the origins of the *Ungrund* will prove to be useful when later offering a full exposition of Hegel's treatment of the unconscious, for we may be able to conceptually contrast what differentiates Hegel's unique contribution from other perspectives which will further aid in our understanding of the role of the abyss in his system. The main focus of this chapter, therefore, will be to highlight some of Hegel's likely historical sources on the abyss that will serve to prepare us for a systematic treatment of his position, which is later to follow. This becomes significant because the metaphysical status of the *Ungrund* plays a central role in Hegel's overall philosophy of spirit, a comprehension of which may hold the secrets to the soul.

HISTORICAL ORIGINS OF THE ABYSS

Hegel himself did not originate the notion of the unconscious abyss. Rather, he took it over in large measure from Boehme, neo-Platonism, and Schelling. The concept of the abyss (*Abgrund, Ungrund*) derives from Boehme's theosophic Christianity. Inspired by the study of Plotinus,[2] Boehme radically reconceptualized God as the *ens manifestativum sui*, "the being whose essence is to reveal itself."[3] Boehme developed an elementary form of dialectic. In this dialectic, positive and negative polarities emerge out of the Godhead's original undifferentiated non-being (*das Nichts*), and these unfold through orderly stages of manifestation as it ascends toward absolute self-consciousness.[4] At one time, scholars thought that Boehme's term *Ungrund* originated in the Gnostic "abyss," since there are shared similarities between the two.[5] But Koyré has cogently disputed this claim, interpreting Boehme's notion of the abyss as the "ground without a ground."[6] Before the divine *Ungrund* emerges, there is no source of determination, there is nothing; the *Ungrund* is merely "unfathomable" and "incomprehensible."

The *Ungrund* is the uncertainty which precedes the divine will's arousing itself to self-awareness.[7]

Furthermore, Boehme's *Ungrund* acts as a subject who desires: "it 'seeks,' it 'longs,' it 'sees,' and it 'finds'."[8]

While Hegel does give testimony to Boehme,[9] he probably owes more to Proclus (through Creuzer), Plotinus, Erigena, and Schelling.[10] Boehme's impact on Schelling was considerable;[11] and Schelling was among the very first philosophers to underscore the importance of the unconscious and the role of irrationality in human experience. However, it was two arch-rationalists, Leibniz and Kant, who paved the way for this development. In the *New Essays on Human Understanding*, Leibniz propounded a theory of unconscious "*petits perceptions*."[12] Kant, in his *Anthropology*, discussed the nature of "obscure presentations" (*dunkele Vorstellungen*) that remain just below the level of conscious awareness.[13] Schelling's revision of Kant's and Fichte's transcendental idealism together with his own philosophy of identity (*Identitätsphilosophie*) and philosophy of nature (*Naturphilosophie*) led to one of the first systematic conceptualizations of the unconscious.

BOEHME'S INFLUENCE ON HEGEL

Perhaps remembered more for his legend than his ideas, the seventeenth-century philosopher, mystic, and theosophist, Jacob Boehme (1575–1624), is considered an intellectual giant among early German philosophers. As a forerunner of the German Romantic movement, Boehme was an inspiration to poets and intellectuals and was also praised by philosophers such as Baader, Schelling, Schopenhauer, and Hegel—leading Hegel to further credit Boehme as "the first German philosopher."[14] Through Boehme, German philosophy had come into its own. Heralded as the self-proclaimed *Philosophus Teutonicus* or the *Philosophus der Einfältigen* ("philosopher of the simple folk"), Boehme's major works include the *Aurora* or the *Morgenröthe im Aufgang* (1612) and *Mysterium Magnum* (1623).[15] Known for his supposed insights into the divine nature, the origin and structure of the universe, and the hidden mysteries of the Bible, Boehme was above all concerned with the human subject, and particularly the soul.

In *Forty Questions on the Soul* (1620), Boehme provides an account of the origins of the soul and for the first time refers to the mystical being of the deity as the *Ungrund* (the "unground").[16] Prompted by Balthasar Walter, Boehme's friend who had researched the secrets of the Jewish Kabbalah in the Near East, Boehme set out to describe ten forms of the soul. Andrew Weeks informs us that Walter may have influenced Boehme's questions as well as his answers, which correspond to the sefirot or the ten emanations of the Kabbalah, thus providing the prototype for the ten forms the soul may assume. Ten is also of eschatological significance to Boehme, because the number ten contains a one and a null. The *Ungrund* is everything yet nothing, both unification and void.

While Boehme may have borrowed the Kabbalic notion of cosmic evolution that precipitates from the Divine Unity,[17] another major source of influence on Boehme was hermeticism,[18] an occult practice thought to have been known to Boehme through the writings of Paracelsus,[19] a tradition employing the use of alchemical symbols and allegories that explain the Deity.[20] Drawing upon the use of astronomical world-models that were often designed by mathematicians and scientists during his time, Boehme diagrammed his own model of the solar system in *The Threefold Life of Man* (1620). It is in the *Forty Questions*, however, where he provides an intricate interpretation of the subtle symbolism that characterizes the spheres of the Divine Being. Boehme's mystical circle-symbolism stands in a tradition that dates back to Cusanus and ultimately Parmenides.[21] Symbolized by Boehme's mystical configurations of the Divine Being, the *V* (designating the *Ungrund*) is dialectically opposed to the *A* (for *Anfang* or *Alpha*) which is encased in the empty mirror or eye of eternity, designated by *O*. In constructing the mystical cell of the Divine Being, Boehme further designed a "Philosophical Globe" or "Wonder-Eye of Eternity" that encompasses numerous other philosophical elements constituting his theosophic cosmology. Boehme's "Globe" is designed to show the interface and circumscription of the created world by the mirroring spheres of night and light. Eternity—the Godhead—is the polarization of life and death, light and darkness, being and nothingness.

In *Forty Questions on the Soul*, Boehme moves toward the neo-Platonic pole of his thought, for he focuses on the eternity of forms within the soul. In response to the question: "Where, from the beginning of the world, does the soul originate?," Boehme replies that by way of reason (*aus der Vernunft*), all things have their origin in eternity (III 8/1.3ff). "Before the divine *Ungrund*, there is nothing, no source of determination."[22] Following Koyré's interpretation: "*L'Ungrund* . . . est l'Absolu absolument indéterminé, l,Absolu libre de toute détermination,"[23] (The *Ungrund* is the Absolute, absolutely indetermined, the

Absolute free of all determination).[24] Here we may see the idealism that parallels Hegel's thought. Spirit first awakens from within itself and then takes itself as its first form, only to progressively move away from itself and then back into itself through its many appearances on its long dialectical ascendence toward absolute self-consciousness. Hegel's notion of spirit in its initial unfolding closely resembles the coming to presence of Boehme's Divine Being. Boehme's *Ungrund* is the abyss of eternity that is absolutely indeterminate subjectivity. For Boehme, like Hegel, the unground, as the groundless ground, behaves as a desiring subject that grounds itself within its own determinations through its burgeoning process of becoming.

Weeks notes that prior to the textual occurrence of the noun *Ungrund*, Boehme uses the adjective *ungründlich*, meaning "unfathomable" or inconceivable. This may correspond to the Kantian view of the noumenal realm of pure reason; absolute knowledge of the *Ding-an-sich* is foreclosed from our awareness—it must always remain unknown.[25] As such, the *Ungrund* is ineffable, in a word, indescribable. And as Koyré contends, whatever exists is always in relation to the "impossible."[26] But Boehme was not content with the silent impotence of reason; the impossible must be named and given substantive form. Thus, what is abysmal for Boehme is retrieved from the lair of the unknown and assimilated into the experience of the devout subject.

> "About the final ground of God one cannot be certain." And: "The final ground of God is Uncertainty." In the first instance, the seeking subject is cut off from the unknown object of its contemplation. In the second instance, the subject has recognized its inner longing for the deity as akin to the Divine Unknown . . . the uncertainty and tormented freedom of the self has been recognized in its relationship to the ultimate ground of divinity. The unknown divine object is reflected in the self-knowledge of the subject. The *Ungrund* is the uncertainty which precedes the divine will's arousing itself to self-awareness (though in the deity this "happens" in eternity).[27]

Like Boehme, Hegel was also intent on showing the knowability of the unknown. But instead of relying on the faith of the devout seeker, Hegel argues that there is nothing we can know more easily than the thing-in-itself, because the distinction between the phenomenal and the noumenal is a distinction in thought.[28] For Hegel, Kant's view of the noumenal was "completely abstract, or totally empty." Positing something that is out of reach of the mind is incoherent; if it were out of reach, one couldn't be positing it in the first place. And it is precisely the distinction between what can be experienced and what can only be thought that Hegel is attempting to annul. The very movement of thought hinges on a negative dialectic—something can only be known in relation to what it is not.

For both Boehme and Hegel, the origin of God and Spirit respectively, may be viewed as original Beginning, an eternal abyss from which both awaken to their own immediate determinateness. As Hegel states: "The beginning of spirit is therefore nothing but its own being, and it therefore relates itself only to its own determinations" (*EG* § 440). Similarly for Boehme,

> God is in Himself the *Ungrund*, as the first world, about which no creature knows anything, for it stands with its body and spirit in the ground alone: Even God would therefore not be manifest [*offenbar*] to Himself in the *Ungrund*; but His wisdom has from eternity become His ground, for which the eternal will of the *Ungrund* has lusted, from which the divine imagination has arisen.[29]

Boehme, like Hegel, points to the notion that the *Ungrund* is the presupposition for the manifestation of God (or Spirit) to occur. Like God who would not be manifest to himself in the abyss itself, Spirit also must emerge from its unconscious fountain to take its initial forms as soul and consciousness. For both thinkers, the *Ungrund* is "the first world," the *underworld* that precedes all else from which desire and thought arise. Yet this underworld is eternal—as original Being, God and Spirit may not be properly said to have a beginning or end, even if they are coextensive with the temporal unfolding of world history.[30] In the *Aurora*, Boehme says, "In his depth (i.e., in the *Ungrund*), God himself does not know what he is. For he knows no beginning, and also nothing like himself, and also no end."[31] God and Spirit respectively, must project their own essence into the world in order to arrive at complete self-actualization as the coming to presence of pure subjectivity. It is only when God and Spirit encounter their own opposition as self-willed independence that self-consciousness (self-revelation) occurs. Within their dialectical polarities, perhaps the *Ungrund* is also an *Überwelt* (overworld), the supernatural space where under and over are equivocated, for they are one and the same. For spirit and the deity, they "seek," they "will," and they "lust" for "wisdom," a longing to complete themselves. Here we may further see a symmetry between the *Ungrund* and Freud's tripartite notion of the soul (*Seele*); reason (mediated by *Ich*) and higher levels of self-consciousness (*Überich*) develop out of natural desire (*Es*) from its primordial subjectivity. Furthermore, for Hegel and Boehme, spirit is self-positing—the deity may only manifest itself through an act of will.

The mystical speculations of Boehme draw on the use of antithesis to explain the *Ungrund*. "God's emergence out of pure oneness into differentiated actuality required a confrontation with opposition. It was out of this creative struggle that the sensible universe issued forth."[32] God is a world beyond this world and beyond direct knowledge as such, yet the divine object is mirrored in the self-knowledge of the subject. As the soul impregnates itself by reflection, yearning, and imaginative faith, the believer approaches knowledge of the divine by "transforming itself into the mirror of the hidden God."[33] Furthermore, God comes to know himself as "ground" through his desire for self-actualization: "His wisdom has from eternity become His ground, for which the eternal will . . . has lusted" (IV 127/II.3.5). This statement by Boehme may suggest that the deity had experienced eternal wisdom that had at some point been alienated from his being. As alienated knowledge, the *Ungrund* awakens from within itself only to desire what had been previously both eternal and estranged. Here we may see an allusion to the desire for recognition that is such a prevalent theme of the Hegelian corpus—the deity desires *itself*, its own self-recognition. The alienation dialectic is a central process whereby recognition is achieved. In fact, the Christian story of man's fall and redemption is itself an alienation dialectic that stands behind both Boehme and Hegel. Yet for Boehme, the *Ungrund* is originally a primal "darkness," a nocturnal will that proceeds through a series of developmental stages that forms the world-creative process. It is through this self-unfolding that the deity initially draws into itself, into its darkness before it manifests as a creative will. The initial withdrawal into itself forms the core of being, which becomes the ground (*Grund*) of all subsequent stages.[34] The process of God's will toward manifestation as a spiritual "hunger" for "wisdom" may also be said to prefigure Hegel's account of unconscious spirit that awakens from within its "nightlike abyss" and "intuits" itself as feeling soul before it unfolds toward the Concept as its absolute self-knowing. Both philosophers employ a dialectic that emerges from undifferentiated unity and passes through a process of differentiation and reunification, constituted in and through a dialectically self-articulated holism. It is Hegel, however, who places more emphasis on the dynamic circularity of the drive toward reason, while Boehme's dialectic is less rational and more volitional, thus becoming more attractive to Schelling's conceptualization of the divine will and the ontology of irrationality.

At this point it becomes important to emphasize the essential metaphysical similarities and dissimilarities between Boehme's divine being and Hegel's concept of spirit. Like subjective spirit, Boehme's *Ungrund* is a desirous subject who seeks to become fully self-actualized. It is only through a self-imposed aspect of limitation that the godhead can emerge and experience his epiphany in nature so he may become self-conscious. Edward Allen Beach explains this process:

> In the finite creature . . . God found his own revelation reflected as in a mirror. Böhme reasoned that because God desired to reveal himself to himself, and because revelation required a sensible (i.e., experienceable) embodiment, therefore God had to become sensible in order to satisfy his need for self-revelation. Thus, the dialectical drive toward self-awareness within God's originally inchoate will was what gave rise to the spiritual as well as the material universe.[35]

But unlike Boehme whose god is only known sensuously, Hegel's spirit is ultimately the embodiment of absolute totality. As pure self-consciousness, spirit transcends its corporeal, sensuous nature through reason while at the same time it becomes instantiated within the concrete universals that comprise nature and culture.[36] For Hegel, spirit moves beyond intuition to thought that belongs to its self-conception proper, viz., its non-sensuous self-actualization. Nature is only an intermediate step in the process for spirit to realize itself. Yet despite this divergence, the ontology of spirit and Boehme's godhead emerge from a process of self-negation.

There are remarkable similarities between the initial stages of spirit and the deity's coming into being: (1) Both emerge from an initial darkness, a nocturnal abyss that contains the potentiality of becoming actual and concrete; (2) Both seek self-manifestation, a longing or desire to know itself; (3) This necessarily gives rise to a negative dialectic. The darkness of the will conflicts with its will to manifest, which sparks the creative process, or in Hegelian terms, spirit moves from its initial intuition of itself as inner feeling to external sensuousness as consciousness and eventually self-consciousness through the process of negation; (4) Moreover, the initial movement of drawing in upon itself is present in both concepts and forms the foundation or ground of all succeeding stages to transpire; (5) Both spirit and the deity achieve self-recognition through the form of concrete self-alienation; and (6) Both seek to acquire (or return to) an original unity.

The positive significance of the negative that informs the dialectic is unmistakably a central aspect of both systems. However, Hegel's dialectic is significantly distinct, and more rigorously articulated, from Boehme's who relies on a firm antithesis between god's three distinct wills. Although Hegel's dialectic offers the theoretical sophistication of a formally logical system, Boehme's emphasis on conflict, self-destruction, and lack informs the very process of becoming, the driving force behind Hegel's articulation of *Geist*. For Boehme, the primal abyss of God undergoes a suffering due to the "darkness" that envelops his will, thus preventing him from becoming manifest to himself. Analogous to the indeterminate Void in Buddhism or to the *ain soph* in the Kabbalah,[37] the "no-thingness" of god's undifferentiated unity underwent its initial differentiation through the experience of "longing" or "hunger," a hunger to know itself, to become manifest—"the craving to draw into itself" (*die Sucht, in sich zu ziehen*).[38]

Boehme argued that there must be a transition from the unmanifest (non-being) *Ungrund's* need to become manifest to itself and the coming-to-presence of a manifest being that stands in opposition to itself. Like unconscious spirit, the unmanifest *Ungrund* precedes all existence and is completely undifferentiated (homogeneous), yet it paradoxically has the innate propensity to divide itself into contraries, and thus pass from an undifferentiated unity into a self-differentiated multiplicity. In the deity's initial inwardness, as inverted will, will-as-desire, Boehme reasoned that there must have been a prolonged longing that was incapable of being satisfied, and thus took its form as a fierce "fire" of chaos that burned internally without giving light. The inner blaze was the quality of the divine wrath or bitterness (*Grimmigkeit*) that turned on itself and consumed its own substance. Such self-consumption gave rise to a self-destruction that took the form of a painful anguish which the deity suffered.[39] And after the divine bitterness turned its destructive drive toward itself, a dramatic reversal occurred. "The anguished negation of free self-manifestation was itself negated: with a violent thunderclap, that harsh first principle overcame its own harshness, and a joyous light supervened. This symbolized the emergence of harmony and order out of original chaos."[40] Boehme speculated that the polarization of the two wills was mediated by a third will that formed the creative impulse in which the universe evolved. The bifurcation of the positive and negative wills of the godhead is the necessary condition that sustains the cosmos. Negativity and conflict form the very foundation for all subsequent stages to occur.

The ontology of the *Ungrund* has important implications for Hegel's system, a system that feeds off its own circularity as spirit elevates itself to the pinnacle of self-actualization. The *Ungrund* becomes the primal ground of spirit, its original being, an edifice that always informs the shapes of Spirit. While Boehme's reasoning was far from systematic or exacting, he nevertheless attempted to account for the emergence of existence out of possibility and multiplicity out of unity, a task Hegel's system specifies. Conceiving of the divine principles based on the supernatural fusion of psychological and alchemical properties rather than on formally logical or objective laws, Boehme's theosophy may be said to be merely a preface to Hegel's system, a preface that nevertheless appears over and over again in a new guise. By emphasizing the experience of absence, craving, striving, and conflict that characterizes divinity and human consciousness, Boehme was a harbinger for modern philosophies of the will.

HEGEL'S NEO-PLATONIC SOURCES

The exact nature of the historical influence on Hegel's conception of the unconscious may never be fully known. There is some debate regarding just how much Hegel was directly influenced by Boehme—ranging from a profound indebtedness to Boehme, to the claim that he was merely a peripheral figure. David Walsh argues that Boehme's impact on Hegel was considerable, which substantially influenced his conception and subsequent articulation of *Geist*. His claim relies on four factual elements: (1) Hegel's endorsement of Boehme within his *Vorlesungen über die Geschichte der Philosophie*;[41] (2) a thank-you letter Hegel wrote to one of his former pupils for sending him an edition of Boehme's collected works, a letter in which he praises Boehme;[42] (3) two essays from Hegel's Jena period, one on the Trinity and the other on spirit; and (4) the various thematic similarities that exist between Boehme's theosophy and Hegel's philosophy. Perhaps the strongest evidence comes from Hegel's early years at Jena when his mature thought was first beginning to take shape.[43] Hegel's textual admiration for Boehme also shows his support, a support however that is always riddled with reservations about the completeness of the Silesian theosoph's philosophy, a system that lacked logical rigor and consistency.

While Walsh makes a compelling case for Boehme's direct influence on Hegel's system, Eric von der Luft attributes more significance to neo-Platonism. Despite Hegel's testimonial to Boehme and the striking similarities that exist between Hegel's treatment of the triplicity of trinities in the Jena fragment and Boehme's conception of the three principles constituting the godhead,[44] Hegel explicitly rejects Boehme's mystical treatment of religion as mythological "picture-thinking"[45] and grows increasingly more critical of Boehme's contributions as his thought matures.

> Because mythologized religion, theosophic religion, a religion of nature, tends
> to lose the individual in contemplation of an infinite or transcendent beyond,
> Hegel, for whom the rational individual is the ultimate locus of spirit, and es-
> pecially of free spirit, has no choice but to reject such religion and to substitute
> for it a knowledge that both explains and includes the full richness of this indi-
> vidual developed from spirit as consciousness.[46]

While there are thematic similarities in Hegel that can be traced back to
Boehme, such similarities may also be traced farther back to neo-Platonic
thinkers such as Eckhart, Erigena, Proclus, and Plotinus.[47] Although Walsh
places Boehme in a tradition that goes back as far as Gnosticism, due to his lack
of formal education[48] Boehme was probably not familiar with these systems of
thought. It is not known whether Boehme had been exposed to the general
ideas of gnostic and neo-Platonic thought, but presumably he could have been,
though perhaps not to the details. Given such ambiguity, Boehme may be said
to have formulated his own tradition of natural-mystical theosophy independently. Hegel, on the other hand, would have been familiar with the more classical, strictly philosophical neo-Platonic texts, which were a likely source for
his ideas.

It may be argued that Hegel's generic conceptualization of the dialectical
self-unfolding of spirit and Boehme's account of the process of self-revelation
as the coming into being of God is a standard neo-Platonic idea. Von der Luft
points out that in *The Elements of Theology*, Proclus tells us that the One must
give of itself or else lack fertility and honor (Prop. 23) and that the One is
equated with the Good and must produce the manifold phenomena of nature in
order to become complete (Prop. 25). John Scotus Erigena in *On the Division of
Nature*, Book 1, further describes how God shows himself to rational creatures
each according to its own capacities and that he moves from within himself and
toward himself.[49] Boehme's and Hegel's characterization of the process of God's
and spirit's own self-recognition may be said to be present in Erigena's dialectic
in which

> God proceeds from Himself as uncreated creator, through his self-manifesta-
> tions as created creators and created noncreators, and returns to Himself, thus
> realizing and fulfilling Himself as Himself, as the uncreated who does not cre-
> ate because He then no longer needs to create.[50]

These dialectical characterizations of the activities of Spirit and God may be all
said to originate and emerge from an unconscious *Ungrund*. The coming to presence of self-consciousness through inner contemplation, separation, projection,
and self-recognition as self-reintegration is a general structural organization (as
process) of spirit and Boehme's deity. The Divine Essence of Boehme's godhead
as the Being whose essence is to reveal itself is not only present in Erigena's text,
but is articulated by Plotinus in the *Enneads*[51] where god as the One must manifest and cause its own essence which is to reveal itself.

Boehme's postulation of the polarities of God's will, at once both loving and wrathful, may be seen as a correlate to standard Plotinian "theodicy." For Boehme, evil was a residue of God's original "darkness" and was part and parcel of God's creative process. For Plotinus, evil is the outward extreme of God's dialectical manifestation, "matter conceived as a negative factor, *when* the soul turns toward it, away from the One, instead of remaining faithful to its ultimate source, and directly *before* the soul realizes the sterility of this choice, and initiates its epistrophic dialectic."[52] Von der Luft convincingly shows that Hegel's use of the positive significance of the negative cannot be primarily derived from Boehme's theosophic speculation and is more likely attributed to the cosmology of Proclus and Plotinus whom Hegel would know quite well since his friend and Heidelberg colleague, Georg Friedrich Creuzer, prepared standard editions of both philosophers.

Hegel was too broad and systematic a thinker to have borrowed concepts limited to only one or even a few sources. Because Hegel never offered a formal theory of the unconscious abyss, allusions to Boehme and neo-Platonism are not surprising and may be seen as a product of Hegel's own dialectical assimilation of philosophical knowledge that had formed a sediment on his thinking. But as with any current of thought dealing with first principles, metaphysical turns of thought may be ultimately traced back to antiquity on some archaic or unrefined level. Yet Hegel was an independent thinker and his dialectic lives up to its name. Hegel's system surpasses his predecessors while simultaneously canceling but preserving their insights. What is most interesting about the influence of the *Ungrund* that figures so prominently in Hegel's system, albeit unintended by him, is that it forms the foundation for spirit to manifest. Because the retentive element of the dialectic prefigures the self-unfolding of spirit in all its subsequent stages, the unconscious is always present in the most exalted forms of spirit, although in a preserved and subordinated mode.

Drawing on the ontological speculations of Boehme and the neo-Platonists, Hegel could not elude the inclusion (even unconsciously) of an implicit theory of the unconscious that plays such a central role in the metaphysics of spirit. While Hegel's system is a formally articulated rational enterprise, the presence of the concept of the unconscious allows for an elaborate articulation of desire and irrationality (which Schelling heavily emphasized) as well as a theory of abnormal psychology that Daniel Berthold-Bond[53] has so brilliantly illuminated within Hegel's philosophy. Therefore, the unconscious is instrumental in the normative processes of cognition, emotion, and mental adjustment as well as in illness.

Although Hegel was influenced by theosophic and neo-Platonic thought, as we have seen, he shows greater affinity for Aristotle rather than neo-Platonism in regarding *nous* (νόοζ) as absolute and underived.[54] In fact, Hegel maintains a clear allegiance to Aristotle with respects to the soul, the principle of internal teleology, the unification of form and matter, the process of the actualization of pure thought, and in elevating *Sittlichkeit* to the apex of human reality through self-realized freedom.[55] Although I will not elaborate on these comparisons here, Hegel's reappropriation of Aristotelian teleology allows him, through his Logic, to introduce an inner principle of self-derivation in which all particularization is developed from within the universal. This is why Hegel enlists Aristotle in his initial discussion of the soul: the soul in its implicitness is the "*sleep* of spirit;—the passive nous of Aristotle" (*EG* § 389), a simple universality. As with Aristotle's *de Anima*, Hegel's depiction of the soul moves from immediate potentiality to mediated actualization through the modification and differentiation of its nascent corporeality. Thus, the soul, as with spirit, is the process of moving from indeterminate, undifferentiated immediacy to determinate, differentiated mediacy. And this is partially why Boehme and neo-Platonists are attractive to Hegel: spirit becomes a self-generating movement.

The implications of Hegel's theory of the *Ungrund* far surpass those of Boehme's by providing a systematic and rigorous justification for the dialectically self-articulated process of human consciousness and subjectivity. As a result, the unifying and synthetic nature of the dialectic finds its origins in an unconscious teleology that underscores the positive significance of negation as spirit elevates itself to its highest potentiality-for-Being.

The positive significance of the negative is a cardinal element in the organization of the *Ungrund* and subsequently the self-manifestation of Spirit. This point opens potential vistas that merit careful exploration, a point that will be emphasized and examined over again throughout the scope of this project. If the *Ungrund* is indeed negativity as Being-in-and-for-itself, then it is essential to the dialectic and may be seen as the fertile source of all psychic reality. This notion poses difficulties in reconciling the dual intentionality of spirit as an upward synthetic and unifying movement and a destructive and regressive drive that is both the source of all rational and irrational determination. The dialectic as determinate negativity is both constructive and destructive, harmonious and chaotic, insofar as all harmony exists within unrest and upheaval and all chaos within a unifying purposeful order. The disharmonious unity that comes with spirit's sublation is itself a paradox. Negative activity is both the power of death and desire and the elevation of spirit as it cultivates a unity through pure self-realization. The *abyss* therefore becomes the darkness of the "not" which undercuts itself and becomes the source of all. Unlike Nietzsche, this is not an abyss we must confront in order to make sense out of our lives, rather, it is an abyss we are continually emerging out of, only to sink back into as finite individuals. It is this "tarrying with the negative" that defines the life of spirit who "wins its truth only when, in utter dismemberment, it finds itself" (*PS* § 32). Such can be said for the quest of self-consciousness: not only does Spirit find its culmination in the unity of aesthetic, religious, and rational life, its very attainment is contingent on the epigenesis and exaltation of the unconscious soul.

THE SPECTRA OF FICHTE

The premiere idealist, Johann Gottlieb Fichte (1762–1814) is known as "the philosopher of the *I*."[56] Such a narcissistic characterization is accompanied by the biographical fact that he truly had an ego worthy of his subject matter. Notwithstanding, Fichte was Jena's resident genius during the time Schelling and Hegel arrived on the scene. As the foremost successor to Kant, Fichte instigated the philosophical tradition commonly known as German Idealism. In fact, it was Fichte's anonymously published *Critique of All Revelation*,[57] initially thought by many to have been Kant's, that first won him a post at Jena—only to lose that same post in 1799 for his controversial political and religious lecturing, just a year after Schelling had been appointed to the faculty.[58] Fichte's as well as Schelling's influence on Hegel was considerable, and it may even be said that Fichte and Schelling were mainly responsible for dividing German thought into the disciplines of Spirit and Nature, a division Hegel sought to reconcile.

Fichte's emphasis on the primacy of the I (*Ich*) or Self (*Selbst*) deserves special attention not only for its inauguration of the idealist movement, but because this emphasis had a direct impact on Hegel's thinking on spirit. While not formally stated by Fichte, the notion of the unconscious is deeply embedded in his *Wissenschaftslehre* (1794), a text Hegel knew intimately because the *Difference Between Fichte's and Schelling's System of Philosophy* (1801), commonly known as the *Differenzschrift*, was his first acknowledged philosophical publication.[59] However, Fichte's theory of the unconscious is largely overshadowed by his attention to self-consciousness. As Eduard von Hartmann (1868) puts it:

> [E]lements of the Unconscious are to be found in Fichte, but they appear only casually, as vague hints scattered here and there, and these promising thought-blossoms were soon buried under the later growths without having borne any fruit.[60]

Because Fichte offered no formal account of the unconscious structures and operations of the self-positing self in his *Wissenschaftslehre*, we will need to examine its latent or implied presence with respect to the *Ungrund* and its implications for Hegel.

Fichte's *Wissenschaftslehre*, literally the "Doctrine of Science," but customarily translated as the "Science of Knowledge,"[61] closely resembles Kant's transcendental idealism, but it is more appropriately interpreted as a radicalized reappropriation or systematic correction of Kant where all objects of possible experience are grounded or are necessarily conditioned by some nonempirical activity of the subject.[62] The *Wissenschaftslehre* attempts to address three central issues: (1) that Kant's formulation of apperception was incomplete; (2) which may be remedied by offering an account of the autonomous self-positing activity of the self as the foundation of subjectivity; (3) that is furthermore responsible for resolving the practical question of moral freedom. Fichte's *Wissenschaftslehre* stands for a doctrine of systematically grounded knowledge that is itself the proper role and task of philosophy, thus making philosophy the eminent science. For Fichte, philosophy is *Wissenschaftslehre*. Like all modern philosophers, Fichte, no less than Hegel, was concerned with ultimate knowledge, or absolute knowledge regarding knowledge—the self, nature, God, and freedom were major metaphysical preoccupations.

Fichte's *Wissenschaftslehre* is a theory of self-consciousness, what Dieter Henrich has called Fichte's "original insight,"[63] because Fichte was the first philosopher to consider the actual conditions or ground that make self-consciousness possible without taking consciousness as its supposition. Following Kant, Fichte was concerned with justifying the nonempirical ground of experience through transcendental deductive or a priori maneuvers. Taking over Kant's analysis of the ground and scope of knowledge, Fichte focuses on the "feeling of necessity" that accompanies our intentional representation of objects, and elevates freedom to the pinnacle of the mind's operations—the *I* freely posits or asserts itself absolutely—the representation of reality is entirely attributed to the human mind. Fichte's emphasis on freedom as the foundation for mental activity was an attempt to circumvent the problematic division of Kant's theoretical and practical philosophy, a distinction that demanded serious attention and revision through an integrated theory of mind.[64] The role of freedom was such an ultimate concern for Fichte that he himself credited his philosophy as the "first system of freedom."[65]

While I have no intention of offering an extended interpretation or critique of Fichte's system, it will be necessary to examine his implicit theory of unconscious mental activity and determine whether this had had any impact on Hegel's thinking. It is well known that Hegel thought poorly of Fichte; in the words of H. S. Harris: "Toward Fichte, Hegel had always been rather cool."[66] Yet despite Hegel's reproach of Fichte in the *Difference* essay, an issue I will address later, as well as in chapter V of the *Phenomenology*,[67] there are many currents of thought that overlap in Hegel's philosophy and therefore merit our attention.

In the *Wissenschaftslehre* (§§ 1–3), Fichte discerns three fundamental "principles" (*Grundsät*) or transcendental acts of the mind: (1) the *I* posits itself absolutely; (2) then counterposits itself through negation as a ~ or not-*I*; (3) only to reconcile its division by counterpositing once again the divisible *I* from the divisible not-*I*, thus taking account of the mutual limitation between the *I* and the not-*I* as its mediated solution. It will be necessary to carefully examine each of these principles in order to bring Fichte into closer dialogue with Hegel and explore the possible compatibility of Fichte's model of self-consciousness with Hegel's theory of unconscious spirit.

In the first principle, Fichte demonstrates that the *I* is entirely the result of its own activity;—it does not presuppose an original being or ground other than this activity itself. Its very being *is* activity, the activity of its self-positing, hence its own becoming. The *I* is therefore "unconditioned"; its own activity is its ground. Fichte states:

> Hence what is *absolutely posited*, and *founded on itself*, is the ground of *one particular* activity . . . of the human mind, and thus of its pure character; the pure character of activity as such. (*W* § 1: I, 96)

For Fichte, as for Hegel, the self is pure activity (*Tathandlung*). From Fichte's account, the "pure character of activity" or as Hegel describes it, this "unrest that is the self" (*PS* § 22) is what ultimately constitutes the foundation of the mental.

The "Act" as Fichte describes, is the activity of the *I*—an assertion, an animate act of will. This assertion is simply a "self-assertion," an "absolute" and "necessary" affirmation of its existence—at once both being and ground. "It is at once the agent and the product of action; the active, and what the activity brings about" (*W* § 1: I, 96). The affirmation or willful self-assertion of "I" is the animation of the soul—an animism—the animus of *anima*. Such self-positing is the animating motive, intention, or purpose of the soul as activity.

Recall from our previous discussion of Boehme as well as Plotinus, the *Ungrund* precedes the will's arousing itself to self-awareness—the being whose essence it is to reveal itself. Thus, self-affirmation as "I" is the primordial act, an underground activity that is itself the ground of its original being. At this stage, Fichte's absolute self may be compared to the unconscious functions of Kant's transcendental unity of apperception—the impersonal unifying agent of all mental activity that directly knows but cannot be known directly. But the presence of the *Ungrund* within Fichte's self-positing *I* may also be inferred because it reveals the primordial activity of the self's unconscious recognition of itself as it "imposes" a "form" on itself—the form of object—thus grounding its own existence (*W* § 1: I, 97). This "substrate" or *Ungrund* is a form of consciousness without having "real" or externally actualized sensuous consciousness. Fichte is suggesting, as does Hegel, that the self *projects* itself—"I" asserts itself through primal activity—the posit (*setzen*)—and gives itself form, a sense of unconscious self-consciousness. The projection of consciousness from unconsciousness—an unconscious *Ich*—may be clearly seen in Freud who in *The Ego and the Id* adduced that "[t]he ego is first and foremost a bodily ego; it is not merely a surface entity, but is itself the projection of a surface" (*SE*, 19, 26). The *I* initially projects itself into being, a being it had only known unconsciously.

When the self posits itself unconsciously, it gives itself a ground—a "*something*"—on which it can further act on its own activity. The point Fichte is trying to make is that through positing, the self gives itself its own content as itself; hence, the self has an original sense of unconscious self-consciousness. However, such rudimentary self-consciousness is not the same as the self-consciousness of oneself as an object for consciousness, rather this unconscious self-awareness is a form of self-consciousness of the *act* of being oneself who posits. For Fichte,

> The self exists only insofar as it is conscious of itself. . . . You cannot think at all without subjoining in thought your self, as conscious of itself; from your self-consciousness you can never abstract. (*W*, § 1: I, 97)

Fichte explains what Kant left unanswered: the a priori ground or condition of the "I think" of consciousness and subjectivity itself is activity, and activity is what constitutes the self. "Being" and "doing" are the same, insofar as the activity of positing is a doing. In Fichte's words, "*To posit*" and "*to be*" are "perfectly identical" (*W* § 1: I, 98). For Fichte, the mind does not merely project static or fixed categories onto experience as Kant suggests, rather, like Hegel's viewpoint, it actively structures experience, hence itself, through a fluid dynamic process of positing. Such positing initially takes place unconsciously, and the *I* is aware of such activity even if it is not fully self-conscious of itself as a subject who takes itself as a subject.

This initial pre-familiarity of the absolute self as unconscious self-consciousness takes place within the realm of *interiority* before consciousness becomes externalized and assumes its regular course of development. "*The self exists for itself*"—necessarily—it "*begins by an absolute positing of its own existence*"(*W* § 1: I, 98). But this "begins" is an eternal beginning of the self-asserting will that proclaims "I am!," or more aptly, "I!" At this level of self-assertion, an unrefined self-consciousness is already implicit in the act of positing which becomes explicit once it is posited; there is an unconscious recognition that the "I" exists, which wants to express itself. This position is not unlike Hegel's notion of unconscious spirit that emerges from the abyss of its own "inwardness" and "internality" (*EG* § 453) only to intuit itself as soul that feels itself through its own activity.

Fichte is particularly vague about the relationship between the absolute self having consciousness let alone unconscious self-consciousness. Presumably, the absolute self is conscious and necessarily has to be or it would not be a self. But given that Fichte does not even define what he means by "positing," our attribution of unconscious self-awareness must be viewed within the context of what Fichte does not directly say but what nevertheless may be inferred about the original positing activity of the self. The difficulty of interpretation is largely due to the opacity of the text itself, but unconscious agency must be presupposed if the absolute self is to be able to posit itself at all.

Because the self posits itself absolutely, it does so without the use of mediation, hence the posit is simply the expression of its self-affirmation as pure generative activity. Fichte states: "The I posits itself *absolutely*, i.e, without any mediation."[68] The self-consciousness involved here would thus be prereflective. This would imply that nothing exists prior to the positing activity—the self must emerge as self-consciousness, albeit unconsciously. As Dieter Henrich puts it, "[T]here would not be any Self-Subject prior to self-consciousness; rather, the subject, too, first emerges at the same time as the whole consciousness expressed in the identity 'I = I'."[69] There is an immediacy to the posit—the entire self materializes all at once; thus, for Fichte, "self-consciousness is immediate."[70] Therefore, the question of original ground *is* the act, the I *is* the positing itself as self-grounding, which necessitates its becoming aware of itself for itself as the self takes itself as its object. Fichte alludes to this: "[N]o object comes to consciousness except under the condition that I am also conscious of myself."[71]

This immediate form of self-consciousness is important for our understanding of the unconscious organization of the self, for in its immediacy unconscious self-consciousness is not epistemically accessible to conscious reflective awareness. Fichte tells us: "That immediate self-consciousness is not raised to consciousness nor can it ever be. As soon as one reflects on it, it ceases to be what it is, and it disappears into a higher region."[72] As we will see, the spectra of Fichte's theory of self-consciousness has further implications for Hegel's notion of the abyss, a topic we will take up later when we examine Hegel's reflection thesis of self-recognition. In the meantime, let us turn our attention to the role of negation in Fichte's model of self-consciousness and see how it influences Hegel's dialectic.

In Fichte's second principle, The *I* engages in counterpositing (*entgegenset-zen*) itself to itself as a not—a negation. At this stage, the self enters into a conflict with what it is not—its opposite. "Opposition in general is posited absolutely by the self" (*W* § 2: I, 103). The ~ *I* is opposed to the *I* and thus forms a firm antithesis. This opposition immediately propels the self into a psychic conflict with itself; although the negation is posited by the *I* and for the *I*, it is nonetheless *other* than the *I*. Hence, in Fichte's second principle or act of the mind's positing, the self is made aware of its limitation, its finitude—its *nothingness*.

Upon engaging in this new act—negating—there is a doubling of the positing; yet this doubling is a continual series of positing that stands in *relation* to both affirmation and denial, identity and difference, self and not-self. Fichte notes: "Opposition is possible only on the assumption of a unity of consciousness between the self that posits and the self that opposes. . . . It is only in relation to a positing that it becomes a counterpositing" (*W* § 2: I, 104). Hence, the self's initial activity opposes itself—its own activity—which in turn is negative activity. This negation is also an absolute determination of opposition, an absolute standpoint of what is not—of "nonexistence." It is not hard to see the impact of Fichte's account of negativity on Hegel's dialectic. Fichte's "*principle of opposition*" or "*category of negation*" is the stock and trade of spirit's laborious movement. The violent character of negativity, negation, and conflict is the essential driving force of the dialectic itself. In fact, for Hegel, "*being* and *nothing* are the same" (*SL*, 82)—a pure unity of becoming. Without negation, the dialectical motion of thought would not be possible. Like Fichte's self-asserting *I* as pure activity, of "unrest," spirit is a stream—it flows.

Fichte maintains that the act of counterpositing conditions the self as "matter," that is, with respect to content, but remains "absolutely unconditioned in form" (*W* § 2: I, 104). What he means by this is that the act of self-positing gives the *I* substance—a "*something*" in which the *I* and not-*I* or self and non-self are counterposited. Therefore, the act of opposing is "*materially* conditioned" because being an act at all, it is in relation to another act and thus is grounded as an existent being. The fact that "we act *so*" and not otherwise is unconditioned "*formally*" because we don't know how other than to act. For Fichte, the activity that forms the relation between the absolute self and the absolute non-self poses an ontological tension, that is, opposition introduces a gap between identity (already "presuppose[d]" by the self-positing of the self) and difference that must be resolved by a "decree of reason" (*W* § 3: I, 106).

The dialectical tension between the self and the not-self "mutually *limit* one another," hence each opposite is limited by the other. If reason is to succeed, it must find a way to reconcile and overcome such mutually limiting finite positions. Fichte maintains that the task of the third principle or mental operation is to seek their unification—a unity already contained in the first principle. The idea of limit through negation also contains the notion of divisibility—the "*capacity for quantity* in general, not any *determinate* quantity" (*W* § 3: I, 109). Here both the *I* and the not-*I* are "*absolutely posited as divisible*." Therefore, the *I* counterposits in the *I* the divisible *I* and the divisible not-*I*; thereby the conflict imposed by opposition is neutralized if not nullified, at least in principle, through the relation of mutual limitation.[73] For Fichte, the concept of divisibility unifies the opposing self from the non-self—opposition is synthesized.

At this point, we may say that Fichte gives conceptual birth to the well-characterized yet often bastardized triad: *thesis—antithesis—synthesis*. Fichte asserts:

> Just as there can be no antithesis without synthesis, no synthesis without antithesis, so there can be neither without a thesis—an absolute positing, whereby an A (the self) is neither equated nor opposed to any other, but is just absolutely posited. (*W* § 3: I, 115)

This dialectic is attributed to Hegel by many analytic philosophers, most notably Karl Popper, yet it is such an imprecise and watered-down appraisal of Hegel's method that anyone with a favorable attitude toward transcendental idealism is appalled by its oversimplification. For Fichte, the synthetic process presupposes an opposition—the initial act is the generation of difference—which demands reconciliation. The ultimate ground has no ground, only self-affirmation or assertion—completely unconditioned by anything other than its own activity—then it proceeds to generate its own self-opposition within itself only to seek a resolution of conflict through a synthetic function, which then gives rise once more to opposition, and thus this process continues toward absolute unity.

Fichte is ultimately concerned with the complete abolition of all contradiction united in a single absolute unity of consciousness—a unity from which the self emerges and one in which it arrives through an onerous strife to terminate opposition. Fichte clearly anticipates Hegel's grand synthesis or complex holism. He declares:

> —All syntheses established must be rooted in the highest synthesis which we have just effected, and be derivable therefrom. In the self and not-self thus united, and to the extent that they are united thereby, we have therefore to seek out opposing characteristics that remain, and to unite them through a new ground of conjunction, which again must be contained in the highest conjunctive ground of all. And in the opposites united by this first synthesis, we again have to find new opposites, and to combine them by a new ground

of conjunction, contained in that already derived. And this we must continue so far as we can, until we arrive at opposites which can no longer be altogether combined, and are thereby transported into the practical part of this work. (*W* § 3: I, 115)

Fichte ultimately characterizes the self as an infinite "striving" (*streben*). This is especially important for Fichte's "practical" or ethical philosophy, for such striving for an ideal unity of both theoretical knowledge and moral action is the goal. However, the infinite striving of the self arises out of its inability to complete itself in the world of knowing, which initiates its subsequent move to action where the conditions for satisfaction may come only in the infinite future.

The self's infinite striving has implications for Fichte's theory of freedom. For Fichte, the self is ultimately free—freedom being the source of the self. But the self is not so perfect that it does not have to strive: we strive because we cannot achieve pure knowing, thus instituting the transition to the practical realm. Yet Fichte paradoxically views the self as infinitely free, but as self-determination, freedom by itself is divine while striving is not. Fichte argues that the movement from indeterminacy or infinite freedom to empirical determination is necessary because the absolute self is nothing if it is merely itself. Thus begins the self-determination of the self initiated on the level of theoretical knowledge. This enterprise remains incomplete, however, which triggers the transition to Fichte's theory of action.

But even before Fichte articulates his ethical theory, the conflict between freedom and limit is seen to be reconciled in theoretical knowledge through the powers of imagination (*W* § 4, III: I, 209–217). For Fichte, imagination becomes the ultimate ground of freedom and thus provides a stable unity for the self's ability to overcome contradiction. The infinite striving or ultimate task of the self is to overcome the causally and mechanically determining objective world and to achieve an absolute standpoint of knowledge as embodied freedom. Like the synthetic thrust of Fichte's system, imagination "is what gives strength and completeness to the whole; it must be a system, and it must be *one*; the opposites must be united" (*W* § 3: I, 115). Imagination is therefore the basis for the entire work of the mind. Such an infinite, unbounded striving or desire for the absolute unity of opposition—a single unity of consciousness—is the hallmark of Hegelian absolute knowing. Although this skeletal structure of the Fichtean dialectic is taken up and refined by Hegel, Fichte's influence is nonetheless profound. Fichte's treatment of imagination is further relevant to Hegel's emphasis on "intelligence as [an] unconscious abyss" (*EG* § 453) that is operative throughout the stages of theoretical spirit, a subject we will attend to carefully when examining Hegel's account of imagination. For Hegel, the unconscious is intelligent and intelligible. But even Fichte recognizes that the aboriginal ground of psychic life has an unconscious foundation, at once disclosed through imagination, and known through "intellectual intuition." He states:

Into the infinite beyond . . . there is projected a determinate product of the absolutely productive imagination, by means of a dark, unreflected intuition that
does not reach determinate consciousness. (W § 4, III: I, 235)

Here Fichte is very clear that there is an unconscious "determinate product"
(e.g., images and thought) at work in the imagination that is "projected" by a
"dark," or as Hegel says "nightlike" abyss which Fichte labels as an "unreflected
intuition." This dark intuition is none other than an unconscious region of the
mind where the free agency of the intuited self is active and determining—willing the content of productive imagination, beneath the "reach" of "determinate
consciousness." This underworld is the ground of freedom—the *Ungrund*—al-
lowing higher forms of consciousness to flourish—unified in its depths. We can
see parallels to Kant's transcendental unity of apperception, the "I think" that accompanies all representations.[74] There remains a powerful connection to the
transcendental unity, because Fichte's absolute self functions as a unifying unifier, an unconscious organizing mental agent.

The unconscious is responsible for the most basal ground of cognition and
imagination. Fichte's ego may be further related to Kant's notion of intellectual
intuition as a self-intuiting operation—the positing of its self to itself. As a borderline construct standing between conceptual and experiential knowledge,
Fichte's reliance on intellectual intuition attempts to explain the very process by
which the *I* comes about in elevated consciousness. For Fichte, intellectual intuition is therefore the initial structure of the self itself as process. Like Kant's
pure apperception, Fichte's self-intuition is tantamount to the "I think" that accompanies all representations—the very feature that makes consciousness possible.[75] The absolute self, the self-positing *I* that "exists insofar as it is conscious of
itself" is an original unconscious self-consciousness that is a form of "unreflected
intuition." The point here is, that as a particular kind of self-consciousness, the
absolute or unconditioned ground of the self as subjectivity is unconscious
agency. The subject cannot exist apart from its own self-awareness of itself.[76] The
I is unconsciously "self-grounded."

In the realm of this "infinite beyond" that Fichte attributes to the depths of
imagination—where Freud would credit the unconscious ego—lies the striving,
the yearning—a desire for unity, a *wish*. It is in this mystery of activity that we may
find the original *I*—the soul that intuits itself. As we will further see, this characterization of the absolute self asserting itself within its "dark" nether-regions may
be attributed to Hegel's feeling soul. Moreover, this "immediate self-consciousness"
that Fichte attributes to the self-positing *I* may be advanced by our treatment of
Hegel's understanding of unconscious spirit. If the primal self knows itself intu-
itively, that is prereflectively—before mediated self-consciousness occurs—then we
may say that the original form of consciousness is a self-consciousness that is properly understood as unconscious and thus belonging to an unconscious self.

It is important to understand that Fichte's prereflective[77] self-consciousness
is not a mediated self-consciousness where the self reflects on itself as an object

and/or subject of consciousness, rather, the positing self is a nonrepresentational self-awareness that is the transcendental condition or possibility for consciousness. Therefore, this original unity of self-consciousness as the pure formal *I*, is the condition for the possibility of experience (hence, rational and reflective absolute self-consciousness), and the agent and archetype of consciousness. Fichte's insights are of even further importance when examining Hegel's recognition theory of self-consciousness, for if unconscious spirit intuits its own being before it emerges in higher shapes of consciousness, then spirit occupies the same ontological space as Fichte's absolute self—it is aware of itself unconsciously. Whether spirit as self-positing is a self-constituting existence or substantive self-determination will need further exploration, for this would seem to imply that spirit, like Fichte's absolute positing self, thinks itself into existence.

Fichte's immediate, intuiting self-conscious self brings Hegel's feeling soul into close proximity with our future analysis of unconscious spirit. Hegel, however, would think poorly of such talk because not only did he dissociate himself from Fichte in the *Difference* essay, in the *Science of Logic* he specifically rejects, or more appropriately sublates, both "positing" and "external" reflection in favor of "determinate" reflection that later becomes the topic of "speculative" thought. But as Robert Pippin points out, Hegel could never purge himself of Fichte for his theory of subjectivity is dispersed throughout Hegel's system as well as his speculative treatment of thought as a "self-determining activity."[78] For Hegel as for Fichte, thought is ultimately free. In the *Encyclopaedia Logic*, Hegel himself says:

> [T]hought is free and withdrawn into itself, free of all [given] material, purely at home with itself. When we think freely, voyaging on the open sea, with nothing under us and nothing over us, in solitude, alone by ourselves—then we are purely at home with ourselves.[79]

Fichte's influence can be clearly seen in Hegel's treatment of determinate reflection in his main *Logic*—thought is self-determined:

> Essence is at first, simple self-relation, pure *identity*. This is its determination, but as such it is rather the absence of any determination.
> Secondly, the proper determination is *difference*, a difference that is, on the one hand external and indifferent, *diversity* in general, and on the other, is opposed diversity or *opposition*.
> Thirdly, as *contradiction*, the opposition is reflected into itself and withdraws into *ground*. (*SL*, 409)

While here in the "Doctrine of Essence," thought is now reflective, hence beyond Fichte's initial prereflective self-consciousness, but the dialectic of identity, difference, and contradiction as ground remains a familiar Fichtean theme. And for Hegel, "resolved contradiction is therefore ground, essence as unity of the positive and the negative" (*SL*, 435). In the end, "the positive and the negative are the same." For both Fichte and Hegel, the unity of affirmation and negation are achieved in a higher synthesis.

Hegel's breach from Fichte's philosophy as well as Schelling's was immediately clear after the *Difference* essay appeared, yet as we have seen, Hegel could not help but take over several key concepts in Fichte and put his own spin on them. Yet what remained Hegel's lifelong complaint against Fichte was Fichte's emphasis on a mere *Sollen*, the infinite striving of the self that ensured an endless process rather than a completed whole. "But why should an endless endeavour *not* be the ultimate truth of our condition?"[80] By 1800, we do know that Hegel did have a preliminary philosophical position of his own that he sketched out in an essay of which only one-twentieth of the whole remains—two sheets typically referred to as the *Systemfragment*—a document exceedingly difficult to interpret.[81] But in those two pages, Hegel expressed that the task of philosophical reflection was to reconcile antinomies, which made it necessary for philosophy to pass over into a religious consciousness in order to complete this task. Fichte's theory of the absolute self was used as an example to illustrate his position.

When Hegel's identification with Schelling's philosophy of Identity became more apparent, Fichte's focus on subjectivity over the natural world lost its appeal. Hegel's treatment of Fichte in the *Difference* piece may be interpreted as a critical, yet constructive evaluation of his philosophy; but by the time Hegel wrote *Faith and Knowledge*, his view of Fichte became more conceptually scathing to the point that it has been interpreted by many as a destructive polemic.[82] At the heart of Hegel's reasoning for the rejection of Fichte lies the same problem he had with Kant: the epistemological insistence that we can never know reality completely, in-itself. The Kantian *Ding-an-sich* or the Fichtean *Anstoss* is a steadfast limit, obstacle, or "check": the mind is always precluded from absolute knowing. In Hegel's estimate, Fichte's *Wissenschaftslehre* then becomes a justification for rational faith. As we have previously noted, for Hegel, there is nothing that we know more certain than the thing-in-itself, for in order to think it at all is to presuppose that we already know it—we have already crossed beyond the limit by virtue of positing it. For Fichte, reason is condemned to a "bad infinite"[83] crusade that is never terminated nor does it ever truly find itself; reason must be suspended in favor of faith—a conceptual move that Hegel just can't buy. Unlike Fichte, Hegel sees spirit through to its end—to the completion of its coming to presence as pure self-consciousness—absolute knowing, or perhaps more appropriately, absolute conceiving.[84]

Another problem with Fichte is that his self-positing self does not account for the brute facticity of the world that confronts us with the unexpected complexities and dynamic relations that Hegel's dialectic of spirit takes into account. Fichte does not give reality or the givenness of the world its proper due. It is for these reasons that Schelling's theory of Nature superseded the limitations inherent in Fichte's system. Yet despite the genuine problems in Fichte's critical idealism, Hegel is greatly indebted to him for providing some groundwork that Hegel himself later took up and refined in his own speculative science.

Systematic differences aside, we can clearly see a number of parallels between Fichte's absolute ego and Hegel's notion of subjective spirit: (1) Both are a pure activity of becoming in which their very being *is* activity; (2) Both form their own ground through a process of self-grounding as self-determining agents; (3) Both "project" themselves as a self-imposed form; (4) Such projection is a self-affirmation or assertion of their being whether conceived of as "positing" or "intuiting"; (5) Both emerge from a state of "internality" and "inwardness," from a "dark" or "nightlike" mine of the mind; (6) where they have sensibility as an "unreflected intuition" that "acquires a substrate" without having any "real consciousness."

Hegel's reliance on the negative activity of the dialectical evolution of spirit may also be partially informed by Fichte's triadic dialectic encompassing the synthetic unification of identity and difference as well as his emphasis on the "principle of opposition" or "category of negation." The self-imposed tension of limitation, finitude, and nothingness as negativity sets the stage for growth and provides the impetus for a synthetic movement that seeks reconciliation in the form of a higher unification. For Fichte, limitation through negation introduces divisibility into the internal structures of the ego. For Hegel, spirit disperses itself as a plurality within a dynamically informed self-articulated unity or complex whole. Both Fichte and Hegel are concerned with the complete abolition of all contradiction united in a single absolute unity of consciousness. Ego and spirit emerge from within themselves as a spontaneous[85] act of assertion or autonomy, a "self-determining activity" that is "free." From this initial act, both generate opposition and labor arduously to end it, weathering a gauntlet until, in its quest, it broaches pure self-consciousness. But for Fichte, the self always remains an infinite striving, a longing—a yearning to complete itself. As we will see in Hegel, deep in the bowels of the abyss, spirit pines, *it* yearns. Just as negativity, internal upheaval, and violence become the driving brigade behind the dialectical progression of spirit, desire (*Begierde*) becomes the general engine of history, forging the path of natural consciousness from its archaic infancy, becoming more intimately aware of itself as process.

Because Fichte offers no textual references to the unconscious, which may only be inferred, my general comparison of the absolute self and the abyss must be viewed with caution. While the pure activity of the self-positing *I* shares similarities with unconscious spirit's burgeoning process of becoming, Hegel is careful to situate the process of the coming into being of the soul within his anthropological treatment of spirit and thus addresses the role of the abyss more directly from the standpoint of his logic. Through the methodological consistency of the internal unfolding of the soul, Hegel is able to articulate with more clarity the logical model by which his doctrine of spirit rests. Once the architectonic functions of spirit are systematically prepared, Hegel is furthermore able to explicate the psychological operations of thought and desire that necessitate the active inclusion of the abyss, a central feature of mind Fichte's *Wissenschaftslehre* leaves unanswered. This will become evident in our next chapter when Hegel describes the soul's initial transition from indeterminate to determinate being.

ENTERS SCHELLING

By the time Friedrich Wilhelm Joseph von Schelling (1775–1854) was twenty-three, he had been given a professorship at Jena, thereby earning himself the well-deserved title "prodigy" for the rest of his life. Close friends with Hegel while he was a theology student at Tübingen, Schelling was influential in helping Hegel initiate his academic career. In fact, it was Schelling who invited Hegel to come to Jena to prepare himself before applying for a teaching license, and soon Hegel was known as his disciple and coadjutor—a partnership that led to their collaboration as co-editors of the *Critical Journal of Philosophy*.[86]

Schelling's *System of Transcendental Idealism*[87] of 1800 and Hegel's *Phenomenology* of 1807 may be said to be parallel attempts to overcome (*aufheben*) the traditional oppositions of subject and object, sensuality and reason, consciousness and nature.[88] Schelling's *System* attempts to present a history of human consciousness by retracing the origins of the self-construction of reason, a preliminary and abortive attempt to capture the all-embracing vision that Hegel's *Phenomenology* claims to provide, viz., absolute knowing. For Schelling, the purpose of his *System* was "to enlarge transcendental idealism into what it really should be, namely a system of all knowledge" culminating in the identity of subject and object in aesthetic consciousness, a thesis he developed in his philosophy of identity (*Identitätsphilosophie*) and philosophy of nature (*Naturphilosophie*).[89] Schelling was among the first to dissolve the subject-object dichotomy calling for a philosophy of Identity between absolute subjectivity and absolute objectivity: nature—mind, were identical.

Following Fichte, Schelling's *System* is an attempt to reconcile the dualism inherent in Kant's distinction between the phenomenal and noumenal realms of reality by replacing them with a single ontological, transcendental psychic agency that actively creates both subjective and objective poles of experience.[90] This alleged unitary, productive activity, however, does not appear in our empirical experience, rather, consciousness finds itself confronted with a recalcitrant incongruity, contradiction, or gap between the mental and the object world, between subjective and objective being, which in turn creates intractable limitations to the power and range of knowledge. In order for the primordial psychical agency to achieve unlimited knowledge of itself as infinite, it must first confront its limitations and surpass them. As Edward Allen Beech informs us:

> Only in the experience of an infinite becoming, a perpetual going beyond and overcoming of limits, can the implicit infinitude of the generative activity be realized. Hence the original unity has to become a temporal duality in order ultimately to return to itself as a higher unity.[91]

This is a striking anticipation of Hegel's abolition of the Kantian *Ding-an-sich*, where the very act of confronting limits and experiencing them as such already entails their overcoming. From the *Encyclodaedia Logic*, Hegel (1817) states:

> Something is only known, or even felt, to be a restriction, or a defect, if one is at the same time *beyond* it. . . . [I]t is precisely the designation of something as finite or restricted that contains the proof of the *actual presence* of the Infinite, or Unrestricted, and that there can be no knowledge of limit unless the Unlimited is *on this side* within consciousness. (*EL* § 60)

For Schelling and Hegel, consciousness and its opposite are conjoined in a single mutually inclusive unity. This claim advanced by Schelling situates the polarities of consciousness and limit within an all-encompassing dialectic: the limitation that separates also binds; one cannot be conceived of without the other—each side merely reflects half of the totality. Hence, what lies beneath or beyond consciousness contains its very nature, and conversely what permeates the confines of nature is consciousness itself. The limit is therefore suspended, the boundary subsumed: inner world and outer world become one.

Schelling's *System* offers an ontological account of mind that no philosopher until him had dared to postulate—the unconscious became the *sine qua non* of psychic life. While having its rudiments in neo-Platonism, advanced by Boehme, posited by Leibniz but merely implicit in Fichte, Schelling was the first to offer a coherent and systematic theory of the unconscious. His insistence on the primacy of the unconscious may be summed up by comments such as this: "[N]ature begins as unconscious and ends as conscious" where "unconscious activity operates . . . through the conscious" (*STI*, 219). Nowhere do we encounter a more transparent account of the centrality of the unconscious until von Hartmann and Freud.

Schelling was an orthodox disciple of Fichte before he developed his own speculative philosophy of nature, yet Fichte's impact on Schelling's thought would always remain imbedded in his theory of consciousness. Self-activity is the principle constituting feature of *Geist*, which is first and foremost an unconscious activity. For Schelling, "the self is originally *mere* activity" (*STI*, 36) which is self-constituting, thus "nonobjective" (*STI*, 26). The self is originally pure "inwardness" as self-consciousness—pure thinking. "The self is nothing distinct from its thinking; the thinking of the self and the self as such are absolutely one" (*STI*, 26). In anticipation of Sartre, the self is "not a thing," rather a pure process that is dynamic, telic, and self-energizing—an agency burgeoning with innate potencies. Following Fichte, Schelling envisioned the self *as* self-consciousness, an original unconscious unity of being as thought self-enacted through "intellectual intuition"—the embryonic moment that initiates the productive process toward an "objective" or synthetic unity of conscious and unconscious activity in "aesthetic intuition." Initially the self intuits itself, it feels itself as thought through its own activity.

Just as Fichte's absolute ego may be said to be derived from Kant's concept of intellectual intuition advanced in § 77 of the *Critique of Judgment*,[92] Schelling makes self-consciousness an original condition of knowledge that is unconscious prereflective awareness.

> The *self* is such an intuition, since it is *through the self's own knowledge of itself* that the *very self* (the object) first comes into being. For since the self (as object) is nothing else but the very *knowledge of itself*, it arises simply out of the fact *that it knows of itself*; the *self itself* is thus a knowing that simultaneously produces itself (as object). (*STI*, 27)

Thus, the self is originally an "inner sense" that is self-producing—original knowledge. Michael Vater points out how this paradoxical concept is not properly a cognitive state for it bears no relation to empirical consciousness, nor is it a faculty or activity *in* the subject, rather it *is* the subject.[93] This original knowledge is what Kant would call "*intellectus archetypus*,"[94] an archetypal knowing that creates or produces as it cognizes. For Schelling, the unconscious is the proper domain of mental activity; the self is pure internality—everything is produced *inside*.

Schelling was deeply engaged with the problem of *Beginning*—original *Grund*. While Hegel elaboratively attends to the problem of ground in the *Science of Logic*, Schelling is concerned with that which *precedes* beginning—an Eternal—"unconsciously impelled to seek itself, a self-sufficent will [that] *produces* itself in eternity."[95] Unlike Fichte, Schelling notes that before the ego, there is a non-ego, a preceding unconscious ground. "There is no ego without the non-ego, and to this extent the non-ego is before the ego. That which is, because it naturally is, has therefore no reason [*Grund*] to desire to be."[96] Before a rational ego emerges, there is an irrational, or perhaps more appropriately, an *a*-rational beginning.

After moving away from his philosophy of identity that characterized his early period toward his "positive philosophy,"[97] Schelling sought to understand the question of origin proper—will, intentionality, with its productive and intuitive capacities, is an abyss. From *Ages of the World* (1813), Schelling naturalizes the *Ungrund*:

> This will *produces itself* and is therefore unconditioned and *in itself* omnipotent; it produces itself absolutely—that is, out of itself and from itself. Unconscious longing is its mother, but she only conceived it and it has *produced* itself. It produces itself not *out* of eternity, but rather *in* eternity (which is no different from how a will unconsciously produces itself in a man's mind without his effort, a will that he does not make but only *finds*, and that only when found becomes a means for him to externalize what lies innermost within him).[98]

The will unconsciously produces itself, a yearning—it longs, it finds. This longing itself is equated with fertility, a "mother," yet it is merely the *act* of conception—a child must grow on its own independently from its source, venturing beyond. But Schelling equivocates his terms: to "conceive" is to envision, formulate, contrive, design, create, fashion, initiate, generate—*produce*, an "unconscious longing." But isn't such longing the very nurturance it needs to "find" itself, only then to "externalize"—to launch, to separate itself from its maternal dependency? Here we may see Schelling grappling with the problem of original ground, of finding an adequate explanation to the question: what precedes beginning? He settles for "longing." Longing is a hunger, a voracity—*it* craves, pines, covets, thus *desires*. This unconscious mother desires to produce itself, thus end the lack, fill the hole in its being. It impregnates and conceives itself, then gives its own birth. The pure activity of the primal self—the soul—is itself desire, being in relation to lack. From Schelling to Sartre and Lacan,[99] desire may be said to animate the life of spirit, to which darkness falls.

Schelling's revival of early modern theosophy is no less due to the influence of Boehme who had a profound impact on his comprehension of unconscious ground, as well as did the Christian theology and mysticism of Franz von Baader.[100] Boehme's *Ungrund* is like Schelling's unconscious will—hunger, an eternal longing, mother. It seeks itself and it finds, but it never stops yearning, this is its nature. For Schelling, the will is "unconsciously impelled to seek itself . . . it must by nature seek itself. . . . This is a seeking that remains silent and completely unconscious, in which the essence remains alone within itself, and is all the more profound, deep, and unconscious, the greater the fullness it contains in itself."[101] Such primordial activity that constitutes the animation of spirit acts as an impulse, a wish to complete itself, a "desire to know." What is unconscious ground but its own ground, a stirring, unrest, a compulsion—*Trieb*. Longing, this compulsory drive, is the principle activity of desire. Desire is *an* abyss, unbounded.

Slavoj Žižek identifies the "rotary motion of drives" that constitutes Schelling's unconscious will as a "blind . . . undifferentiated pulsating" beginning that is itself its own beginning.[102] In its inception, the abyss is a vicious cycle of motion, movement, and energy as drive, just waiting to appear. The problem Schelling faces, as does Hegel, Žižek notes, is the problem of "phenomenalization." How does the *Ungrund* appear to itself and for itself? How does it come to presence, come into being? Unlike Kant, the realm of the noumenal is the self's starting point, the *in-itself* is the presupposition of spirit. It becomes a matter of articulating itself, of willing itself *to appear*. So the question is not: what is *beyond* the phenomenal?, it is: what is *before*? Furthermore, how and why does this primordial (in-itself) undifferentiated being divide and split itself off from itself, thus creating the space to appear (to itself), to produce its own appearance?

Schelling locates this ultimate foundation, the "origin of all things" in that psychic space that precedes beginning—a nothingness that *is*. It is this "vortex of drives" where Žižek also places primacy, a "chaotic-psychotic universe" of longing, the *real* psychical reality.

Is, however, the primordial vortex of drives not the ultimate ground that nothing can precede? Schelling would entirely agree with that, adding only that the point in question is precisely the exact status of this "nothing": prior to *Grund*, there can only be an abyss (*Ungrund*); that is, far from being a mere *nihil privativum*, this "nothing" that precedes Ground stands for the "absolute indifference" qua the abyss of pure Freedom that is not yet the predicate-property of some Subject but rather designates a pure impersonal Willing (*Wollen*) that wills nothing.[103]

And it is precisely in this act of decision where you find freedom, a mad freedom, a freedom of the *not*. Schelling says that the unconscious will does not "make" itself, it only "finds." Therefore, will does not emerge *ex nihilo*, it is already there, eternal. It discovers its own disclosedness, and in such discovering it discloses, it produces. This generative activity is the fountainhead of unconscious agency as unbridled freedom. Freedom is *the* abyss.

If unconscious will or spirit precedes all and is thus the ground of its own ground, we must then redirect Schelling's question about the proper status of this *Ungrund*. Is the abyss an entity, an agent in-and-for-itself of its own free being, or is it merely psychic space, a cavern of the mind where thoughts, images, intentions, and conflicts are warehoused? This is a central issue we will take up with Hegel because his anthropological treatment of the feeling soul must be contrasted with his psychological analysis of theoretical spirit, thus accounting for several kinds of unconsciousness. For Schelling and Hegel, the *Ungrund* is not the gnostic abyss Lacan attributes to desire as the *ineffable*, where the symbolic cannot breach that which is indescribable, thus remaining unspeakable—to which silence (*hush*) is our only resort. Nor is the abyss "out there," disembodied, but rather it is internality itself, pure "inwardness."

Schelling, like Hegel, naturalizes the unconscious as corporeal and historical: "Nature is an abyss [*Abgrund*] of what is past, but the oldest thing in it is still the deepest, what remains even if everything accidental and acquired is taken away."[104] And like Freud, the *Ungrund* has a relationship to its past; repression is the "deepest" content struggling to either remain buried or return; it wants to surface, to appear, to relieve its tension. And for Schelling, "all consciousness has what is unconscious as ground, and, just in coming to be conscious, this unconscious is posited as past by that which becomes conscious of itself."[105] Freud also echoes this sentiment: "The repressed [past] is the prototype of the unconscious. . . . We can come to know even the *Ucs.* only by making it conscious" (*SE*, 19, 15, 19).

The primacy of negation, disorder, and tempestuous activity characterizes the inner world of spirit and is thus the catalytic might behind its appearances. Such force may be known as destruction, death, suffering, and disease—mental anguish characterized by striving, longing, and lack. Yet it is this very core character of suffering and lack that propels the *Ungrund* to transcend itself, a desire to move beyond fragmentation, chaos, and despair to a comprehensive unity of self-awareness where the promise of—the *wish* for—solace resides. Hence, through the power of its own hand, it transforms its ground while living underground. Schelling states:

> The true original and primary power of everything corporeal is the attracting essence which gives it form, limits it in position, and gives body to something that is in itself spiritual and intangible. To be sure, this latter continually contradicts the corporeal and makes itself known as a volatilizing, spiritualizing essence which is hostile to all limitations. But it appears everywhere only as

something issuing from the original negation, and, on the other hand, that attracting power appears as its mainstay, its real ground.[106]

The attracting power of negation is "real ground," a volatile essence that is itself the positive significance of the negative.Unconscious spirit is therefore a dynamic activity of becoming, a spiritualizing-materializing of essence as appearance, a point Hegel makes emphatically in his *Logic*.[107]

Perhaps psychic space—this abyss—may be "conceived" by itself, as Schelling suggests; that is, the abyss conceives itself, it generates and produces its space, expands its yawning gulf, to which Hegel would most certainly agree. If the essence of the abyss is to will itself, to affirm (or posit), to produce itself to appear, this would suggest that it also fuels its own lack, an inner chaos, and the gap widens. In this sense we may say that the abyss is not necessarily a lack of being, but rather a relation to lack, a relation it has *to itself* which it generates from within and seeks to resolve, to fill. The unconscious is not merely a porthole to consciousness, nor is it only a receptacle of consciousness, it is both. Therefore, the abyss is both an agency and a store, the container and the contained, both substance and void, its own cosmos.

FROM THE *UNGRUND* TO THE ABYSS

Throughout this chapter we have seen the historical role the *Ungrund* has assumed in the archeology of understanding human consciousness. Whether we refer to the inner mind and its psychic activities as spirit, will, self, ego, apperception, or soul, each being assigned diverse facets by different philosophical traditions, we have unequivocally seen the explanatory force of the concept of the unconscious. From neo-Platonism, to Boehme, Fichte, and Schelling, we have witnessed the rise of modern philosophies of the will that eventually led Freud to elevate the unconscious not only as the provenance, but as the pinnacle of mind—"true psychical reality."[108]

Hegel remained deeply engaged in Fichte and Schelling throughout his life, an engagement that preoccupied his own thinking, leaving a lasting residue on his philosophical system. Their influence is not only evident from Hegel's early writings and their role in his lectures on the history of philosophy, but their thoughts also linger in Hegel's own treatment of unconscious spirit, which, although ambiguous, he takes up and makes his own. Perhaps Hegel's sparse references to the unconscious were quite deliberate: he wanted to distance himself from Schelling's system, one Hegel found to be overly romantic, labile, and lacking in logical rigor, where Schelling's Identity thesis was merely an "empty formalism" and his Absolute a "night in which . . . all cows are black."[109] Furthermore, Schelling used the word *unconscious* excessively, whereas Hegel used it carefully and methodically, with the sustained patience of philosophical discipline. But perhaps Hegel didn't quite see its value, how it serves an indispensable architectonic function. Hegel was a committed rationalist; how could irrationality be a driving force behind reason?

After preparing the historical context for Hegel's understanding of unconscious mental activity, the relationship between the *Ungrund* and the abyss may now be taken up within Hegel's system, which is the focus of our next chapter. Boehme's emphasis on the *Ungrund* as original ground plays an important role in Hegel's treatment of the abyss, yet one that surpasses Boehme's theosophic attributions. For Hegel, the abyss is not only original ground, it also signifies the depth features of psychic topography, the primordial cognizing functions of the mind, and an unconscious agency that is responsible for the operations of thought, feeling, imagination, and the higher capacities of spirit. But in the historical overview we examined, philosophy of the abyss prefigures Hegel's thinking on the subject, theories he knew well because he studied them with precision. These antecedent models greatly impacted his own intellectual development, a fact that not even the most loyal Hegelian can ignore. Yet what Hegel does with these concepts in his own texts—despite the fact that they were advanced by his predecessors—is another matter and deserves our close inspection. While we may speculate about the degree and kinds of influence these early thinkers had on Hegel's philosophy, they remain only our speculation. What Hegel says in his texts is of crucial import and represents his authoritative word on the matter. It is only by a careful exegesis that we may be able to understand what concepts have been taken over from others and rightfully made his own.

Throughout our retracing of the *Ungrund*, we may see a universal philosophical preoccupation with the ultimate explanation of ground. The question of Origin, of Beginning proper—a true Genesis—becomes situated in the realm of the abyss. Hegel's comprehensive treatment of ground and all its implications are clarified in his *Logic* where the operations of thought are attributed to *conscious* spirit. By logical extension, however, we may say that a prereflective *unconscious* "essence determines itself as ground" (*SL*, 444). Hegel takes immediate consciousness as his starting point for the analysis of ground, yet by his own epigenetic treatment of spirit, that is, his structural and dynamic elaboration of spirit's development, consciousness must have certain ontological preconditions that make the appearance of consciousness possible, a necessity claim that Hegel himself would concede. By his own account, spirit first experiences an unconscious intuition of itself as the life of feeling, and in this experience affirms it very being. The free activity of consciousness therefore presupposes the activity of unconscious constitution.

In determining its own ground, unconscious essence "proceeds only from itself . . . [thus becoming] an *affirmative being* [*seiendes*] as the identity of essence with itself as ground" (*SL*, 445). The ultimate ground has no ground, only its self-affirmation which is the grounding of its own ground. The will or self-affirmation—the posit—in its initial act becomes a *negative flow*, the animation of the *not*. "*Ground is essence that in its negativity is identical with itself*" (*SL*, 447). It is from this original cosmos of negation and chaos that unconscious spirit wants to appear as its own creative self-expression—as thought—on the other side of darkness.

Within the *Ungrund*, spirit thinks the unthought. But in order to be made actual, thought must make its transition from the depths of the abyss to conscious reality. It is impelled to surface. Spirit must appear as the embodiment of thought, which remains unthought until the veil of night is converted to dawn. It is in this aurora that such surfacing appears as actuality. The *Ungrund* thus becomes actual as it punctures beyond its self-enclosed bottomless void through its own volition and "emerges from the groundless, that is, from its own essential negativity or pure form"(*SL*, 478). The underworld of tumult and nothingness then becomes the inner world of affirmative tangible thought that is itself intangible spirit. As a self-constitutive procreative activity, unconscious spirit is pulsating desire, a desire that makes thought possible. Thought first lives underground.

TWO

UNCONSCIOUS SPIRIT

HEGEL NEVER USES the term *Ungrund* to refer to the unconscious although he was very familiar with its significance in Boehme and Schelling, as we have seen. It is surprising that Hegel did not directly mention the *Ungrund* in his treatment of Boehme in his *Lectures on the History of Philosophy*. When he summarizes Boehme's position on God's self-revelation, he specifically refers to knowledge of the being or selfhood [*Ichts*] of self-consciousness within the spirit as opposed to nothingness [*Nichts*][1] but he does not address Boehme's further treatment of the *Ungrund* even though he relied on Boehme's texts where it specifically appears.[2] But Boehme also uses the term *Abgrund* (abyss) to designate the divine omnipresence of the deity,[3] a term Hegel himself uses to characterize the unconscious mind. While the *Ungrund* has a specific explanatory force for Boehme, its significance for understanding the problem of original ground is germane to our application to Hegel. It is important to note however, that the abyss serves several functions for Hegel, disclosing different forms of unconsciousness, the notion of original ground bearing only one meaning.

Hegel uses the German nouns *Schacht* (pit, mine, or shaft) and *Abgrund* to refer to the unconscious abyss in several key passages in his psychological treatment of theoretical spirit, each carrying with it different meanings, but most of the time he simply uses the word *unconscious* (*bewußtlos*). Petry informs us that Hegel may have taken over the reference to an "unconscious abyss" from the works of J. F. Herbart (1776–1841), a contemporary whose work Hegel was familiar with.[4] However, as we have seen, the introduction of the abyss may be properly said to have been motivated by multiple philosophical sources and thus its sole attribution to Herbart seems unlikely. When Hegel does mention the word *abyss*, he is often referring to psychic space, a place where images are "preserved unconsciously" in the bowels of the mind. The use of this imagery may be interpreted as Hegel's abbreviated attempt to propose a depth psychology that Freud was later to provide, because Hegel allows the abyss to serve many psychic functions that traverse the plane of mental topography, thus bringing forth images, affect, and presentations to bear upon the operations of imagination, fantasy, and memory that hover within the spheres of preconsciousness and conscious awareness. But he also equates the abyss with an agency or entity that is spirit's original being—"intelligence as this unconscious abyss [*Bewußtlos Schacht*]" (*EG* § 453)—where "images of the past [lie] latent in the dark depth of our inner being" (*EG* § 454, *Zusatz*). In fact, Hegel recognizes the significance of unconscious agency as early as the *Phenomenology* where he equates "*unconscious* Spirit" with the "force and element"—the *Trieb* behind the maturation of "universal self-conscious Spirit" (*PS* § 463).

It is interesting to note that despite the introduction of the unconscious in the *Phenomenology*, there is barely mention of the abyss (*Schacht*) in the 1817 first edition of the *Encyclopaedia*, and it was not until the 1827 second edition that it was first discussed.[5] Furthermore, Hegel's 1827 treatment of the abyss alters significantly in the third edition of 1830 where he adds further elaborations to the notion of the abyss in both the main text and in his remarks. Whereas the word *unconsciously* (*bewußtlos*) was only referred to in parentheses when first introduced in § 453 of the 1827 edition, by 1830 the parentheses were removed and it was made a proper part of the text. Here Hegel also specifically equates intelligence "*as this*" unconscious abyss, a comment that was left out in 1827. What is clear from the texts is that the notion of the abyss was growing on Hegel. He identified it in 1827 and even mentioned it in his lectures of 1827–1828,[6] but by 1830 he felt he needed to add more to it. We can see from this that the conceptual importance of the abyss was being rethought and incorporated into his system in a more thorough way. One can only speculate what he might have done with this concept if it were not for his untimely death a year later.[7]

In the stage of Recollection discussed in the *Encyclopaedia*, Hegel is struggling with how we move from a particular image we sense and recall, to something that is universal and thus which can stand for a number of directly intuited sensations. This struggle is evident by the fact that textual changes from 1827 to 1830 were substantial enough to warrant even changing the order of some of the movements in the transition from Intuition to Presentation. It may be argued that in speaking of unconscious processes within the realm of intelligence, Hegel does not mean the same unconscious processes that we get with Freud. The psychological processes of intuition, presentation, and thought are much closer to consciousness than Freud would want to emphasize and may largely be seen as preconscious activity,[8] which is mentation and concomitant psychic material that is capable of being made conscious if one's attention were properly drawn to it. But this would not prohibit Hegel's description of the abyss from functioning in different modalities or assuming other forms of psychic appearance; thus, we may see a closer parallel to psychoanalytic depth psychology than one is first led to believe.[9]

In order to see how Hegel's treatment of the abyss approaches a concept similar to the psychoanalytic unconscious, we must extrapolate back to Hegel's discussion of what is truly *pre*-conscious in his system, that is, the ontology and inner organization of psychic life prior to the appearance of conscious spirit. Hegel's anthropological analysis of the feeling soul provides us with the most uncontested evidence that he had anticipated a dynamic unconscious agency, which was later made intelligible by Freud by the turn of the century. For Hegel, spirit is an epigenetic construct, a "progressive development" (*EG* § 387) that dynamically evolves and becomes more structurally self-elaborate, and not simply an expansion of a preformed entity. It emerges from within itself and develops out of its most elementary foundation, its *Ungrund*. By Hegel's own textual account of the soul, the abyss becomes the original ground of spirit.

ON THE STRUCTURE OF
THE *ENCYCLOPAEDIA GEIST*

Hegel's structure of the *Encyclopaedia* at times appears arbitrary and even disjointed. Why does he begin with the Logic and then progress to Nature and Mind? Furthermore, what are his justifications for structuring the subject matter of the *Philosophie des Geistes* in the order of Anthropology, Phenomenology, and Psychology? More specifically, why does he discuss habit and illness in the Anthropology but not memory? It could be argued that his system would flow better if the Logic came after Psychology because the operations of pure thought rely on psychological processes. Moreover, why the need to separate Psychology from Phenomenology when the ability to fix attention, perceive presentations, etc. are necessary operations of the phenomenology of consciousness?

Hegel himself in the Introduction to the *Encyclopaedia* and the *Science of Logic* preliminarily discusses the relation between the operations of intelligence, sensation, representation, and pure thought. From this account, he suggests that one can use the psychology to interpret the logic. Furthermore, in the *Nürnberger Schriften*,[10] Hegel comments that one could understand his system through the Psychology as well as through the Phenomenology, although he does distinguish between getting to the standpoint of absolute knowing and the systematic development of that knowledge which is the distinction between the *Phenomenology of Spirit* and the system as outlined in the *Encyclopaedia*.[11]

In the *Encyclopaedia*, Hegel is not describing a progression from what is nearest to us consciously to what is more remote—this is the task of the *Phenomenology*. Rather, he is developing what he conceives to be the most elementary aspects of spirit, which is to be presupposed in whatever follows; as the elementary becomes more complicated, each stage builds on the previous ones. Because the whole approach to Hegel's system is one of philosophical understanding, the Logic comes first in order to clarify the structure of rational thinking. Once Hegel addresses the ground, scope, and essence of pure thought, then he turns to that which is quite other than thought, namely, Nature. Spirit, in turn, presupposes nature and builds on the natural, thus accounting for the rationale behind the structure of the *Encyclopaedia*.

In the *Philosophy of Spirit*, Hegel appears to follow the same strategy that informs the schema of his overall system: (1) Anthropology examines the immediate inchoate self as soul; (2) Phenomenology looks at consciousness where there is a distinction between the self and what it is conscious of; and finally (3) Psychology examines those structures and operations of the self whereby the self and object are integrated into the framework of thinking and willing. Hegel needed to start with the Anthropology because it elucidates the formal conditions for consciousness and higher modes of spirit. As such, Anthropology is concerned with the pre-objective and the nonpropositional conditions of consciousness, hence it explains the structural preconditions or ground of spirit and the dynamic operations that make the appearance of consciousness possible.

This is not to say that Hegel might not well have wanted to approach matters differently under different circumstances. In his lectures he wanted to follow the schema he had set out in the *Encyclopaedia*. But certainly he was prepared to revise his organizational structure as he became aware of more detailed information, thus accounting for the changes appearing in his 1827 and 1830 revisions. One can see him doing that in the lectures on religion, where he did not have the straightjacket of the *Encyclopaedia* theses to structure his course. Furthermore, Hegel's system is a circle and hence can be entered at any point.[12] It may simply be a matter of personal choice where he starts the exposition in any given case. This implies that everything is a necessary condition of everything else measured by their mediational differences. It also implies that there are intimate connections between elements of the system, and no one element can stand alone as the single source of any other. There is clearly a logic to the organization of the *Encyclopaedia* and its important subdivision, the *Philosophie des Geistes*, despite the fact that there may well be other ways of structuring his system. But one does need to distinguish between moving from what is nearest to us in experience to what is farthest, and working from the conceptually most simple to the more sophisticated and complex, only then to recognize the pattern that Hegel takes to be universal—moving from a simple immediacy to considering how it appears when that immediacy breaks apart, and then on to what happens when the two sides are integrated. This latter element is essential to his understanding of a "scientific" approach to the subject matter.[13]

While Hegel explicates the process and organization of thought in his Logic, he is acutely aware that he must account for the ground that makes thought possible. This is the central aim of his Anthropology. Hegel states: "Philosophy lacks the advantage, which the other sciences enjoy, of being able to *presuppose* its *ob-jects* as given immediately by representation. And, with regard to its beginning and advance, it cannot *presuppose* the *method* of cognition as one that is already accepted" (*EL* § 1). In an attempt to advance the method of cognition that he justifies in the Logic, Hegel must deal with the notion of its origin. This is why he turns his attention to anthropology in the final part of his system. But as early as 1808, Hegel was occupied with the place of the soul in his philosophy:

[A]n introduction to philosophy has to consider above all the different constitutions and activities of spirit through which it passes in order to arrive at a science. . . . The theory of spirit considers spirit according to the different species of its consciousness and according to the different species of its activity. The former can be called the theory of consciousness, the latter the theory of the soul.[14]

In the Anthropology, Hegel addresses the "activities" of the soul, which further paves the way for understanding the higher phenomenological and psychological activities of spirit.

THE EPIGENESIS OF
UNCONSCIOUS SPIRIT

Hegel's Anthropology begins with a detailed analysis of natural spirit or the emergence of the soul, hence the anthropology becomes an engagement with the question of nature. Here Hegel is concerned with the problem of beginning, the "immediacy of spirit," spirit that is "involved in nature, related to its corporeality. This foundation of humanity . . . is the general object of anthropology" (EG § 387, Zusatz). This "foundation" that Hegel is concerned with imports a universal ontological claim—spirit is first and foremost an unconscious embodiment. Spirit is originally fused with its material nature, which it seeks to overcome as an immaterial hence spiritual embodiment. This initial instantiation of spirit has the character of negativity and conflict for spirit is confined to the form of nature. In fact, the question of the meaning of nature for Hegel is central to our understanding of the abyss. The implications of spirit's natural foundation are significant for understanding the general negative organization of the dialectical drive toward vanquishing opposition as well as providing a conceptual framework for a theory of abnormal psychology. Hegel explains: "Out of this immediate union with its naturality, the soul enters into opposition and conflict with it. It is here that the conditions of derangement and somnambulism belong. This follows from the triumph of the soul over its corporeity" (EG § 387, Zusatz). Unconscious spirit is at first a bodily ego that enters into opposition with its immediate symbiotic unity as nature. Its task is to become immaterial to itself, that is, materiality is sublated, hence surpassed yet retained in its higher structure, but this result is a labored achievement. In fact, the cardinal purpose of the soul's development is to liberate itself from its corporeal chains.[15] As Murray Greene informs us, the portrait of the soul's development may be best characterized as a "liberation struggle" (Befreiungskampf).[16] But Hegel's dialectical narrative of the soul's fight to free itself from the confines of nature is also a saga of the unconscious struggling to free itself as consciousness. In its initial natural state, soul is "not yet spirit" (EG § 388), it has to mature, yet it is spirit "implicit," thus presupposed. It is only by "achieving immateriality" that the soul "passes over into spirit" (EG § 389, Zusatz) as concrete subjectivity.

Hegel outlines the soul's progression from its (*a*) natural embodiment to (*b*) feeling its "individuality" with its "immediate being" where it is merely for itself abstractly to (*c*) an actuality where its immediate being is "formed within it" as corporeality (*EG* § 390). Therefore, the natural soul, feeling soul, and actual soul, are three moments of spirit's genesis. Initially, the unconscious soul is the "*sleep* of spirit," a "passive nous" as the "possibility of all things"which is a singular substance or the particularizing of spirit (*EG* § 389). Yet this passivity is itself immediately active as spirit "rouses itself from the somnolent state in which it finds itself as soul, since in this state difference is still shrouded in the form of lack of difference and hence unconsciousness" (*EG* § 389, *Zusatz*).

It is in this initial state of indifference that Hegel situates the generic condition for both health and madness which hinges on spirit's ability to manage opposition and conflict, as well as its relation to external reality. Spirit awakens to find itself as the "life of nature" enthroned within its unconscious corporeality. Here Hegel recognizes a base materialism; spirit is thrown into the brute givenness of the body, a facticity spirit cannot deny but only surpass. Spirit is at first a complete unity or totality that lacks difference. It is an entirely universal, self-enclosed autistic immersion in nature which is the "immediate substance" of spirit as a "pulsation, the mere inner stirring of the soul"(*EG* § 390, *Zusatz*). At this stage there is no positing of difference or individuality that is opposed to the natural and hence is not determined nor determinate nor is it a particular or actual being. This requires unconscious spirit to move from a state of undifferentiation to differentiation. Just as being must pass over into determinate being in the *Logic*, the natural soul must pass over from indeterminateness to a determinateness. This initial form of determinateness is itself naturality, but it is merely a "transitory *condition*," spirit asleep. Sleeping spirit is not in a totally passive or peaceful state, however, there is an internal "stirring" that gives rise to a "*natural awakening*, to the opening out of the soul" (*EG* § 390, *Zusatz*). Hegel explains that this awakening is not the activity that fills waking consciousness, but rather it is merely the natural condition of the soul being awake.

Hegel's metaphorical use of sleep and awakening allows him to account for the soul as a restless activity. In its sleeping nature, the soul is simply unconscious—not awake, but sleep does not imply there is no mental activity. Spirit is always active even when it is only implicit to itself—it thinks, senses, and feels while it dreams. "Thinking remains the basis of spirit in all its forms" (*EG* § 398, *Zusatz*). Its restlessness compels itself to awake because it cannot rest, its nature is activity as such. In some ways unconscious spirit is like an anxious insomniac who is never able to sleep peacefully for it is plagued by a profound negativity. It is precisely this negativity that impels spirit to surface from its depths, a hibernation from within which its night thoughts take flight.

The awakened soul eventually comes to feel itself as life, as a sensuous actual being. This progression involves a series of sublated movements that constitute the coming into being of subjective spirit as an intuiting, self-determining ego. This unconscious ego as determinate being-for-self is a "*thinking being* and *subject"*(*EG* § 412, fn) which precedes its transition to consciousness. In this transition to consciousness, however, the ego forges an even wider gap, an expansive abyss between its unconscious life and its now newly experienced conscious sensuousness. Unconscious spirit is never abandoned for consciousness, but rather is co-extensive with consciousness as both realms influence the activity of the other. This is evident from Hegel's understanding of recollection, where images, thoughts, and affects are retrieved from the dark cellar of the abyss, as well as his conception of psychopathology, and the law of the heart which informs our actions and character. But as I will show, unconscious spirit assumes a primacy in Hegel's system. The unconscious as original ground informs and paves the shapes of consciousness toward a higher unity, a unity it fights within itself. This is the "tremendous power of the negative" (*PS* § 32) that is itself the positive life force of the psyche. In order to provide a systematic account of Hegel's architectonic theory of unconscious spirit and its indispensable role in his system, it will be necessary to closely examine how the abyss dynamically informs the dialectical unfolding of the soul.

THE ANTHROPOLOGICAL ABYSS

The first textual reference to the abyss occurs, not in the Psychology, but in the Anthropology section of the *Encyclopaedia*. For Hegel, the soul necessarily comes into confrontation with its corporeality, which it must set over against its ultimate immaterial nature. In order to accord reconciliation between the material and spiritual aspects of its being, the nascent ego must progress from its unconscious feeling mode to reflective consciousness, which thereafter commands spirit's quest for pure self-consciousness where subjective and objective polarities are unified. Before the move to consciousness, unconscious spirit first comes into dispute with its simple determinacy as matter, and thus ensues an opposition between the subjective ego and its reciprocal relation to the body. Hegel informs us that: "The ego, this abyss [*Abgrunde*] of all presentations, as what is thoroughly simple, as singleness, is set in absolutely stark opposition to matter i.e. to the many, to what is composite" (*EG* § 389, *Zusatz*). Here Hegel equates the abyss with the unconscious ego which is a singularity set against its material instantiation. In its self-identification, it becomes opposed to its mere bodily form and thus constitutes its immateriality.

The use of the term *Abgrund* is contrasted to the use of the word *Schacht* which also appears in the Anthropology when Hegel describes the indivisibility of the ego in the context of the feeling soul as a "featureless mine" (*EG* § 403). Petry notes that Hegel's use of the term in this context may derive from the fact that the shaft (*Schacht*) of a mine was originally a rod used to measure its depth.[17] But Hegel uses the term again when he considers the recollecting of content pertinent to the condition of magnetic somnambulism, a form of amnesia Freud would probably describe as hysterical repression. Hegel refers to this as a form of "disease" in which the "soul is aware of a content it has long since *forgotten*, and which when awake it is no longer able to recall consciously" (*EG* § 406, *Zusatz*). While this psychical condition is discussed in a context that presumes subjective spirit's transition to conscious awareness, Hegel notes that this type of forgetting is the result of "deposited . . . knowledge into the abyss [*Schacht*] of our inner being," which we have "no power over" nor are we "in possession of." These repressed contents "have gone to sleep in our inner being [and] often come forth during illness."[18] All of these references to the abyss involve spatial images that presume an unconscious agent and not merely a storage facility for our experiences. The two references to the "ego" as "*this* abyss" and a "featureless mine" are the strongest allusion to unconscious agency, while the third reference to the notion of sleeping images and content in our "inner being" suggests a power to the mind that is beyond conscious control, for how could one explain forgotten memories coming to light if there was not an inner unconscious agent guiding such processes.

The fourth and final reference to the abyss in the Anthropology comes in Hegel's discussion of mental derangement. Hegel specifically refers to a process of "fixation" where psychic organization cannot progress past a particular stage of development. This occurs in the "self-absorption" of natural spirit when it acquires a particular content that becomes a "*fixed presentation*." "This fixation takes place when spirit which is not yet in full control of itself becomes *as* absorbed in this content as it is *in itself*, in the abyss of its *indeterminateness*" (*EG* § 408, *Zusatz*, 2).

Here we may see how Hegel has anticipated several key psychoanalytic concepts such as the self-absorption of primary narcissism, the fixation of the drives, and psychotic regression to a symbiotic and undifferentiated indeterminateness of the natural soul. In "On Narcissism: An Introduction," Freud tells us, "[T]he development of the ego consists in a departure from primary narcissism and gives rise to a vigorous attempt to recover that state" (*SE*, 14, 100) when desire has been "withdrawn from the external world [and] has been directed to the ego" (*SE*, 14, 75). Reminiscent of Fichte's absolute self, before the ego directs its psychic investment toward a particular attachment to the object world, the ego is originally a self-absorbed narcissistically enveloped unity that takes itself as its own object. Freud similarly notes that a "particularly close attachment of the instinct [*Trieb*] to its object is distinguished by the term 'fixation' . . . [which] puts an end to its mobility" (*SE*, 14, 123).[19] This is truncated spirit, self-enclosed in its own narcissistic cocoon where it only takes itself as its object.

Hegel's reference to spirit's self-absorption in the "abyss [*Abgrund*] of its *indeterminateness*" refers to the earliest condition of the natural soul's undifferentiation from its corporeality. While we will discuss Hegel's theory of psychopathology in a later chapter, it is important to note how this original undifferentiated oneness or unity of unconscious spirit serves as the stepping stone for the inception of the unconscious ego. Spirit's immediate shape is the natural soul, its material embodiment, yet this embodiment is itself a mental activity of sleeping spirit which we may say is the seed of ego. While Hegel does not directly say this, such implications may be inferred. Because spirit is always thinking, which remains its basis in all its forms (see *EG* § 398, *Zusatz*), ego must be present (even if only rudimentarily) in order for there to be thought at all. *Geist* is self-generative and active: spirit "rouses itself." Thus, for Hegel, "the beginning of spirit is therefore nothing but its own being, and it therefore relates itself only to its own determinations" (*EG* § 440). As a self-relating soul, presupposed spirit is already a presupposed inchoate ego with an inchoate idea of itself as the object of its self-relation. It "intuits" itself and "feels" its own being, an ego activity that is already constituted in the soul, for spirit exists first as activity itself. It is merely the task of spirit to awaken as ego and mature. Hegel's self-articulated progression of the soul may be compared to Freud's developmental model: "[T]he ego cannot exist in the individual from the start; the ego has to be developed. The . . . instincts [*Triebe*], however, are there from the very first (*SE*, 14, 77). Spirit exists first as activity, an essence as force or drive—an impulse to arouse itself as ego which becomes its essential form, a self-determining desire. Though the soul progresses from its material to its immaterial embodiment as ego, its dialectical configurations become more complex and dynamically constituted, thus expanding the range and power of spirit's self-determining activity.

My equation of the self-absorption of the natural soul's undifferentiated unity with primary narcissism is further described by Freud as constituting the conditions for the "oceanic feeling"—the unbounded, limitless bond with the universal.[20] Indeed, the symbiotic union of the ego within its abyss may be compared to an ocean. An ocean is a vast and expansive encompassing body with a seemingly endless surface, below which opens into an underworld of colossal configurations—a dark and interminable void. There are many beautiful things in the sea that coexist in a shared unity, as well as the most frightful creatures. The abyss, like the ocean, is an aesthetic creation engendering countless images, emotions, urges, and thoughts that invade the pleasure centers of our imagination, wishes, and most cherished ideals. But it is also the primary source of our suffering, at once containing both the monstrous and the sublime. "[A]nd some sufferings that one seeks to expel turn out to be inseparable from the ego in virtue of their internal origin" (*SE*, 21, 67). In its dark side, there is a real horror to the unconscious, for you can never get away from the *Thing*.

Hegel's anthropological references to the abyss provide us with textual evidence for original unconscious ground, the driving force behind the appearance of spirit. With the exception of one direct textual reference to the abyss (*Schacht*) in the context of the feeling soul, most references in the Anthropology section come from the *Zusätze* or Additions to lectures Hegel gave while teaching at Heidelberg and Berlin, while his psychological references to the abyss, on the other hand, do not. Many notable scholars find the *Zusätze* to be very trustworthy and reliable records of Hegel's lectures and are thus invaluable sources for understanding his thought. Yet it may be argued that the Additions have been manipulated or conflated by Hegel loyalists and that they do not match the intellectual sophistication of his proper philosophical text. Despite the general consensus that his lecture material is valid,[21] we may do better by staying with his psychological treatment of theoretical spirit, thus providing us with his clearest ideas on the abyss. However, Hegel's anthropology of the soul is an ontological thesis about the unconscious origins of spirit, while theoretical spirit is concerned with the articulation of conscious psychological processes. It is best at this point to stay on ontological rather than psychological ground. Whatever position the reader may adopt toward the *Zusätze*, we will need to examine Hegel's ontological treatment of the soul and observe how unconscious spirit provides the preconditions and architectonic function for theoretical spirit to emerge.

NATURALIZED SPIRIT

Hegel's project may be said to be an attempt to trace and articulate the dynamic movement of spirit ascending toward increased freedom; as such, he must show how spirit emerges from its natural immediacy and supercedes it in thought and action. Thus, Hegel acknowledges the prehistory of reason in nature and specifically the pre-objective form of the subjective soul. The question of nature is important for Hegel because he must show how spirit is dependent on nature yet is free. At first the soul is a complete simple, natural totality that must free itself from its mere corporeality, but freedom is not the renunciation of nature, only its sublation. In fact, feeling remains a central organization of spirit, which is why Hegel desires to include our natural selves within his overall conception of reason and spirit. For Hegel, freedom is among other things freedom from natural determination. We are free but we are natural beings; thus, freedom is the process of transcending nature while incorporating it in its spiritual embodiment. Having attained freedom from its mere natural, necessarily determined corporeality, spirit is actively free to determine itself as a dynamic, intelligible self-articulated complex whole.

In its natural embodiment, the soul is the immediate substance of spirit, which is an entirely "universal" immediate "singularity," a subjective being with "natural determinatenesses." The universal soul is to be "grasped as a totality, as being a likeness of the Concept" (*EG* § 390, *Zusatz*). Here Hegel is referring to the soul as it would be present in all self-conscious beings, but he must first take this generality and describe the way in which it comes into being as particularized souls before it may achieve a complex totality. His method is to try to elucidate the developmental unfolding of how the soul comes to understand the world and show how its conceptual understanding becomes progressively sophisticated. Therefore, we need to conceive of the soul first in its most general aspects and determine how that stage of mind develops.

Hegel informs us that initially the universal soul is not "fixed as *world soul*," hence as if it were an absolute subject that incorporates the whole world, but rather as a singular solipsistic unity that only knows its natural or given immediacy. Since Hegel is making his transition from the final stages of the *Philosophy of Nature*, the simple determinations of nature such as climate and geography are at this stage idealized by the soul. Natural determinations have a "free existence" prior to any ideational content of external objects, which is the function of consciousness, but the soul treats them as natural internal objects, thus these determinations pertain to the soul as its natural "qualities" (*EG* § 391). Therefore, natural objects are determined and exist apart from the soul's immediate being before it incorporates them into its internal structure, but Hegel doesn't necessarily assume that the empirical world is simply given. He must account for how the soul comes to this determination and therefore starts from an internal rather than an external reference point. It is only by way of advancing toward the Concept that the soul can come to grasp the unity of itself with nature.

Hegel compares the soul in its quiescent state to a microcosm that is not aware of the entirety of nature but only has the *form* of being subjective, "of being a particular impulse [*Trieb*], and which as a being is in him unconsciously" (*EG* § 391, *Zusatz*). Here we see the origins of spiritual drive as an unconscious determining agent. Hegel's treatment of the soul's natural qualities is addressed largely in the *Zusätze* and presents how the various "natural objects" manifest themselves as specific qualities of the natural order such as the innate awareness or sensing of "planetary" and "telluric" life, as well as the differences in climate, seasons, temperatures, and times of the day that are only partially realized as "vague moods" (*EG* § 392). While these advanced forms of sensation and awareness require consciousness, Hegel is setting the stage for what makes these conditions possible, first conditioned into the substance of the soul. At this level there is nevertheless some elementary unconscious internalization (*Erinnerung*) of these natural conditions, a point Hegel makes later about the fetus in the womb.

The universal life of nature is what constitutes the soul as a "life of *motion*." Here Hegel draws on cosmology, astronomy, biology, and natural spirit's terrestrial relationship to the solar system as well as our common kinship with animals as "instinct"—"finite being's unconscious sympathies with this life of nature."[22] For Hegel, these "general" or "vague" moods are linked to many natural innate dispositions as well as mental illness such as "depression." Hegel explains these divergences of plurality largely from the standpoint of conscious reflection, yet he still remains tied to his epigenetic model. Spirit is first and foremost a natural spirit; it must be accounted for as a naturalized being. Here Hegel is developing a progressive classification that becomes increasingly more intricate and arcane. At this level in his Anthropology he is looking at those aspects of the soul that build most directly on the framework of nature he has already expounded in part two of the *Encyclopaedia*. In his *Logic*, the universal always determines itself into its particulars. This model provides the logical congruity for Hegel's next step in explaining the unfolding of the natural soul. At this point, Hegel's analysis explores ways in which souls are distinguished from each other.

The universal natural soul divides itself into a multitude of specific "concrete differences" and "particularizes" or instantiates itself as natural individual "*spirits*." This is very important for our understanding of unconscious *Geist*, for there is an internal splitting, separation, and externalization into a plurality of singular particulars. When examined closely, this serves as three distinct moments that constitute the initial movement of the dialectic. First, as an internal division or the *act* of splitting itself within itself, second, as a differentiation hence separation of itself from what it is not, and third, as an externalization of itself into particular entities. Therefore, unconscious spirit moves from a state of undifferentiation to differentiated determinate being. This is such an important step for spirit that it is surprising Hegel addresses this movement in only one sentence in § 393. He then quickly jumps to explain how this accounts for the natural reality of the external world such as geographical continents, racial variety, terrestrial polarity between the lands and the seas, and the flora and fauna.

We may interpret this movement in Hegel from the vantage points of two primary perspectives, namely, metaphysics and his logic. As an anthropological thesis, Hegel is attempting to account for the original ground of the natural soul and the structural preconditions that allow for the very movement of thought, hence the unfolding of spirit itself. In this sense, his Anthropology is an ontological project. Hegel's division of the universal, particular, and singularization of spirit is moreover a metaphysical enterprise that is the counterpart to his logic where the dialectical treatment of being, essence, and conceptual understanding form the systematic method by which he is able to account for Natural Philosophy and the Philosophy of Spirit. Hegel already adheres to a form of realism in his *Naturphilosophie*, and in his *Philosophie des Geistes*; spirit is a material embodiment within a plurality of naturally determined objects it encounters.[23] Moreover, Hegel himself specifically refers to his Anthropology as a "metaphysical treatment" of the soul (*Metaphysik als Seele*) (*EG* § 408). However, the issue becomes one of understanding just how spirit actually encounters nature. Following his *Logic*, which informs the method of his system of science, Hegel is attempting to arrive at the correct way of comprehending how the world really is constructed.

In his *Science of Logic*, Hegel sought to replace metaphysics with his objective logic, which was designed to account for ontological concepts such as pure thought, the soul, the world, and God but without importing a presupposed substratum to account for their existence. Hegel's logic considers these concepts "in their own proper character . . . the determinations themselves according to their specific content" (*SL*, 63–64). Hegel repeats his intention in the *Encyclopaedia Logic* when he says that "*logic* coincides with *metaphysics*, with the science of *things* grasped in *thoughts* that used to be taken to express the *essentialities* of the *things*" (*EL* § 24). The interrelationship between abstract forms such as a concept and causality may only be established within logic itself. At this level Hegel is attempting to displace traditional metaphysics under the rubric of his own method, which he takes to be a superior means of describing reality. There is no mention in the text that he intended for the logic to be extended as a metaphysical principle of the creation of all reality. But this does not mean that this conclusion cannot be inferred.

At the moment in the text where Hegel introduces into the natural soul the notion of geography, terrestrial bodies, racial diversity, and the animal and plant species, we must remember that he had already covered this ground in the Natural Philosophy, therefore these things do not need to be *created* at this stage by the natural soul, for they had already been explained. Recall that the division of the *Encyclopaedia* into three books was the result of Hegel's editors due to their efforts to supply his lectures to the main body of the text. Ideally the *Encyclopaedia* should read as one text, and not three distinct texts. Anthropology flows out of Nature, which Hegel sought to explain. From this standpoint, it would seem to follow that he is attempting to articulate how spirit responds to and appropriates the natural world, a world that he holds to be the actual external conditions for spirit to manifest. "What is external is *implicitly* what is true, for the true is the actual and must exist" (*EL* § 38, *Zusatz*). However, Hegel ultimately places priority on the mental determinations of immaterial spirit that stands above its material counterpart while always being in it.

Despite the evolutionary thrust to Hegel's system, he denies a theory of modern evolution, claiming that nature can produce no internal changes within itself for this is only possible through the mental activity of spirit.[24] While Hegel's philosophical approach finds evolution congenial, this is reserved for the domain of spirit. Even though Darwin had not quite arrived on the scene, there were contemporaries and predecessors who advocated theories for natural, biological evolutionary forces, claims that even date back as far as Empedocles. From the *Philosophy of Nature*, Hegel makes his point unequivocally:

> Nature is to be regarded as a *system of stages*, one arising necessarily from the other and being the proximate truth of the stage from which it results: but it is not generated *naturally* out of the other but only in the inner Idea which constitutes the ground of Nature. *Metamorphosis* pertains only to the Concept as such, since only *its* alternation is development. (*PN* § 249)

Hegel continues to reject any theory of origination, variation, and evolutionary change that accounts for the natural process of lower organisms giving rise to higher developmental species. The reason for this is that he wants to preserve the generative self-determining power of the spiritual. From this account, Hegel's metaphysical position of spirit animating nature applies to the natural soul. But if we interpret his logic as a surrogate for metaphysics then we would do best by showing how Hegel's method accounts for a coherent comprehension of the world.

Hegel is not necessarily describing the generation of the universe in the *Encyclopaedia*. It may be argued, however, that when it comes to cosmic questions, Hegel becomes rather Christian: The Logic is God before creation, the expulsion of pure thought into externality is the initiation of nature, while spirit then develops out of nature.[25] Hegel is ultimately a monist with the recognition that nature and spirit represent different levels of qualitative complexification. Spirit is self-conscious life while nature is material life. Spirit ultimately overreaches nature while incorporating it into its internal structure as a self-directed activity. When Hegel introduces the mechanism by which implicit spirit moves from an undifferentiated immediacy to a differentiated determinate being-for-self, he is applying his logical analysis of how a universal applies to a particular.

We must understand how vital this initial activity of the natural soul is for Hegel. Following his logical method, he is attempting to isolate the most primitive features that define humankind and particulary how internality finds expression before consciousness emerges. In this movement of the natural soul, Hegel attempts to show how multiplicity, variation, and singularization flow from a monistic universal undifferentiated unity. Because spirit may only emerge from the initial standpoint of its natural internality, it is a self-contained simple totality, albeit lacking complete totality, which is its task to fulfill. By dividing itself and externalizing its being into a complex multiplicity of singular instantiations, Hegel is able to show how particulars derive from a universal essence.

At this point we may ask: Why didn't Hegel start with the brute facticity of the plurality of the world and show how unity evolves out of multiplicity? Instead of taking the empirical position of particulars as his starting point, Hegel has to start with an undifferentiated unity, thus a universal, even though this universal is still simple and embryonic. An initial universal unity of the natural soul must be posited in order to *account for* particulars and their origin. Here Hegel is tackling the question of original ground. If you start from the empirical position of particularity or multiplicity and then abstract an essence from them as did Aristotle, then you jeopardize the internal consistency of a developmental hence architectonic model. As a developmental monistic ontologist, Hegel shows congruity, which is the logical structure to his system. This is a process that unfolds from within, and is thereby not an empty formalism where a generic template or structure is applied to phenomena. His developmentalism also has epistemological advantages. What spirit knows first is its immediate internality. By starting from the inside and then moving toward externality and then back into internality, Hegel maintains the logical coherency of his system. To presuppose the outside is to beg the question. From this account, Hegel is better able to capture the internal unfolding of the embodiment of spirit within reality.

Thus, nature is originally passive spiritual activity or motion that is actively self-awakening, which then divides or differentiates itself into infinite particulars that it alienates or externalizes, which it then seeks to reincorporate back into its inner being. Ultimately, Hegel sees spirit through to its end; the natural soul is sublated as materiality is subsumed within immaterial spirit thus becoming more complex, variegated, and holistic in its return to its original unity—a process of reingesting its singular manifestations or plurality into a totality that is now mature, robust, and all encompassing. But this is a long excursion; natural spirit has a lot of work to do.

After spirit awakens from its internal slumbers as a subjective naturalized activity, it projects its universal particularizations or qualities and discharges itself into concrete being as actual nature. Hegel is very clear that the universal soul is a productive self-defining activity:

Just as light disperses into an infinite multitude of stars, so the universal soul of
nature disperses into an infinite multitude of individual souls, the only difference being that whereas light appears to have a subsistence independent of
stars, it is only in individual souls that the universal soul of nature attains actuality. (*EG* § 390, *Zusatz*)

It is through the activity of individual subjectivity that the initial fragmented
unity of natural spirit is taken back up into the unity of individual human souls.
We must caution, however, that subjectivity at the level of the natural soul is
very hollow and lacks articulation. It is more appropriate to say that the soul has
an internality that has the potential of becoming a subject to itself but is not yet
fully realized as such. Hegel explains in his Introduction to the *Philosophy of
Spirit* that the way in which implicit spirit or the logical Idea originally determines itself is revealed in spirit's move from its internal immediacy to its externalized determinate being which is the coming into being of nature itself.
Technically, the idea or its comprehension is estranged from itself at this juncture; it now becomes spirit's objective to incorporate nature back into itself
thereby elevating itself to a higher unity. Hegel explains:

> The externality, individuation and immediacy of nature is therefore sublated by
> the Idea, by the spirit implicit and dormant in nature, which creates for itself a
> determinate being corresponding to its internality and universality, and so be-
> comes the intro-reflected being-for-self of self-consciousness and awakened
> spirit, i.e. spirit as such. (*EG* § 384, *Zusatz*)

In these passages we have been exploring, Hegel is attempting to formulate the most archaic way in which spirit begins to idealize nature by taking it
into its own life, not the brute given of reality, but as something to be integrated into some kind of whole or unity. Mind implicit, slumbering within nature, overcomes its externality by making "an existence *conformable* to its
inwardness and universality" (*PM* § 384, *Zusatz*). It is through the move from
internality to externalization that spirit emerges as a self-determining, self-
conscious "being-for-self in the face of unconscious nature, which conceals as
much as it reveals of it" (*EG* § 384, *Zusatz*). This is the point where nature is
made a general object for spirit with the externality of nature then brought
back into the internality of spirit as its own self-awakening. "It makes this a
general object, reflects upon it, takes back into its internality the externality of
nature, idealizes nature, and so gains being-for-self in its general object" (*EG*
§ 384, *Zusatz*). We can see that spirit at this stage has already attained for itself
a form of unconscious self-awareness, an "intro-reflected" or prereflective "self-
consciousness" whereby it takes itself as its own object in nature as a "being-
for-self." When Hegel tells us unconscious spirit is intro-reflective, he is
pointing to the immediate awareness of the soul's self-identification as an intuitive reflection into its self (*Reflexion-in-sich*). Here lies an introduction of the
faculty by which the processes of mediation and reflection are constituted. This

is the initial pre-familiarity the soul has with itself, but being only an abstract immediacy, spirit is far from being an absolute unity.

This initial pre-familiarity or self-relation the soul has with itself is a paradoxical construct for Hegel. At once, implicit spirit opposes itself to unconscious nature, which also manifests spirit. Thus, while it overcomes its mere implicitness and makes itself a determinate being, it is nevertheless still unconscious. Moreover, natural spirit as determinate soul attains for itself a form of unconscious self-awareness. Hegel himself calls this awareness "self-consciousness" despite the fact that spirit remains unconscious (*EG* § 384, *Zusatz*). We may say that this is justified on the grounds that self-relation precedes object-relation insofar as awareness of opposition is contingent upon awareness of self in order to differentiate between self and otherness. If identity is determined in opposition to difference then spirit must at least have a prior self-familiarity or quasi-awareness of itself before determinate difference is established. But this awareness is far from being a sentient self-consciousness that belongs to a reflective mind; it is a prereflective, hence nonpositional and nonpropositional self-consciousness that takes place underground. This form of unconscious self-consciousness points to the fact that Hegel is carving out a foundation which is the most primeval and uncultivated conditions that make the later development of self-consciousness possible. This originally comes about from the ways in which spirit overreaches nature and molds the most basic feelings of the soul.

The awakened spirit at this point does not know its unity with nature or with the implicit spirit within nature and thus stands in opposition to its externality. There is still a division between the inner and the outer; the other of nature is contrasted with the internality of spirit. While the natural soul attains an elementary form of self-consciousness through intro-reflectiveness, this inadequate unity subsists in nature in an "external, empty, superficial manner, that at the same time there is also a falling apart of the two terms" (*EG* § 384, *Zusatz*). Spirit in its being with itself is also not with itself but with the other—its natural counterpart, insofar as this unity of implicit spirit in the other has not yet attained it own being-for-self. Spirit then "posits nature" as its world, an intro-reflectedness, and thus denies nature's form as distinct from itself thereby turning that which is opposed into that which posits. Hegel further explains, however, that this positing of nature by what it takes to be itself is actually its presupposition and hence nature remains independent of spirit as an immediate presence. "As such it [nature] is therefore a becoming posited which precedes reflecting thought. From this standpoint, nature's being posited by spirit is therefore still not absolute, since it merely takes place in reflecting consciousness" (*EG* § 384, *Zusatz*). At this level, spirit is still limited by nature, hence finite, because it has not yet grasped that nature is only part of the infinite spirit that created it by means of which nature subsists. Spirit has still not grasped its unity with its counterpart. Only in its long transition to absolute knowing will natural spirit be sublated into the infinite.

THE DESIROUS SOUL

Nature for Hegel is a complex organization of interrelated parts and processes. From physical to chemical and biological configurations, nature is the conglomeration of interdependent material entities that reflect a complex whole. In spirit's externalization of itself as particularizations, nature only appears as individuated parts that are subjective self-expressions. At this level of the soul's development, the unity of interdependence is only implicit; it is not until this unity becomes more progressively complete that it is more fully introjected into each entity, which gradually becomes more responsive to its environment and the external events that comprise world activity. However, the process of internalization is already underway, which moves the organism more toward sensibility. At the level of sensuous organization, there is more of an intense self-relation the organism has with its own internal unification, and the process of reincorporation of its self-externalization into the profusion of nature has begun. We have already seen how the soul senses and relates to changes in its environment such as climate, temperature, time, and seasonal variations, and this takes place in all animate creatures thus affecting their internal states. Yet it is through individual minds that the soul feels.

Once awake, the universal natural spirit disperses its qualities into externality only to have them shaped by the natural changes of individual subjects that inevitably occur throughout the "stages of life." These stages are largely the product of social relations, the idiosyncrasies of individual interests, temperament, mood, disposition, and personality, and intellectual and ethical character. By this stage of development, consciousness and self-consciousness are presupposed. However, the form or maturity of self-conscious spirit is in question here: the soul is still connected to its natural states and alterations and has not yet achieved a full spiritual liberation that we may properly call objective. The soul is singularized into individual and familial or collective subjectivity as natural determinations that account for particular physical and mental differences, which are further influenced by life experiences.

The individual soul enters into opposition with itself as the other, which naturally leads subjective spirit to seek and find itself in a sexual relationship with the other. For Hegel, the sex-relationship is at once both a natural difference of subjectivity and activity and a universal that achieves union through passion and love, which further acquires ethical significance as the family. The individual soul remains at one with itself in its sensation with the other and its universal relation to the opposition of the external world. Sex distinctions institute both a firm antithesis due to the natural qualities of difference as well as a simple unity formed in the identification with the genus. In the stages that characterize the drama of life and the process of aging, change is a constant enterprise with nothing remaining fixed or stagnant. As the individual subject persists through the course of life experiences, everything is "fluid." The sex-relationship, on the other hand, is set in "firm" difference; the first being a simple unity, the second being a firm opposition. We may see that the dialectic unfolds continuously through all these appearances becoming more mature at each stage. At this point there is division and opposition but as mutually interdependent and contrasted aspects of psychic reality.

Hegel extends this contrast to the states of waking and sleeping. Individuality constitutes the awakening of the natural soul as a being for itself by means of confronting its natural determinateness, namely its self-absorbed life of sleep. Waking is the *"primary component"* of the singular soul for it distinguishes itself from its original undifferentiated universality. Just as sleep replenishes conscious functioning, it does so "negatively"—rest is a withdrawal from the determinateness of the world of singularities to the indeterminateness of "the universal essence of subjectivity, which constitutes the substance and the absolute power of these determinatenesses" (*EG* § 398). Hegel is very clear that the absolute power of determination lies in that unconscious region of the mind—the abyss of indeterminateness—where the latent activity of the natural soul, which is spirit implicit, "rouses" itself from its immediate determinate corporeality.

We can see how Hegel recognizes the contradiction inherent in the notion of determinism: spirit is both naturally constituted and free. At once spirit finds itself as material embodiment but is already activity in its implicitness that is capable of confronting its own confined original natural state and emerging in opposition as a determinate being. What is the "primary component" is the *impulse* to wake, to express itself as a free agent. As in social and sex-relations, the awakened soul relates itself not to a simple unity but rather "through the mediation of opposition" (*EG* § 398, *Zusatz*). And with each mediation, there emerges a new immediate. Dialectical rigidity falls away through mediation but always reinstantiates itself in the new immediacies or contingencies it both encounters and generates.

In the sleep of the soul, spirit is inherent but has not yet achieved determinate being. It is only through its own self-affirmation that spirit emerges. But what constitutes the *need* to awake; what drives spirit to reveal itself? Is perhaps need itself—*desire*—the gestation of spiritual activity, at once both natural corporeality and the inherent immaterial possibility to become other to itself? Spirit hungers, it wants to be fed—to feed itself. In the instants *before* spirit awakens, it experiences an impulse, it yearns to surface, a desire to *be*. Like Boehme's *Ungrund*, spirit undergoes an extreme tension, a primeval chaos, *lack*.[26]

In "Instincts and Their Vicissitudes," Freud describes four principle features of a *Trieb*, namely, its (*a*) pressure, (*b*) aim, (*c*) object, and (*d*) source. The pressure or force (*Drang*) corresponds to its urge or wish, which Freud identifies as its "very essence" (*Wesen*). "Every drive is a piece of activity"(*SE*, 14, 122). The aim (*Ziel*) of a drive is unwaveringly to achieve "satisfaction," the fulfillment of which results in a reduction in the amount of tension it experiences. The object (*Objekt*) is anything that is capable of being used through which its aim may be achieved and it is the most fluid or variable aspect to a drive, while the source (*Quelle*) is somatic processes or any "part of the body and whose stimulus is represented in mental life by a drive" (*SE*, 14, 123). Freud is very careful to note that the exact nature of a drive's source may not be fully known by organic reductive explanations such as those that refer to chemical or mechanical forces, rather, in mental life we can know them only by their aims. Furthermore, "sometimes its source may be inferred from its aim," which is the "need" itself.

Freud's depiction of a drive captures the very process by which spirit awakens as natural soul. Spirit is pure activity—an impulse to awake as determinate being. Indeed, spirit is a constant force or pressure as essence that takes itself as its own object, the aim of which is to fulfill itself, hence achieve self-completion, a primordial need for satisfaction. Freud further tells us that a drive "never operates as a force giving a *momentary* impact but always as a *constant* one" (*SE*, 14, 118). Spirit is continual dynamic energy that can only know itself as a being that is alive and desires. Its will to wake is the manifestation of such desire that finds itself as nature. Hegel, like Freud, cannot deny the body, which may be taken as its source but only known as its aim, its own stimulus as need. Yet for Hegel, the ultimate source of spirit is the Idea, which is logically prior to nature and mind, however, "the moment of its particularity or of its initial determining and otherness, [i.e.,] the *immediate Idea* as its reflexion, [is] itself as *Nature*" (*EL* § 244).

Spirit simply wants to affirm its own being, to discharge. In its state of sleep, of implicitness, spirit undergoes a violence from within, a permeating tension as undifferentiated void. It seeks to fill that void through self-differentiation as determinateness. Pure negativity is its ground and thus becomes the driving pressure behind its search for self-satisfaction. As spirit undulates through its various shapes of appearance, it achieves momentary pleasure as sublation hence reducing its tension, however mediation always collapses into a new opposition which re-institutes tension that serves as its platform throughout its upward momentum. The cycle of negativity and circular motion of drive is the dialectic of desire spirit may never completely purge. This primal negativity has the character of death and destruction as spirit perennially confronts opposition and limit in its quest to transcend it.

The intimate relation between Freud's thesis on the nature of drive and Hegel's characterization of unconscious spirit is further complemented by the significance both give to negativity and death. The primary significance of destruction is never so present as in Freud's postulation of the death drive (*Todestrieb*), the engine that powers psychic life. For Hegel, spirit is always "tarrying with the negative"—confronting death, for, "Spirit is not the life that shrinks from death . . . but rather the life that endures it and maintains itself in it" (*PS* § 32). Ultimately, spirit, like the death drive, wants to return to itself and recover its original unity in a higher form. Negativity is always the base agitation of any organism, the destruction that constructs life.

For Freud, destruction plays a significant role in psychic development to which "*the aim of all life is death*" (*SE*, 18, 38). But paradoxically, the death drive leads to the construction of self-preservative and life-enhancing processes. Freud tells us of two competing forces in human nature: the will toward life and the will toward death, manifested as Eros or libido, the sexual force responsible for erotic life, and its antithetical companion conceived under the drive toward destruction.[27] This dual class of innate drives comprise those that seek to preserve and unite and those that seek to kill and destroy. "Neither of these drives are any less essential than the other; the phenomena of life arise from the concurrent or mutually opposing action of both" (*SE*, 22, 209).[28] Furthermore, they scarcely operate in isolation, each borrowing from the resources of the other as an accompanied or alloyed counterpart, drawing a certain quota from the other side, which in turn modifies its aim or is even used to achieve its aim.

This union between life and death is the ontological fabric of the human mind to which all other dialectical polarities arise, including the universality of love and hate. Self-preservation is clearly an erotic impulse but it must have aggression at its disposal in order to accomplish its task; just as in love, the aggressive drive is utilized in order to gain mastery and possession over an object, which the attachment to it brings about. While the self-preservative drives stand in stark opposition to destructive ones, the two are dialectical complementarities that effect their confluence. These dual forces may be compared to the structural dynamic of the Hegelian dialectic with negativity begetting progression in the service of achieving higher aims. Just as Being is in opposition to Nothing, so is life to death, two sides of a symmetrical relation, their necessary unity.

In *Beyond the Pleasure Principle*, references to ego-instincts and death-instincts are used almost interchangeably. For Freud, the ego is characterized by its comportment to libido in the service of the pleasure-principle as well as its comportment to the death drive in response to the primal anxiety it generates which imperils the integrity of the organism. In contrast to Hegel's monistic posture, Freud postulates two distinct sources that the ego assumes bipolar positions toward. While there is a dialectical separation between the two classes that stand in antithesis to one another, the ego may adopt a dual identification with the two drives that may be preserved in violent opposition (depending upon which class is most operative at any given moment) or may become merged through an ego-mediated confluence, (e.g., sexual sadism).

While offering no formal commitment in his initial introduction to the death drive postulate, Freud surmises that the "compulsion to repeat" is *beyond* the pleasure motives of libido and is situated in the organism's proclivity toward death, that is, to return to its quiescent inorganic state of tranquility. In fact, the death drive presumably exists *before* the pleasure-principle. Preceded by a careful disclaimer under the title of "speculation," Freud ventures to hypothesize that the death drive may be developmentally prior to libido, therefore the pleasure-principle, and that the early stages of ego genesis are formed in response to the conservative needs of the organism to regress to its inanimate beginning. From this standpoint, the origin of the death drive appears to be a defensive maneuver characterized by its tendency to orient itself back to its tensionless nativity. Freud conjectures: "The tension which then arose in what had hitherto been an inanimate substance endeavoured to cancel itself out" (*SE*, 18, 38). As living organisms became more complex evolutionary systems, the influence of external demands forced the organism to adopt more circuitous routes to its own death. Freud asserts:

> For a long time, perhaps, living substance was thus being constantly created afresh and easily dying, till decisive external influences altered in such a way as to oblige the still surviving substance to diverge ever more widely from its original course of life and to make more complicated *detours* before reaching its aim toward death. (*SE*, 18, 38–39)

From this passage it follows that external reality itself impinges upon the organism's primordial motivation and forces it "to ward off any possible ways of returning to inorganic existence other than those which are immanent in the organism itself" (*SE*, 18, 39). Such tendency to respond to extrinsic threats with its own self-preservative impulses in the service of securing its own path toward death *at its own hands* suggests the rudimentary structures of ego development that are dialectically constructed to serve aims of both life and death. Thus, the ego wishes to live and die by its own fashion. "These guardians of life, too, were originally the myrmidons of death" (*SE*, 18, 39). Hence, the paradoxical situation of the organism's own propensity toward death is interrupted by an external source of danger that threatens its blissful rest, namely, life itself, which it responds to with its own impulse toward life (self-preservation) which is phenomenologically experienced as the binding of psychic energy to the pleasure-principle.

While the death drive only appears bound, the question remains whether on the topographic and ontological level there are indeed two classes of drives that abide in dialectical conflict with one another, or whether they are merely two appearances of the same drive. Following Hegel's progressive unfolding of spirit, the appearances of life and death would flow from a monistic source. Freud, however, maintains rigid bifurcation between the two classes due to the exclusivity of the sexual drives, which are oriented toward pleasure.[29] The death drive, on the other hand, produces anxiety, not pleasure, and the ego's response to such anxiety is in service of binding the psyche in order to safeguard against dangers or external threats that jeopardize its homeostatic placidity. Neurotic repetitions and trauma dreams, for example, are for the sake of inducing anxiety, not pleasure, so that the wounds of the psyche may be bound—what binds the psyche is anxiety. What makes the ego a sufficient shield against stimulation from libidinal forces is a ready charge of anxiety against pleasure. Within this context, the ego is a defense against pleasure, whereas repetition and trauma are in response to death drive derivatives. The death drive is not a stimulus to the pleasure-ego, rather, a breaching of the ego. Therefore, the death drive is a stimulus to anxiety whereas anxiety is understood as central to the ego's formation.[30] Without the death drive, there would be no ego.

Freud conjectures that life itself is a disturbance in the quiescent state of inorganic matter, which must have emerged from some charge that aroused it from its somnolent rest. The origin or essence of such disturbance, however, remains unknown. He states, "The attributes of life were at some time evoked in inanimate matter by the action of a force of whose nature we can form no conception" (SE, 18, 38). Freud suggests this "force" was an external event rather than an internal motive, linking the rise of the preservative drives to a fortification against threat from an encroaching environment. Is it possible, however, that such a psychic event be an internal one, thus the origin of its own arousal? This would certainly be Hegel's view. This would require not merely an ego's developmental response to the id, but rather their equiprimordial existence. While Freud's death drive has been largely rejected on biological grounds,[31] it does not mean that the destructive and regressive inclinations of the psyche are not present equiprimordially as ego, ontically positioned alongside libidinal forces. If the self-preservative drives can be looked at as nothing but the organism's own path to its self-determined death, then life is organized as the refusal to die by exogenous forces, for external reality would deprive it of its own pleasure.

At first glance, the self-preservative drives emerge in very complicated organisms out of the death drive, and in effect are merely its defensive response to external danger, which eventually take on their own life principles extricated from the death drive and bound to libido, and which are instantiated, sustained, and mediated by the ego. This assumes that libido is originally the defensive creation of the drive toward death that mutates and takes on its own being as higher complexities of organic life loom. As the organism becomes a more complex and intricate mental system, these two classes maintain an austere relation in radical opposition to each other in regards to their object goal (death versus life), but, strictly speaking, not in their aim. Upon closer analysis, while each class has a specific goal, the aim remains the same, namely, drive reduction, hence pleasure. It is the role of the ego, however, to determine the objects of gratification and the necessary detours needed in the service of the pleasure aims of the id. Following from this reconceptualization, there appears to be one source of motivation with regard to the aim of the psyche, viz., tension reduction; the forms in which the aim is fulfilled, however, appear to fall on the side of life and death, with object choice determined by the ego.

It is important to note that for Freud, tension reduction means a momentary attainment of satisfaction that is never complete in itself, for there are always desires that remain unfulfilled in the abyss and continue to drive psychic processes; like spirit, the mind is pure unrest. We may be able to partially extend this notion of pleasure to the dialectic of spirit: what spirit takes to be truth in each of its shapes collapses into singular moments, thus there is an ebb and flow of satisfaction and despair as spirit slowly elevates itself to a higher truth. As Hegel states, "the *satisfaction* of desire is . . . *singular* and *transient*, which is perpetually giving way to the renewal of desire . . . [and] since its goal is *never* completely attained, [it] only gives rise to an *endless progression*" (EG § 428, *Zusatz*). And even after attaining satisfaction in absolute knowing, spirit still desires more. But we need to be cautious not to blindly equate Freud's pleasure-principle with

Hegel's notion of satisfaction. While pleasure motives may be said to operate within the passions and hence to be associated to spirit's psychological or empirical embodiment, satisfaction is a much broader concept for Hegel associated with "the ego's self-integration" in self-consciousness (*EG* § 428).

Both Hegel and Freud would contend that impulse or drive is the engine of the psyche and that the ego develops out of drive, yet unlike Freud, Hegel already sees the ego's implicit existence from the start; it is only a matter of it becoming more mature. He asserts: "[T]he being-for-self of the individual soul has to be taken as already determined as the ego of consciousness and the spirit of understanding." Spirit awake "is essentially that of the concrete ego" (*EG* § 398). But the truth of spirit as pure activity has sleeping and waking as potential dialectical activities already implicit within its structure as its immediate being. For Hegel, "awakening is brought about by the lightning stroke of subjectivity breaking through the form of spirit's immediacy" (*EG* § 398, *Zusatz*)—spirit determines itself into awakening. The moment of awakening is a "*self-discovery* which in the first instance only progresses into sensation," a progression from night to day. In the darkness of the mind, difference is obscure for internal states are undifferentiated while, like the light of day, waking allows the soul to distinguish itself from otherness and enables differences to emerge. Discovering the duality of its own opposition with itself and the world is what constitutes its natural embodiment.

SENTIENCE

After progressing from an undifferentiated to a differentiated determinate being, the waking soul discovers its own content-determinations within its dormant nature as sensation. The sentient soul knows itself as a sensuous embodied being, which is the immediate unity of its somatic processes with nature. The awake soul immediately senses itself and thus constitutes the immediate acquaintance or familiarity it has with its own nature. In its concrete apprehension of itself as a sensuous, hence natural entity, the sentient soul now "achieves *actuality*" (*EG* § 399, *Zusatz*), yet the complete transition from sensation to full actuality requires several further steps.

Inherent in the very impulse to wake is a determinant activity, and it is through this activity that spirit crosses over from its implicit to its explicit state and therefore becomes a concrete actual being. By bringing itself into explicit being, spirit attains for itself an "initial fulfillment" by virtue of being actualized. Hegel explains that the sentient soul "proves" itself as a being-for-self not merely because it is a being for itself but also by "*positing* itself as such, as subjectivity," which is the inverse negativity of its immediate determinations. It is in the act of affirming itself that spirit "asserts itself within the manifoldness" of its own "inwardness" and thus sublates itself by moving from the opposition of its mere implicit immediacy to actual subjectivity (*EG* § 399, *Zusatz*). Like Fichte's absolute self that posits itself as an affirmative being, spirit defines itself as "*true* individuality."

The sensuous soul's mental activities may be the most archaic organization of unconscious processes—the abyss initially senses itself within its own inwardness thus affirming its being. Hegel is clear: "In sensation, spirit has the form of a subdued stirring in its unconscious and understanding individuality" (*EG* § 400). Here Hegel identifies the unconscious as an agent with individuality that understands. This understanding however is confined to its immediate determinateness, which is undeveloped in respect to its content and is its most particularized property characteristic of its naturality. Revealed in its immediate natural form, the content for sensuous spirit is transient and limited since natural embodiment will only reveal qualitative and finite determinations.

Hegel imbues unconscious sensation with foundational properties that infiltrate every subsequent developmental stage of spirit. "Everything is in sensation . . . it is in sensation that everything emerging into spiritual consciousness and reason has its source and origin" (*EG* § 400). Once again, Hegel anticipates Freud's emphasis on the somatic source and organization of the body as the sensory stimulus behind drives. Furthermore, Hegel suggests that the origin and source of anything is the most primary and immediate manner in which something appears. In its externalization, spirit appears as its aim—its purposefulness or desire to appear as a differentiated determinate being-for-self that actively posits and affirms its own being, hence obtaining "fulfillment." Sensation is subsumed or devolves into enlightened spirit, but it always informs the emergence of new appearances and is retained in all levels of sublation.

Hegel even equates personal value and principles with sensation for they "must be in the heart, they must be sensed" and not restricted to the "head" (*EG* § 400). From this standpoint, we may say that morality is sensed and made more intelligible as ego or perhaps superego, but for Hegel, the law of the heart is the "criterion of what is good, ethical and religious" as well as what is "evil, bad, godless, base, etc" (*EG* § 400). At this stage in spirit's development, unconscious sensation is its "most characteristic property." Valuation, whether base or pristine, is just as much unconsciously constructed as are our most conscious cherished ideals. Hegel situates the embryo of perversion as well as ethical enlightenment in the unconscious. And with Freud, not only do the most bestial characteristics reside in the unconscious, but also "the formation of the ideal, into what is highest in the human soul" (*SE*, 19, 36).

Sentient spirit has its origin in unconscious sensation and even possesses an inchoate form of ego organization. Hegel is very clear in specifying the existence of an unconscious ego at the stage of sensation:

> In sensation however, despite the subdued [unconscious] nature of being-for-self in such a form, content such as this is a determinateness of my entire being-for-self, and is therefore posited as my most characteristic property. That which is its own is inseparate from the actual ego, and this immediate content of the same constitutes this inseparability precisely in so far as the ego is not determined as the ego of consciousness, and certainly not as the freedom of rational spirituality. (*EG* § 400)

Hegel distinguishes the nascent unconscious ego from its conscious rational counterpart by the level of sophistication and freedom spirit attains for itself in conscious life. Spirit nevertheless retains sensation as its most basic experience, which becomes ever increasingly enriched and complex as the mine of images, presentations, affects, and thoughts become unconsciously harbored, organized, contained, and expressed as spirit moves from its immediate sentience into consciousness. Here we may see how Hegel advances the thesis that the unconscious is the womb of the self, which gives birth to a conscious animate being and then advances on to a parallel level or co-extensive process of development where unconscious and conscious spirit are mutually informing the reality of the other. This is the fundamental opposition that Hegel may never formally dissolve. Admittedly, this claim introduces a conundrum, for it would seem to suggest that spirit fights within itself its own process of becoming: the abyss resists being surpassed by the dialectic, its proper integration into the Absolute. This becomes a central issue when Hegel discusses madness, for the drive toward truth is eclipsed by the nostalgic desire to retreat back to earlier shapes of the feeling soul. Whether this is a condition reserved for subjective spirit or whether it equally applies to universal Spirit, we will have to carefully address, for the truth of desire may operate on parallel levels of consciousness.

Spirit must always retain both a conscious and unconscious organization for presumably the abyss cannot be totally sublated, only certain aspects of its content. And certainly the unconscious ego may not pass over and dissolve into the conscious ego except insofar as certain mental contents may be made available to conscious awareness but not the unconscious ego itself, for this would cleave Hegel's commitment to a developmentalism he is so conscientious to provide, one that is free of contradiction in its systematic attempt to explain spirit's maturation. If the unconscious ego evaporates into consciousness then there would be no psychic agent present to make images from the abyss available to conscious spirit. Sensation, affect, thoughts, and presentations are always "unconsciously busy" for Hegel—much takes place behind the back of consciousness. Hegel would not allow himself to commit to a position that would contradict his own system. If everything were conscious and readily available to the fund of spirit's self-understanding then Hegel would have no need to introduce the abyss in the first place—everything would be transparent. Furthermore, Hegel needs an unconscious agent to account not only for the normative aspects of consciousness, recollection, memory, and imagination, but also to explain psychopathology and the various forms of mental operations that psychoanalysis would label as defense mechanisms, subjects Hegel addresses throughout his *Encyclopaedia*.

If unconsciousness were sublated into consciousness and ultimately into self-consciousness as absolute spirit, then spirit would be perfect—omnipotent. But then spirit would not need to encounter the world of contingency any longer; the word *finitude* would not be in its vocabulary. If spirit were to attain this level of *Aufhebung*, then it would never need to move beyond itself, it would not need to surpass itself any longer—the dialectic would vanish entirely for spirit would no longer encounter opposition nor would it continue to desire. A proper appreciation of spirit in its absolute context must account for the world of change and contingency. While through repetition, old forms are constantly being rejuvenated, their appearances take on the form of novelty. This is the creative element to mind. If spirit were absolutely self-actualized in that it no longer required the contingency of experiences in the world, then it would be dead. Without the continual presence of the dialectic, unconsciously as much as consciously constituted, Spirit would simply cease to be.[32]

In the last paragraph of the *Phenomenology*, Hegel even alludes to the manifestation of spirit's internality as the projection of its "depth" and wholeness. We may infer that insofar as spirit is the self-realization of its totality, the abyss is a co-extensive being of spirit:

> Their goal [absolute knowing] is the revelation of the depth of Spirit, and this is *the absolute Concept*. This revelation is, therefore, the raising-up of its depth, or its extension, the negativity of this withdrawn 'I', a negativity which is its externalization or its substance; and this revelation is also the Concept's Time, in that this externalization is in its own self externalized, and just as it is in its extension, so it is equally in its depth, in the Self. (*PS* § 808)

Spirit seeks to reveal itself from its "depth" as it appears in pure self-consciousness, but this realization and externalization of its interior—from its abyss—is not the termination of its internality, only its "extension" that "is equally in its depth," namely, unconscious spirit.

With respect to its inceptive ego, the sensing soul also has more fundamentally the animal characteristics that we may properly call drive or instinct, meaning that which is innate and naturally given. Drive cannot be dissociated from spirit at any level, only sublated, or in Freudian terms, sublimated. Freud saw sublimation as a vicissitude (*Schicksale*) or fate of the drives, but he also saw it as a specific defensive process against the drives (*SE*, 14, 127). The fate of a drive in sublimation may be generally extended to the principle of *Aufhebung* where earlier impulses are mediated and transformed into a higher unity. While sublimation is a specific process for Freud, the two concepts share a general compatibility. In fact for Freud, "The most important vicissitude which a drive can undergo seems to be *sublimation*; here both object and aim are changed, so that what was originally a sexual drive finds satisfaction in some achievement which is no longer sexual but has a higher social or ethical valuation" (*SE*, 18, 256). This position is comparable to Hegel's:[33] natural desire finds higher forms of cultivation and refinement as reason and ethical and religious consciousness. Hegel is not shy in informing us that "it is also necessary to remind people that while man's thinking is the most characteristic property distinguishing him from beasts, he has sensation in common with them" (*EG* § 400). Desire is the basal foundation of spirit, a sensuous drive that "is common to the animal as well as the human soul" (*EG* § 400, *Zusatz*). Yet its sensuous content is hardly adequate to the human spirit; it must move beyond its mere natural immediacy and confront the limitations inherent in its finitude.

In its natural corporeity, the soul progressively moves from the immediate sensation of its internality to its external encounter with the natural world, which gives rise to affect and feeling. The soul's inner sensations of qualitative differences such as gravity, heat, and touch are also accompanied by quantitative variations that give rise to "*intensive* magnitude[s]" of pressure and measure. Here Hegel warns us that sensations determined to be pleasant or unpleasant, thus giving rise to satisfaction or dissatisfaction brought about in the awakening of impulses by affections, are determinations that rely on conscious reflection, however the simple "external sensation's being *unconsciously* related to spiritual inwardness" gives rise to inner moods that are analogous to those in animals. These moods of the soul are "something known of which the subject is not yet fully conscious" (*EG* § 401, *Zusatz*). Here Hegel is situating the locus of natural instinct or desire within the sensuous soul which accounts for drives that later inform conscious intention, reflection, emotion, and need.

UNCONSCIOUS FEELING

Sensations are immediate, single, and transient determinations posited by and for the soul in a stage where it is identical with its substantiality. For Hegel, these determinations are not simply moments of sensing however, but reflect the implicit totality of the soul's sensing substantiality, and therefore in this respect it feels itself as self. "[U]pon the immediacy of feeling's determinateness, feeling refers more to the selfhood involved here" (*EG* § 402). Sensation already has within it the form of a mediated dynamic. When the soul senses, difference becomes determinate; in order to know that one senses, sensation must be mediated by a cognizing agent, albeit cognition at this stage would be a quasi-cognition in the form of an incipient ego. From the transition of mere sensation to determinate feeling, the soul attains a certain liberation from its immediate naturality. Now the soul has simple ideality as a feeling individual that must posit its subjectivity and "take possession of itself" as "self-mastery." "In that it feels, the soul is no longer merely naturally individualized" (*EG* § 403). The shift from (*a*) slumbering undifferentiated spirit to waking differentiated spirit, then from (*b*) immediate natural sensation to discriminative feeling marks the mediatory dynamic that begins to take shape at this most elementary level of ego organization of the soul. Negation serves the function of mediation as the feeling soul differentiates itself from its mere natural form.

At this point in the soul's development, Hegel tells us that while the negation of the real is a feature of the positing ideality, that which is negated is also preserved and maintained despite the fact that it does not yet exist. Here we may see the germ of the canceling hence surpassing but at once preservative moment of the dialectic taking place as early as feeling is sensed by the ego in its infancy. But at this layer, "the ego is completely indivisible,—a featureless mine [*Schacht*], in which all is preserved without existing" (*EG* § 403). Because the ego at this stage is devoid of content other than its own sensuousness, it is barren, a "featureless" or characterless pit. It is only when the ego attains consciousness that the mine or abyss is supplied with ample images and presentations that can be recalled in the more advanced stages of intelligence. The indivisibility of the ego Hegel speaks of here pertains to the fact that the ego has not yet achieved consciousness and is only bound to its interior. When the ego makes the transition to consciousness we may then say that it is properly divided, a splitting of itself at its own hands.

The subjectivity the ego possesses at this unconscious level cannot be conceived of in the same way normal consciousness is construed; however, we must concede that there is some crude form of division even at the level of sensation, for the soul could not institute its conversion from symbiosis to differentiation without instituting an internal negation hence a separation within itself. This internal splitting of the ego takes place gradually, but soon takes on a doubling function that builds on itself, manifesting different qualitative degrees of internal division and corresponding affect. As the doubling progresses, separation, projection, incorporation, and reunification occur, which configures the core movement of the dialectic of drive and desire. As the intrinsic division, externalization, and reconstitutive process becomes more complex, the repetition of the generic template of the dialectic becomes superimposed on each progressive experience it encounters in the world of contingency. It is important to note that the ego initiates its own activity from within itself and attempts to assimilate its natural internality in which it finds itself as a feeling sentient being. As this process gains momentum and shifts more toward externalization, the ego acquires more sophistication, plasticity, and mastery on its acclivity toward consciousness.

We may speculate that one of the reasons Hegel saw the soul as the incubation of madness derives from the fact that the ego is initially a self-enslaved psychotic unity with a featureless interior marked by fragmentation and internal conflict. The horror of fragmentation and negation constitute the initial break from its merged undifferentiated union with its interiority to its self-externalization as plurality that it must now assimilate and gain control over in its quest for "self-mastery." It is this initial thrust from symbiosis to multiplicity and then back into reunification that constitutes the initial formation of the dialectic that the unconscious ego initiates through its own self-directing activity. The inward division and chasm the ego is eventually able to create and maintain in its break into consciousness signifies the remarkable ability the ego has at forging and sustaining two realms of psychic reality that are based on fundamental opposition—the inner and outer is a firm antithesis that may only broach a unity under special circumstances such as sleep or psychopathology. The dreaming soul is a case in point, where Hegel suggests that "it attains to a profound and powerful feeling of the *entirety* of its *individual* nature, of the *complete compass* of its past, present and future" (*EG* § 405, *Zusatz*). The conscious awake ego is in fact alienated from its primordial counterpart that lays concealed and buried in its depths yet is always present to furnish the conscious ego with its presentations and affect, although the conscious ego remains unaware of the unlimited quarry of content in its interior. The acknowledgment of this continental divide and the co-extension between the conscious and unconscious ego is supported by Hegel when he says that one "can never know the true extent of the knowledge he possesses . . . . This simple inwardness constitutes individuality, and it persists throughout all the determinateness and mediation of consciousness subsequently posited within it" (*EG* § 403). The unconscious is always present and is acknowledged by the conscious ego as its implicit inner self.

During the inception of the individual feeling soul, it is "entirely exclusive, and posits difference within itself" (*EG* § 404). What is differentiated is not yet an external object as in consciousness but rather the internal object of its substance as a sentient totality. In this basic division, it feels itself as a "monad" and takes its own being as its content. Hegel refers to this stage as the "darkness of spirit" for its determinations have no conscious or understandable content apart from its merely formal nature. The soul has being only as abstract form but appears to itself as a state, one that developed spirit may "relapse" back to during times of illness, a regressed wish to return to its original symbiotic unity.

Hegel situates this original unity of soul in the symbiotic "psychic" relationship of the unborn child in its mother's womb who is the soul's surrogate self as concrete subjectivity (*EG* § 405). Here in this unity "is the being of this germ of feeling which, in its enveloping simplicity, contains not only what is in itself *unconscious*, natural disposition, temperament etc., but also maintains, through habit . . . all further bonds and essential relationships, fates, principles—everything that pertains to character, and in the elaboration of which self-conscious activity has played its most important role" (*EG* § 405, italics added). Hegel shows how the feeling soul is the seat of spirit's natural dispositions and the reservoir of spirit's future experiences that become maintained through habit. Feeling constitutes the inner determination of the soul and what we call disposition or "heart." Here we may see another application of Hegel's reference to the abyss; not only is it the psychic depths of the soul where images and presentations are stored, but all of life's experiences and "essential relationships," including the fabric of "character" and "principles" and most importantly unconscious "feeling." This may be illustrated by referring to one of Hegel's examples: "In the relationship of parents with their grown-up children however, something that is undoubtedly magical has revealed itself in so far as children and parents who had been long separated and did not know each other, have unconsciously felt an attraction for one another" (*EG* § 405, *Zusatz*).

Here it may be said that Hegel is attempting to account for features of unconscious activity Freud was later to describe as transference. The abyss becomes the reservoir of all our "essential relationships" which may become activated unconsciously when the ego encounters a certain stimulus. And for Freud, "This produces what might be described as a stereotype plate (or several such), which is constantly repeated—constantly reprinted afresh—in the course of the person's life," which we project onto every individual we encounter (*SE*, 12, 99–100). Hegel's assessment of the feeling soul further anticipates unconscious attributes that Freud had arrived at only after his repeated theoretical speculations had been challenged in the face of new clinical evidence. Hegel sees feeling states, moral character, and ethical principles already constituted in the sensuous soul as a logical inclusion, hence as potential, while Freud's metapsychological postulations of the superego and unconscious emotion were the result of mature theoretical revision.

In his essay "The Unconscious," Freud specifically rejects the idea of unconscious emotions, but by the time he wrote *Civilization and its Discontents*, unconscious feeling is of major importance. This is somewhat surprising since he was fully content to grant the mind the presence of unconscious ideas—an advanced ego capacity—yet saw feelings as conscious constructs. He did however view affect as a somatic organization tied to sensuousness, as did Hegel. But what is clear from Freud's notion of unconscious ideas is that he views them as a cognizing activity, a position that aligns with Hegel's. Furthermore, ego ideas are mental (re)presentations of drives; drives become the content for the unconscious self as ideas. Freud states:

> A drive can never become an object of consciousness—only the idea that represents the drive can. Even in the unconscious, moreover, a drive cannot be represented otherwise than by an idea. If the drive did not attach itself to an idea or manifest itself as an affective state, we could know nothing about it. (*SE*, 14, 177)

Following Hegel and Freud, drives or impulses must instantiate themselves first as sensation or affect and then as concrete ego states, the ego already implicit in sensation. Affect and ideas are unconscious transformations or mutations resulting from the internal divisibility and externalization of drive activity. Hence Hegel and Freud would be in agreement that in order for thought to be made actual it has to *appear* as essence, essence being its logical idea. But unlike Freud who maintains that a drive cannot be an object for consciousness, thus employing something that looks like a *Ding-an-sich*,[34] Hegel shows how drive appears as essence, for nothing could exist unless it is made actual. For Hegel, appearance is essence; "Essence must *appear* . . . since the essence is what exists, existence is appearance" (*EL* § 131). As early as the *Phenomenology*, Hegel shows that the coming into being of higher forms of subjectivity are mediated by its previous appearances: "The inner world, or supersensible beyond, has . . . *come into being*; it *comes from* the world of appearance which has mediated it; in other words appearance is its essence and, in fact, its filling" (*PS* § 147). Drive appears as ego, hence a mediation, and as essence, ego is its sublated shape.

The abyss is the original locus of an ego that feels whose next step is to divide itself internally only to awaken through its initial inner split by virtue of the fact that it possesses particular feelings. This is an important advance for the feeling soul because as individuality, it is a subject that posits its feeling determinations as singular sensations while at the same time it amalgamates them as a unity. It is at this point that the feeling soul constitutes an *unconscious self-awareness*. Hegel clearly states that the soul "is immersed in this particularity of sensations, and at the same time, through the ideality of what is particular, combines with itself in them as a subjective unity. It is in this way that it constitutes self-awareness, and at the same time, it does so only in the particular feeling" (*EG* § 407). The feeling soul attains for itself an immediate form of unconscious self-consciousness of a particular feeling state. Again we may see how the burgeoning soul as the incipient ego gradually acquires more familiarity with itself as an unconscious agent.

Hegel imbues the feeling soul with a sense of self that approximates some neonatal form of awareness, although such awareness cannot be compared to conscious self-realization and is only confined to the realm of sensation. Hegel is confronted with the immense difficulty of superimposing language that is intrinsic and common to our conscious understanding on an inner self that is implicitly there but has not yet achieved conscious actuality. Yet this inward non-actualized self exists by virtue of its sentience and determinate activity. His only recourse is to explain the primitiveness of the mind by inferring a parallel process of mentation that approximates consciousness *as if it were* in possession of such faculties. This quasi self-awareness is indeed an unconscious prereflective self-consciousness, yet it is not a reflective agent. We must proceed cautiously about the degree of internal awareness and autonomy the soul has achieved for itself in the stages of feeling, but Hegel is nevertheless attempting to articulate a primal ground of the psyche that has its origins in the somatic organizations that constitute the basic structures of subjectivity.

At this point, we may say that the feeling soul has an unconscious self-relation to its own immediate inwardness in the form of internal division and particularization. Awakened spirit is still shrouded in the night of the mind and only knows its sensuality, an instinctual awareness or intuition of itself as an animate being.

> What we have called genius is instinctive, active in an unconscious manner, in opposition to particular determinations. Other oppositions fall within reflection within consciousness.—What we have before us here is feeling subjectivity, which realizes itself, is active, proceeds forth from simple unity as liveliness. This activity belongs to the determination of liveliness, and although it awakens opposition within itself, it also preserves itself by sublating it and so endowing itself with a determinate being, with *self-awareness*. This activity is the expression of drive, of desire, its determination or content being drive, inclination, passion, or whatever form this content is given. (*EG* § 407, *Zusatz*)

Hegel reinforces the notion that instinct, drive, or desire is the essence of the nature of unconscious organization. It is important to note that for Hegel, as well as for Freud, instinct is not a fixed, rigid, or inflexible mechanism, but rather a natural determinateness that is malleable, telic, and dynamically constituted, finding expression through its feeling subjectivity. The core element of the feeling soul is an active aliveness, the expression of drive (*Trieb*) or desire (*Begierde*) which is its determination and content.

Errol Harris points out that Hegel's use of the term *genius* is to be understood in the context of the ancient Greek meaning of *daimôn*—the spiritual animating forces of the psyche having their sense and direction emanating from unconscious pressures.[35] Hegel shows how the very impulse, urge, or pressure within spirit is itself its own innate nature as "liveliness." Impelled to wake from its implicit state—this "stirring" in the soul, spirit sets up dialectical polarities within itself and sublates them *because it wishes to do so—for the sake of which*, thus attaining a free self-awareness. This form of realization however, is only in the form of a sense of feeling or a "self-feeling" (*Selbstgefühl*). As the feeling subject emerges from what is merged—its original unity—it generates its own opposition within itself, surpasses but preserves such opposition, and gives itself determinate being that is now aware. This awareness however, is not a reflective awareness by which the soul knows itself as a self-conscious subject who takes its own self as an object set over against its externality, for it is still confined to its own immediate inwardness. What the soul realizes is that it simply *is* and it feels, its being is activity itself—drive.

THE ACTUAL SOUL AS EGO

Recall that when the soul first attains unconscious self-consciousness in the form of feeling, this self-consciousness is a prereflective, nonpropositional form of awareness. At this point we may say that naturalized spirit has made its transition from its mere corporeity to the self-awareness of its corporeal nature, which we may further attribute to an unconscious agent we call ego. As we have noted, ego organization appears gradually, slowly moving from its implicit internal state to becoming an actual entity. It does not simply pop up as an end product, but rather developmentally evolves from its immediate potentiality and slowly materializes as a cognizing state of intentionality, which involves the ever increasing assimilation and organization of internal drives. Like spirit, ego itself must be implicit within the natural soul thus gaining more acuity, potency, and awareness as it emerges from slumber to wakefulness, symbiosis to individuation, sensuousness to thought, resulting in a form of intellectual intuition, or what Hegel calls "unconscious intuiting" (*EG* § 409). When the soul acquires its initial awareness of itself unconsciously, we may say that ego is present, for in order for there to be any awareness at all it must be apprehended by an individualized being that is already engaged in the elementary process of mentation. The immediate familiarity the soul experiences of itself as sensuousness is at once both an intuitive and intellectual activity insofar as it thinks, a self-feeling as unconscious intuition and a cognizing awareness as a thinking ego. Hegel himself sees this process as constituting the prerequisite for consciousness:

[T]his pure being, which is being-for-self, or entirely pure and *unconscious in-tuiting*, in that the particularity of corporeity, immediate corporeity as such, is sublated within it, is the basis of consciousness. It inwardly assumes the na-ture of consciousness in that it is posited as the being-for-self of a subject. (*EG* § 409, italics added)

Here Hegel is palpably clear in showing that the unconscious is the root of con-sciousness and every higher activity of spirit that is to be made manifest—"un-conscious intuiting" is the "basis of consciousness"—a basal cognition. "In the *Soul* is the *awakening* of *Consciousness*" (*PM* § 387). This architectonic process as a whole forges the original groundwork of spirit and is thus the necessary pre-condition for consciousness to appear.

Furthermore, the move from drive to sensation to ego forms the template or original model for consciousness to unfold. This is evident by Hegel's treat-ment of the phenomenology of consciousness, which moves from an undiffer-entiated unity to particularization, perception, and finally self-consciousness with each progression involving a dialectically self-articulated elevation of awareness. The dialectical organization of the unconscious becomes more com-plex as ego integration begins to take shape, hence moving from feeling to con-sciousness proper. Consciousness, however, is also quite an elementary form of spirit, and it is only through its steady acclivity to absolute knowing that uncon-scious spirit will become more refined and robust as the "heart" or drive behind spiritual valuation, because whatever is experienced consciously is equally pre-served within the abyss of its determinations.

Again we may see the logical consistency in Hegel's method, which he ap-plies from within the dynamic progression of spirit itself: unconscious spirit emerges from (*a*) undifferentiated unity to (*b*) sensation then to (*c*) conscious-ness, while conscious spirit moves from (*a*) undifferentiated sense-certainty to (*b*) differentiated perception then to (*c*) understanding. This method is the same structural dynamic all the shapes of spirit utilize on its developmental ascen-dance; first as the inward unfolding of unconscious activity, which moves be-yond its self-enclosed cave, only secondly to encounter the world of conscious sensation and the higher tiers of thought.

When the soul projects its internality into externality and thus takes its in-ternality to be identical with its external corporeal nature, then we may say that the soul has achieved actuality. We have seen that this process requires three suc-cessive movements with several intermediate steps beginning with: (1) the soul as initially mere being, unseparated from its natural immediacy; (2) only to awaken as sensation and thus make its transition into feeling, which requires the soul to separate itself out from its immediate undifferentiated unity and hence determine itself for itself in an abstract manner; (3) in which it develops out of this separa-tion into a mediated unity with its corporeal nature and is now for itself as a con-cretely existing ego. Here the actual soul attains "concrete self-awareness" in its "higher awakening as *ego*" and is now a being-for-self as abstract universality and a thinking subject (*EG* § 412). As "thought and subject," the soul or ego is "specifically the subject of its judgment" in which it now excludes itself from its natural totality of the external world and thus relates itself to this totality, which is reflected within its being (*EG* § 412). It is at this stage of reflection that the soul now attains consciousness.

Recall that the epigenesis of the ego appears in incremental stages, gaining fuller presence and elaboration as the soul begins to engage in active mediation. Within its body, the soul as organic retains a limitation, which constitutes a withdrawal of its power. In recognizing the limitation of its power, the soul "reflects itself into itself" and thus divides itself from its corporeality, which it expels and sees as "*alien*" to itself. "It is through this *intro-reflection* that spirit completes its liberation from the form of *being*, gives itself that of *essence*, and becomes *ego*" (*EG* § 412, *Zusatz*). Here Hegel is following the same analytic sequence he outlines in his *Logic*. The developmental character of the ego is evident in that the ego is already implicit in the act of "intro-reflection" as a prereflective self-consciousness. Hegel himself states that "the soul is already *implicitly ego* in so far as it is subjectivity or selfhood" (*EG* § 412, *Zusatz*). The prereflective activity of the soul clearly marks the emergence of the unconscious ego, which becomes the prototype of the mediated reflective activity the shapes of consciousness are to assume later in the course of spirit's development. By tracing the emergence of the ego situated within the dynamic unfolding of the soul, hence the anthropological sphere of spirit, we may see how the unconscious becomes an indispensable entity for Hegel which serves as the original ground for spirit to appear. It is only when spirit surfaces from its corporeity as ego that its essence appears and thus the ego becomes a general object for itself as an actual concretely existing being.

Hegel's articulation of the soul's development from its (*a*) immediate naturality to (*b*) feeling then to (*c*) actuality anticipates Freud's epigenetic treatment of the ego. For both Hegel and Freud, the inchoate ego is originally encased in a unity and is therefore modally undifferentiated from external forces—the inner and outer are fused in a symbiotic organization. From *Civilization and its Discontents*, Freud informs us:

> [O]riginally the ego includes everything, later it separates off an external world from itself. Our present ego-feeling is, therefore, only a shrunken residue of a much more inclusive—indeed, an all embracing—feeling which corresponded to a more intimate bond between the ego and the world about it. (*SE*, 21, 68)

Just as the natural soul moves from an undifferentiated unity to a differentiated determinate being, ego boundaries gradually become more contrasted, constructed, and consolidated throughout its burgeoning activity. Freud notes that originally an infant is unable to distinguish between its own ego and the external world as the source of stimulation and sensation. But eventually the organism comes to discern its own internal sources of excitation, such as its bodily organs or somatic processes, from external sources of sensation (e.g., mother's touch, breast, etc.), which become set apart and integrated within ego organization. It is not until this stage in ego formation that an object is set over against the ego as an existent entity that is outside of itself.

The ability to distinguish inner from outer reality requires the appropriation of mediational capacities from the ego that perform the function of judgments. By the time the soul becomes a concrete actuality, according to Hegel, the ego is "the subject of its judgment." For Hegel, the affirmative function of a judgment hinges on the determinate power of negation. This is further echoed in Freud's discussion of an ego judgment that "affirms or disaffirms the possession by a thing of a particular attribute; and it asserts or disputes that a presentation has an existence in reality"; but before judgments are consciously formed, inner and outer are one: "[W]hat is alien to the ego and what is external are, to begin with, identical. . . . The antithesis between subjective and objective does not exist from the first" (SE, 19, 236–237). The act of negation is itself a projection of an inner state, an expulsion of the inner into the outer. The soul's expulsion of its corporeity as the affirmation of its spiritual being-for-self as "free universality" is seen by Hegel to be the *decisive act* of the ego's determinate judgment, although at this stage it is confined to an unrefined level of thought.

It is important to note that when Hegel and Freud speak of the "ego" they use the same German word *Ich*. As a personal pronoun, the *I* as ego is viewed by both as a personal subjective agent. Hegel, as does Freud, shows the ego's progression from its immediate unconscious unity to its internal division, projection, and introjection as the ego punctures through to conscious awareness. It is through these architectonic movements that the ego differentiates between what is internal to itself and thus truly belongs to itself from what is truly external to itself as experienced through its newly acquired consciousness, namely, the plurality of objects that emanate from the external world, a world that is still the self's own. But before the phenomenology of objects is made available to consciousness, Hegel shows how the ego slowly cultivates a steady progressive organization of mental capacities that make consciousness possible.

The activity of differentiation constitutes the turning point in the formation of a determinate psychic agency. While inner drive, impulse, or desire commences the awakening of the soul from within itself—drive being its very essence and thus equated with the dialectic itself—the act of division or individuation from its immediate unity becomes the initial teleological function of a cognizing agent that, while still enveloped within its sensuousness, is still nevertheless a deliberate and determinate will or affirmative being. It is in this intermediate stage of differentiation—already a mediation—that the inceptive ego gradually takes on the nucleus of its core dialectical structure of negation in the service of affirmation, a process of sublation it sees through to the awakening of consciousness. We may say that this intermediate shift from undifferentiation to differentiation culminating in the intro-reflected or prereflective awareness of its determinate being is the transition from an unconscious division to a preconscious pre-familiarity of the soul with itself; such preconsciousness however retaining all the characteristics of a dynamically formed unconscious agent. Dynamically, spirit is still unconscious at this stage, with consciousness constituting its logical antithesis; descriptively however, we may say that spirit has advanced to the intermediate arena of making itself a cognizing sentient subject in which preconsciousness—its prior form—is its appropriate shape.

For Freud, the preconscious is distinguished from the unconscious only in a descriptive manner; in the dynamic sense they remain undifferentiated.[36] In *New Introductory Lectures on Psycho-Analysis*, Freud states: "[W]hether we are using the word [unconscious] in the descriptive or in the dynamic sense, we make use of a permissible and simple way out. We call the unconscious which is only latent, and thus easily becomes conscious, the 'preconscious' and retain the term 'unconscious' for the other. We now have three terms, 'conscious', 'preconscious' and 'unconscious', with which we can get along in our description of mental phenomena" (*SE*, 22, 71). Freud's distinction may be applied to Hegel's development of spirit, for as we have seen, within the ego's unconscious formation it gradually and "inwardly assumes the nature of consciousness" (*EG* § 409).

Prior to consciousness proper, unconscious spirit begins to acquire the essential features of consciousness as thought, mediation, and intentionality become more crystalized. However, this shift from the purely unconscious activity of initial differentiation and determinate negation to unconscious sensation and feeling may be attributed to the ever-increasing construction and assimilation of conscious ego structures, which we may descriptively call preconscious. In this sense, the inner ego organization and preparation effecting spirit's transition from the unconscious soul to the conscious ego may be seen as the prototype of conscious sensation. If unconscious spirit internally assumes the nature of consciousness as Hegel asserts, then consciousness itself may be said to be the externalization of the unconscious, because there could be no consciousness without an a priori ground serving as its template. We may then speculate that consciousness is the fruition of unconscious maturation, thus consciousness is the instantiation of unconscious structure. This has further implications for the developmental progression of spirit: consciousness may be said to assume the structure of the unconscious in a more animate, dynamic, and complex manner whereby unconscious self-familiarity is converted from prereflective to reflective self-conscious realization. From this standpoint, the nature of consciousness lies on a continuum, with unconscious processes expanding into conscious ones that are further capable of sliding back into their original domain as repression and regression become operative. What we have gathered from our analysis of the soul's initial unconscious self-relation is that self-consciousness precedes consciousness, which is only made more explicit in spirit's eventual actualized potential as absolute knowing. From self-conscious immediacy and universality spirit emanates, and to self-conscious universal realization spirit returns, only in a higher and more evolved form.

The mediated interaction between the soul's internal division and its projected externality within its internality presupposes a prereflective nascent awareness of its own being as a determining subject, only made more specific as the soul proceeds toward external consciousness. Therefore, we may conclude that the ego develops forth from a series of internal splits and projections which it externalizes within itself—externality still being confined to the soul's internal totality—until the ego matures to a level of increased separative and integrative order in which it continually divides and splinters itself off within itself only to unify itself in its next moment, insofar as each unification is a reunification. The ego achieves unconscious self-recognition when it becomes increasingly more aware that it is an agent performing this process of division and (re)unification, a process still shrouded in abstract emptiness and sensuous embodiment but nevertheless the formative prototype for a model of consciousness the soul transfers from its inward casing to its external arousal.

It is through the destruction of its immediate being that the soul institutes its animate activity, initially as sensuous embodiment, then as ego. But as Hegel explains, the awakening of the ego is that of a "*higher kind*," as opposed to its mere natural awakening, one in which the ego is the "*lightning*" that "consumes its naturality" (*EG* § 412, *Zusatz*). As ego, the soul raises itself above its singleness limited by sensation and posits itself as the ideality of naturality—its ideal nature, hence an individuated self-relating universal or "*abstract totality liberated from corporeity*" (*EG* § 412, *Zusatz*). The self or ego is now the actualized determinate being of the soul that posits its corporeity within itself and conversely views itself in its otherness, and is thus its own self-intuiting.

THE LOGIC OF THE UNCONSCIOUS

One of the more interesting aspects of Hegel's developmental treatment of the soul is the way in which a mediated dynamic forms a new immediate. This process not only informs the basic structure of his *Logic*, which may further be attributed to the general principle of *Aufhebung*, but this process also provides the logical basis to account for the role of the unconscious. The process by which mediation collapses into a new immediate provides us with the logical model we can clearly glean from the soul's transitions from nature, to feeling, then to actualized ego. And it is precisely this logical model that provides the internal consistency to its specific instantiation within unconscious spirit. As an architectonic process, spirit invigorates itself and breaths its own life unconsciously as a self-determining generative will that forms the edifice for all else to unfold. It is this internal consistency that provides us with a coherent account of the circular motion of the progressive drive toward higher manifestations of psychical development. Unconscious spirit builds upon its successive shapes and layers and constructs its own monolith.

Hegel allows for many distinctions to be made between the different forms and levels of unconscious activity in the Anthropology, Phenomenology, and

Psychology of Spirit, ranging from the standpoint of unawareness in general, to psychic space, to the telic functions of an unconscious ego with determinate being. It is the last that is the most significant in our understanding of the abyss, for not only does unconscious spirit reside within the nocturnal *Ungrund*, it remains the nucleus or dynamic agent that guides the dialectical functions of desire, thought, and reason, thus canceling opposition while simultaneously transcending yet preserving its immediate forms through sustained mediated syntheses. It is important to reemphasize that unconscious spirit is always present in any activity of spirit, whether we consider the phenomenology of consciousness or the psychological processes of intelligence, imagination, and reason, for the abyss is their presupposition. While we can examine or dissect spirit in its moments, we may not exclude the presence of the abyss in any treatment of spirit, for the Anthropology, Phenomenology, and Psychology are interconnected activities—the unconscious soul forms the ground of all higher modalities.

These interconnected structures and processes make the abyss a fluid and dynamic ground that is constantly transforming itself as it encounters new contingencies, therefore generating new desires and complexities of thought and valuation encountered in each moment. The logic of the dialectic forms the internal configurations of all shapes of spirit, which we may say is its proper essence, without which Spirit could not exist. The dialectic of spirit first appears unconsciously and is thus generated unconsciously from within the soul itself. It is this movement and the mechanics of the dialectic *as process* that provide the logical basis for an unconscious ground, one that is precipitated and superimposed onto all forms of mental activity.

A logical analysis of the operations of unconscious activity may be found in Hegel's general treatment of mediation within the soul where he traces the systematic application of his logic within its unfolding. Each opposition the soul encounters it mediates, which in turn generates a new immediate that it must further surpass and digest into its internality. By following this dialectical pattern, the soul steadily divides and separates itself out from its otherness when it encounters each new immediate shape, and then in turn reconstitutes itself through mediation until it achieves determinate being-for-self as a concrete ego set over against its mere natural embodiment which has become incorporated into its inner structure. Hegel explains:

> It is therefore through the separation of the soul from its corporeity and the sublation of this separation, that this *inwardness* of soul and *externality* of corporeity emerge as a mediated unity. It is this unity, which relinquishes its being brought forth as it becomes immediate, that we call the *actuality* of the soul. (*EG* § 411, *Zusatz*)

No longer confined to the limits of bodily sensation, the soul as ego now attains cognizing capacities as its ideal nature, which it further expounds upon as it continues to confront new immediacy.

Hegel's use of mediation within the movements of the soul has been properly prepared in the *Science of Logic* as well as the *Encyclopaedia Logic* which prefaces the Anthropology. In the *Logic*, Being moves into Nothing, which then develops into Becoming, first as the "passing over" into nothing, second as the "vanishing" into being, and third as the "ceasing-to-be" or passing away of being and nothing into the "coming-to-be" of becoming. Becoming constitutes the mediated unity of "the unseparatedness of being and nothing" (*SL*, 105). Hegel shows how each mediation leads to a series of new immediates which passes over and ceases to be as that which has passed over in its coming to be until these mediations collapse into the determinate being of *Dasein*—its new immediate. Being is a simple concept while becoming is a highly dynamic and complex process. Similarly, *Dasein* is a simple immediacy to begin with which gets increasingly more complicated as it transitions into essence and conceptual understanding. It is in this early shift from becoming to determinate being that you have a genuine sublation, albeit as a new immediate, spirit has a new beginning.

We may see how Hegel uses this method as the basic framework for the unfolding of unconscious spirit. In the soul's transition from undifferentiated unmediated being to differentiated mediated being, the soul must divide itself from what it is not—its *nothingness*—as the coming-to-be of its determinate being, with the act of its initial separation already constituting its determinative power. As the soul awakens to find itself in its immediacy, it has already mediated its immediacy in that it finds itself through the act of division. In its division it passes over into nothing, its otherness, ceasing to be what it was as it comes to be what it already is—a determinate being. The soul continues on this circular albeit progressive path conquering each opposition it encounters, elevating itself in the process. Each mediation leads to a new beginning, and the soul constantly finds itself confronting opposition and overcoming conflict as it is perennially engaged in the process of its own becoming. In the *Logic*, the whole process is what is important as reason is eventually able to understand its operations as pure self-consciousness, however, in its moments, each mediation begets a new starting point that continually reinstitutes new obstacles and dialectical problems that need to be mediated, hence eliminated.

But thought always devolves or collapses back into the immediate. This dynamic is a fundamental structural constituent that offers systematic coherency to Hegel's overall philosophy of spirit as well as its specific relevance to unconscious spirit and the soul. The methodological congruity of the logic allows for its systematic application to the unconscious and gives logical order to the mediative activity of the soul, otherwise Hegel runs the risk of potentially having a plethora of immediate concepts or relations that can be generated independently from the soul. It is not merely that concepts mediate each new immediate, but rather that mediation attempts to resolve earlier problems unto which new immediacy emerges. Mediation is therefore an activity performed from within the soul and not engineered by extrinsic forces that in turn make new experience possible.

Hegel's logical analysis of spirit perpetually engaged in the process of mediation begetting new immediacy is the same structure in the *Phenomenology* where consciousness first encounters sense-certainty before perception is achieved as a mediated unity, where reason is effected as the sublation of self-consciousness. In the natural progression of the soul, as with the phenomenology of consciousness, unconscious spirit educates itself as it passes through its various stages, preserving its experiences within the nocturnal abyss of the mind. The soul brings its collective retained history to bear on each successive shape, and while practically barren at this early embryonic level, it nevertheless starts to amass its experiences, thus reorganizing its interior cupboards, and the abyss begins to fill.

Hegel sees this general structural dynamic throughout all contexts of spirit, giving the movement of spirit its logical substance. What is happening in each mediatory shift of spirit is that in each new immediate encounter it faces, it brings forth within it unconsciously all of its past mediation that has already taken place, thus forming the backdrop onto which spirit interprets and resolves its new reality. Each immediacy has a new kind of claim that tests spirit's past shapes, which in turn must be put into practice in the novel experience it confronts. Spirit is faced with the tussle of having to take each new immediate and integrate it within its preexisting internal structure, thus incorporating each novelty within its subsisting mediatory faculties. This structural dynamic takes into account the ubiquitous nature of contingency, for spirit is not simply extending a part of itself as mediation that is already there, it has to incessantly vanquish each new experience it encounters in all of its freshly discovered and unacquainted future environments. The ongoing process of confrontation is the leviathan of spirit's journey, with each encounter signaling a spewing forth from the well of what it has already incorporated from its past, thus defining the context for each new stage, which also defines what confronts spirit as unexpected reality.

This model holds true for unconscious spirit that has to take each experience of novelty and assimilate it into its psyche—its personality. And here we may see Hegel once again in the company of Freud: there is always an element of our history that informs our relation to novelty and influences the way in which reality impacts us, that is, how we respond to it; the dynamics of wish and defense, transference, and character formation are the collection of our unconscious histories. Hegel's treatment of the soul accounts for an unconscious teleology that is free, what psychoanalysis would call "psychic determinism," not as a materialist interpretation of mind naturally determined by mechanical causal laws, but rather one that freely takes into account the unexpected in its appropriation of its past experiences. The psychic determinism of spirit is therefore the freely determining power of the ego. There is a degree of choice unconscious spirit assumes as it becomes more mature, a teleology defined, not as a preordained goal, but one that finds novel ways of incorporating novel encounters into its self. In this sense there is no absolute fixed end point that has been predesigned or preprogrammed into spirit, for spirit defines its intentions and purposes in each moment. It is through the interaction of each mediated immediacy that choice is defined, whether existing in spirit or in nature, for as Hegel says, "the true teleological method—and this is the highest—consists, therefore, in the method of regarding Nature as free in her own peculiar vital activity" (*PN* § 245, *Zusatz*).

The soul, being part of nature, is free vital activity that becomes more convoluted and circuitous as it becomes increasingly more permeated by the spiritual. And as John Findlay points out, Hegel's teleology of spirit as the self-conscious ideal is "the ultimate meaning of everything," a meaning however that does not lie at the beginning of thought and being nor at a presupposed end, for the end is a transformed achievement—"the logical and ontological Alpha of the cosmos, but only after it has first emerged as its logical and ontological Omega."[37] William DeVries also affirms that "Spirit is what is self-determined, . . . a self-productive activity."[38] Hegel's teleology is all inclusive, equally stressing the beginning, the process, and the end product as spirit's unactualized potential moves through a process of actualizing the potential to the emergent actuality itself—all one, equally necessary and reflective totality.

Through the interaction of mediated immediacy, teleology becomes defined in each moment, with each immediate being only a moment in the process of unconscious spirit's development. As unconscious spirit passes into new stages, it takes on new forms as the self expands and incorporates larger aspects of its experience into its inner being, preparing itself for its next confrontation, guaranteeing there will always be a new stage.

In Hegel's discussion on determinate being in the *Logic*, the escalating shift from mediation to immediacy ultimately carries spirit into dialectical engagement with the finite and the infinite, a combat with the Fichtean "ought" in which there is always a beyond.[39] Hegel cannot accept this mere *Sollen* of the ego as an endless endeavor, for spirit must get beyond the ought, a beyond that is itself finite; "For in the ought, the limitation as limitation is equally implied" (*SL*, 133). Yet this finite position is equally beyond or in opposition to that which is free from limitation, which marks the shift to the infinite which is the affirmative determination as negation of the finite. However, as Hegel points out, this shifting back and forth from finite to infinite determinations is merely alterations or moments of the "*one-sided* infinite" and is not self-sublated until it is viewed "as a *single* process—this is the *true* or *genuine infinite*" (*SL*, 137). Hegel shows that the progression to infinity is "like the ought, the expression of a contradiction which is itself put forward as the final solution" (*SL*, 150). But rather than get ensnared in infinite progresses of infinite regresses, thought moves back and examines the process.

What we see is an infinite pattern: first, the finite moves over into the infinite, second, the infinite becomes finite, and third, the finite slides once again over into infinitude. However, it is this pattern itself that contains both finitude and infinity as contrary moments of each merging into the other. This pattern is genuinely infinite for it is a self-maintaining process; each alteration collapses into a new moment, which is its being-for-self in its mediacy. By standing back and seeing the recurrent pattern as a new dimension, spirit is enabled to effect the transition to a new immediate that is truly sublated.

Despite the fact that spirit attains an appreciation of genuine infinity, this does not mean that the contingency of finitude vanishes; spirit is always faced with the relative novelty of each new shape. But it approaches each new opposition not as a static antinomy doomed to a stalemate, rather as a self-contained pattern; the infinite generates new finites as a fundamental repetition of itself—a self-maintaining process that generates its own process. While unconscious spirit is not aware at this stage of its infinite fundamental pattern within its finitude, the procreative movement of the dialectic informs the relation between a mediated immediacy as an internally self-generating dynamically articulated process. Because consciousness is the self-sublation of unconscious activity, the logic of the dialectic of consciousness provides us with the prototype for understanding the underlying functions of the abyss.

TOWARD PSYCHOLOGICAL SPIRIT

Hegel's dialectical articulation of how mediation forms new immediacy provides us with the logical model for understanding the activity of unconscious spirit. This is of special significance as we begin to turn our attention toward the psychological operations of consciousness, thought, and imagination, which is the topic of the next chapter. The logical and phenomenal description of the unconscious represented in the Anthropology provides us with a necessary ontological ground that makes all subsequent shapes and the higher activities of spirit possible. As in the *Logic*, immediate being becomes determinate being, and so the unconscious soul moves from undifferentiation to differentiation, implicitness to explicitness, immediacy to mediacy as determinate being. As implicit spirit in its immediacy, being transitions into nothing—its negative—and therefore divides itself and separates itself out from its other, which is also being that is in relation to what it is not, and hence the soul becomes a determinate being-for-self as the affirmation of the negative, which is spirit made explicit. The positive significance of the negative is the process of its own becoming as unconscious spirit wakes into free determinacy. Also in the *Logic*, the universal always determines itself into particulars, just as the soul awakens from its simple unity and disperses its being into particularities, only to incorporate its plurality back into its internal structure.

Hegel sees the dynamic of mediatory immediacy throughout all progressions of unconscious spirit, each stage becoming more intricate and labyrinthine as the soul moves from sensuousness to thought. Spirit is first and foremost an unconscious embodiment that must subjugate its corporeality and emerge as subjective thought. Negativity comprises its original unity, for implicit spirit is first of all a "stirring" "pulsation," simply restless "vital activity." Spirit must raise itself from its conflictual implicitness to actual feeling ego, internal tension being the very instrument of progression. The negative character of drive sets the soul to engage in an internal division. There is a primordial hostility to the negative, a discord responsible for spiritual health as well as psychopathology. The ability to contain, mediate, and utilize conflict in its abyss is the power of the spiritual harnessing the unconscious soul has in its initial moments of life.

Because spirit exists first as activity—its essential force as drive—spirit has within it the self-determining desire to "rouse" itself into wakefulness and thus pass over from indeterminateness to determinateness. In its initial division and externality, unconscious spirit already has the seed of an inchoate ego that thinks even at the stage of sensuous feeling. As Hegel himself reminds us: "Thinking remains the basis of spirit in all its forms" (*EG* § 398, *Zusatz*). The very activity of internal division requires the presence of ego, even if at this stage it is merely a simple composite, because differentiation necessitates an agency performing such functions; and if there were no agency, separation and individuation could not be possible let alone made actual. The real issue for Hegel becomes showing how the primitive features of mind gain sophistication through a cognizing activity. We may say that the real question of differentiation involves distinguishing between drive and ego. If drive or desire is internal impulse, force, or pressure as pure activity, then ego must assume its form, because, as Hegel carefully takes means to prepare, spirit is an epigenetic achievement with each shape evolving out of lower ones.

Desire is, first, natural desire in the bodily form of sensations, affect, and feeling, but in order to perform an internal division and project itself into externality to begin with, the soul must have a preliminary psychic organization, which we may call ego. In order to successfully make the conversion from undifferentiated symbiosis to differentiated subjective being, a crude subjective ego must already exist so to *act* at all, let alone acquire a provisional understanding of itself as a determinate being. Perhaps we should call this crude mental organization the *pre-ego*, for it is only a matter of making the ego more actual and cognizant that is Hegel's task. However, this is a grey area for Hegel because he situates these primal telic operations within the heart of darkness, within the pit of unconscious spirit under the name *soul*. Presumably the soul at this level is a quasi-agent as the unifying unifier; it is not until the ego appears that spirit attains true personality. However, the natural soul already possesses "individuality" as "subjectivity," an agent teeming with quiescent potentiality, thus unconscious ego is its presupposition. In this sense we may advance the claim that drive and ego are *equiprimordial* constructs within the abyss of the soul and ontologically undifferentiated. In its transformation to feeling and concrete ego, the abyss swells and expands until it is divided into a firm and irreversible polarity brought on by a *second awakening*, the bursting forth of consciousness proper. Consciousness becomes the day while the unconscious remains the night, alternating moments of mental life each slipping into one another, each the dawn of a new-found horizon.

The sleep of spirit is an undifferentiated void with the inner ambience of violence. It experiences the primeval chaos of an intense longing to fill its empty simplicity, desire being its form and content, the desire to fill the lack. Through the drive toward self-differentiation, unconscious spirit defines itself as a determinate being for itself and thus effects the passage from the universal to the particular, from a unity that lacks difference to differentiated plurality and singularity. There is an antediluvian cycle of negativity that we may say belongs to the prehistory of conscious spirit, a circular motion of the drives that constitute the dialectic of desire. Awakening as sensation from its nocturnal slumber, the feeling soul remains the birthplace of what is the substance of the "heart," for the abyss is its original home.

Ego is unconsciously present within the sentient feeling soul and is already a neonatal form of self-awareness. Both a sensuous and cognizing agent, unconscious spirit intuits itself as an "intro-reflected" or prereflective self-conscious being, intro-reflection being the process or mechanism of unconscious spirit's immediate self-awareness and self-identification. In its alteration from mere immediacy to determinate mediate being, the soul senses its self as an impression, already containing the rudiments of ego-awareness in its self-intuiting. In its ego explicitness before the soul makes its final trajectory to consciousness, unconscious spirit has already undergone a splitting of its interior in manifold accounts by its own hands. In each incremental process of splitting that accompanies sublation, there is an internal division, projection, and (re)introjection of its particularization back into its internality. Each introjective maneuver is a reincorporation of its projected interior that takes place through an identification with its alienated shape(s) it takes to be an exterior object however possessing its internal qualities. Such identification may be said to be the truncated recognition the soul has with itself through the process of intro-reflection as a preliminary form of self-consciousness, only that the ego has undergone a splitting as an element of defense against its unconsciously perceived conflict, which subsists due to the negative tension of the dialectic.[40]

This continual process of internal separation, projection, and introjection as reincorporation is the general structural framework for the defensive process psychoanalysis has come to label as "projective identification."[41] The ego projects its internality as alienation, comes to recognize and identify with its alienated qualities, then takes hold of and repossesses its earlier disavowed shapes. It is through this continual elevating process that both the content and the developmental hierarchy of spirit become more complex and sophisticated. Unconscious spirit comes to take itself as its own object through intro-reflection once it projects its interior as its exterior then "reflects upon it, takes back into its internality the externality of nature, idealizes nature" (EG § 384, Zusatz), and thus effects a transition back into reunification. Spirit is continually engaged in this dialectical process in all its shapes, however at this level in the soul's development, unconscious spirit displays an early form of self-recognition through its projective identification as mediated intro-reflection. This model of unconscious self-consciousness as self-recognition becomes the logical template for Hegel's mirror theory of self-consciousness outlined in the dialectic of desire and recognition advanced in the

Phenomenology. This proves to be of theoretical significance in defending Hegel from charges launched by his critics that his reflection theory of self-consciousness omits a pre-familiarity spirit has with itself which becomes a necessary prerequisite for self-recognition, a topic we will address further in a future chapter. Although Hegel discusses desire and recognition in his phenomenological treatment of consciousness, it is already prepared in the Anthropology as an ontological feature of unconscious spirit. The soul is desirous—the abyss is unconsciously self-aware, with desire as *Trieb* and intro-reflection providing the logical prototype for desire and self-consciousness to emerge in conscious spirit.

Our survey of the soul shows the unequivocal ontological fabric necessary for consciousness and the higher regions of spirit to appear, all having their origin in the unconscious abyss. The soul's use of mediation in its initial activity also provides us with the logical model for an unconscious agency further justifying the teleology of the ego. The early presence of mediatory organization, intro-reflective self-recognition, and thought instantiated within the sentient soul is transferred and superimposed on conscious spirit as its logical counterpart—the abyss becoming an ever increasing and encompassing mental force in the progression of spirit. The dialectic of desire and self-consciousness is already prepared within the underground soul, which assumes more profound shapes in spirit's phenomenological and psychological development. In the underworld of spirit's incipient nature, the unconscious becomes the indispensable psychic foundation: before spirit achieves absolute knowing, the abyss is where spirit is home.

THREE

HEGEL'S PHILOSOPHICAL
PSYCHOLOGY

REASON IS ALSO A WISH. Could it be possible for spirit to be in excess of reason, that is, beyond reason's grasp? If we could envisage for a moment that spirit
was in excess of reason, then what would constitute that excess? Does spirit resist reason? These are indeed difficult questions to sustain because it would suggest that spirit is beyond reason, thus beyond itself. It would require us to
suspend thinking dialectically, to envision excess nondialectically, to suppose that
excess would exceed the dialectic.[1] If we may persist with this almost impossible
question, then we may be led to venture that reason is beyond, or perhaps behind, itself. Would this not be fantastic—merely a fantasy that spirit could exceed itself, exceed its own rational structure? But if we could imagine spirit in
excess of reason then perhaps we would conclude that spirit would indeed have
some imagination, because for Hegel, "phantasy is reason" (*EG* § 457).

Hegel is often criticized for his tenacious commitment to rationalism—the
real is the rational and the rational is the real.[2] This aphorism is admittedly mis-
leading, but in the face of palpable irrational processes that saturate human relations, the metaphysics of a grand and all-encompassing synthesis based on
liberated rational freedom appears to be rather wishful. In the words of Charles
Taylor, "[N]o one actually believes his central ontological thesis, that the universe is posited by a Spirit whose essence is rational necessity."[3] But what is the
essence of Spirit? As the coming to presence of pure self-consciousness, spirit is
the dialectic of desire, thus a burgeoning process of Becoming, culminating in
the holistic comprehension of its truth—the rational actualization of its potential. As Errol Harris puts it: "To be rational is to press ceaselessly onward towards
the full realization of spirit. . . . This urge is the essence of the real."[4] This *urge*,
this desire, is the essence of spirit's nature.

Spirit is constant motion, a restless dynamism, pure self-conscious activity. If
Aristotle is correct in saying that reason is what distinguishes us from beasts, then

we must address what makes reason possible: "All men by nature *desire* to know."[5] Reason—absolute knowing—is exalted desire, Spirit's actualized potential. For Hegel, reason does not preclude desire, but rather reason is the logical extension of its fulfillment. While Hegel would contend that spirit is oriented toward rational self-conscious self-completion, he would also add, contentment. The pleasure of contentment is as much a consequence of self-actualized reason—its passion—as is passion itself.[6] Henry Harris tells us that "to speak of the antithesis between reason and the passions would be awkward for Hegel, because it would involve the abandonment of the *speculative* standpoint at the very beginning."[7] For Hegel, "Inclinations and passions . . . have their foundation in the rational nature of spirit" (*EG* § 474). The passion toward reason—its truth—is spirit's cardinal motive. It is in this move from desire to reason that we may hear the echo of Freud's dictum: man is a wishing animal. Reason is also a wish.

PROLEGOMENA TO HEGEL'S PSYCHOLOGY

A proper appreciation of Hegel's philosophical psychology is advanced not merely in theoretical spirit, but in the larger scope of his theory of desire and mutual recognition as well as his treatment of abnormal mental processes. While these issues are the topics of future chapters, it becomes our primary task here to address how Hegel understands the psychological processes of intelligence including intuition, imagination, phantasy, and how the process of consciousness and thinking itself is rendered possible. Just as the Anthropology provides the ontological fabric for the phenomenology of consciousness, self-consciousness, and reason to unfold, Hegel's psychology is the necessary connection for his logic and the operations of pure thought.[8]

Psychology is normatively thought of as the comprehensive assessment of mind primarily pertaining to the functions of psychobiology, cognition, emotion, individual and social behavior, and our relation to the environment. As such, psychology is interested in the nature and structure of consciousness. While consciousness for Hegel is described as an appearance or shape of spirit, consciousness itself does not stand ontologically distinct from spirit's psychology nor does it unfold as an independent process, rather the two are mutually inclusive and separated only by the way in which we study their temporal appearances. As consciousness is sublated into higher stages, the psychological processes governing conscious operations themselves become more refined and integrative.

Hegel's *Phenomenology of Spirit* is largely an attempt to explain the coming into being of the ever-increasing complexities of self-awareness, insight, social consciousness, and our understanding of the human race. In pursuit of the Delphic decree, "Know thyself!," spirit educates itself to truth—pure self-consciousness.[9] But Hegel's *Phenomenology* far exceeds a mere exposition of consciousness and includes a historical, cultural, ethical, political, aesthetic, and religious account of humankind. For these reasons, a psychological analysis of *Geist* becomes displaced by a phenomenological project. In an advertisement published in 1807 summarizing the significance of the *Phenomenology*, Hegel himself writes: "This book demonstrates how *knowledge arises*. Psychological explanation, as well as the more abstract expositions of what is basic to knowledge, should be replaced by the phenomenology of spirit."[10] But Hegel's *Phenomenology of Spirit* remains only a partial account of his mature system of science, which he saw necessary both to distance himself from and to remedy by offering a philosophy of spirit that placed anthropology, phenomenology, and psychology firmly within his systematic philosophy.[11] Furthermore, the *Encyclopaedia* version is a truncated and exceedingly different account from his 1807 work, showing how it plays a vastly different role in his mature system.[12] Preceded by the Anthropology, the *Encyclopaedia* Phenomenology only accounts for the first five chapters of the *Phenomenology of Spirit*, whereby the treatment of reason is given the briefest summation, preparatory for his discussion on psychology. It becomes quite palpable that Hegel had entirely different intentions for the two works. While the Jena *Phenomenology* begins with the sense-certainty of consciousness, he makes no attempt to account for its presupposition, thus revealing his changing attitudes on the subject, which he either was not interested in or had not considered at the time, but after reflection, sought necessary to rectify. The Anthropology, on the other hand, prepares the ground for consciousness to arise, involving an extensive exploration of the unconscious soul.

Drawing on his *Logic*, Hegel's theory of unconscious activity becomes the ontological model for his theory of consciousness and the advanced stages of theoretical spirit as each immediacy is sublated into a higher unity within its self-maturation.[13] But the way in which Hegel arrived at this model was in all likelihood the result of his application of his theory of consciousness and the logical operations of thought to unconscious structure. We have demonstrated that Hegel grew increasingly more preoccupied with the abyss later in his life. In order to offer a coherent, holistic, and internally consistent systematic philosophy he had to account for the presupposition or ground of consciousness that he omitted in the *Phenomenology*.[14] He further had to provide a logical analysis of the soul that did not contradict his logic of consciousness. We have seen how Hegel manages to accomplish this task by applying his developmental model of sublation, which informs the principles of his *Logic*. As a dialectician, Hegel shows how each immediacy must be confronted with mediacy which in turn begets a new immediacy. Just as Being must move into determinate Being (*Dasein*), the soul must move from an indeterminate immediate to a determinate being-for-self, from undifferentiation with its universality to a differentiated particularization. Thus, Hegel's logical model becomes the ontological justification for the unconscious element of spirit's nature.

Through our analysis of Hegel's Anthropology, we have seen that unconscious spirit takes its initial major forms first as soul, then as consciousness. As consciousness, the ego is a concrete actuality, but being only a new immediate, it still remains an "abstract formal ideality" (*EG* § 414) and hence merely "*subjective self-certainty*" (*EG* § 413). It now becomes the task of the ego to move from its immediate self-certainty to immediate sense-certainty, thus its breach into the object world.

It is important to note that at this point of breaching into external sensuousness, a gap is forged between the now two existing parallel realms of mental activity, namely, unconscious and conscious spirit. While Hegel does not inform us of this directly, these ramifications may be drawn. This conceptual endeavor broaches the question of the degree to which the abyss resists integration into the dialectic. While generally we may suspect that the unconscious would have to be eventually incorporated within absolute knowing, perhaps there are elements of the abyss that elude absolute incorporation. With qualifications we may pursue this possibility based on the ego's transition to consciousness further supported by Hegel's theory of intelligence. Through Hegel's treatment of theoretical spirit, we may see his fullest appreciation of the unconscious mind and its indispensable necessity in the anatomy of spirit. If consciousness as awareness lies on a continuum, then we may speculate that each realm is operative within its own psychic topography divided by two different mediums: one of pure inwardness, and the other by its added relation to external reality. While consciousness is the medium oriented toward absolute knowing, the abyss remains the inner eye of spirit.

Until now, I have attempted to show that Hegel provides an account of the unconscious dimensions of spirit that are implied throughout various sections of his texts. But it now requires us to move beyond simply giving expository voice to what Hegel says to addressing what he could have said more directly. While I will remain faithful to what Hegel actually says in the text, it will be necessary to extrapolate what can be further inferred from his terse comments about unconscious processes. What is implied needs to be stated more cogently and systematically, thus giving structure to what remains unsaid by Hegel but is nevertheless warranted by his overall comments on the abyss. This will require us to investigate the psychic division of consciousness and determine the degree to which the unconscious remains a dynamic organization throughout all shapes of spirit. In order to advance this thesis we must examine more closely Hegel's developmental paradigm of the ego and its relation to consciousness as well as his psychology, and determine how unconscious forces continue to operate within conscious processes, a functional dynamic that brings him in closer dialogue with Freud.

THE STRUCTURE OF MIND

Having provided a critical evaluation of Hegel's Anthropology, we are now able to examine more broadly his view of the structure of the mind. What becomes initially important in our discussion is to understand the role of ego development and its relation to conscious and unconscious processes. The ego becomes the central issue in understanding the functions of mind and remains the locus of spirit's activities. What is particularly significant is how the ego operates as both a conscious and unconscious transcendental agent. This requires a critical analysis of how the phenomenon of consciousness arises in the ego (*Ich*) and how unconscious processes assume a parallel organization within psychic topography that continues to operate and influence conscious processes. The splitting of consciousness into two bipolar regions within a unified model of spirit may be understood from the standpoint of the ego's breach into consciousness.

We must first determine how the ego dislodges itself from the soul and thus becomes an independent functional agent capable of ascending toward pure self-consciousness. What is the film, so to speak, separating ego from soul? From Hegel's account, this would appear to be consciousness itself. In its move from self-certainty[15] to sense-certainty, spirit fashions a new world, and this very breach into consciousness forges a gap between the interior of soul and the exterior of ego. Yet just precisely how is this process accomplished? Perhaps our clue is to be found in the notion of "intro-reflection."

In Hegel's discussion of the ego's actual emergence from its natural embodiment as soul, the ego has to confront its corporeal confinement and inwardness. He states: "It is through this *intro-reflection* [*Reflexion-in-sich*] that spirit completes its liberation from the form of *being*, gives itself that of *essence*, and becomes *ego*" (*EG* § 412, *Zusatz*). Intro-reflection or reflection-into-self is a process that is further revealed throughout spirit's advanced cognitive activity, such as in understanding consciousness and self-consciousness, the "*internality* which is for itself and a universal" (*EG* § 422). Then why does it show up as an unconscious process, which Hegel directly states in the Anthropology? It appears that the process or operation of intro-reflection is nothing other than inward self-reflection, spirit's reflecting itself into itself—*die subjektive Reflexion-in-sich* (*EG* § 414). In the soul, self-reflection takes place unconsciously. This is a mediatory process—the template for conscious self-reflection—that spirit engages in within the soul, only to become more variegated and robust in later development. Initially, this involves the soul's recognition of self-identity or a self-identification with itself, an internal verification or affirmation through negativity that it exists as thought thinking itself, albeit implicitly. It is for these reasons that it supercedes its material nature and is ego—"I!" As Hegel says, the soul "reflects itself into itself and expels the corporeity as something that is *alien* to it" (*EG* § 412, *Zusatz*). The soul knows that it is more than just its materiality and thus moves beyond itself as ego, to become a freely thinking being. This requires the soul to alienate itself from its natural state and opt for a higher instantiation. In fact, the soul instantiates itself as ego, it defines itself under different terms and psychic conditions and thus gives itself a new existence.

We need to precisely understand how Hegel prepares the ground that initiates consciousness, that is, the conditions for sense-certainty. The soul becomes a conscious ego, but how? We know that the ego expels the corporeity that limits the soul which it wins over its self-confinement, but it is the breach into consciousness itself that constitutes a significant advance the ego gains over itself, the sublation of the soul. While not yet at formal self-consciousness, consciousness is implicitly aware of itself as conscious in the way the soul is not. This breach is generated by reflection.

In Hegel's discussion of reflection in the *Science of Logic*, reflection is external to what it considers, but it thereby determines what is essential. There is already a kind of negativity or distancing relative to what it is examining. "Essence is reflection, the movement of becoming and transition that remains internal to it, in which the differentiated moment is determined simply as that which in itself is only negative" (*SL*, 399). It relates negatively to its own negativity for negativity is its very nature. In this sense, there is a doubling function of the self—the self reflects and the self is reflected upon. Absolute reflection or reflection as such starts as a simple immediacy (nothing) which is posited as presupposed (something), set over itself as an external, hence negated, then sublated determining reflection. Burbidge says: "At first [reflection] starts from that which is nothing in itself—a nonentity—and by dissolving its illusory character posits as its conclusion what the premise is not. Then it presupposes an independent, immediately given being, which, as essential, is to be distinguished from inessential thought. Now it determines its own starting point."[16] Essentially, reflection is the ability to make distinctions, an activity the soul undergoes as early as its move from undifferentiated universality to differentiated determinate sentience.

Intro-reflection comprises a unique maneuver or mechanism—not as a fixed or rigid causal law—but as a dynamic and fluid determinate activity. Hegel's model of reflective consciousness is prepared by the ontology of unconscious intro-reflective processes, the structural form that is superimposed upon, that is, operating within conscious reflective processes. Hegel's logical model in all its forms follows a generic process: first there is immediacy, followed by mediacy, which begets new immediacy. This process is developmental and ascending in that each new mediated immediacy affords itself a higher elevation of determinate freedom and self-understanding. As we have seen in the Anthropology, spirit is initially "asleep," "implicit," yet it is *activity itself*—agency, a self-assertion that "rouses itself" from sleep in which it discovers itself as soul (*EG* § 389). What is the agent responsible for the activity itself, the self-arousal of the soul? In that the soul arouses itself it must undergo this initial primitive process of the intro-reflection of its self into itself in order for there to be a shift from the immediate to the mediate form of soul. Soul is the self-identity or the self-certainty it has of itself and is the assertion of its identity. While soul is the initial *product*—the externalization of implicit spirit, the rousing is the initial *act* due to the "inner stirring of the soul" (*EG* § 390, *Zusatz*). So here we have the germ of the dialectic: immediacy reflects into itself as mediacy creating a new immediate. As each mediated immediacy gains increased complexity, awareness, and determinate freedom, the soul moves toward the parameters of consciousness.

Hegel's developmental sequence of the soul provides us with a clear outline of his unconscious ontology that makes consciousness and self-consciousness possible. There are four main movements constituting the soul's epigenesis that may be viewed as shapes or phases of spirit's maturation: (1) natural soul; (2) sentience; (3) feeling soul; and (4) ego as actual soul; culminating in (5) consciousness; and finally (6) self-conscious spirit. The first four movements constitute unconscious spirit while the last two comprise conscious spirit. Taken together, they form Spirit's holistic totality. (See Figure 1.)

SPIRIT

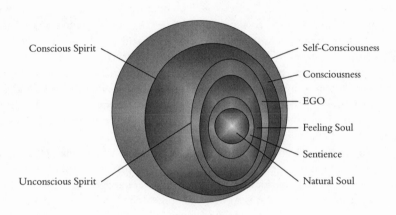

FIGURE 1

In its awakened natural embodiment, the soul proceeds to divide, project, and re-internalize itself through a series of increased capacities and operations of intro-reflection within the dialectical thrust that constitutes its activity. Each respective phase of the soul's burgeoning structure is merely a transitory condition, progressing from its corporiety into sentient being—the sensing of its self-embodying particularization—to the life of feeling, then to concrete actuality as ego—the template of consciousness and self-conscious realization. Higher stages are the result of the expansion of the core, levitating the soul from its "psychic physiology" (EG § 401) to spiritual liberating consciousness. Consciousness itself is now a new opposition—a polarity unto which unconscious spirit arose. Now being an external sensuous being, consciousness becomes a new frontier for spirit, leaving the inner world of darkness to abide in an abyss that it fills with presentations and images of its new found life. As spirit expands in its experience and self-understanding, so does its interior, which becomes the reservoir of all its deposits. This process of expansion is a dynamic self-articulated complex holism that encompasses the totality of Spirit, hence Hegel's thesis is an ontological treatise on the nature of mind. Spirit is all encompassing. Hegel ostensibly shows, as does Freud, that consciousness develops out of the unconscious.

When viewed systematically, Hegel's theory of the unconscious mind advances our understanding of the ontology of Spirit. Although Hegel himself did not offer a formal analysis of the unconscious as a distinct topic within his system of science, his references to the abyss and his ever-increasing recognition of unconscious processes in general developed in the *Encyclopaedia* allow us to say that he anticipated a great discovery that psychoanalysis would later make more intelligible. While the abyss is only prepared in Hegel's texts, we still grasp his growing preoccupation with the significance of the unconscious, which provides us with a clearer window into his system of science and our overall comprehension of spirit. As a speculative science, Hegel's philosophy is enriched by his inclusion of the unconscious, for in the words of Alfred North Whitehead: "Speculative Philosophy is the endeavour to frame a coherent, logical, necessary system of general ideas in terms of which every element of our experience can be interpreted."[17] For Hegel to offer such a detailed, logical analysis of the soul that is both coherent and necessary to his system is to at least account for every possible element of our experience even though they all may not be fully addressed.

For both Hegel and Freud, the mechanism as process by which mediation occurs is through the agency of the ego. As we have previously seen, Hegel situates agency within the soul from the start; the very activity of implicit spirit rousing itself to wakefulness is an ego function. While this is merely the undifferentiated inchoate ego merged with its natural immediacy, the move from indeterminate symbiosis to determinate differentiated being-for-self is a mediated achievement no matter how primitive it may be at this stage. This preliminary psychic organization would correspond to a crude subjective ego feeling and flourishing as cognizing activity. Hegel himself tells us as early as his discussion of the natural soul that "the individual soul [*Seele*] has to be taken as already determined as the ego [*Ich*] of consciousness and the spirit of understanding" (*EG* § 398). Elsewhere, Hegel states: "It is true that the soul is already *implicitly ego* in so far as it is subjectivity or selfhood" (*EG* § 412, *Zusatz*). As the soul winds its way through its various upward dialectical configurations toward consciousness, its inner reality gains determinate strength through self-assertion and negation of opposition until the soul actualizes itself as *I*. The actualized soul is ego, now broaching consciousness in a form proper to it. As Hegel tells us, "[U]nconscious intuiting . . . is the basis of consciousness" (*EG* § 409).

We now have a model of ego development that may be juxtaposed to Hegel's stage progression of the soul. The coming to presence of the ego is analogous to one big internal expansion into determinate external consciousness. Spirit is a steady ego expansion that eventually becomes, as it were, a big eye, seeing and understanding everything, most of all itself—pure self-consciousness. But the eye of spirit doesn't see the seeing, there remains an inner eye behind the veil of consciousness. The core expands, spiraling outwardly, boring into consciousness as the projection of its interiority, yet at the same time a portion of itself remains within the abyss. (See Figure 2.)

SPIRIT

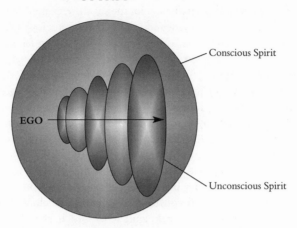

FIGURE 2

Yet this process may also be paradoxically represented as an inner digging into it-self through internal division, negation, and intro-reflection, an inwardizing that is itself externalizing—both a vortex and an eruption. The ego must carve intri-cate configurations in its splitting, slipping in and out of itself within its self, forging layers of determinate negation as a circular upward grinding motion, in-corporating more and more, until it achieves victory as sensuous consciousness, a second awakening, rebirth. Spirit becomes a profound self-elaboration as ego moving from its "affections" and "psychic physiology" (*EG* § 401) to determi-nate free thought. And for Freud, as it is for Hegel, the ego is first a body-ego: "[I]t is not merely a surface entity, but is itself the *projection* of a surface" (*SE*, 19, 26, italics added). The ego projects its surface—sensuousness. Freud is in agree-ment with Hegel when he further says, "[T]he actual ego . . . is turned towards the external world, it is the medium for the perceptions arising thence, and dur-ing its functioning the phenomenon of consciousness arises in it" (*SE*, 22, 75). Both Hegel and Freud are clear that the ego has unconscious a priori conditions that make consciousness possible.

   The breach into consciousness is the decisive factor in the splitting of psy-chic topography. Spirit now attains two realms of consciousness with different modes of perception, thus two different psychical realities within one encom-passing structure. The reawakening of the soul as ego into consciousness is the "concrete self-awareness" of subjective "thought" insofar as the ego separates it-self from the object world through reflective judgment. For Hegel, the "soul . . . posits its being over against itself . . . as ego . . . [and] excludes from itself the nat-ural totality of its determinations as an object or world *external to it*" (*EG* § 412);

as too for Freud, "the ego is setting itself over against the rest" (*SE*, 22, 58). The soul's birth into awakened consciousness is the expanding of its psychic universe, forging an even wider valley inside its abyss. Conscious spirit becomes an ever-increasing incorporation of the outside, which it engulfs and digests, and in this process its inside grows. Spirit's self-expansion as the epigenetic process of its structural evolution is not merely the enlarging of a preformed interior, but instead a steady ego progression of determinate and purposeful freedom. The shapes or "stages" of the soul, as Hegel refers to them, are not rigid categorical stages that operate by fixed causal laws determined by nature, but rather they are dynamic, flexible, and adaptable processes of self-expression.

This brings us once again to the question of the ego's relation to the abyss. Is the ego the incarnation of the abyss? Is the abyss the unbounded void of the ego's creation? Can they be both? If the abyss is the product of the ego, then this would challenge Freud's conviction that the ego develops out of the id. However, if the abyss is to be seen as belonging to the soul in all its modalities, then we may be justified in saying that the ego becomes more modified and differentiated in its development and indeed grows out of natural desire, something analogous to the id. Yet another line of inquiry may indeed equivocate the ontological distinction between the ego and the abyss. Is it possible that the ego can initially emerge as natural desire but become modified in later forms that transcend its materiality? Here Hegel would likely agree: ego being implicit in the natural soul already presupposes its being. Recall what Hegel says: "[T]he soul is already *implicitly ego*" (*EG* § 412, *Zusatz*). When the soul becomes actual the ego transcends its naturality. What is the ego and what is the abyss are merely moments within spirit's developmental temporal sequence, thus the ego's relation to the abyss may be the relation to its previous form that is preserved within itself. This previous form, however, remains alienated from conscious spirit, while unconsciously the ego is merged within its nightlike unity. This is to say that the unconscious ego is something quite different from our waking conscious ego, yet it remains behind the back of consciousness, internally operating as a synthesizing agent or process.[18] The distinction between the abyss and the ego may then be in one of its aspects a distinction between nature and unconscious determinate will. The ego can hardly deny its material embodiment and the impulses arising within it, but through sublation it moves beyond mere materiality to spiritual affirmation, thus desire becomes transmogrified as subjective volition.

The relation between the ego and the abyss may be further addressed by examining the notion of drive. While not a particularly Hegelian question, it becomes interesting and important to locate the locus of drive. Do drives themselves spring forth from the ego or does the ego emerge from the drives? Perhaps it is fair to say that the ego emerges as drive, ontologically equiprimordial with drive yet differentiated by its appearance. Our inquiry into Beginning may lead us no further than Boehme's *Ungrund*, but we are obliged to pursue it. Unconscious spirit is a groundless *activity* that can be readily seen as being its own ground. If drive as activity and process is inseparable from agency, hence from the ego, and the ego is at bottom pure activity, then perhaps we are justified in saying that drive and ego are identical, or at least that ego becomes the modified portion of drive; this makes the two ontologically identical. Drive requires ego organization in order to have any potency and the ego expresses itself as drive or desire, and ultimately rational desire. Following this account, perhaps the unconscious ego and the abyss may be conceptualized *as* the same intrapsychic space that the soul inhabits at this early primitive stage of spirit's being.

If unconscious spirit is essentially the budding life of the ego, then would it not be more proper for us to refer to the abyss within the ego—the abyss within our self? The real ontological question is: "When does the ego actually exist?" It can't simply pop up as the actual soul without having gone through its own prenatal development. If spirit is implicit in the soul, then the ego is its presupposition. In this sense the unconscious ego and the abyss would be identical at a certain stage in development. Yet for Hegel, identity always involves difference. For descriptive purposes it is important to distinguish between the ego and the abyss and maintain their equiprimordial status, reserving the designation "abyss" to encompass all unconscious states including drives that may be discerned to exist apart from the unconscious ego, such as natural desire as well as material alienated or repressed from the conscious ego. But if desire is originally said to belong to the natural soul in the form of bodily impulses or urges that are constitutionally determined, desire may only appear through the mediation of the nascent ego as soul which it apprehends as sentience and feeling. If ego organization is the necessary condition for the experience of desire, and the ego is both the medium and expression of desire, then the ego and the abyss may be said to be originally merged, only to later undergo differentiation from their original symbiotic unity. The *I* of the abyss is spirit's original primitive unity, only to reawaken as conscious ego.

Insofar as spirit is a holistic activity of the self-understanding of its determinate totality, we are led to the belief of the inseparability of the ego—and our sense of self—from all domains of mental life. Even when content is banished to the abyss, it is not so completely alien that it does not come back to us in some form, which Freud so meticulously chronicled. Even in the case of the ambiguity surrounding the proper origin of the drives, which are envisioned by Freud to be completely alien to the ego, the ego is the medium for the drives, hence they could not appear without such mediation. It is within this relation, however, that the notion of true alienation is preserved, for presumably the unconscious ego does not recognize all drives as emanating from itself despite that it is from within itself that drives emerge. The same may be said for repression: alienated content, affect, impulses, wishes, or conflict may be banished as something foreign or menacing, thus tossed into the lair and critically checked or censored. We may speculate that during such determinations, the ego is beyond its earlier shape of animality or natural drive, hence it is a more evolved agent that sets itself over against its immediate corporiety and when confronted with foreign impulses arising from its previous sublated shape, it does its best to incorporate and modify them in order to make its inner reality more properly organized and transmuted within its own structure. It is precisely because the ego has evolved as a spiritual rather than a material entity that it no longer sees its natural impulses or striving as the determinations of its own will. If the ego could speak to itself through intro-reflection, perhaps it would say: "I am no longer *that*, but *it* is now *me*." The ego is obliged to acknowledge what it once was that still yearns within it. Ego is nature but it is more than that: ego is a spiritual being capable of transmuting nature as its own. As sublated nature, desire becomes mediated. Unbounded (unmediated) desire may only appear bound.

It is worthwhile noting that Hegel, or Freud for that matter, never intended to reify psychic processes so that they appear compartmentalized or spatially located, as my earlier illustrations seem to suggest. To borrow Freud's caveat, these concepts are merely a scaffolding so we may climb up and get a better view of the architecture. We should "not mistake the scaffolding for the building" (*SE*, 5, 536). "We cannot do justice to the characteristics of the mind by linear outlines . . . we must allow what we have separated to merge together once more. You must not judge too harshly a first attempt at giving a pictorial representation of something so intangible as psychical processes" (*SE*, 22, 79). Here we may be reminded of Hegel's strictures on picture-thinking. Furthermore, we should not reify these concepts as actual spatial entities, or for that matter, as entities at all. While it is true that desire occupies a certain mental space, its trajectory spans throughout all psychic topography. It is important to keep in mind that mental topography metaphorically represents the domains of desire. While desire is characterized by its spatial relations, in actuality, desire and all its modalities are temporal processes. Thus, the self is the unity of the processes that constitute psychic life.

Our analysis and extrapolation of Hegel's general model of the mind and ego processes in particular prepare us for a careful evaluation of his philosophical psychology. Although perhaps not intended by Hegel, I am not under the persuasion that the ego is equivalent with consciousness, nor that the ego and consciousness are coordinate and therefore must arise together.[19] Making the ego tantamount to consciousness does not account for the myriad unconscious processes that infiltrate the ego, which Hegel carefully explicates in his Psychology, nor does it do justice to the ego's prior evolutionary life. Consciousness must be preceded by an unconscious agent that experiences, thus providing a necessary (albeit not sufficient) a priori ground for the phenomenon of consciousness to arise. Hence, Hegel's narrative of the soul accounts for the coming to presence of unconscious subjectivity realized as ego. The ego becomes the vehicle or mental process in which the phenomenon of consciousness arises, thus accounting for the ego's relation to the external world. As the operations of consciousness become more intricate and elaborate, spirit's psychological organizations do as well. As Hegel shows, the abyss becomes even more apparent in the operations of intelligence, recollection, imagination, and phantasy. But before we delve into the psychological processes of the "so-called faculties of spirit" (*EG* § 442), it is necessary to offer a preparatory study of Hegel's theory of consciousness in order to appreciate the diverse intellectual operations of theoretical spirit.

HEGEL'S THEORY OF CONSCIOUSNESS

As I have mentioned, there is a great deal of scholarly debate over the role and differences between the Jena and later versions of the *Phenomenology*. M. J. Petry, among others, argues that the *Encyclopaedia Phenomenology* represents Hegel's mature theory of consciousness.[20] This is further echoed in the *Berlin Phenomenology*, which is an exposition of the *Encyclopaedia* version Hegel delivered in the summer term of 1825. In these accounts, it may be argued that Hegel provides a more analytical and rigorous inspection of the unfolding of consciousness and self-consciousness, with the *Jena Phenomenology* having been selectively reappropriated into his mature system. The beginning framework of his revised program may be seen as early as 1808, in which many main features of his later theory of consciousness were apparent in the syllabus he drafted for his pupils at Nuremberg.[21] Notwithstanding the value of the Jena work, taken together, the *Encyclopaedia Phenomenology* and the *Berlin Phenomenology* provide an equally if not more comprehensive elaboration of Hegel's doctrine of consciousness. For the prefatory purpose of examining Hegel's psychology, it becomes important to provide a brief account of Hegel's theory of consciousness offered in the *Encyclopaedia*.

For Hegel, consciousness (*Bewußtsein*) is distinct from the soul (*Seele*) and the unconscious (*Unbewußte*), yet as we have seen, consciousness is an outgrowth of the unconscious soul and is hence the soul's appearance as ego. "*Consciousness* constitutes spirit at the stage of reflection or relationship, that is as *appearance* . . . ego is consciousness" (*EG* § 413). But as self-certainty, the ego is an immediate being or subject that must confront its otherness, namely, its object. "In the first instance the ego is only the wholly abstract subjective being of simply formal, contentless self-differentiation. Consequently, the *actual* difference, the *determinate content*, finds itself outside the ego, belonging entirely to the *general objects*" (*EG* § 413, *Zusatz*). Before sense-certainty, the ego's object is the natural soul itself, what the ego was but no longer is in its presently evolved shape. Recall that the ego is the sublation of the soul. Hegel states: "The ego, the reflection of the soul into itself, separates this material from itself, and in the first instance gives it the determination of being" (*EG* § 418). By confronting the natural soul and denying its suffocating restriction to the corporeal, the ego attains its own independence, no longer belonging to the soul but to itself. That is why Hegel compares the ego to "*light* which manifests another as well as itself" (*EG* § 413). In the sense that the ego reveals itself to itself, its other is also revealed to itself as an independent shape, its dark counterpart. Because the ego thinks in a form that is now proper to it, its determinations are no longer of the soul but are determinations of consciousness. For these reasons, Hegel attaches greater potency to the conscious ego, which now has the capacity to confront the manifold of objects while the natural soul remains entombed within its "childlike unity" of internality.

What is clear is that the ego graduates from its natural determinacy to determinant freedom, but being only a simple formal individuality, it has a long trek till it achieves its truth. Hegel states in the *Encyclopaedia* that the goal of spirit as consciousness is to raise its self-certainty to truth (*EG* § 416). Like the soul's progressive unfolding, this requires spirit to advance through a series of shapes beginning with (*a*) *consciousness* as such, where sense, perception, and understanding have a general external object, then (*b*) *self-consciousness*, where desire, self-recognition, and universal self-consciousness have the ego as its general object, culminating in (*c*) *reason* as the unity of consciousness and self-consciousness determined in and for itself—the Concept of Spirit (*EG* § 417).

Like the natural soul's initial apprehension of its immediacy, Hegel consistently views the initiation of consciousness as the manifestation of "the sheer *being* of [a] thing" (*PS* § 91) to a subject that only knows its simple and immediate sense-certainty. From the *Phenomenology*, Hegel shows that sense-certainty is nothing more than the immediate experience of an empty or abstract yet concrete content as "knowledge of the immediate or of what simply *is*" (*PS* § 90). As an immediate connection, "consciousness is '*I*', nothing more, a pure 'This'; . . . [a] single item" (*PS* § 91). In the *Encyclopaedia*, Hegel says virtually the same thing: "Initially, consciousness is *immediate* . . . having *being* . . . as immediately *singular*" (*EG* § 418). And in the *Berlin Phenomenology*,[22] he tells us, "[W]e are conscious of something, of a general object, of immediate general objects i.e. of the sensuous being of general objects" (*BP* § 334).

Consciousness as such is sensuous consciousness of a presence or impression with spatial and temporal singularity, simply the "*here* and *now*." But as Hegel continues to describe this process: "Strictly speaking this belongs to intuition" (*EG* § 418). Here we may see the inextricable interrelatedness between consciousness and the psychological operations of theoretical spirit that preoccupies Hegel's later psychological analysis of the ego. The ego senses that something is external to it by reflecting into itself, thus separating the material from itself and thereby giving it the determination of being.

Hegel sees three primary stages of consciousness: (*a*) sensuous, (*b*) perceptive, and (*c*) understanding, with consciousness itself being the first of three developmental stages of the phenomenological unfolding of spirit resulting in self-consciousness and reason respectively. In immediate sensuousness—the empty or abstract recognition of being, consciousness then proceeds to grasp the essence of the object, which it accomplishes through perception. The essence becomes the general object of perceptive consciousness where singularity is referred to universality. There is in fact a multiplicity of relations, reflectional-determinations, and range of objects with their many properties that perceptive consciousness apprehends, discerns, and brings into acuity (*EG* § 419). Having mediated the immediacy of sense-certainty, sensuous thought-determinations are brought into relation with concrete connections to universals, which constitutes "*knowledge*" (*EG* § 420). This linking of singulars to universals is what Hegel calls a "mixture" that contains their mutual contradictions (*EG* § 421). Because singularity at this juncture is fused with universality, contradictions are superceded in understanding consciousness. Understanding consciousness is the unity of the singular and the universal in which the general object is now raised to the appearance of being for the ego. In the next stage, self-consciousness arises where the ego takes itself as its own object, and the process continues until spirit wins its truth in pure reason.

In the *Berlin Phenomenology*, Hegel offers further elaboration on four distinct aspects of consciousness including (*a*) everyday consciousness, (*b*) empirical consciousness, (*c*) ordinary consciousness, and (*d*) comprehending consciousness.[23] Everyday consciousness is simply the subject's relation to objects or elements of experience, such as sensations, perceptions, etc. When Hegel refers to empirical consciousness, the general object of inquiry becomes the subject's conscious experience itself, which gets further elaboration in his psychology which is an analytical examination of consciousness in general. What Hegel calls ordinary consciousness is the model of consciousness he associates with Kant and Fichte in which there is always a limit imposed upon the ego and its claim to knowledge, as opposed to comprehending consciousness, which is the consciousness that constitutes the basis of his exposition in the *Encyclopaedia*.

Hegel's exposition of consciousness is essentially an exposition of the functions of the ego, which Freud, although conceived differently, also finds as the object of science:

> We wish to make the ego the matter of our enquiry, our very own ego. But is that possible? After all, the ego is in its very essence a subject; how can it be made into an object? Well, there is no doubt that it can be. The ego can take itself as an object, can treat itself like other objects, can observe itself, criticize itself, and do Heaven knows what with itself. (*SE*, 22, 58)

With this assessment Hegel would most certainly agree, with the addition that the completion of science requires that the ego no longer view itself as an object. Both Hegel and Freud were preoccupied with the science of subjectivity and articulating the universal processes that govern mental functioning. It is for these reasons that psychology becomes an essential ingredient in our appreciation of the abyss and why Hegel needed to address the psychological processes of intelligence within his Philosophy of Spirit. Having offered a preparatory survey of Hegel's theory of consciousness, we may now examine the character of the diverse psychological operations of the ego that becomes the subject matter of theoretical spirit. Because of the intimate relation between the psychological processes of intelligence and the unconscious, we will be able to recognize the ground that justifies the reflections, transitions, and logical operations of thought.

PSYCHOLOGICAL SPIRIT

For Hegel, a study of psychological spirit involves understanding very specific operations and processes that fall under the rubric of intelligence, and is thus distanced from other inquiries that are commonly thought of as proper subject matters for the discipline of psychology, such as the nature of the soul and consciousness. As we have said before, this does not preclude the interconnectedness of the anthropological and phenomenological features of spirit, but rather Hegel seeks to draw clearer distinctions particularly between the phenomenology and the psychological operations of cognition. In fact, Tom Rockmore has impressively shown how Hegel's *Phenomenology* is a theory of scientific cognition,[24] one that is not entirely at odds with cognitive psychology today. Theoretical spirit is concerned with the rational and its immediate determinateness, which it has to posit as its own, that is, internally determined as being-in-and-for-itself (*EG* § 443). For Hegel, this is the activity and purpose of cognition under the direction of reason. This intelligent activity is what Hegel calls a "spiritual faculty" (*EG* § 445), again not as a fixed or ossified agglomeration, but as a malleable and determining process of cognition. Intelligence finds itself as naturally determined, insofar as it cannot will itself not to think, and is concerned with the empty form of finding reason. Cognition is therefore the concrete activity of mediating and unifying objects with concepts.

Hegel initially concentrates on three major stages of spirit's psychological activities comprising the main categories of theoretical spirit: (1) intuition, (2) presentation, and (3) thought. While Hegel isolates the contingent events of each intellectual maneuver, he stresses the point that each operation of intuiting, presenting, etc. is merely a moment of the totality of cognizing itself, which underscores the necessity of rational thought (*EG* § 445). Throughout the various sub-stages of each operation, he shows the mutual relations between contingency and necessity and how one prepares the path for the other.[25] First, intelligence has an immediate object; second, material is recollected; and third, it is rendered objective.[26]

INTUITION AND ATTENTION

Intuition (*Anschauung*) is immediate cognizing, a direct and simple apprehension of immediate objects which can be derived from internal or external sensations. Intuition falls into three subdivisions or movements of cognition: (*a*) sensation, (*b*) attention, and (*c*) intuition proper. With the sensation of immediate material, feeling is the initial form spirit assumes, which is the truth and unity of the soul and consciousness. Recall that feeling first appears within the soul, and second within consciousness as a separated or independent object from the soul (*EG* §§ 446–447). In intuition, feeling is free from its dual one-sidedness as soul and consciousness respectively, and now has the implicit determination of being objective as it is subjective, which is the immediate unity of the subject intuiting and the object intuited. Hegel tells us that with respect to content, "*[T]here is more in feeling than there is in thought*" (*EG* § 447), particularly moral and religious feelings, for all that is rational and spiritual in content enters into feelings. "The *whole* of *reason*, the *entire material* of *spirit*, is present within *sensation*. All our presentations, thoughts and Concepts, of external nature, of what is right, of the ethical, and of the content of religion, develop from our sentient intelligence" (*EG* § 447, *Zusatz*). Here lies the compendium of what is in the soul, namely, the sentiments that subjective spirit holds in the heart, which comprises the character of the individual. In sensation, the ego intuits its soul—its previously preserved shape, soul being the reservoir of feelings. But for Hegel, the form of feeling is the lowest in spirit for it belongs to singularity and selfhood, thus lacking the freedom of infinite universality. As such it is subjective, contingent, and particular.

Because intelligence as intuition finds itself determined as the content of feeling, it does not reflect upon its immediate characteristics. This occurs through attention. Attention brings further clarity to the content of intuition, thus the content that is present in its own activity as feeling is brought to consciousness. Here a distinction is made between the attending act itself and its determinate content. As various aspects of the original determination are isolated in their successive moments and brought to light, the content of sensation is determined to be outside the self, what Hegel calls a "self-external" (*EG* § 448), thus an independent object that is for the subject. What was once a simple immediacy has now been fractured by discrete spatial and temporal relations, which intelligence mediates through attention and projects into the forms of "*space* and *time*" (*EG* § 448). At this stage intelligence has still not grasped the specific characteristics that comprise the feeling content, only the distinct moments that are external to the activity of attending itself.

Attention is the initial act of sublation, an overcoming of the simplicity of sensation which Hegel situates as the beginning of spirit's "education" (*EG* § 448, *Zusatz*). There is both a separation and a unity of the subjective and the objective as a single process, yet the difference between these two moments is indeterminate. At this stage, intelligence advances to distinguish subject from object and thus achieves intuition proper. So attention takes note of the unity of both subject and object as well as their difference, which is then internally recalled or "intro-recollected," and in this process it renders access to the specific characteristics of the material that is now properly intuited. Intuition apprehends the essential relation between the act of attending and the object, and thus unifies the initial unity of feeling and the difference of attention. In other words, intuition is apparent when this synthesis has crystalized as an immediate and explicit simple unity.

RECOLLECTION

Intelligence moves from sensation of its immediate material to attention, whereby it fixes the object as well as separates it from itself, to intuition as positing the object externally. At this point, the presentation of a certain object thrusts intelligence into its second main movement, which has three corresponding sub-stages: (*a*) recollection, (*b*) imagination, and (*c*) memory. Presentation (*Vorstellung*) is implicit within intuition because attention is paid to two moments, namely, feeling and the attending act, whereby an object is isolated and related to externally. Attention now becomes introspective and must recollect the content intuited within itself, "within its *own space* and its *own time*" (*EG* § 452). This content initially appears as an image (*Bild*) which is taken up by the ego and disassociated from its external context in which intuition had occurred. Abstracted from the concrete immediacy of intuition, the image becomes contingent or arbitrary and is but a fleeting moment since attention may focus on only one thing at a time.

Essentially, the ego internalizes its presented content by gathering up and separating the external image or impression and then making it part of its internal structure, but being only a transient impression it vanishes quickly from consciousness. "Intelligence is not, however, only the consciousness and the determinate being . . . recollected within it, the image is no longer existent, but is preserved unconsciously" (*EG* § 453). Here Hegel points to the underworld of spirit; intelligence is *not only* consciousness but is a "nocturnal abyss [*nachtlichen Schacht*] within which a world of infinitely numerous images and presentations is preserved without being in consciousness." Hegel specifically equates "intelligence as this unconscious abyss," thus forming the domains of two fundamental realities, the world of the abyss and the world of consciousness.

This is the first textual mention of the abyss within the Psychology, § 453, thus pointing to its relationship to consciousness. Hegel explains how unconscious presentations are preserved within certain "fibers" and "localities" of the abyss, recalcitrant, as they were, to the tangibility of conscious processes, subsisting as intrinsically concrete yet simple universals. Intelligence has "imperfect control of the images slumbering within the abyss" that as of yet cannot be recalled at will (*EG* § 453, *Zusatz*). Hegel himself even concedes that we have no means of knowing the full extent of all that which lies within the unconscious, suggesting that there are certain elements to psychic life that may resist incorporation into the dialectic. "No one knows what an infinite host of images of the past slumbers within him. Although they certainly awaken by chance on various occasions, one cannot,—as it is said,—call them to mind" (*EG* § 453, *Zusatz*). This concession on Hegel's part points to the inner autonomy of unconscious processes and organizations, presumably belonging to the soul—the unconscious ego—and how, from the standpoint of consciousness, they share a divided existence within spirit, thus resisting complete integration into absolute knowing. This suggests that there is always an element of "chance," as Hegel says, and contingency that spirit can never completely overcome.

At this point, we need to distinguish between subjective spirit and absolute spirit. Presumably, unconscious forces within subjective spirit may potentially stultify sublation, thereby leading to an incomplete integration into the dialectic. Generally we may say that the transition from intuition to imagination to thought is a process whereby the natural content of the feeling soul is taken up and conceptualized, thus lending more order to the abyss. Through representational concept formation, there is an increased taming of the unconscious forces, which appear to enjoy an autonomy all of their own. But there is a limitation to conscious recollection that Hegel himself acknowledges: at any given moment, not all material is accessible to conscious self-reflection. Does this mean that the abyss resists the thrust of sublation? This is most palpable in madness, a topic I will address at length in a later chapter. But absolute spirit in the forms of philosophy, religion, and art grasps or represents the meaning of objective (historical) spirit and thus is not a personal or individualistic account of the human mind, but rather is a process that embraces the entire human community that has evolved over time. From this standpoint, subjective spirit as a whole is incorporated into the dialectic as the universal selfhood that represents humankind. Therefore, the unconscious is sublated. But the question becomes: What is sublated?—its content, its structure, its entire being? The abyss is constantly sublating itself, both in terms of its content and internal structure; but does it or any part of it resist its transition to absolute spirit? Or is the abyss itself the embodiment of absolute spirit in the forms of philosophy, religion, and art, an embodiment that is derived from its most primordial unconscious nature? From this standpoint, absolute spirit would have to know, at least in principle, its unconscious life.

However, within subjective spirit itself, we are led to believe that the operative forces of chance and contingency may indeed prevent or lead to a recalcitrance toward sublation. Our task becomes deciphering how subjective spirit in some of its forms resists sublation, which leads to a further contradiction: if absolute spirit is the unity and sublation of subjective and objective spirit, then how can subjective spirit resist such an all-encompassing process? Would this not prevent any transition toward absolute spirit, or does absolute spirit take into account its own anomalies? While the mad mind does not know the absolute standpoint, absolute spirit knows the mad, at least in its truth. Because absolute spirit knows that the abyss resists sublation in its particularizations, it has integrated the abyss into its internal structure.

The Absolute is the realization of the abyss—a return to its original lost unity of the feeling soul in the absolute unity of pure thought, a point I intend to argue further in Hegel's treatment of psychopathology. It is more plausible to say that any resistance toward sublation is confined to the level of the individual, but this could also occur within groups and communities. But from the standpoint of absolute spirit, all knowledge is brought to self-consciousness, for what spirit took to be its truth in its previous moments was merely an unconscious consciousness. Absolute spirit is the actualization of the human race as world history that had been unconscious of its very nature until its transition to absolute knowing. Until absolute knowing, spirit is unconscious, hence unaware of its totality until it achieves its end. But absolute knowing is as much dependent on contingency as is subjective spirit.

Many scholars agree there is a necessity to chance and contingency that spirit requires, thus displacing the notion that absolute knowing frees itself from all contingency or fully completes itself by acquiring pure or absolute knowledge.[27] This should, however, pose no problems for self-actualized spirit. Hegel would probably say that that which is unconscious can be made conscious, and this is certainly the case for absolute spirit. But what about on the level of subjectivity? Can everything be known about the human mind? Perhaps not. More personally, can we know everything about our own unconscious? Psychoanalysis would emphatically say no—analysis is interminable: the unconscious is limitless while knowledge is finite. Here we may venture to say, that which cannot be brought fully to consciousness is simply not very pressing. When unconscious processes produce some effect, then reflection and analysis can bring them to conscious awareness, or at least can determine their power and efficacy even if we are not able to picture or represent them directly. Of course, there will be those people who do not bring such unconscious forces to awareness and others who do through introspection, self-observation, and personal insight. This is precisely the goal from the standpoint of absolute knowing. Here Hegel would be on the same page with Freud; like self-conscious spirit, the task of psychoanalysis is to make what is unconscious conscious, and critical analytic reflection as well as effective therapy often involves bringing such unconscious forces to consciousness in some form or manner. Of course, the two are not the same; one deals with the analysis of one's own personal history while the other deals with the analysis of the world historical development of the human race, yet both involve archeology.

Hegel explains that the act of relating an image to an intuition is what is properly called recollection, hence fitting a particular with a universal. Intelligence collects or gathers into itself what it renders through intuition and then posits its own content distinct from what is external in space and time. In intuition we are directly aware of what is presented in the senses, but the *image* has to be separated from that given presence of sensation before it can be deposited into the pit. Internalization is taking the image out of the space and time of its immediate presentation and incorporating it into spirit's own internal space and time. If that were not performed as part of spirit's conscious activity, the image would never be able to be universalized and transposed into the unconscious. As a result, the previous moments of intuition lose their original spatio-temporal structure, which is collapsed within an unconscious unity. Unconscious activity provides a counterpart to conscious attention. "The one relates; the other distinguishes. The one universalizes; the other particularizes. The one responds to intrinsic characteristics; the other introduces extrinsic relations of space and time."[28]

The images and impressions that are internalized, deposited, and preserved within the unconscious are later brought forth and reissued from within the abyss itself, and thereby related to subsequent intuitions and recollections, which are redeposited back into the pit as attention directs itself elsewhere. This process has particular implications for imagination and phantasy, because conscious perception triggers a free play of associative images and material that are unleashed from the interior of the soul and *re-presented* to consciousness. In these situations, the unconscious ego responds to its intuited content by re-presenting previous images and impressions it gathers up from the bowels of the mind. Here the past comes to present as the surfacing of latent content, but being only a transient recollection it can vanish quickly back into its lair.

> The images of the past lying latent in the dark depth of our inner being be-
> come our *actual possession* in that they come before intelligence in the bright,
> plastic shape of an intuition, a *determinate being* of *equivalent* content, and we,
> helped by the *presence* of this intuition, recognize them as intuitions we have
> already had. (*EG* § 454, *Zusatz*)

We are beginning to get a picture of intelligence as a metapsychological process spanning over two distinct but interconnected landscapes undulating through a divided yet inextricable domain, each division the inversion of the other. Hegel's metapsychology of the abyss points to that seemingly featureless void that lies *beyond* or *behind* the conscious operations of spirit but is indeed responsible for its dynamic operative force. Beneath the perceptual surface hides a complex underworld, each behaving like two different agencies: an observing layer where the nuances of sense perception function over a deep, dark yawning chasm with unknown psychic communities and wild underground weather.

The images generated within the abyss have their own dynamic beyond conscious control. The diverse multiplicity of presentations may generate isolated aspects of vastly different images, which may have some nebulous similarity or may be completely disparate to immediate intuition, thus the network of spatio-temporal relations generated by the unconscious may be insignificant *or* crucial. It is through attention that consciousness acquires the discriminating capacity to discern and introduce significant relations. "Intelligence is therefore the power of being able to express what it possesses, and no longer to require external intuition in order to have this possession existing within itself" (*EG* § 454). As Hegel says, "The image is mine, it belongs to me" (*EG* § 453, *Zusatz*); while first immersed in the night, it is now distinguished as recollected content.

To recall an image is to repeat or *re-present* an intuition, and this is why it is free of immediate intuition because it is "preserved unconsciously." We recognize in immediate intuitions images we have experienced before. While consciousness isolates a specific feature, it relates it to the universality of unconscious recollection. Representation is therefore the synthesized product of relating an immediate intuition to an unconscious universal, which becomes an object for consciousness. It is in imagination, however, where the process of relating one representation to others is intellectually carried out.

IMAGINATION

In imagination, representations are related to one another in the flow of consciousness which becomes linked with other images, affects, and thoughts as they are generated and manipulated by the ego's activity. Retrieved from the abyss, they are now technically under the ego's control, but with qualifications. Imagination also assumes three forms or sub-stages, namely: (*a*) reproductive imagination, (b) associative imagination, and (c) phantasy, which is further sub-divided into (1) symbol, (2) sign, and (3) language. First, representations are re-produced from the abyss but fall under the direction of the ego as "the issuing *forth* of images from the ego's own inwardness," which it now governs (*EG* § 455). The line of demarcation that divides the unconscious ego from the con-scious ego is now breached. Images are not only retrieved but issued forth from the ego itself, assuming that unconscious material is externalized into conscious apprehension, or as Hegel puts it, "excogitated . . . from the generality of the abyss." This process immediately initiates an association of variegated images and features that are related to further presentations which may be either abstract or concrete and varying in content and form, thereby the range of intellectual con-nections expands. Within this multiplicity of associations, the synthetic functions of intelligence are already operative as thought implicit within intelligence. Imagination in general determines images. As a formal activity, the reproduction of images occurs "*voluntarily*" (*EG* § 455, *Zusatz*); it does not require the aid of an immediate intuition to effect this process as in the case of recollection, which is dependent upon the presence of an intuition. Distinguished from recollection, intelligence is now "self-activating."

In his comprehensive treatment of presentation, John Burbidge notes that associations are not in the conscious possession of intelligence, but rather they simply seem to happen.[29] It is not until phantasy comes on the scene that the ego gains full control in manipulating images; but in associative imagination, he claims, the ego does not determine the relationships between images. What is im-portant here is to understand how associations just seem to happen. In light of the reproductive function of intelligence, Burbidge's assessment of the role of the ego must be revisited. As Hegel says, images are generated out of the inwardness of the ego, or the internality of the I (*innerlichkeit des Ich*), but it is unclear why phantasy should be the point when conscious determination and control over images occur. It certainly may achieve its full control at that stage, but we must readdress whether conscious forces come to bear immediately in imagination or whether the intellect simply moves from one image to another in association as a process that just "happens." If those moves are not determined by the ego, then they must be determined from activity within the abyss; yet at the same time the inwardness of the ego, hence the unconscious ego within the abyss, must be pro-ducing such associations behind the conscious ego's back. The question must be pushed to the degree of isolating that movement that distinguishes consciousness from unconsciousness. Is the stream of consciousness directed by the ego? It de-pends upon where we locate the ego. The flow of images is generated internally by the ego, but not consciously directed at this stage. It is only later from the con-scious initiative of the ego that images and their relations are generated through phantasy so that we may properly say there is a shift from the mere succession of associative images to being in control of those images that are willfully produced.

Throughout Hegel's treatment of theoretical spirit, he is attempting to de-scribe how the implicitness of ego functioning and consciousness itself become self-consciously appropriated as the result of the active initiative of the self. This is a further elaboration of spirit's quest for freedom, the crux of which is to become more free from nature. But the nature of the precise shifting of ego states becomes the critical question. We need to distinguish between the generation of images within the abyss and the temporally subsequent stage of generating the connection between images. If the ego does not control the relationships between images in association, then we need to determine at which juncture the unconscious ego ceases to be the director behind the scenes. This ceasing to direct by the unconscious ego would have to give way to a transition as the coming to direct by consciousness. That is to say, the unconscious ego is itself a presentation—it presents itself as a presenter.

Imagination is another critical point in which there is a breach into consciousness, indeed, an undulation back and forth between transient moments of conscious and unconscious mentation. As a transcendental agent (process), the unconscious ego must transfigure and reappropriate itself into a new form: it appears as consciousness. This involves the perpetual dialectic of internalization and externalization insofar as each process constitutes the reinternalization of its projected externality as the ego oscillates between its two media of internality and perceptive consciousness. The ego's reinternalization of itself or withdrawal from conscious perception back into imagination typifies how the ego can slip, or more appropriately, retreat from the standpoint of consciousness to unconscious determinate activity. There is a redirection of its attention from external sensuousness to an internal apperception, so to speak, or focus upon its inner operations and its unlimited internalized objects. Intelligence has to draw on the pit for images but the ego must bring connections fully to consciousness so that they can be manipulated. While the abyss is busy at work in generating associations, only when the ego directs its attention do associations come under its control that it gains possession over for itself in consciousness. This activity happens in a fraction of a second; and it is in that fraction that the space between unconsciousness and consciousness is abridged. Hegel does not directly say this, but its process can be inferred.

However, the question of the breach—the puncturing into consciousness—is important here. How can the ego shift from being within the abyss to being within consciousness and yet still remain within the abyss? This shift could only have logical congruity if a portion of the ego were to undergo transformation or differentiation and become modified to adapt to external perceptive consciousness while still allocating and executing operations from within the abyss. While the ego bifurcates itself into two psychical regions, bearing in mind these are temporal processes, fashioning internal and external modifications, it nevertheless has the capacity to organize multiple networks of synthetic, affective, and sensory activity. The multiple parallel processes of ego organization act in accordance with a unifying principle that allows ego states to operate simultaneously with respect to the functional capacities and stimuli that dominate each domain. Conscious and unconscious processes not only operate on parallel levels of complexity, they *interpenetrate* one another. Because the conscious ego is an assignment, allocation, or modification from its unconscious counterpart, consciousness becomes the extended periphery of the ego's expanded structure. As an appropriation or distribution of its essence, sensuous consciousness becomes another medium for the ego's expression. Each domain of the ego could scarcely operate in isolation, because both borrow resources from the other as an accompanied or alloyed counterpart. Yet it is during the phenomenon of imagination that the boundary separating the inner from the outer becomes relaxed.

As our detailed analysis of the soul has shown, ego formation does not just pop up at the end as consciousness, but rather it is prepared, it has a prenatal life, what Hegel subsumes under the term *implicit*. But it is more explicit as an unconscious agency than Hegel wants to say. Therefore, it is fair to suppose that the ego is present to some degree during reproductive and associative imagination but is more fully governing in phantasy. The ego—the inner I—finds expression in consciousness. The critical issue is how things immediately present in sensation become appropriated by the self in such a way that the self can begin to enjoy them on its own terms. This involves the development of a hierarchy of functions. Only gradually will the self become self-consciously aware of what it is doing.

In the stream of consciousness, images saturate our mind from many directions, triggering associations that may be trivial or imbued with residual meaning. We are not consciously constructing, determining, or willing the spate of images, they are merely presented in the theater of the mind as though they were being generated by a film projector. But associative imagination involves interrelating images and is as such a higher activity of intelligence, which goes beyond their mere reproduction to actually positing them and relating images to one another.[30] The ego slips in and out of consciousness; when attention wanes it withdraws back into its interior as if it were lost in its own muse, only to resurface in another form. From this account, it must allot certain portions of its presence and force to multiple domains within psychic reality, and through splitting and division hover within its bifurcated terrains while maintaining its dual existence through its multiple organizations and intellectual processes. Like the seemingly autonomous song that keeps recycling itself which you cannot seem to get out of your head, the ego is playing, and spirit sings.

PHANTASY

Phantasy is the third movement of imagination where the ego fully manipulates its representations and images, drawing lines of interconnection where particulars are subsumed under universals and given the richer elaboration of symbols and signs that effect the ego's transition to memory, the third stage of presentation. Phantasy is a subjective bond the ego has with its contents, and with the introduction of symbolization, allegory, and sign, imagination gains increased synthetic mastery over its presentations that are imbued with "reason." Here the inwardness of intelligence "is *internally determined concrete subjectivity*, with *a capacity* of its own deriving" (*EG* § 456). Within phantasy, there is an imagined existence as hidden unconscious processes infiltrate the creative centers of subjectivity. While phantasy attains its most elaborate articulation in language and speech—as well as in the creative power of art, it does not strictly require words in order to show itself. This may be achieved by the mind's manipulation of its own operations with respect to both content and cognitive functions, such as the confluence of certain feeling states attached to interrelated images. In fact, phantasy is the a priori condition for language: it is a prelinguistic organization that precedes organized conceptual thought.[31]

Phantasy both symbolizes and engenders signs. Initially it subsumes singulars under a universal through symbolization, but because the immediate content is both a particularization and a universal, interpretation remains ambiguous. While not articulated by Hegel, phantasy becomes a central operation in unconscious production, a spewing forth of impulses and desires from the wishing well of the abyss. It may be suspended in space and time, conform to the abyss's will through regression or withdrawal irrespective of the ego's counterintentions, and warp objective reality to the tone of the ego's own subjective caprice. This is why images may be either disturbing or pleasing. The "*symbolizing, allegorizing* or *poetical* power of the imagination" (*EG* § 456) is not confined to the mere subjective, however, it may take an external objective referent as the embodiment of its creativity. This move constitutes "the phantasy of sign making" (*EG* § 457).

Through signification, intelligence is concerned with unifying the relations between determinate content and what it signifies universally. The synthesis of phantasy is the unity of the sign with the universal and its self-relation. Hegel states, "[I]n phantasy intelligence has being, for the first time, not as an indeterminate abyss and universal, but as a singularity, i.e. as concrete subjectivity, in which the self-relation is determined in respect of being as well as universality" (*EG* § 457). This statement suggests that abstract universality itself is a sort of abyss, in that all particularity is lost in it, whether this be the soul's initial immersion with and undifferentiation from nature or its subsumption in universal spirit. Such unification of the sign with universality is seen by spirit as its own activity that is internal and proper to it. Here intelligence gives itself being, which is now within its own capacity to do. Not to be underestimated in its importance, the sign "adds proper intuitability" to images as an objective existent (*EG* § 457). While the symbol refers to the intuition of the content and its relation to its essence and Concept, the sign *designates* meaning in which the content of intuition becomes dissociated to what it signifies (*EG* § 458). In symbolic phantasy, intelligence pays attention to the given content of images, but in sign phantasy it replaces imagined universality with objective affirmation—the presented universal is liberated from the content of images. Hegel tells us:

> The *sign* is a certain immediate intuition, presenting a content which is wholly distinct from that which it has for itself;—it is the *pyramid* in which the alien soul is ensconced and preserved. (*EG* § 458)

Hence, intelligence proceeds from the pit to the pyramid,[32] the soul sublated as intelligence gains more mastery over its self-designating operations. The content of intuition becomes "irrelevant" to what it signifies. Spirit may now focus on the signified universal rather than on the particular features of its intuited content. But before its final transition to memory, imagination must cancel its subjectivity, its internality, and give itself objective being. In this way it unifies "the universal and being, one's own and what is appropriated, inner and outer being, are given the completeness of a unit" (*EG* § 457).

Derrida is correct in telling us that Hegel treats the sign only as a transition.[33] In fact, imagination accomplishes the transition from merely abstract universals to concrete universality as expressed, for example, in art, religion, and philosophy and this is why Hegel accords it with the status of nominal or formal reason (*formelle Vernunft*). Intelligence goes beyond the sign to understanding its meaning. With each new immediate intuition, intelligence moves from unconscious determinateness, which transforms intuitions into images, images into representations, representations into associations, and is thus raised to the level of objective existence and self-determining being as sublatedness. Intelligence is now presented (as presenting itself) with a "*tone*" from the unconscious soul, "which intelligence furnishes from the anthropological resources of its own naturalness, the fulfillment of the expressiveness by which inwardness makes itself known" (*EG* § 459). Sound instantiates itself further in speech, which as the interrelations of words in a system of language that endows the sensations, intuitions, and representations with a "second determinate being," sublates the immediacy of the first. Spirit no longer needs the constant presence of external signs; when they vanish as ephemeral phenomena, intelligence draws upon its inner meaning and "inner symbolism" as it generates and relates to its own processes. Intelligence remains active, it confers meaning through sounds and words and as such becomes a sublated intuition for itself. Networks of meaningful relations are externalized as signs, and when they disappear spirit must reconstitute their significance through its own self-relating activity. Imagination first makes visible unconscious processes in the form of images, then manipulates their relations through phantasy, conferring symbolization and assigning meaning—the name, a word. When the name vanishes, imagination either must create a new name for its set of relations, or it must recollect a previous name and its meaning and attach it to new associations. This requires memory.

Intelligence has moved from its initial task of internalizing intuitions, to its externalization of the abyss through imagination, to which it takes its next shape as memory, the task of which is to integrate its previous two movements. While intelligence gains greater dynamic unity in verbal, reproductive, and mechanical memory, Hegel sees theoretical spirit through to its end, viz., to thought as understanding, judgment, and formal reason. Thought knows itself, it *re-cognizes* itself, which achieves its fullest logical elaboration as pure thinking: thought thinking about itself and its operations. While these are the greater faculties of spirit, they need not concern us here. We have seen the overwhelming presence and indispensable function of the nocturnal abyss throughout the stage of presentation, the necessary precondition for higher activities of spirit to become manifest. Presentations are fleeting and much of memory fades, but it becomes imprinted within the soul and wells up from imagination. Hegel explains:

> The power of memory is replaced by an unchanging tableau of a series of images fixed in the imagination. . . . Not only is spirit put to the torment of being pestered with a deranged subject matter, but whatever is learnt by rote in this manner is as a matter of course soon forgotten again. . . . What is mnemonically imprinted is as it were read off from the tableau of the imagination . . . and so really brought forth from within, rehearsed from the deep abyss of the ego. (*EG* § 462)

As Hegel reminds us once again, intelligence is unconsciously constituted as ego. There can be no doubt about the importance of imagination and its relation to the abyss; spirit is as much dependent on imagination—especially phantasy—as it is on reason. In fact, their relationship is so intimate that it leads Hegel to say, even with stipulations, that "phantasy is reason" (*EG* § 457). Imagination recuperates, expresses, and lends order to the implicit concrete universality of the soul's natural content: imagination—phantasy—is the medium of desire only to flower as rationality. Before intelligence makes its formal transition to reason, imagination becomes the locus of the powers of the mind.

COMPARISONS WITH PSYCHOANALYSIS

Hegel's treatment of the unconscious processes of theoretical spirit brings us in closer dialogue with Freud. Like Hegel, Freud was concerned about offering an integrative and coherent theory of *Geist*; what Hegel called subjective spirit, Freud called soul (*Seele*). Led astray by inaccurate translations of the German term *Seele* rendered as "mental apparatus," "mental organization," or "mind" in English, Freud's humanistic commitments are often eclipsed by a cold and detached scientific lexicon, thus misrepresenting his original text.[34] Like Hegel in his attempt to capture all the complex psychological processes of spirit, Freud spoke of the "structure of the soul" (*die Struktur des Seele*) and "the organization of the soul" (*die seelische Organisation*). For example, in *New Introductory Lectures on Psycho-Analysis*, Freud specifically refers to the three psychic agencies and their structural relations as "the three provinces of the apparatus of the soul" (*die drei Provinzen des seelischen Apparatus*), not "the three provinces of the mental apparatus" (*SE*, 22, 72). In fact, Freud saw psychoanalysis as "the science of the life of the soul" (*die Wissenschaft vom Seelenleben*) (*SE*, 22, 6) and regarded the soul as synonymous with the Greek word *psyche*—not merely mind or intellect, which he situated with the ego, but the unification of the temporal processes of passion or desire (*eros*), morality (*ethos*), and reason or mind (*nous*). Although more robust and intricately defined, Freud's notion of the soul mirrors the Platonic notion,[35] with one exceptionally important added feature—the unconscious. It may be said that Hegel offers his own version of the psyche as spirit, whereas Freud used the term *soul* to describe the complex structures and operations that correspond to spirit's activity.

Built on the unconscious features of the soul, Hegel's theory of spirit shows remarkable similarity with Freud's tripartite structural model of the mind. While I do not intend to advance the thesis that Hegel's theory of spirit or his account of the abyss and its unconscious operations is identical with Freud's model, there are some striking resemblances between ego development, psychic topography, and the role of negativity in their respective systems.

Freud's theories of human nature and most importantly his theory of mind underwent many significant transformations throughout his lifetime. As he moved away from his depth psychology introduced in *The Interpretation of Dreams* toward his metapsychology, the centrality of the ego became the cornerstone for understanding the complexities of the self and abnormal development. The centrality of the ego marks the turning point in Freud's transformation period leading to the introduction of the death drive and his final paradigm regarding the structures and functional operations of the psyche. In fact, Freud's conception of the ego underwent more theoretical adjustments than any other construct. By the time Freud published *The Ego and the Id*, his original topographic model became subsumed within a new functional-tripartite framework emphasizing the dynamic interplay between passion, rationality, and moral judgment.

Freud's eventual inclusion of the ego within the unconscious prompted his abandonment of the reference to the system *Ucs.*' and instead replaced it with reference to the *it*. Adopted from Nietzsche's usage and following the suggestion of Georg Groddeck, a German physician who was attracted to Freud's ideas, the *it* was designated as that region of the mind that is completely unknowable in itself and alienated from the ego (*SE*, 19, 23; 22, 72). The German word *Es* was rendered *id* in Latin, which is the ordinary word for "it." I will retain the use of id simply for conventional purposes, but the notion of a foreign entity residing within the night of the mind has particular significance for addressing the question of alienation. In *New Introductory Lectures*, Freud himself says: "This impersonal pronoun seems particularly well suited for expressing the main characteristic of this province of the mind—the fact of its being alien to the ego" (*SE*, 22, 72). As we have seen, Hegel situates the ego within the unconscious soul and conscious spirit, thus sharing a common theoretical bond with Freud, but concerning the abyss being alienated from the ego, Hegel says nothing. Presumably it is, for each new appearance of spirit is the alienation of its prior shape. But as for each new shape, its old form is preserved within it. However, there are times when Hegel clearly equates the abyss with the ego—he speaks of "the deep abyss of the ego"(*EG* § 462). Perhaps it is fair to say that the abyss is only alienated from its moments, for it is the primordial ground of spirit, a home that spirit retreats to in both the normal operations of thought and intelligence and in the terrors of the sick soul.

The id is so impersonal and foreign that it does not *know* and it does not say *no*, it knows no negation—is timeless—a purely alienated void. Only the ego may have these mediatory privileges. "It is the dark, inaccessible part of our personality . . . a chaos, a cauldron full of seething excitations" (*SE*, 22, 73). Desire is unbounded, an unbridled current—it gushes. The id simply wants to discharge. This assessment may not sit well with Hegel, but since he did not formally attend to this matter in a systematic treatment of the abyss, we are left only to speculate about its proper place and role in the anatomy of spirit. The abyss may in fact be the reservoir of the repressed and the wishing well in which all forms of passions and impulses and untamed desires spring forth without mediation, only to be apprehended and mediated by the ego. But it is certainly true that the unconscious ego also resides in the abyss and brings images and content from its bowels to the light of consciousness, because if the ego was completely alienated from the abyss, nothing would shine forth into conscious awareness. Here there seems to be a merger of the ego and the abyss. And for Freud: "The ego is not sharply separated from the id; its lower portion merges into it" (*SE*, 19, 24). As we will address shortly, for Hegel, perhaps it is more accurate to think of the ego and *its* abyss—its own alienated self, rather than viewing the ego and the abyss as two distinct entities.

Freud's final model of the mind is as follows: (1) The *id* (*Es*) is that which can never be known directly and contains the primal libidinal and destructive drives and passions solely belonging to the unconscious under the influence of primary process mentation and the pleasure-principle. It contains all that is inherited at birth and that which is constitutionally inlaid, as well as wishful impulses, and the residue of repressed content (*SE*, 19, 24; 22, 74–75; 23, 145); (2) The *ego* (*Ich*) is the central organizing feature of the mind standing in relation to sensuous consciousness and perception as well as having transcendental access to preconsciousness and the unconscious proper. With its task of self-preservation, the ego serves as mediator, controls motility, is a protective or defensive shield against internal and external stimuli, and is a censor for id impulses and the conscious self, bringing the reality-principle and secondary process thinking to bear upon the drives (*SE*, 19, 25; 22, 75–77; 23, 145–146); and (3) The *superego* (*ÜberIch*) is an assignment or modification of the ego as the critical faculty and harbinger of ideals. As the product of identification, the superego also has the capacity to reside in all three domains of psychic topography under the direction of the ego representing moral conscience, punitive judgment, guilt, and shame (*SE*, 19, 28–39; 22, 60–69; 23, 146).

Freud's trinity of the id, ego, and superego is a fundamental and familiar pillar of psychoanalytic lore. Freud frequently refers to them as psychical "agencies," "provinces," "regions," "realms," "instances," "systems," and "powers." (*SE*, 5, 537; 22, 72; 23, 146). Taken together, these agencies comprise the necessary features of personality as the ontological fabric of mind. It is important to note that these provinces or agencies are frequently interpreted as three (ontologically) distinct psychical agents, hence separate entities, when they are in fact epigenetic achievements that derive from the same monistic ontology. While Freud himself was ambiguous through much of his early writings with regards to psychic ontology, in his mature theory he is, like Hegel, very clear that the ego develops out of its natural immediacy. In *Inhibitions, Symptoms and Anxiety*, Freud (1926) states:

> We were justified, I think, in dividing the ego from the id, for there are certain considerations which necessitate that step. On the other hand *the ego is identical with the id, and is merely a specially differentiated part of it*. If we think of this part by itself in contradistinction to the whole, or if a real split has occurred between the two, the weakness of the ego becomes apparent. But if the ego remains bound up with the id and indistinguishable from it, then it displays its strength. The same is true of the relation between the ego and the super-ego. In many situations the two are merged; and as a rule we can only distinguish one from the other when there is a tension or conflict between them. . . . [T]he ego is an *organization* and the id is not. *The ego is, indeed, the organized portion of the id*. (*SE*, 20, 97, italics added)

Freud clearly explains that the ego is a modally differentiated aspect of the id that becomes the mental organization of its prior shape—in Hegel's terms, its sublated identity. Elsewhere he says: "[T]he ego is that portion of the id that was modified . . . tak[ing] on the task of representing the external world to the id" (*SE*, 22, 75). This may be said to correspond to Hegel's ego of consciousness, where the material of sensuous perception is mediated, stored, and retrieved from the inner mine. The ego's main feature is that it is a mediatory synthesizing agent: "[W]hat distinguishes the ego from the id quite especially is a tendency to *synthesis* in its contents, to a *combination* and *unification* in its mental processes" (*SE*, 22, 76, italics added). Both Hegel and Freud adhere to a developmental ontology: the mind acquires increased dynamic complexity and organization as modally differentiated shapes of earlier processes assume new forms. Freud's recognition that organized psychic processes develop from unorganized hence undifferentiated natural determinations insulates him from criticism that his theory of mind purports three ontologically distinct agents that participate in mutual causal relations. Because the trinity of the three provinces are modally differentiated forms or shapes of its original undifferentiated being, each participates in the same essence and thus none is an independent nominal agent. Rather, they are interdependent forces that *appear* as separate entities, when they in fact together form the unification of the dynamic temporal processes that govern mental life.

While Freud's theoretical model was crafted and repeatedly recast based on clinical case evidence falling under the constraint of empirical observation, his theory of mind also has a logical coherency that may in part be compared to Hegel's developmental treatment of the soul. Freud shows, like Hegel, that the ego must develop out of its natural corporiety, thus it undergoes differentiation and modification. The move from the unorganized and undifferentiated immediacy of the id to the organized and differentiated mediacy of the ego and then the superego shows the logical transition in the ego's increased capacities at determinate freedom and negation. As Hegel was discontent with the limitedness of the soul's materiality, Freud "remain[s] on psychological ground" (*SE*, 5, 536), thus making several attempts to distance himself from earlier materialist commitments advanced in the unofficial and unpublished *Project for a Scientific Psychology* (*SE*, 1, 295). By 1900 he had officially abandoned his materialism for a psychological corpus and was careful not to conceive of the mind in the reductionist terms of anatomy, chemistry, or physiology (*SE*, 15, 20–21).[36] Psychoanalysis was to be the investigation of "*psychical* reality" (*SE*, 5, 620), a point Hegel would applaud as a more proper estimate of *Geist*.

To what degree is all that which corresponds in Hegel to Freud's id merely alienated forms of unconscious spirit, therefore disassociated ego states cast into the *shaft* of the soul? What theoretical relation does the abyss have toward the id? It would appear that the two are identical: the repressed most certainly, as well as the stockpile of life experiences, images, presentations, and memories that survive decay, but also conflicted psychic states, especially those belonging to the tormented soul. But whether we may attribute an impersonal agency to the abyss that *remains* alienated from spirit, Hegel would probably say no. Following the logic of the dialectic, the abyss must be subsumed within spirit, it devolves into absolute knowing. Yet Freud always maintained an epistemological boundary surrounding the nature of absolute knowledge claims. In *An Outline of Psycho-Analysis*, one of his final publications, he avouched the limitations to the powers of human consciousness with elegant simplicity: "Reality will always remain 'unknowable'" (*SE*, 23, 196). This could have been Kant speaking.[37]

Hegel would have frowned upon this: the unconscious is known by virtue of the fact that we posit *it*. Freud repeatedly informs us of the unknowability of the unconscious (*SE*, 19, 23; 23, 144–145), which he maintained from the start: "The unconscious is the true psychical reality; *in its innermost nature it is as much unknown to us as the reality of the external world*" (*SE*, 5, 613). Yet what we know is *that* it appears and also presumably *how* it appears, which is on common ground with Hegel. The unconscious abyss—the soul—appears as ego, to which Freud's famous epigram echoes: "Where id was, there ego shall be." (*SE*, 22, 80). A more appropriate translation of Freud's *Wo Es war, soll Ich werden* is "Where it was, there I shall become." Here Freud points to the significance of the transformation of the relation the ego has with its instinctual life,[38] a mediated differentiation that restructures intrapsychic relations—the task of psychoanalytic treatment itself. This process of the coming to presence of the *I* constitutes the self-liberating dynamic of the mind. Like Hegel who describes spirit as the self-articulated determinant freedom over its natural immediacy, the task of ego development for Freud is to achieve freedom over the alien forces harbored within its instinctual nature.

While Hegel saw the soul as being the most elementary aspect of spirit, for him the soul always remains that deeply hidden dimension of our common humanity—"the deep abyss," what Freud thought was largely unconscious. It is important to note that both Hegel and Freud, while offering differing accounts, provide closely similar conceptualizations of the role of the unconscious in mental life and the structures and processes of human subjectivity. It is not my intention to provide an exclusive comparison between Hegel's psychological account of theoretical spirit and Freud's treatment of the soul, but there are some further remarkable resemblances between Freud's understanding of perceptual processes and Hegel's description of presentation.

In chapter VII of *The Interpretation of Dreams*, Freud offers his first formalized theory of the organization of the soul and its conscious-unconscious relations. Referring to consciousness and the unconscious as two distinct "instances" (*Instanzen*) or "systems," he specifies that they need not stand in such a relationship to one another as one would expect if they were arranged in some spatial order. But "the excitation passes through the systems in a particular *temporal* sequence" (*SE*, 5, 537). Thus, the soul has a "sense or direction" in that all "psychical activity starts from stimuli (whether internal or external) and ends in innervations" or a process tended toward discharge (*SE*, 5, 537). For Freud, the soul is an apparatus comprised of two poles, with sensory capacities on one end and motor activity on the other. As sensations and perceptions enter the systems, they impinge upon the psychical apparatus, which leaves a memory trace before traveling to the motor end, which activates physical activity. "Psychical processes advance in general from the perceptual end to the motor end" in which "a trace is left in our psychical apparatus of the perceptions which impinge upon it" (*SE*, 5, 537–538). This memory trace, however, does not take place at the perceptual end of the system, but rather behind the back of immediate consciousness where "a second system transforms the momentary excitations of the first system into permanent traces" (*SE*, 5, 538).

We may already observe a general similarity between Hegel's account of intuition as the internalization of sensations and Freud's account of the perceptual system. While Hegel's elaboration of the intuitive functions of sensation are more meticulously defined than Freud's, they may both be said to account for the same process, namely internalization. We have already determined for Freud, as well as for Hegel, that perceptual consciousness is a phenomenon that arises *within* the ego (*SE*, 22, 75), consciousness being the manifestation of the unconscious soul. In his mature theory of mind, Freud states, "We have said that consciousness is the *surface* of the apparatus of the soul [*des seelischen Apparatus*]; that is, we have ascribed it as a function to a system which is spatially the first one reached from the external world" (*SE*, 19, 19). Consciousness for him is a developmental achievement with sensory-perceptual capacities as its definitive term. Within this context, both Freud and Hegel are realists, that is, they pre-

sume the existence of the external world. For Hegel, intuition is the direct apprehension of objects; for Freud, objects of perception impinge upon consciousness, the conditions for which arise within the ego. Note here that Freud
does not subscribe to a Lockean model of the universe where active forces impinge on a passive mind, but rather thinks that a priori organizations make perception possible, a theoretical position that is consistent with Hegel.

Recall that with the sensation of immediate material, feeling is the initial form spirit assumes, which is the unity of the soul and consciousness.
Freud further concurs with Hegel on this point: "All perceptions which are
received from without (sense-perceptions) and from within—what we call
sensations and feelings—are Cs. from the start" (SE, 19, 19). Hegel first situates feeling within the anthropological soul, which is reconstituted again in
sensation. Freud also came to recognize "unconscious feelings" (SE, 19, 22)
which may further be brought to consciousness. For Hegel, intuitions must be
incorporated, organized as representations through imagination, recorded in
memory, and externalized or re-cognized in consciousness, as unconscious
processes generate synthetic associations that are properly comprehended.
Freud acknowledges a similar process:

> Our perceptions are linked with one another in our memory—first and fore-
> most according to simultaneity of occurrence. We speak of this fact as "associ-
> ation". . . . We must therefore assume the basis of association lies in the
> mnemic systems. (SE, 5, 539)

For Freud and Hegel, the perceptual system has no capacity for memory and it is
only through the mediation of another system (imagination) that associative
traces are retained. While Freud does not speak of imagination, association is the
result of excitations being transmitted from certain mnemonic points to others
that open facilitating pathways toward more unconscious processes. "It would of
course be a waste of time to try to put the psychical significance of a system of
this kind into words. Its character would lie in the intimate details of its relations
to the different elements of the raw material of memory" (SE, 5, 539). Freud
uses association in terms of denoting the relations between various images and
memory traces that may be further imbued with word-presentations, symbols,
signs, and ideational and emotive derivatives such as wishes. While the perceptual
system is without memory capacities, thus freeing sensuous consciousness to attend to the multitude of sensory qualities, the associative elements are processed,
retained—leaving "a variety of permanent records"—and are "in themselves unconscious." While they can be made conscious, "there can be no doubt that they
can produce all their effects while in an unconscious condition" (SE, 5, 539).

Hegel and Freud both underscore the mediating activities of the unconscious underlying the encoding processes of sensations, associations, and memory. In his early depth psychology Freud simply refers to this activity within the
system Ucs.; Hegel on the other hand, locates this activity within imagination,

thus unconsciously producing "all their effects." Recall: "What is mnemonically imprinted is . . . read off from the tableau of the imagination . . . [and] brought forth from within, rehearsed from the deep abyss of the ego" (*EG* § 462). For Hegel, the actual ego—individuated soul—is the birthplace of consciousness endowed with the capacities for receiving sensations and perceptions. Perceptual consciousness for Freud is also attributed to the ego's activities by its relation to the system *Pcpt.-Cs.* (sense-perception), which he tells us is "the outermost superficial portion of the apparatus of the soul" (*SE*, 22, 75). This position may be compared to Hegel's on two accounts: first, the actual ego is an individuated or modified portion of the soul, and second, sense perception is an elementary hence superficial aspect of spirit's mental structure. Sense perception is directed toward the external world, perception arising within the ego itself. As we addressed earlier, the ego is the modified portion of the id adapted to receive stimuli as well as to defend against stimuli. "The relation to the external world has become the decisive factor for the ego; it has taken on the task of representing the external world to the id" (*SE*, 22, 75). Here again we may see two parallel streams of thought overlap with Hegel's conception of the abyss. First, the ego emerges out of the abyss (id) into consciousness while a portion of it remains buried within the night of the mind; and second, the liberated ego represents external images, impressions, and experiences within its deep inwardness, therefore it relates externality to its own internality.

THE DAWN OF DECAY

Throughout this chapter we have examined the intelligence of the abyss and its relation to ego development, consciousness, and psychological spirit. From its natural determinacy the soul awakens as a steady ego progression breaching into consciousness and thus raising its intelligence through intuition, presentation, and thought. Unconscious spirit constitutes the burgeoning life of the ego, which severs its domains through its puncturing into consciousness leaving an aperture in the inner vortex of the soul. As a steady ego expansion, spirit attains two worlds within one: consciousness is the decisive point of psychic fracture— the splitting of psychic topography. Spirit now attains for itself two mediums and two realms of mental life, sensuous and perceptual consciousness mediated by the ego's relation to the external world, and the inwardizing of the abyss mediated by the unconscious ego's relation to its prehistory and the fecundity of images, linguistic processes, and sensory contents derived from its new-found existence outside of its interior. The ego's relation to the abyss is a relation to its own self and that psychic space within itself. What appears foreign to itself is what is estranged from itself: it can be alienated and unrecognizable—the *it*—or it can be intimate and personal, but in any event *it* is still "mine."

When the boundaries between the inner and the outer dissipate, the ego returns home, back into its original unity. In imagination—phantasy—the thin line between the inner and the outer begins to fade: the *I* of the abyss is the silent dialogue the soul has with itself. The same is true for the dreaming soul, asleep within its original lost unity, recovered, reconstituted—even if only for a moment—a confluence between the inner and outer is subsumed within the underworld. In imagination—the artist of the dream—there is a contraction of the ego back into its interior, bringing the wealth of its experiences to bear upon the soul. And for Hegel,

> the human soul in the state of dreaming is not merely filled with *single* affections, . . . it attains to a profound and powerful feeling of the *entirety* of its *individual* nature, of the *complete compass* of its past, present and future, and that it is precisely on account of this sensing of the *individual totality* that mention has to be made of dreaming when the self-awareness of the soul is being considered. (*EG* § 405, *Zusatz*)

The dreaming soul knows its totality, the ego is reunited with itself and recovered from its external breach. And like Freud who also tells us, "[T]he dream is a result of the activity of our own soul" (*der Traum ein Ergebnis unserer eigenen Seelentätigkeit ist*), Hegel shows that in dreaming we possess the "complete compass" of our being, the deep apprehension and feeling of our "entirety." It is in the centers of our imagination that the union between the abyss and the ego is effected, and this imagination is at once both the synthesizing agency behind the scenes of consciousness and the amplitude of the inner soul.

In the next chapter we will extend our investigation of Hegel's philosophical psychology and address those conditions and mental processes that lead to deviation from the normative psychological functions of theoretical spirit. While Hegel's theory of psychopathology by no means provides a psychiatric taxonomy on the spectrum of mental disease, he does offer a general theory of neurosis that has its origins in the life of unconscious spirit derived from the feeling soul, thus leading to the phenomenon of madness. It is in the prehistory of spirit's unconscious unity that the sick soul finds itself imprisoned in the terror of darkness, a darkness that taints even the light of the liberated ego. It is also here that the dialectic of desire shows its double edge, struggling to overcome the antithetical forces that propel spirit toward both progression and regression, transcendence and withdrawal back into its pit.

The intimate relation between desire and reason is bridged by imagination, hovering like a dove in the realm of phantasy where passion becomes imbued with intelligence. There is a real intelligence to the unconscious, one that conforms to the logical structure of spirit; and even in the throes of insanity irrationality has its reasons. Presentation is that stage where spirit hovers over itself, or more appropriately within itself, wanting to take flight toward reason but resisting separation from its nocturnal peace, a dove. And in the mist of decision—or its absence—you find madness.

As Hegel recognizes, our dispositions and desires breathe through the lungs of our presentations. "All presentation, and to an even greater extent the passions, derive a particular affiliation in respect of the various dispositional determinations such as gaiety and gloominess" (*EG* § 455, *Zusatz*). Imagination has no boundaries, no fixed end points, it merely oscillates between oppositions, summoning desire aimed toward fulfillment—the fulfillment of a wish; and when it is frustrated, it lapses into phantasy in both happiness and psychic pain. In the "*pun*," Hegel tells us, "the deepest passion can indulge in such play," a point with which Freud would certainly concur, "for a great mind knows how to set everything which confronts it in relation to its passion" (*EG* § 455, *Zusatz*). Here I am reminded of Freud's doctrine of transference;[39] the libidinal eye is vigilant toward everything it confronts, especially when it "is not entirely satisfied by reality" (*SE*, 12, 100). The sick soul, imprisoned, unable to confront reality, is held hostage by its own archaic pain, its archetypal chaos—negation. If negation is the central ingredient that holds the soul imprisoned, then we are all sick. When imagination is not subjugated by the horrors of the abyss, spirit moves beyond its confinement to discover its truth; from the pit to the pyramid, "phantasy is reason," a wish.

FOUR

THE DIALECTIC OF DESIRE

IN "THE 'UNCANNY'," Freud tells us a personal anecdote of when he once encountered an unsavory old man on a train, until he realized that he was staring at his image in a full-length mirror at the end of his compartment.[1] This experience of misrecognition points to the uncanny powers of projection and personal alienation, a theme that preoccupies spirit's self-estrangement lost in the intersubjective field of the Other. For Hegel, self-consciousness initially does not recognize itself in the face of the other; it is only through the struggle for recognition that spirit eventually comes to identify with its alienated structure and properly reclaim its desire as its own. But as Hegel informs us, even in alienation, "the self-conscious subject knows itself to be *implicitly identical* with the general object external to it" (*EG* § 427, *Zusatz*). As alienated desire, self-conscious spirit is aware of its own liberated ego even if such awareness is unconscious. From this standpoint, there is a real uncanniness to self-consciousness, for there is a familiar unfamiliarity with its primordial lost self-certainty manifest within the gaze of the other. Alienation is thus the appearance of absence, of *lack*, a repetition as the return of its original pre-familiarity with its unconscious nature, a return of the repressed.

The problem of alienation and spirit's struggle for recognition has received overwhelming attention in the Hegel literature, influencing the rise of Marxism and critical theory, French phenomenology, and the psychoanalytic movement initiated by Lacan. Within this context, there has been almost an exclusive fixation on the master-slave dialectic introduced in the *Phenomenology*. It is interesting to note that Hegel's treatment of desire and recognition is contrasted differently in the *Encyclopaedia Phenomenology* and the *Berlin Phenomenology* from that of his Jena period. The most notable difference in his later writings is his scant discussion of self-consciousness in comparison to his original work, and that his famous section on "Freedom of Self-Consciousness," thereby explicating stoicism, skepticism, and unhappy consciousness, has been entirely purged.

135

Hegel's master-slave discussion, or what we may refer to as lord and servant, and more generally the "*relationship* of *mastery* [*Herrschaft*] and *servitude* [*Knechtschaft*]" (*EG* § 433), is given the briefest summation in the *Encyclopaedia*. This is undoubtedly why almost all interpretations of desire and recognition rely exclusively on the Jena *Phenomenology*. It is interesting to note that the terms *master* and *slave* may be translated differently, although most scholars agree that the actual arguments in the two books appear to be essentially compatible. *Herrschaft* is customary translated as lordship, although supreme rule, reign, and governorship are the main implications. *Der Herr* means Lord, also God, but today it is used as a polite address for any male, thus, Mister. At Hegel's time, however, "*Herr*" was reserved for wealthy landowners, sometimes of nobility, not for the average man. In his days, one would have expected the servants of a count and countess to refer to their employers as "*die Herrschaft*."

Knechtschaft is typically rendered as bondage; however, it is difficult to find an exact English equivalent for *Knechtschaft*. Today, the word bondage has sexual connotations and this is far from what Hegel had intended.[2] *Knecht* means farmhand, but it is often translated as servant, serf, or slave. A *Knecht* is someone who works the land without owning it, but who is a free man—not a slave, although poor. *Knechtschaft* is a state of living in material dependence on another person, often without the ability to leave, and working for them under austere circumstances. *Knechtschaft* can also be symbolic: for instance, one could say that someone who lives in a country that offers no freedom of speech and no human rights lives in servitude. The exact translation of "serf" would be *ein Leibeigener*. *Der Leibeigener*, in contrast to the *Knecht*, would physically be a property of his *Herr*, and work his land. He could be sold, but generally only together with the land. *Der Sklave* is the translation of "slave" and obviously means that the person is considered a thing. While *Knecht* refers to a singular person, *Schaft* suggests the relational involvement of several people or what John Russon calls the "institutional"[3] character of this situation.

In standard discussions of Hegel's theory of self-consciousness, desire is portrayed as self-consciousness itself, the truth of self-certainty. Although this position is explicitly outlined by Hegel himself in the *Phenomenology*, this was long before he introduced the *Encyclopaedia* where he traces desire back to a much earlier instantiation. The traditional literature ignores the Anthropology, which provides a systematic groundwork that accounts for the presuppositions that inform his mature theory of self-consciousness. If one were only to concentrate on the *Phenomenology*, desire is viewed as exclusively occurring during the stage of self-consciousness when it is in fact prepared in the soul; thus, its appearance in self-consciousness is a resurfacing of its earlier shapes. Hegel uses desire in a very specific context in the *Phenomenology of Spirit*, but by way of our previous analysis, desire suffuses the very unconscious configurations that comprise the soul. Therefore, it may be said that *desire* is the proper *essence* of spirit with reason being its exalted outgrowth: reason is the knight of desire. While desire appears in its multiple and variegated forms, reason and desire are ontologically identical.

SELF-CONSCIOUSNESS REVISITED

Hegel has been criticized by contemporaries such as Dieter Henrich, Manfred Frank, and Roger Frie for his model of subjectivity, which relies on the reflective medium of the other for self-recognition. In Hegel's early position, the condition of the possibility for the attainment of self-consciousness is constituted by the relation to the other. He maintains that in order to experience self-consciousness, consciousness must first recognize the consciousness of the other in a process of mutual recognition. This is problematic, for self-consciousness is not the result of the dynamic of reflection, as he suggests in the *Phenomenology*. However, this account precedes Hegel's mature system which thereafter affords us the ground or precondition of consciousness and thus allows for a different interpretation of self-consciousness and intersubjectivity altogether. But before we revisit Hegel's theory of mutual recognition, it is necessary to revive a previous issue that was introduced by Fichte.

Fichte understood that self-consciousness cannot be adequately explained by a reflection thesis whereby the self reflects upon itself, for the reflection model is inherently circular.[4] This is because there is no necessary criterion for identification that allows self-consciousness to recognize its own image in the mirror reflection of the other. The reflection model of cognition presupposes what it sets out to explain. For Fichte, self-consciousness is given in a spontaneous act of positing and thus escapes circularity. According to Manfred Frank, "[S]elf-consciousness present[s] itself from the very beginning as a relation that comes about only on the precondition of a grounding identity that escapes the play of all relations."[5] The very condition for the possibility of self-conscious reflection and recognition is that the self must already be familiar with its own self.

As Fichte demonstrates, consciousness must have some prior pre-familiarity with itself in order for it to recognize itself in the mirror reflection of the other. Without such a prereflective, pre-familiar association with itself, it would not be in a position to recognize or know itself. As Frie puts it: "If this were not the case, there would be no way of knowing that the reflection of myself in the other is in fact my own consciousness."[6] If I did not know my own consciousness, how would I be able to recognize another as myself in my otherness? Following Fichte, consciousness must already be familiar with itself before reflection into the other. Reflection (of myself into another) can only identify that which is already familiar. Fichte's formula, "the self posits itself," is the manifestation of immediate self-consciousness as consciousness of an act. As consciousness encounters itself in the other (as exemplified in the master-slave dialectic), it may only know that the other is like itself through having some rudimentary self-knowledge of itself. Hence, recognition of the self in the interpersonal realm must presuppose a prior form of self-consciousness; thus, self-acquaintance precedes intersubjective relation.

Despite this alleged shortcoming typified in the *Phenomenology*, Hegel's notion of the unconscious soul provides us with a solution to this criticism. Given the centrality of the abyss, self-awareness is borne out of unconscious activity and is not the exclusive product of the mirror recognition of self-consciousness. In fact, spirit initially emerges from within the feeling soul and intuits itself as such, only to take its next form as sensuous consciousness. Therefore, there is an elementary form of self-recognition prior to the appearance of consciousness and self-consciousness proper. Such unconscious self-consciousness is the "self-certainty" of the soul as a "determinate being-for-self" which constitutes the basis for spirit to dialectically unfold, and thus be able to recognize its own consciousness in the consciousness of another. While intersubjectivity enriches spirit's dialectical growth, the abyss of subjective spirit originally provides the touchstone for self-reference and differentiation. From this standpoint, unconscious self-familiarity (no matter how archaic and unrefined) precedes self-conscious spirit and is the precondition for thought to occur.

Hegel's explicit account of the coming into being of the soul may be said to be compatible with Fichte's absolute self, with one exception: Fichte's account is thoroughly undialectical—the initial act is that of positing, while Hegel's account is thoroughly dialectical. Unconscious spirit first "rouses" (*EG* § 389, *Zusatz*) itself from its sleeping nature due to the "inner stirring" of the soul (*EG* § 390, *Zusatz*). This original act of arousal is the self-manifestation of its self-certainty. The awakening of soul is the assertion and particularization of its self-identity defined in its movement from undifferentiated indeterminate unity to differentiated determinate being. Unconscious spirit is a self-generative activity instantiated in a self-relating soul. This is why Hegel tells us that "the beginning of spirit is therefore nothing but its own being, and it therefore relates itself only to its own determinations" (*EG* § 440). Similarly, Fichte tells us, "[T]he self *exists* and *posits* its own existence by virtue of merely existing" (*W*, § I, 96). Both assume the primordial being of the soul or the self as a subjective agent. As pure self-relation, the soul is self-consciously aware of its self in its unconscious milieu.

For Fichte, the self-posit is a spontaneous act of self-assertion, the "original unity" of "actuality and freedom."[7] For Hegel, implicit spirit undergoes a "stirring" or a "pulsation." This restlessness is the pre-activity before unconscious spirit actively asserts itself as soul. We may infer that Hegel points to the tremendous negativity that saturates spirit even in its implicitness. This reminds us again of Boehme's *Ungrund*, the primeval chaos—"the negative is the self" (*PS* § 37). In Hegel's discussion of evil in practical spirit, he refers to Boehme. "[In] life and to an even greater extent in spirit, there enters an ought to be, negativity, subjectivity, ego, freedom, constituting the principles of evil and pain. — Jacob Boehme conceived of *egoity* as *agony* and *torment*, and as the *source* of nature and of spirit" (*EG* § 472). This pre-activity—the agony and torment of spirit—may be said to be that which lies *before* the spontaneity of Fichte's self-positing "*Act*," because unconscious spirit in its negativity is nothing other than pure activity, the "primordial, absolutely unconditioned first principle" (*W*, § I, 91). Unconscious spirit as soul asserts itself as deliberate determinate being. Why does spirit pulsate, why does it stir? Because it desires, it *lacks*.

It is important for us not to conflate Hegel and Fichte, but merely to point out the pre-activity of unconscious life that exists in their respective philosophies. We must keep in mind that Hegel always thinks in relational terms, while Fichte initially does not. There is no better example of this difference than acknowledging the way in which Fichte conceives of the self-contained self-positing of the self. For Hegel, any such activity must be constructed out of the oppositions of fluid processes. But despite their theoretical differences, the self attains self-certainty prior to self-conscious reflective awareness.

Hegel reminds us that the "unconscious intuiting" (*EG* § 409) of the soul is the basis of consciousness, hence self-relation or pre-familiarity is prepared long before self-conscious spirit grapples for its own self-recognition. He furthermore shows that self-certainty, first as soul, then as the ego of consciousness, must continue to mediate opposition through its own self-related activities and thus move from simple self-certainty to immediate sense-certainty. As consciousness, "ego is spirit's infinite self-relation, it is so in that it is *subjective self-certainty*" (*EG* § 413). Self-relation as negativity remains the form for each mediated dynamic to be effected. Also recall that recognition occurs during presentation within the imaginative functions of theoretical spirit. Spirit recognizes prior shapes that are internalized through intuition and projected from within its abyss, including affective states that are deposits of the feeling soul. Therefore, the quest for mutual recognition has an unconscious prehistory as desire is transposed and infused within self-conscious spirit. With Hegel's elaboration of the unconscious soul, criticism of his reflection model of self-consciousness becomes inconsequential.

The acquisition of a prior form of self-awareness through spirit's initial unconscious contact with itself as soul may be said to be spirit's original self-consciousness. Spirit is aware of itself unconsciously as an agent that intuits and feels itself before it posits itself in consciousness, which is its next shape. Self-consciousness constituted through intersubjectivity, therefore, becomes more fully actualized as spirit progresses toward absolute self-understanding. While self-consciousness becomes more elaborate and refined in relation to the other, it is already preestablished—its unfolding is already unconsciously prepared.

DESIRE AND DRIVE

In consciousness, the self understands its world but not itself. In self-consciousness, the ego now takes itself as its general object, which it must win as an objective certainty. While consciousness is concerned with the external world, self-consciousness is concerned with its internal world, the life of desire. The crucial issue in self-consciousness, however, becomes the relation between object and subject. The first appearance of self-consciousness is self-knowing constituted in the act of reflection: "[S]elf-consciousness is the reflection out of the being of the world of sense and perception, and is essentially the return from *otherness*" (*PS* § 167). Hegel explains two distinct moments of reflection: first, as the distinguishing of self from other—the positing of difference—and second, as the unity of the self with other—the identity of non-difference. Taken as a totality, this unity constitutes desire as life.[8] Hegel says: "Through this reflection into itself the object has become Life" (*PS* § 168). What the self desires is living as opposed to just being, hence it desires the other. The life of desire becomes a process of overcoming difference, its otherness, and through experience it comes to see that otherness is an independent object.

In the *Phenomenology*, desire has a special meaning for Hegel associated to the conscious self: "[S]elf-consciousness is *Desire* in general" (*PS* § 167). To be aware of oneself is to be aware that one wants, this constitutes life; but life is always juxtaposed to the negative—its opposition: to live is to want and to want is to suffer, for desire is constantly immersed in absence, in lack. Kojève tells us: "The very being of man, the self-conscious being, therefore implies and presupposes Desire. Consequently, the human reality can be formed and maintained only within a biological reality, an animal life. But if animal Desire is the necessary condition of Self-Consciousness, it is not the sufficient condition."[9] Natural desire is instantiated in the body[10] and in the family through communal affiliation where it is generated and sustained. Self-consciousness naturally wants to be satisfied and to be happy, but it ultimately discovers that it wants to be free.[11] Desire is desire for self-externalized freedom, but this can only come about by the mutual recognition of subjects each of us confronts.

Desire ultimately desires unity, the unity of the disparity between the self with its world and the self with its self.[12] There is a disparity between what actually exists and what the self wishes there to be. But self-consciousness is dependent upon the other for full self-recognition; it can no longer maintain the inner privacy of its narcissism. The self duplicates itself in the other, and finding itself outside of its self in the other, it alienates its internal being from its very possession. The self is lost in the other and so must recover its self from its lostness in order to regain its original unity. Desire becomes a circular motion of the drives, a projection outward, a constant craving.

Essentially, desire confronts what it wants, an independent object, as well as a subject—its other; and through this confrontation, self-consciousness must transform itself into true certainty of its own being by destroying the independence of the other, and thus give itself objectivity, "for self-certainty comes from superseding this other" (*PS* § 175). Consciousness therefore has to come to know itself in its otherness; the other is what mediates objective self-certainty, but only insofar as the negation of the other is a negation of the ego's self-projection into the other. Negation, destruction, supersession once again becomes the principle of *Aufhebung*, the sublation of self-consciousness as universal recognition—the self knowing its self in the other.

In the *Encyclopaedia Phenomenology*, Hegel states, "[S]elf consciousness appears at the *first* stage of its development in the form of *desire* [*Begierde*]. Here . . . desire still has no further determination than that of a *drive* [*Trieb*], in so far as this drive, without being determined by *thought*, is directed toward an *exter-*

nal object in which it seeks satisfaction" (*EG* § 426, *Zusatz*). Self-consciousness is immediately immersed in contradiction as the negation of consciousness yet at the same time remains consciousness. In order for the ego to give content and objectivity to the abstract knowledge of itself, it must free itself of the sensuous restrictions of consciousness, sublate its objectivity within itself, and posit itself as identical with such objectivity. As Hegel tells us, these two moments "constitute the identification of the consciousness and self-consciousness . . . ego = ego" (*EG* § 425).

Initially, immediate self-consciousness is only implicitly aware of itself as an abstract self-identity. The determination of *I = I* is still not posited as actual; however, given self-conscious spirit's pre-familiarity with itself as unconscious self-consciousness, we may say that its immediate self-awareness of itself has been forgotten only to be recovered, hence recollected, in the eyes of the other. Since self-consciousness is at the same time consciousness, thus the opposite of itself, it is faced with an immediate contradiction it is forced to overcome. The immediacy of abstract self-consciousness still has the form of being which is the "*conditioned* negation of the immediacy of consciousness" (*EG* § 425, *Zusatz*) and is still not the absolute negativity which is the affirmation of the negation of the negation. Because the ego is still ensconced within an inward undifferentiation, its inner form is the internalization of that which lies without. While it contains negation within itself, it also contains negation outside of itself as the external object or non-ego which constitutes consciousness.

The contradiction must be overcome by annulling the dependence the ego has on external reality. Instead of self-consciousness being externally bound to consciousness, consciousness becomes subsumed within self-consciousness as it infiltrates and dissolves the contradiction within it. This requires three stages in order to reach this goal: (1) First, self-consciousness collapses into its new immediacy as simple self-identity with consciousness, which is itself a contradiction since it is related to an external object. The general object has the appearance of independence, which is its nullity, and this constitutes desire. (2) Second, the objective ego encounters another ego, which gives rise to the intersubjective relationship between one self-consciousness and another leading to the process of recognition. (3) Finally, the two independently existing selves become mutually identical, which is the culmination of universal self-consciousness.

Self-consciousness in its immediate singularity is desire, which appears as drive, simply impulse, urge, compulsion, or appetite. Desire hungers, it craves. It is very important to note that desire has its origin, not in self-conscious spirit, but in the natural soul, thus constituting the generative basis of the dialectic. Desire becomes the general engine behind the evolution of spirit, hence history and absolute knowing. Drive is the essence of desire, insofar as if it were removed, desire could not attach to objects for satisfaction, thus it could no longer be. The aim of desire is simply to achieve satisfaction, to gratify. Hegel tells us in the *Anthropology* that the self-awareness of the feeling soul is the unconscious activity of its aliveness, which it endows with determinate being.

"This activity is the expression of drive, of desire, its determination or content being drive, inclination, [or] passion" (*EG* § 407, *Zusatz*). Drive becomes the constitutional force behind the acquisition of habits and character formation. "Self-awareness, in that it is immersed in the particularity of such feelings or simple sensations as desires, impulses, and passions and the gratification of such, is not distinguished from them" (*EG* § 409). He further states, "[T]he content of sensation, deriving from *without*, while alternatively having its origin *within*, in the will or drive, is . . . the objectivity of the soul" (*EG* § 410).[13] Here we may see why Hegel says, "self-consciousness is Desire" (*PS* § 174); desire is originally the unconscious self-awareness of the feeling soul.

However, Hegel does make an attempt to draw a distinction between desire and drive; while desire is something simple and seeks only to satisfy a particular momentary impulse, drive has a general holistic process as determinate will. Hegel says, "*desire* . . . is something *single*, and only seeks what is *single*, for a single, momentary satisfaction. *Drive* on the contrary, since it is a form of *volitional intelligence*, goes forth from the *sublated* opposition of what is subjective and what is objective, and as it embraces a *series* of satisfactions, is something of a *whole*, a *universal*" (*EG* § 473, *Zusatz*). While desire is the manifestation of immediate craving, *Trieb* is the general force behind the generation of spirit—the drive to know. Hegel's distinction lies in the immediate preoccupation of satisfying a particular desire versus the general thrust of spirit as attending to a "series" of impulses that want fulfillment. Because desire can only achieve fulfillment in its singular moment, it "is transient [which] gives rise to further desire" (*EG* § 428). For Hegel, there is always a "renewal of desire, . . . its goal is *never* completely attained, [it] only gives rise to an *endless progression*" (*EG* § 428, *Zusatz*). Desire is something that is never completely satiated, hence it is *being in relation to lack*. While drive may attain satisfaction, desire is unbounded immediacy.

In many ways, this is a surprisingly contradictory conclusion. One would think the opposite seems equally warranted—that desire may be satisfied but a drive never fulfilled. If desire wants a particular, such as a concrete object or the fulfillment of a wish, obtaining it satisfies the desire completely. Yet procuring a particular never truly satisfies desire because it is soon gone, fulfillment dissipates almost immediately. Desire is constantly reprinted afresh. Thus, only the universal, even though it involves an apparently insatiable drive, can yield final satisfaction.

When self-consciousness confronts another, it sees the conditions for the possibility of its fulfillment and hence desires what it does not possess. This is brought about by an act of identification. This begins with the child's relation to its parents. It recognizes the parental imago and wishes to be recognized in return, thus satisfying its desires. Hegel says, "[S]elf-consciousness exists . . . only in being acknowledged" (*PS* § 178). Children recognize their parents and take them to represent the fulfillment of their ideals. Therefore, not only does the child want to be recognized, hence its desire recognized and fulfilled, it also wants to be the other. This process is nicely summarized by Freud: "Identification is known . . . as the earliest expression of an emotional tie with another person. . . . A little boy will exhibit a special interest in his father; he would like to grow like him and be like him, and take his place everywhere. We may say simply that he takes his father as his ideal" (*SE*, 18, 105). To identify with another is to identify with a particular value as a form of self-expression or identity. The other is imbued with value, an ideal. We wish to possess this ideal, to *be* this ideal that the other represents.

THE THROES OF RECOGNITION

We all seek recognition; this is a basic human need.[14] The ego is affirmed by the other, but not at first. There is originally the experience of inequality, whether this be the child's relation to the parent or the bondsman's relation to the lord. H. S. Harris argues that the concept of recognition is the bare Concept of Spirit itself;[15] spirit passes from the recognition of the human lord to God as Absolute Lord. It must emerge from its momentary state of inadequacy as it educates itself to truth.

Desire immediately apprehends what it is not from what it would like to be, hence the self-conscious self starts from a place of inequality and deficiency. Hegel asserts:

> The self-conscious subject knows itself to be *implicitly identical* with the general object external to it. It knows that since this general object contains the *possibility* of satisfying desire, it is *adequate* to the desire, and that this is precisely why the desire is stimulated by it. The relation with the object is therefore necessary to the subject. The subject intuits its *own deficiency*, its own onesidedness, in the object; it sees there something which although it belongs to its own essence, it lacks. (*EG* § 427, *Zusatz*)

When Hegel says that the self knows itself to be "*implicitly identical*" with the other, he is pointing to the pre-familiarity of self-consciousness with its "own essence"; the self identifies with itself in the other, but being only an immediate, it is fixated on absence or what it lacks that the independent object possesses. The process of recognition commences when the self identifies with the other, that is, identifies *its* alienated shape in the other, which it must win back through a genuine struggle. The subject is opposed to an object but the object is imbued with the self's subjectivity which it must recapture and claim as its own, thus making its self objective.

The other of self-consciousness is indeed the projection of the self, but because this projection takes place behind the back of self-consciousness, hence is pre-reflective, the self does not initially recognize itself in the other. Hegel supports this claim: "Self-consciousness is faced by another self-consciousness; it has come *out of itself*"(*PS* § 179). But the self has "lost itself" in the other being, which it comes to see as its own self. Because the self is lost, it is in a genuine state of despair and ambiguity. In order to recover itself, it must aggress upon its otherness, supercede the independent object, and thus prove the truth of its own essence as objective self-certainty. But its supersession of the other is also a supersession of itself, for the other is the self. Therefore, the sublation of the self in recognition is none other than a return to its self.

The process of the ego's self-integration is a negative movement. It vanquishes the other and achieves satisfaction as objective actuality. "Desire is therefore generally *destructive* in its satisfaction, just as it is generally *self-seeking*" (*EG* § 428). Once again we see the "tremendous power of the negative"; everything is about death and destruction—the sustenance of life. Death saturates life; the entire structure of the world is replete with opposition and contradiction that must be destroyed in order to achieve self-affirmation. Death is our inner being.

Such inequality of recognition first exists when two opposing self-consciousnesses confront one other. Each wants to be what the other only represents, thus each is determined to slay the other's independence in order to give its own self value; "each seeks the death of the other" (*PS* § 187). This is exemplified in the master-slave dialectic where the lord dominates the bondsman who is made into a serf and forced to give up his self-determination.[16] A familiar pillar of Hegelian theory, the slave must renounce his own desire for the lord's desire or he will surely face his own death. But ironically, the master depends on the slave for nurturing and harvesting the land and is thus not completely free, because both his life and enjoyment rest on the slave. The slave serves as the being against whom the master defines himself as superior, but given his dependency on the slave, the master lives a contradiction.

The master's will is enslaved by its actual conditions while the slave, in relinquishing his independence, gains it—the slave still owns his own mind and is free in his thought. He is free to work the land and develop his craft through which he can remake himself afresh as master of the soil, while the lord may only achieve satisfaction through the slave, thus his satisfaction is not his own. Working the land gives life to the slave while the master is dependent upon the productivity of his otherness, which he fails to fully recognize and appreciate as human. The slave is merely a "thing," an object or instrumental means to be used and exploited. But despite the fact that the master can always beat the slave, his power of mastery is illusory because the slave has grown indifferent to threats of pain and death and is beyond the master's manipulation of his mind, having escaped into stoic indifference. Because the other is not fully recognized for its own worth and its own value, the self remains alienated from its truth.

It is important to reemphasize that Hegel's treatment of self-consciousness and the struggle for recognition in the *Phenomenology* is presented differently in the *Encyclopaedia* and the *Berlin Phenomenology*. The most noticeable distinction is the brevity of the latter works. In the *Encyclopaedia*, the discussion from recognition to universal self-consciousness is contained in only six paragraphs and one remark, excluding the additions, and little additional elaboration is offered in the Berlin manuscript. Furthermore, all references to stoicism, skepticism, and unhappy consciousness are eliminated. This terse account suggests that perhaps

Hegel wanted to distance himself from his earlier commitments outlined in the *Phenomenology*, or else that he thought he had treated the subjects adequately beforehand. Despite the fact that the *Phenomenology* stands on its own as a major philosophical treatise, we should use caution when inferring from Hegel's early work; his mature system speaks a slightly different tongue. Yet despite Hegel's later texts, it will be necessary to examine the *Phenomenology* along with the *Encyclopaedia* version. The *Phenomenology* proves to be especially instructive when examining the extreme despair and spiritual unhappiness self-consciousness endures, for it is in Hegel's treatment of stoicism, skepticism, and unhappy consciousness that we find a general theory of neurosis, a topic I will shortly address.

For Hegel, the subjection of the other to the domination of desire is a "thoroughly selfish *destructiveness*" (*EG* § 428, *Zusatz*) that is only concerned with its immediate satisfaction. In the *Encyclopaedia*, self-consciousness first posits itself as an ego in its otherness that stands in opposition to itself. Secondly, it places itself over against the ego of otherness as its own distinct ego and thus raises itself from the selfish destructiveness of immediate desire. Recognitive self-consciousness is the immediate confrontation of two egos, each extending its self into the other. During this moment, the self has an "immediate intuition" of itself as well as the recognition of an "absolutely opposed and independently distinct object" (*EG* § 430). Hegel is very clear that the self projects its own ego into the other and recognizes its own self as well as the opposing ego. This leads us to offer a competing reinterpretation of his original position espoused in the *Phenomenology* where some interpreters have attributed to the other the causal powers of self-conscious recognition. This claim has been inferred from statements such as these: "Self-consciousness . . . exists for another; . . . it exists only in being recognized" (*PS* § 178); "For the other is equally independent and self-contained, and there is nothing in it of which it is not itself the origin" (*PS* § 182).

However, Hegel also says that consciousness comes "*out of itself*," at the same time remains "within itself," is "*for itself*," and is "aware that it at once is," while "the self outside it, is for *it*" (*PS* § 184). There is a double movement to self-consciousness where each sees the other do as it does, thus appearing as the same action. But before the recognition of an independently existing ego is determined by each subject, the ego of otherness is projected from the ego of each self-consciousness. While the other is a necessary condition that brings about self-recognition, it is not a sufficient condition. This rests on the activity of the ego.

Recall that the ego already is aware of itself, first as the unconscious self-acquaintance of the soul, and second as the ego of consciousness, even if such awareness is still not raised to its truth of pure reason. But nevertheless, the soul initially moves from indeterminate unity to determinate being-for-self then to self-certainty as the actual ego, only to have consciousness move from self-certainty to sense-certainty. Self-certainty is a condition of every stage of the development of spirit. Self-certainty is the early phase of any emergent condition of consciousness, a stage of primary narcissism, when it thinks it is the world and sees nothing beyond itself. It is through opposition and bitter experience that it turns from this self-enclosed stage to eventually attain its truth, which is at once its demise. When Hegel speaks of the self losing itself in the other, it has already lost itself and recovered itself many times as each mediated dynamic forms new immediate relations. Intersubjective self-recognition is the ripening of self-consciousness, and hence is the formal extension of the sublation of the ego.

While desire is the first proper stage of self-consciousness, recognition is its second. The immediacy of desire is sublated with recognition, but desire does not disappear as such, rather it is an "*endless progression*." Desire will always be operative within the self and materialize in response to certain interests, inclinations, or passions, but it also evolves as a more general thrust of spirit, what Hegel locates as drive, for "self-consciousness acquires the drive to display itself as the free self, and to be there as such for the other" (*EG* § 430). The process of recognition is saturated with conflict. Two selves oppose the independence of the other and in so doing assert their independence. As each overcomes the immediacy of the other, each self gives determinate being to its freedom so it may be recognized as an immediacy. Put simply, two mutually confronting selves appear as physical things to each other that act independently hence freely, which both recognize as being before the other.

But freedom is something that must be fought for, it must be achieved or proven. This is why Hegel sees the tussles of recognition as an altercation—a struggle, for it is "a matter of life or death" (*EG* § 432). Each self-consciousness throws itself into the perils of death where each is equally exposed to annihilation. Each is willing to risk its own life in order to be recognized by the other—in order to receive validation. And when we encounter opposition and invalidation, we simply wish the other would vanish. But self-consciousness is also motivated by self-preservation and weighs its odds before directly engaging in conflict. Hegel discusses the crude negation of the other through annihilation, such as hand to hand combat, but this can be easily extended from any raw display of violence to the intellectual realm of conceptual argumentation—we all know when to pick our battles. Here we are reminded of Freud's distinction between the self-preservative drives of the ego having their origin in eros and the destructive derivatives of the death drive. In self-preservation as in aggressivity, both converge upon one another borrowing resources from the other side. For Hegel, the self "is equally committed to the preservation of its life . . . the existence of its freedom" (*EG* § 432). But the "*absolute* proof" of freedom is found in death; one self-consciousness is left standing while the other has perished. Yet this too poses a great contradiction, for the self has effaced the very conditions for recognition: while it demonstrates its superiority, its existence cannot be recognized by its dead antagonist, therefore it is a vacuous freedom.

Because often one of the contestants prefers life to death, he will show deference in order to preserve his own self-consciousness. As a one-sided negation, this is the initial appearance of inequality; one self recognizes and submits to the superiority of the other. Hegel characterizes this process as the relationship of mastery (*Herrschaft*) and servitude (*Knechtschaft*). The servant relinquishes his own self-will for the will of the lord's; the lord remains only self-conscious of his own needs and not the needs or free independence of the servant. We may say that the lord, in his denial of the other's needs, is enveloped in a primary narcissism where he only takes himself, hence his own ego, as his object. This selfishness of self-consciousness may be compared to the Kierkegaardian aesthete who has not yet contemplated the ethical—the servant is not recognized as the rational self-consciousness of the universal ego that has the right to be free.

The sublation of self-consciousness moves from immediate desire to recognition, thus the base destruction of the other is replaced by its acquisition and maintenance; mindful of its own desires, the master secures a community of need in which the servant is used as a means to an end to provide for the self's satisfaction. Yet here, independence and dependency unite themselves. But it is due to the unique position of the servant that self-consciousness advances itself. The master is only concerned about his fulfillment; the servant, on the other hand, while forced to acquiesce to the lord, gives up the immediacy of his desire and hence sublates it; thus begins the transition to universal self-consciousness. Because the servant is no longer confined to the immediate shape of self-serving desire, his desire expands to include that of the others' desire and thereby "he raises himself above the selfish singularity of his natural will" (EG § 435, Zusatz). For Hegel, this is "the beginning of wisdom" and the beginning of true freedom.

While Hegel's master-slave dialectic is a direct allusion to the historical contingencies of man alienated from his true self only to emerge as a more civilized being with the abolition of the institution of slavery, the depiction has symbolic implications for any institutionalized practices of oppression and domination, such as the patriarchal and androcentric infrastructures that govern interpersonal relations between the sexes[17] and sociopolitical policies that contribute to the subjugation of disadvantaged groups. Within the psychological realm of social development, the dialectic of mastery and servitude is a natural and necessary process of psychic growth. As each of us progresses through the life cycle, the quest for mastery becomes a lifelong pursuit. This advances from the most primitive stages of ego development where children struggle to gain control through advanced capacities to manage and manipulate their body, internal desires, the demands of the environment, the object world including their attachments and relatedness to others, and finally the mastery over their own mind and fulfillment of their ideals as adults. This necessarily requires dependence upon and servitude to others, including submission to authority. This is a process we must all encounter. We must renounce our primary narcissism and relate to a world governed by rules and standards for civil and social behavior, and freely contribute to that world. A child shows deference to parents out of fear which grows into love, and through identification comes to internalize the desires and values they espouse. Hegel tells us: "The quaking of the singularity of the will, the feeling of the nullity of self-seeking, the habit of obedience,—this constitutes a necessary moment in the education of everyone" (EG § 435, Zusatz). A child learns discipline and self-control first through the axillary ego of the parent—reality itself is prohibitive; then, through identification, the child develops its own ego organizations at mastering its internal impulses, physical and psychomotor development, and the environmental demands of external reality. Through this process, freedom becomes more actualized. Hegel avouches: "In order to be free, in order to be capable of self-control, all peoples have therefore had first to undergo the strict discipline of subjection to a master" (*EG* § 435, *Zusatz*).

Obedience is only the beginning of freedom, where submission takes place not to a universal, rational will, but to the particular and contingent will of another subject. This constitutes the first movement of freedom, a negative relation to the singular self-seeking desire of another. The positive relation occurs when the servile self-consciousness frees itself from both its own singularity and the master's will and hence grasps the universal will of self-consciousness that is in-and-for-itself. Universal self-consciousness is "affirmative"; one knows oneself in the other and does not differentiate oneself from the other (*EG* § 436). Being both universal and objective, each recognizes the freedom of the other, and through reciprocity, each knows itself to be free.

Recognition is a mutual enterprise of equality, the intersubjective sublation of the self within the other as an objective unity. If self-consciousness truly sees itself in another, then it would not want the other (self) to die or be enslaved when the other is actualized within the self. Recognition is the sublation of desire, it is an identification with an ideal and perhaps even an empathy for the autonomy of mutually existing selves. We recognize in others what we do ourselves, that is, we act freely. This involves relinquishing the other as a tool for our own self-recognition and thus sublating our oppression and objectification of the other as a "thing" to that of a freely determinate being-for-self. In this way we recognize that each recognizes the freedom of the other—freedom belongs to all.

The process of emancipation is never simple. The master's release of the servant constitutes the completion of his freedom. Seeing that he, while separate and independent, is identical with the servant, he can no longer enslave the other and his own self within the other. The other is raised to the standpoint of human equality and as freedom is valued for itself. Subjectivity becomes subsumed within objectivity as a unity constituting the universal. The freeing of the other is concomitantly the freeing of the self, which is ultimately "the substance of what is ethical" (*EG* § 436, *Zusatz*). It is here that self-consciousness makes its transition to reason as the being-in-and-for-self of the unity of the subjectivity of the Concept with its objectivity and universality: opposition is united.

Hegel's treatment of desire and recognition advances our understanding of psychic development. The deficiency, inequality, and supersession of self-consciousness is a normative process of self-development. While each individual commands a certain mastery over another in skill, knowledge, character, or deed, each individual also stands in an inferior or subordinate relation to a higher authority, as does the solitary subject to the objective institutions that govern civil society. As Hegel reminds us, each of us must be subjected to a master as part of our education, and nowhere is this so evident as in a child's relation to his parents. In the most optimal conditions, parents extend their own egos into the soul of the child, thus fulfilling (or depriving) its needs and desires. When children advance in their own sense of achievement and self-mastery, parents must let them go free to live their lives by their own choices and self-determinations. This is an exercise in identification, empathy, and love—the true expression of the ethical. But mutual recognition always remains an intersubjective process: the child in turn must acknowledge the parent, which remains an obligation of love. And when life achieves a form grown old, the mother who gave her self for her child will forever long for validation that she was indeed a gentle master.

NEUROTIC SPIRIT

In the *Encyclopaedia*, Hegel offers an abbreviated account of the toils of self-consciousness, whereas in the *Phenomenology* he focuses more closely on spirit estranged from itself. It becomes important for us to now turn our attention to the theme of alienation and despair, because as self-consciousness struggles for its freedom it must endure the anxiety, uncertainty, and confusion associated with its neurotic constitution. Before self-consciousness finds its unity in reason, it dwells in the shapes of stoicism and skepticism until it eventually realizes that it can find no place to hide from its anxiety and anquish and thus is forced to embrace its unhappiness. In Hegel's discussion of the freedom of self-consciousness, we may find a general theory of neurosis in the way in which spirit comes to terms with its conflicted psychic states. From a psychoanalytic perspective, spirit's forms of self-alienation may be construed to be products of defense, and personality being the constellation of defense and desire is expressed primarily through the ways in which it copes with its inner conflicts and the actual reality of a hostile environment. This takes different forms throughout the history and education of spirit that appear throughout the evolution of culture (*Bildung*). The enslaved self knows its freedom first as stoicism.

The stoical serf attains a certain degree of freedom over his enslavement by an alien consciousness insofar as he is free in his thoughts. The stoic is free in his own thinking, and in having no control over his social position, his only recourse is to "withdraw from the bustle of existence, alike from being active as passive, into the simple essentiality of thought" (*PS* § 199). Thus, the stoic renounces his desire, emotions, and passions which are of no importance and holds steadfast to the one thing that he may have some semblance of control over—his mind.

In stoical freedom there is a retreat from the actual world to the inner world: the slave has the concept of freedom but not the lived concrete reality of freedom, thus he gives up his natural existence. But in letting nature go free, free thought has no content in itself apart from what it is given in experience. Hence, the negation of existence is only partial; the withdrawal from existence is only an inwardizing, it is not an absolute negation of existence. This is only achieved through skepticism.

Skepticism is the actualization of the negative, what stoicism only had as its concept. As the pure negativity of free self-consciousness, skepticism is "the concrete thinking which annihilates the being of the world" (*PS* § 202). All reliance on sensory perception and the empirical world of experience is to be negated; the freedom of self-consciousness requires the total suspension of judgment. Skeptical self-consciousness maintains an absolute negative relation toward all otherness, toward desire and work. The skeptic admits that he knows absolutely nothing, and in this assertion of free thought makes objective reality and his relationship to it disappear. In this sense, skeptical self-consciousness is the sublation of stoicism because it generates a higher freedom in the act of pure negation, while the stoic may only find an illusory solace in the abstract thought of freedom, which he resigns as fate.

But spirit pays a price in both its forms of stoicism and skepticism; it lives in denial of its full existence. Both shapes of self-consciousness are illusory defenses for coping with life's vicissitudes. What the stoic really desires but cannot have is conveniently reinterpreted as that which he did not really desire in the first place. In psychoanalysis, this is referred to as a reaction formation.[18] The stoic withdraws from life in order to live within a narrowly controlled and purified world of his own ordering. This is accomplished by a strict denial of emotions and passions that, while clamoring for release, are compartmentalized and strangulated; thus, the stoic levels down his world to a reality devoid of natural consciousness. Any serenity the stoic enjoys is purely an inwardizing, a complete retreat from the actual world. The freedom of self-consciousness is therefore limited by its own denial; he does not confront life fully and on his own terms in such a way that he can learn and grow through experience and suffering.

The retreat from the actual world into the self-enclosed cocoon of the inner world is an act of disconnection, a dissociation from the very source of pain and suffering that bonds the serf to enslavement by the master. There is a form of masochism to stoicism; while the slave gains freedom in his thoughts, he sacrifices his natural relation, responsiveness, and openness to the real. Thus, "whether on the throne or in chains" (*PS* § 199), his world is sharply curtailed even if his "aim is to be free." While stoic disconnection can be interpreted as a source of great inner strength—the triumph of the human spirit—it can also be viewed, from the perspective of different models of human flourishing, as the self-retardation of emotional and moral growth. Because stoic strategies of detachment and neurotic withdrawal undermine a person's capacity to embrace a large range of intrapsychic and interpersonal experiences, one is barred from truly living life and is thus alienated from one's own humanity.

Hegel views skepticism as a sublated response to stoicism and as an attempt to gain even more freedom than the mere internal withdrawal from the deprivation of the natural world. But the skeptic takes denial to the edge of the absurd: reality is destroyed by thought, it is given no existence. Negation dwells only within its onesidedness—pure death. Nothing can be known except nothingness; what is certain is uncertainty itself. Hegel himself sees this as a self-generated, self-sustained thought disorder: skeptical consciousness is a "confused medley, the dizziness of a perpetually self-engendered disorder. It is itself aware of this; for itself maintains and creates this restless confusion" (*PS* § 205). As universal negation, all singularity and difference are obliterated; but lost in its confusion, skeptical consciousness constricts its comportment to spontaneous negativity which is separate and single, and thus it falls back into contingent preoccupation.

Hegel sees this form of consciousness as an "unconscious, thoughtless rambling" vacillating between the two extremes of self-identical self-consciousness and contingent consciousness. The skeptical consciousness does not unite these two thoughts, it simply repeats them as a rigid and immobile contradiction. Yet the skeptic himself is a walking contradiction. Skeptical consciousness affirms the nullity of the senses yet it still senses; it denies ethical standards yet lets them rule its conduct. It applies its negative attitude toward everything: when identity is highlighted, it points to difference; when difference is determined, it sinks into disavowal. The skeptic lives a lie by violating and contradicting his own self-imposed and perverted order of the universe. But this is skeptical consciousness' attempt to assert its independence and self-expression, what Hegel labels as a child's squabble where the only pleasure gained is in contradicting the other.

If skepticism is taken seriously by the subject and is not merely a mental game one plays with oneself for amusement, then this form of alienation and self-deception is bound to break down under the weight of its own denial. Reality can be repressed only so much before it snaps and makes itself felt. When this happens, melancholia sets in, for denial is rendered a useless passion. The skeptic has to eventually face up to its bad faith, its lie. The skeptic is a person who lives in a fragmented inner universe based on a fixed oscillation—a repetition compulsion—attempting to gain mastery over the very source of its suffering, namely, the *daimôn* of desire and irrational passions on the one side, and the reality of social oppression, fear, and bondage on the other. In this state, consciousness is truly on the edge of madness, for if it maintains itself in skepticism for long, all boundaries lose their demarcation and thought plummets into the bowels of decay. Skeptical consciousness lives in inner contradiction and thus all reference points are blurred with negation. It is forced to attempt to resolve its contradictory nature or face insanity; and in the face of that decision it finds madness. At the extreme, skepticism is a delusion, it violates all objective evidence to the contrary. While psychosis is one possibility, Hegel outlines its neurotic trend, the path of unhappy consciousness.[19]

As a self-inflicted symptom, skepticism is no better off than stoicism: both live in the illusory haven of denial, hence a state of wish-fulfillment. For the stoic, the self is purged of its own naturality, and for the skeptic, the actual is not allowed to exist. Although stoic consciousness denies its emotional life—its suffering—in an attempt to control its suffering, the skeptic needs to hold onto its suffering, its chaotic existence. But skeptical consciousness undergoes a deep despair. Once it reflects on its condition, it becomes aware of its self-contradictory nature. Self-consciousness duplicates itself as a duality. What was formerly divided between lordship and bondage is now seen as one. But this is still not yet an actual unity, for the unhappy consciousness must sit with its contradictory duality.

The unhappy consciousness is not at peace with itself because it remains a divided self, an "*inwardly disrupted*" split entity. As Hegel puts it: "Unhappy Consciousness itself *is* the gazing of one self-consciousness into another, and itself *is* both" (*PS* § 207). Initially, unhappy consciousness sees only opposition; the two self-consciousnesses are alien. But because it is both and is aware of its own self-contradiction, it lingers in agony. "Consciousness of life, of its existence and activity, is only an agonizing over this existence and activity, for therein it is conscious . . . only of its own nothingness" (*PS* § 209). The extreme despair that self-estranged spirit feels may be more adequately equated with dysphoria—a restless, agitated depression. It no longer withdraws like stoicism nor annihilates like skepticism, for it is ill at ease with surpassing these two previous moments. At first its self-relation is one-sided; it identifies with the finite and transient world of the changeable and thus takes itself to be an unessential being. Consciousness is at the same time conscious of the unchangeable universal and essential being, but does not yet take this essence as its own. The individuality of the other is identified as the unchangeable, but through this identification it comes to know itself to be an individual as well, thus constituting the reconciliation of the individual with the universal. But in order to annul its spiritual despair, spirit has to first pass from opposition to unity.

Spirit finds itself caught in a dilemma: to struggle with the other for recognition is to become ensnared in a death trap. If consciousness defeats one side of its polarity it really defeats itself, for "victory in one consciousness is really lost in its opposite" (*PS* § 209). The goal of the unhappy consciousness is to transform the unchangeable alien reality to a relation in which it becomes one with it. Unhappy consciousness resides in an intermediate space between the abstraction of pure thinking and the concrete actuality of individuality, and it knows itself to be this thinking individuality. But what it does not know is that it is merged with the unchangeable essence of the universal within its individuality. It does not know this as pure thought, for it is only a movement toward pure thinking. What it knows is only what it senses in its heart: it feels in the pure heart what the mind only knows as a "chaotic jingling of bells"; it has still not grasped the Concept.

The pure inner feeling of the heart knows itself to be identical with the infinite, but does not (rationally) comprehend it as such; the object appears alien to it. This is a great source of suffering for the unhappy consciousness because it pines for recognition from its other, its self, and for unity and wholeness. It abides in a state that is "agonizingly self-divided," certain that its essence is this pure heart, and "certain of being known and recognized by this object, precisely because the latter thinks itself as an individuality" (*PS* § 217). Spirit wants recognition from the master, and in such recognition it will achieve mastery, validation, unification, and actual freedom. As a movement toward pure thinking, but only known in the feeling soul, unhappy consciousness expresses itself as "devotion." It is devoted to the lord, to serve his desire, and ultimately the Lord thy God. We are devoted to our parents, family, and community, who represent as a social identification the infinite fellowship of universal selfhood. But when the infinite unchangeable is sought, it cannot be found for it remains a *beyond*. When sought in the individual, it is not the universal individuality but only the concrete object of the actual individual, hence the fleeting immediacy of sense-certainty. This is why Hegel says consciousness can only find immediate reality to be "the *grave* of its life"; it has already vanished. When consciousness realizes that the actual unchangeable being cannot be found in the actual individual, it will either abandon its search for the unchangeable individuality as an actual existence or it will try to let go of what has already vanished, and in so doing it may grasp individuality in its universal or genuine form.

Spirit feels its essential being—its self in its heart; this pure heart is its inner being and thus belongs to the feeling soul. Hence, this feeling is a reawakened sensation of its earlier life and the recognition of its primordial being; the pre-familiarity the heart has with itself as soul is reunited in consciousness. This is consciousness of itself as a felt object, and the self-feeling associated with its actual consciousness is taken as existing on its own account. Spirit has returned to its self as an inward affirmation of self-certainty, which is further validated in its second relationship with itself through desire and work. But the unhappy consciousness finds itself as "an *actuality broken in two*" (*PS* § 219); it desires and works but is not united with its alien counterpart which it feels to be identical with itself yet divided and estranged from itself. It is still not completely certain of itself even though it acts, because it is still lost in its nothingness which it takes its own reality to be. Therefore, its own action is considered by itself to be actually doing nothing and hence any "enjoyment a feeling of its wretchedness" (*PS* § 225). This is the self-debasement of spirit, the invalidating and defiling attitude it harbors toward itself. Desire, work, and enjoyment are denigrated to the level of a hog; they lose any significance because they are purged of universality. This is how the "enemy" reveals itself—a debauching self-consciousness confined to its own "petty actions, a personality brooding over itself, as wretched as it is impoverished" (*PS* § 225). The self sacrifices its self, divests itself of its *I* and deprives itself of its freedom by turning itself into a thing. The unhappy consciousness lives in "*misery*" (*PS* § 230), "grief and longing" which is its "common birth-pang" (*PS* § 754). Even when the unhappy consciousness receives recognition from the other—its self—and makes its transition to reason, "its enjoyment remains pain"(*PS* § 230). For Hegel, spirit as self-consciousness ultimately bears "the infinite *pain* of the negation of its individual immediacy" (*EG* § 382), and in its profound unhappiness it is never able to become the *beyond*.

Unhappy consciousness may be said to be the way in which the self turns on itself when it demands too much of itself. The self is unhappy because there is a deep fissure inside its self, an internal split it cannot reconcile: it sees purity and eternity as belonging to itself, but it feels sullied and will die. The ideal of the pure, unchangeable, eternal universal essence is projected into the being of humankind, and that of God, which are external and beyond yet are hoped to be endowed with the solution of the self's internal dilemma. But the same problem arises with God: we cannot live up to the demands we have Him impose upon us. This is why Hegel says the unhappy consciousness is "the tragic fate of the certainty of the self that aims to be absolute" (*PS* § 752); it loses all essentiality and substance, and it lives in grief of not being able to live up to the desire to become God, for "God is dead." God is the projection of the human soul on its way toward reconciling itself with itself, and is but a stage in spirit's development. The Absolute cannot be conceived by means of picture-thinking, but only by immersion with pure thought itself. So unhappy consciousness must tarry with self-flagellation and live in torment of not being complete and whole, of not finding unity, of living in anxiety and despair over its yearning that is bound to *lack* and the "infinite pain" of not being able to reach its ideal, a neurotic compulsion.

Unhappy consciousness is marked by inner division and external frustration—it cannot escape sin. Here we may see how Freud's notion of the superego corresponds to spiritual despair. As a modified portion of the ego, the superego represents ideal perfection and moral condemnation: it is both virtuous and vicious—our internal judge that tries and defends. The superego is a developmental achievement that grows out of the internalization process based on the nature and qualities of our identifications (*SE*, 19, 28–39; 22, 60–65; 23, 146). Both Hegel and Freud contend that character is largely the result of the contents and values a person identifies with and internalizes from their social environment, whether this be social mores, laws, or the ethical life of the family and community. Identification may be said to be the single most important factor in the development of the superego (*SE*, 19, 28), and it is precisely this identification with an ideal that creates so much suffering for unhappy consciousness.

For Freud, identification is "the assimilation of one ego to another one, as a result of which the first ego behaves like the second in certain respects, imitates it and in a sense takes it up into itself" (*SE*, 22, 63). This process is not unlike the struggle for recognition whereby the self recovers its alienated shape in the ego of the other. We are forced to become self-conscious of ourselves when we confront another that stands in opposition to us. Yet through identification, we come to value the other and what the other represents to us, and this process leads to mutual recognition. Identification is based on an attachment to a particular object, person, or set of values and ideals, having its immediate existence in relation to the family, and more specifically one's parents, then later in its relation to the Absolute. In fact, Hegel recognizes the significance of identification and attachment by which spirit raises itself from its unconscious being to the ethical realm of actuality:

> [T]he universal self-conscious Spirit, becomes . . . united with its other extreme, its force and element, with *unconscious* Spirit. . . . [T]he divine law has

> its individuation—or the *unconscious* Spirit of the individual its real existence—in the woman, through whom . . . the unconscious Spirit rises out of its unreality into actual existence, out of a state in which it is unknowing and unconscious into the realm of conscious Spirit. (*PS* § 463)

It is through the mother and father that we learn to be self-conscious, to become our own master, and to value what is true, right, good, and just. It is largely through identification that conscience—the pure heart—is formed, raising spirit from the "underworld" to the "divine law."

Unhappy consciousness constitutes the bifurcation of the human soul into a part that sets standards for itself and requires perfection and another part that systematically fails to live up to such demands. The contradiction that ensues is devastating for psychic health: the self views itself as perfect (i.e., rational, eternal, etc.) and also as hopelessly imperfect, deficient, and finite—both saint and sinner. This problem repeats itself in religion: we think we are made in the image of God but we are inevitably fallen. Unhappy consciousness is mainly fueled by the superego: beset by the reality of an oppressive environment, spirit strives for the ideal, what it feels in its heart, and condemns itself for not being that ideal. The pursuit of the ego-ideal propels unhappy spirit toward reason and the ethical, political, aesthetic, and religious realizations of social order. This is why Hegel refers to the ethical as "The True Spirit" (*PS* § 444).

The superego, constituted through dependence on the family, is the psychological correlate of the Absolute. The Absolute signifies completion, totality, and perfection, and has no tolerance for failure to live up to these principles. This is why unhappy consciousness is besieged by judgment, guilt, hostility, and anguish: it is always at odds with itself—its own ideal. In its quest for perfection, spirit is truly neurotic, because it pursues the ideal with obsessive compulsive tenacity. Freud refers to the superego as the source of "moral anxiety" (*Gewissenangst*) (*SE*, 22, 62), a condition not unlike unhappy consciousness as the beautiful soul. In its contemplative morality, spirit becomes a "lost soul." "In this transparent purity of its moments, an unhappy, so-called 'beautiful soul', its light dies away within it, and it vanishes like a shapeless vapour that dissolves into thin air" (*PS* § 658). The beautiful soul is homeless and empty because it only thinks and judges, but does not act. Hegel tells us that unhappy spirit, while in its state of being lost, engages in a defensive retreat similar to that of stoic withdrawal: "[I]n order to preserve the purity of its heart, it flees from contact with the actual world" (*PS* § 658). While internally pure, the beautiful soul is impotent and hollow.

We may easily appreciate how Hegel's depiction of the throes of self-consciousness corresponds to Freud's notions of psychic conflict and pain. Like the ego, which fights to transcend the id, desire is sublated in recognition. The superego becomes the paragon for idealization, judgment, guilt, and punishment, just as unhappy spirit strives to overcome its internal division of purity and sin. Unhappy consciousness has the added onus of combating its cruel and unjust enslavement, which it must overcome in order to be truly free. Hence, spirit must sublate nature—its confinement to the natural soul, the austere conditions of an unequal society, the self-condemnation of its own inadequacy, and the lure of its own inclinations and passions that threaten to derail its pursuit of liberated self-articulated rational freedom. It is here that Freud's insight is most appropriate: "[W]e see [the] ego as a poor creature owing service to three masters and consequently menaced by three dangers: from the external world, from the libido of the id, and from the severity of the super-ego" (*SE*, 19, 56). It is no wonder that unhappy consciousness is plagued by anxiety.

The unhappy consciousness is *despair*, and in its lament it is acutely aware of its absence of unity that it can never surpass, but in its heart, wholeness remains its wish. When it projects its ideal into the reality of the beyond, it is at once aware that the reality of its ideal is only its projection and self-consciousness is thus but a transient contingent, mutable being. If despair is such a central feature to self-consciousness, one that perennially invades our psychic organization, then Hegel, like Freud, would contend that "we are *all* ill—that is, neurotic" (*SE*, 16, 358). Despair not only informs the condition for self-consciousness, but informs the precondition for madness. Jean Hyppolite has gone so far as to say that for Hegel, "the essence of man is to be mad,"[20] a theme Daniel Berthold-Bond examines with precision in *Hegel's Theory of Madness*. But Berthold-Bond and I ultimately disagree with this claim; there are important distinctions to be made between despair and madness. Yet the two symptoms share a fundamental commonality influenced by the ontology of desire, for even Hegel says that the desire for unity marshals great attempts that "constantly pass into madness" (*HP*, 3, 510). It becomes the topic of our next chapter to examine the parameters of psychopathology and the distinctions Hegel draws between madness and spiritual despair.

TOWARD THE ABNORMAL

What becomes of spirit when it can't effect its transition to reason, when it can't relinquish its quest for unchangeable individuality, when it can't let go of its being that has vanished—its nothingness? What is abnormal in unhappy consciousness is also what is normal, that is to say normative, namely, irrationality and psychic pain. Self-consciousness endures a poignant internal contradiction and suffering that cannot be overcome. The torment of division and alienation, the withdrawal from the world into the self, the obsessional fixation of the confused and dizzy refutation of reality, the self-sacrifice and denial—these are the shapes of the lost soul. When self-consciousness is unable to make its transition to reason, it remains fixated within the irrational, within the life of feeling, and is inclined to regress to the nostalgic recovery of its earlier lost unity, a withdrawal back into the interior of the soul. This becomes the domain of spiritual psychopathology. Spirit devoid of reason is an incomplete or diseased spirit, what Hegel sees as madness, even though madness has its own reasons.

Is it possible that the progressive path of natural consciousness toward unity and wholeness may be achieved by a circuitous regressive route? Spirit as soul emerges from its nocturnal immediacy, asleep within the womb of nature, its symbiotic union. After traversing a long and arduous battle for self-expression and determinate freedom, spirit breaks loose from the chains of nature and achieves spiritual liberation in pure thought and absolute knowing. But if it incurs a snag along the way, or the actual conditions of a bellicose environment are too oppressive, or if the yearnings in the feeling soul are too strong to escape its call because the suffering and the lack are too severe, spirit may wish to retreat back to that which it knows best, to the warmth of its original unity, the tranquility of sleep. This would mean that absolute knowing would have to be abridged, forsaken for a previous primordial knowing, the knowledge of being at one with itself once again. The withdrawal back into archaic universality within its undifferentiated beginning may be one way in which the deranged spirit comes to know peace. When the pain is too great and reality too restrictive and cruel, this may be one way spirit chooses to cope with its predicament, for in its hollow halls of torment and depression, spirit just wants to go to sleep.

If the division of the self in unhappy consciousness cannot be overcome, and if spirit seeks to achieve unity with the Absolute, with God, then perhaps the principle of *Aufhebung* and regression back to symbiosis are two bipolar ways of achieving this aim, one rooted in pathology, the other in health. Are we to understand world spirit as universal fellowship that seeks absolute unity in pure thinking, or is this merely a wish to return to the "oceanic feeling"[21] of symbiosis like a fetus in the peaceful sea of its mother's womb? The very nature of the need for progressive unification may also be dialectically opposed to destructive and regressive inclinations that derive from earlier primitive shapes of our psychic constitution we seek to act out or recover during conflict precipitated by opposition. If the desire for unification is a derivative of our original psychical ontology, then both progressive and regressive desires may be said to emanate from the same mental (symbiotic) configurations, which may further possibly serve the same aim. Both seek unity or peace of a different kind and in a different form: one through the attainment of higher integrated complexities, the other a wish to return to the warm blanket of its initial undifferentiated being—unity is nevertheless their goal. If the drive toward destruction—negativity and death—is responsible for both progress and regress, growth and decay, then one will advance while the other succumbs to the tyranny of its counterpart. Negativity and destruction influence the pursuit of the rational and the self-preservative drives in their quest for unification and mastery even if such unity and mastery are an illusion and retrograde autism confined to the unconscious soul. And so begins spirit's journey back into the abyss.

FIVE

ABNORMAL SPIRIT

In history as in nature, decay is the laboratory of life.

—*Marx*

PSYCHIC DECAY: this is the deviation of spirit, a decay it undergoes by its own hands. Decay, negation—the language of life, confined to its own laboratory as spirit educates itself to truth. The violence that permeates spirit in its historical truth is also the violence that inflicts great suffering upon spirit as it seeks to conquer opposition; and when it can't, it sinks back into the abyss, its original lost unity. Perhaps decay is not a deviation at all, but merely the instantiation of the negative, inverted inwardly, turned on the self, slipping away from the spiritual back into the life of nature, the malady of the sick soul.

What does it mean to be mad? If negativity underlies the diseased mind then perhaps we are all mad, for negativity is the ontology of spirit. But madness has a specific meaning for Hegel primarily associated with extreme forms of mental illness such as insanity and clinical depression. Yet there is an interconnected thread of negativity that conjoins spirit in both health and madness. Insofar that spirit suffers, such as in the despair of unhappy consciousness, we all are neurotic, that is, we are maimed by anxiety and pain. And this can lead to inversion and withdrawal into disordered thinking, to psychosis and melancholia. There is an aggressivity to madness, to the disordered mind. It underlies our being angry—mad, and also derangement, mania, frenzy, and the frantic confusion and agitation of the fool, who lacking restraint and reason in his folly, is no more rational than a rabid animal afflicted by the craze of an infection. These are the categories Hegel ascribes to abnormal *Geist*, what modern psychiatry would label as forms of thought disorder.

Hegel's views on abnormal psychology are confined mainly to the Additions in his Anthropology section of the *Encyclopaedia*. As a result, his treatment

159

of the domains of psychopathology is delimited, loosely organized, and at times consists of piecemeal associations to then current theories that were advanced by the rise of late-eighteenth-century medicine. By today's standards, his typology of mental illness appears rather simplistic. Daniel Berthold-Bond has greatly advanced our understanding of Hegel's theory of abnormal psychology and provides systematic rigor to what remains otherwise dissociated from mainstream Hegel scholarship. I do not wish to duplicate his important work here, but rather to show how Hegel's notion of the unconscious abyss is as responsible for mental disease as it is for the normal operations of mind.

THE ONTOLOGY OF MADNESS

Hegel's theory of psychopathology does not rest upon pure empirical observation, the categorization of symptoms or the external features of illness, nor does it rely upon clinical case studies, but rather on the conceptual, theoretical, and philosophical discernment of the underlying processes and meanings that constitute the diseased mind. However, Hegel is very clear that his speculative outlook is not at odds with empiricism, instead, "experience" becomes the standpoint of "*speculative thinking*" (*EL* §§ 7–9). In the *Philosophy of Nature*, he also states: "Not only must philosophy be in agreement with our empirical knowledge of Nature, but the *origin* and *formation* of the Philosophy of Nature presupposes and is conditioned by empirical . . . science" (*PN* § 246). Just as Freud is concerned with the "sense of symptoms" (*SE*, 16, 257) that modern psychiatry had ignored in its preoccupation with labeling clinical phenomena, Hegel is concerned with the inner meaning and ontology of madness grounded in the speculative or rational standpoint that seeks out deeper explanations of disease.

A philosophical exploration of madness and its parameters is essentially an ontological project. Rather than offer a litany of clinical signs, symptoms, and behavioral traits or patterns that belong to the appearance of illness, Hegel addresses "the Concept of derangement in general."

> The *particular kinds* of derangement are usually distinguished in accordance with the *manifestations* of this illness rather than an *inner* determinateness, but this is inadequate to philosophical consideration. We have to recognize that even derangement *differentiates itself internally* in a *necessary* and therefore rational manner. (*EG* § 408, *Zusatz*)

Hegel recognizes that in order to understand the phenomena of illness, we must be able to appreciate its internal ontology or structure. This is very akin to Freud's focus on the unconscious etiology and inner dynamics of psychic conflict. Because of all the multiplicity, varied courses, and divergent appearances of mental disorders, Hegel advices us to focus our attention upon the "wholly *universal differences of form* which emerge in derangement." For Hegel, the abnormal mind is the *return*—a repetition—of its previous shape, the immediacy of the formal undifferentiated feeling ensconced in the soul. Thus, the deranged mind "has already been displayed as *spirit which is confined*, spirit which has *lapsed into itself*" (*EG* § 408, *Zusatz*).

For Hegel, the processes of madness may be said to be (1) the result of a fixation in the feeling soul leading to truncated ego development, what psychoanalytic object relations theorists would label as a form of developmental arrest, or (2) the result of a regression back to the interiority of the feeling soul once ego differentiation has been achieved. The feeling soul is the subject's "sentient totality" that remains the "darkness of spirit" confined within a constricted inner world "into which the development of the soul may relapse after having advanced to the determination of consciousness and understanding" (*EG* § 404).

The "darkness" that Hegel speaks of is the unity the soul has with its natural corporeality, which it takes as its object, not external to itself, but rather its own substance as subject that remains "enclosed" within its own "particular world." All determinations for the soul are "entirely formal," lacking in content or understanding. In the feeling soul, the dark spirit is a contradiction of both universality and individuality. "It is the incongruity involved in the truer existing in a subordinate and more abstract form of spirit which constitutes illness [*Krankheit*]" (*EG* § 404). Hegel explains that in order to understand mental (spiritual) illness, one first has to consider the "abstract formations of the soul," and only through such consideration can the diseased mind be explained. Here Hegel is not appealing to clinical evidence of the symptomatology that accompanies the deranged mind, but rather is interested in understanding the underlying ontology that becomes the condition for illness.

Hegel first looks at the feeling soul in its immediacy as the relationship with the mother merged in her womb. Hegel considers this relationship to be neither exclusively corporeal nor spiritual, but rather "psychic" (*psychisch*), the "undisturbed" symbiosis the soul has with its natural life. When Hegel refers to this original symbiosis—the "unity of the soul" that is undisturbed and undivided, he is referring to the inviolate undifferentiated oneness the soul has with itself (*EG* § 405): there is no division between inner and outer, self and other. We may say that this state of unity is the primordial condition and experience of *peace*, the very state the soul wishes to reclaim when burdened and tormented by the chaos of negativity whether generated from within itself, administered from a hostile external reality, or due to the interaction of both.

Hegel sees the mother as the child's "genius," which is the entire totality of determinate being, "selfhood," "life and character," and concrete subjectivity. As a psychic relationship, the feeling soul absorbs all that which the mother endures, including "violent dispositional disturbances and injuries etc. experienced by the mother . . . within which the child assumes its predisposition to illness, as well as its further endowments in respect of bodily shape, temper, character, talent, idiosyncrasies etc." (*EG* § 405). Here Hegel clearly states that the child acquires certain predispositions toward personality and adjustment including illness during "conception," biologically as well as psychologically. Whatever the mother experiences during her pregnancy, for instance, anxiety, physical discomfort, hormonal, bodily, and emotional flux, etc., the unborn child will absorb it as if it were its own. Within this immediate being of feeling lies what is endowed in an "unconscious" manner as well as everything that comprises one's "principles" and character, which is maintained through habit. It is also in the feeling soul where Hegel situates the law of the "heart or disposition." The unconscious feeling soul is the seat of subjective spirit and contains within it the essence of humankind including the germ of psychopathology.

The life of feeling is where spirit "may relapse as into a state of illness" (*EG* § 405, *Zusatz*), because it is in feeling that subjective spirit is first constituted, its original home. And whether this home be the oceanic feeling within the mother's womb, the instinctual attachment and dependency the infant has on her warmth, love, and nurturance—what Hegel calls "the embodiment of the mother's inner affections"—or the home of childhood that is imbued with the idealized relations of being cared for and protected by its omnipotent parental imagos, when spirit is confused, persecuted, or in pain, it evokes the feelings it once knew and would like to re-gather and re-experience in its affliction, a soothing wish. Hegel believes the soul of the unborn child is fused with the soul of the mother as an "undivided union," one an actual being-for-self of a self, while the other is only a formal being-for-self in the process of becoming self. Here there is no division or mediation for the soul of the fetus; it is enveloped within a pure unity offering no resistance to an opposition.

Hegel refers to the feeling of totality within the soul and its relationship to this totality as "magical." He not only speaks of this in relation to the fetus within the mother's womb, but also in dreaming and in relation to the individual's genius as a felt self-totality. The internal self-relation of feeling totality, such as in the undifferentiated determinateness of the unborn child, or in dreaming where one's "*entirety*" is felt, is what "I am *inwardly*" (*EG* § 405, *Zusatz*). The magical power of the felt totality of one's inwardness is what Hegel attributes to the uniqueness of character that determines a person's "actions" and "*destiny*." In the feeling soul there is both a duality and an indivisibility, whether this be in the mother-fetus dyad that is one, in the world of dreams where presentations are acquired passively despite subjective spirit's self-relation, or in the soul's genius as the unity of its previous shapes.

For Hegel, the formal, empty and undifferentiated unity of the feeling soul is an ontological condition of madness: "As form . . . the life of feeling is a disease" (*EG* § 406). The mind fixed in the soul's formalness is sequestered in a dark universality, contentless, abandoned to an empty immediacy. In normal development, the soul moves beyond this empty immediacy, but in abnormality it is either developmentally retarded, as in autism or psychosis, or it slips back to its archaic existence in these primitive feeling states from the more advanced stages of spirit's progression. This latter appearance is the most common path of illness. The logical movement of the dialectic is suspended in a fixation and/or regression to the form of feeling where it becomes paralyzed, not in the sense that it is totally immobile, but checked or limited, oscillating between empty and disturbing presentations.

In sickness, there is a repetition of the formal immediacy of feeling as a self-enslaved preoccupation with the soul's own inner sensations and thoughts that do not venture beyond its interiority. The dialectic becomes suspended; it no longer drives to surpass or sublate itself, only to retreat into the abyss of the distortions of imagination and fantasy, recycling the contents of its simple self-relation. The withdrawal back into feeling may be said to be spirit's need to re-capture the original immediacy the soul has with its self-enclosed unity. When confronted by the strain of negation and mediation, spirit seeks a nostalgic re-union with its previous lost shape. We may speculate that this is spirit's feeble and ineffectual way of coping with its suffering as the result of a failed adaptation to reality. By retreating into the bowels of its interior life, it gains some illusory de-gree of mastery over its struggles and anguish, a mastery it cannot obtain in its external relations.

In unconscious unity with feeling, the soul may shelter itself from the in-cubus of reality and reproduce a state of comfort it once knew. This is the most primitive level of spirit's development, one it can control by means of withdrawal and submersion into undifferentiation. Yet this regressive move is a form of nega-tion, a denial of externality, an expression of death. Indeed, it is a self-destructive maneuver oriented back toward spiritual stagnation, to the shell of an autistic pri-mary narcissism. This renunciation of difference and externality is an amplification of the milder forms of stoicism and skepticism to a complete isolation and denial of opposition. Yet this very act of renunciation is itself a negation, the destruction of the new for the security of the old. When spirit is threatened and it cannot cope with contingency, multiplicity, and change, it relapses back to simplicity, uni-versality, and the illusory consistency it had previously surpassed.

When Hegel focuses on the abstract formation of the soul as a nocturnal unity, he is concerned with explicating the meaning of illness by locating the ab-stract form of feeling responsible for abnormal spirit's malaise. By isolating the formal condition of feeling within the soul, he is further able to situate the struc-tural condition or predisposition toward disease. This is the abstract form or primitive state of the "darkness of spirit" that conditions us all to illness as well as health, and is a natural and necessary stage in subjective spirit's development. Thus, for Hegel, the potential for psychopathology is grounded in the abyss. The unconscious becomes the locus of spirit's potential for adjustment and deteriora-tion that spans the spectrum from its most heightened and exalted achievements to its most regressed and decomposed forms.

But the form of feeling is not the only ontological ground for psy-chopathology to arise. The ontology of madness is also rooted in the destruc-tive character of negation. Negativity is as much the essence of spiritual despair and regression as it is the positive force behind the dialectical thrust of spirit's sublation. In negativity lies the ontological duality of spirit's nature. Negation serves a dual function for spirit oriented toward transcendence and decay. This is why we all have within our constitutions the inherent capacity for madness even if we never succumb to the regressive pull of spiritual darkness. In fact, the regression back to feeling is itself the expression of the negative, a negation of externality through denial, retreat, isolation, and atrophy. But the secluded soul is deluding itself into thinking it is protected and safe in the interiority of the pit as it was in the womb, in its undifferentiated beginning. This nightlike unity is in fact a self-imprisoning tomb, the very tomb spirit rouses itself from in the first place because of the restless negativity—the primeval chaos it experiences being confined to its corporiety.

The formal abstract unity of the feeling soul is like a psychotic universe marked by the persecution of void, haunting spirit with the fear of suffocating by the baptism of being immersed in a black hole, the blackness of nothingness. But it is precisely in that nothingness, in that undifferentiated state of oneness, that spirit feels some tranquility, even if only for a moment. Perhaps this is what spirit wishes to repossess when the struggle for absolute knowing appears unattainable. Negativity, destruction, and death are spirit's proper essence, an essence also responsible for the elevation of spirit, the positive significance of the negative.

The ontology of madness, or what Berthold-Bond calls the "*logic of the interior*,"[1] is anchored in the processes of negation and the abstract formation of the feeling soul, itself the generated consequence of negation. The logic of interiority is particularly evident in the stage of the immediacy of the feeling soul where it is submerged in the abstract universality of its sentient nature. To be sure, the soul must pass over into the ego of consciousness from its self-enclosed world or else face a perpetual absence of the content that only external consciousness can provide. If the soul were to remain confined to its feeling immediacy, then the mediated dynamics constituting the logical operations of spirit would be stymied and encrusted in a blind and banal dark universe. This would correspond to spiritual autism, mental retardation, organicity, or a psychotic symbiosis. Subjective spirit indeed surpasses its feeling immediacy and in doing so becomes ego through mediated negation. But spirit's reversal back to its primordial immediacy is what constitutes the inverted or regressive logic of the dialectic. Rather than push forward, it slides backward into the pit, evacuating its will toward progression, instead succumbing to the lure of nature, an exodus from the spiritual.

THE PHENOMENOLOGY OF SUFFERING

Hegel's interest in abnormal psychology was not only theoretical but personal. Hegel himself struggled with bouts of depression,[2] and his sister Christiane and his university friend Friedrich Hölderlin both became mentally ill. Christiane fell ill to a nervous disability that forced her to retire as a governess as early as 1814,[3] after which time Hegel invited her to move into his home "permanently" to recover.[4] Her condition worsened and she was institutionalized after being diagnosed with hysteria (*Hysterie*). She was treated by Schelling's brother

Karl, a Romantic physician enthusiastic about animal magnetism, for more than ten years (1822–1832) after she spent a year in the Zwiefalten asylum.[5] Christiane eventually committed suicide one year after Hegel's death.[6]

Furthermore, the poet Friedrich Hölderlin (1770–1843), Hegel's friend since they were students together at Tübingen, suffered a nervous breakdown, later diagnosed as severe "frenzy" (*Wahnsinn*), the modern equivalent of schizophrenia,[7] and was institutionalized for the rest of his life.[8] Hegel was no stranger to personal tragedy; he had an intimate relationship with pain, which he repeatedly expressed in private conversations and correspondences.[9] Alan Olson has even professed that Hegel's entire treatment of madness in the *Encyclopaedia* is a "sublated" attempt to come to terms with his friend's illness,[10] his own form of therapy.

Daniel Berthold-Bond suggests that Hegel's formal (ontological) philosophical treatment of madness is vastly different from the intimacy or lived (phenomenological) experience of his personal suffering, and that his need to distinguish the abstract forms of derangement from the existential experience of suffering is philosophically warranted. He says, "The absolutely personal and inherently intimate encounter with life's sorrows can never in principle be 'logicized' or philosophically comprehended."[11] Berthold-Bond's point is that abstract or formal philosophical reflection can never adequately capture the pain and horror of the lived experience of suffering; how it appears and is felt by each individual cannot be reduced to the impersonal hands of logic despite its own inherent logic or reasoning. Hegel's own view on this, however, would stress that the immediacy of this experience is not its truth, and its truth is far more important than its immediacy. But all creatures suffer; we are ultimately alone in our pain: it cannot be compared to any other's. While the phenomenology of despair and anguish may resist conforming to a purely philosophical discourse, and indeed may even resist conforming to a discourse at all, Hegel is concerned with specifying the ontological conditions of madness that make the existential reality of psychic pain possible. Philosophic order may miss the experience of suffering, but it does not preclude understanding its formal conditions; in fact, it is essential for such understanding.

THE PSYCHOTIC CORE

Hegel's taxonomy of mental illness is treated almost entirely in his sections on the feeling soul, beginning with magnetic somnambulism (*magnetische Somnambulismus*) in § 406 elicited mainly by animal magnetism, and advancing to several forms of derangement (*Verrücktheit*) in § 408.

In magnetic somnambulism, consciousness is "self-possessed" and relates to the concrete content of itself without mediation. Hegel refers to the hypnotic states of animal magnetism as a primary example. In somnambulism, the subject is immersed in a withdrawn, internally determined world of constricted particular interests and truncated relationships. In this condition, spirit is not free in its thinking and willing, but rather enveloped in the form of feeling which "constitutes the

surrender of the individual's existence as a self-communing spirituality" (*EG* §
406). Hegel mentions forms of sleep disturbance, what clinical psychology refers
to as parasomnia,[12] as well as catalepsy and "other diseases incident to the development of the woman." Here Hegel is implying the propensity toward hysteria
often associated with female development by the modern psychiatry of his day, a
diagnosis further attributed to his sister's illness. Catalepsy and its accompanying
symptoms such as muscular rigidity, lack of awareness of one's environment, and
lack of response to external stimuli, may be attributed to forms of sleep disturbance as well as dissociative disorders such as psychogenetic fugue, and is often
associated with forms of epilepsy, hysteria, and schizophrenia.

For Hegel, consciousness is withdrawn inwardly into a form of solipsism,
what he refers to as a "monad" "degraded" to the state of feeling (*EG* § 406).
Hegel says that in this withdrawal of consciousness to self-enclosed feeling, external reality is suspended for the life of internality because consciousness no
longer "takes its content to be an external objectivity." This is a form of thought
disorder, a regression to the psychic organization of its original self-absorbed
unity. Although the feeling soul inwardly knows its actuality and intuits its totality as genius, it is limited to the deficient world of not understanding the con-
jointness of its contents. Hegel refers to this self-intuiting as a "clairvoyance":
the soul knows its undivided substantiality, yet it lacks knowledge of how its
contents are connected. Hegel explains: "[S]ince its turbid nature precludes the
contents being displayed as an understandable connectedness, this clairvoyance is
exposed to all the contingency incident to feeling, imagining etc., not to mention the alien [*fremde*] presentations which intrude upon its vision" (*EG* § 406).
There is a hallucinatory quality to the meaning of this last sentence: the murky
internality of the soul does not possess the "cognition of universal validity" and
is apt to imagine things it mistakes for reality generated from the abyss, trapped
in the domain of feeling, bombarded with foreign presentations that encroach
upon its walled-in shell. This is why Hegel says clairvoyants who claim to have
extrasensory powers of perception, visions, or prophecies have no capacity to
determine whether they "see correctly [from what] preponderates over their
self-deception."

Withdrawal into the form of feeling becomes the central criterion for all
forms of mental illness for Hegel. Hegel equates the life of feeling to an infantile state of passivity like "the child in the womb." This is why the diseased mind
is prone to magnetism and it further explains why the magnetized subject absorbs and internalizes the intuitions, sensations, and presentations of the other
"as if they were its own." There is no ability to discern or differentiate self from
other. In feeling lies the recovered symbiosis, the undifferentiated oneness between subject and object, like the soul in its natural immediacy. When consciousness retreats to feeling, ego boundaries deteriorate between inner and
outer reality; "[I]t is [thus] uncertain which sensations or predictions are derived,
intuited and brought to knowledge from his own inwardness, and which from
the presenting of the person with whom he stands in relation. This uncertainty

can give rise to various delusions [*Täuschungen*]" (*EG* § 406). A delusion—a fixed and inflexible conviction contrary to the objective evidence against it—is the refusal of mediating consciousness to remain connected to the real world, which has been abandoned (even if temporarily) for the subjective immediacy of feeling.

There is a fluidity of ego boundaries when an individual is in a hypnotic state of animal magnetism, or what Hegel also equates with mesmerism, solarism, or tellurism. In modern language, Hegel is referring to the dissociability of the psyche. In this state, the ego of the magnetized subject becomes merged with the ego of the magnetizer who stands in reciprocal relation. Hegel views the magnetic state as an illness because the ego alienates itself from its own body and becomes impotent at the hands of an "*alien* power." One is reminded of the stage hypnotist who can induce subjects to squat, walk around, flap their arms, and quack like a duck. Hegel believes "the essence of disease *in general* has to be posited as residing in the dividing off of a particular system from the general physiological life of the organism" (*EG* § 406, *Zusatz*). Hegel further tells us, in magnetism, there is a "*breach*" between the soul and feeling from the life of natural waking consciousness and its mediated understanding. Because both functions are common to everyone, Hegel acknowledges that "it is *possible* for this breach to occur in even the healthiest of people." When the ego divides itself off from understanding consciousness and lapses into the feeling soul, it is unable to disengage from the alien power that controls it and thus loses its freedom. But while Hegel admits that it is possible for healthy individuals to fall into disease, he attributes this to a "*particular* endowment" that is "predisposed."

Hegel tells us that the general form of disease in feeling is being lost in the unity itself, where all particularities of feeling have "disappeared." Sensation becomes inverted: the diseased mind becomes "devoid of the differences between subjective and objective, an understanding personality and an external world, and of the . . . finite relationships between them" (*EG* § 406). This assertion meets the generic definition of psychosis: ego boundaries between the self and environment are suspended, one's sense of self is non-apparent, particularity is lost in universality, and the normal ego operations of mediation, judgment, the linking of cause and effect, and synthesis are nullified. But in somnambulism and in the array of hypnotic trances or dissociative states that fall within this class of disorder, there is a regression and fixation to the circumscribed unity of the feeling soul. For Hegel, this remains the abstract form or model of mental illness, even though in somnambulism and its variations it may constitute only brief or transient breaks with reality.

Recall the "magical" relationship the soul has in its immediacy with the formal subjectivity of life. Despite the fact that objective reality is not yet achieved, such as in the case of the soul's fetal status and its relation to its genius, or when it lapses from objectivity to formal subjectivity, such as in dreaming, Hegel nevertheless calls this subjectivity "*real*" insofar as the soul attains a "*twofold*" existence. The first is with the soul's unmediated relationship with its individual, substantial actuality, and the second is with its mediated connectedness to the objective world. But in disease, the soul keeps these two aspects separate and mutually independent: "[D]isease occurs in the *life of the soul* when the merely *soul-like* aspect of the organism appropriates the function of *spiritual* consciousness by freeing itself from it. Spirit then fails to remain in control of itself" (*EG* § 406, *Zusatz*). By reverting back to nature, it merges once again with substantial subjectivity at the expense of abnegating its spiritual elements. The universality it sinks into is thus a lowly and underdeveloped unity of corporiety rather than the objective and freely articulated universality of spirit's relation to the actual world. What is only "soul-like tears itself away from spirit." In feeling, the soul becomes a divided self, a double personality, itself fixated in one element of its doubleness, namely, its corporeity; "and since it is divided within itself, itself becomes diseased" (*EG* § 406, *Zusatz*).

Here we may observe the pathological dimensions of the splitting of the ego. While the ego of consciousness has attained for itself a relationship to the external world through splitting and mediation, in pathology an inversion occurs and the ego retreats to its prior primitive shape, which forsakes its ties to the objective for the secure seclusion of its original subjective immediacy. The splitting or dividedness within the soul itself that becomes detached from objectivity and reattached to subjectivity is a defensive maneuver of spirit. Earlier we have seen how splitting is a normative and progressive process with each sublated shape constituting the ever-increasing internalized complexity and expansive growth of the ego. But the regressive fixation in feeling is just its opposite: there is an undoing marked by reversal, inversion, and decompensation as though spirit were unraveling itself. In feeling, there is a withdrawal back to unconscious spirit, its prenatal life, the presumed motive or telos being to recover its lost unity.

Again we are confronted with that element of spirit that resists itself, its own process of becoming, its higher integration into the dialectic. The reversal back to the soul is what "tears" spirit away from itself, from its sublated thrust to its dark universality. In these moments of division, fixated within its onesidedness, spirit turns on itself—indeed, it turns into itself, into a bleak inwardness. This is itself a form of aggressiveness, a negation of negation into unity, simple immediacy, and indivisibility that is itself divided. This is the inwardness of the unconscious, a complete submersion into the abyss of universality where all particularity is lost. Recall that Hegel is not necessarily concerned with describing all the possible manifestations of mental illness, but rather with accounting for the condition that is common to all forms of disease, which he locates in this "division" of the soul into feeling universality devoid of its connection to objective externality. "[N]early every disease can progress to the point of this division" (*EG* § 406, *Zusatz*). What is philosophically important to Hegel is to "establish the *principal forms* of the *universal* which in various ways shapes itself within them." Psychopathology is a closure of spirit, the simple self entombed in the casket of its own black underground, its own self-burial.

The separation of what is soul-like from objective consciousness is the form that underlies all types of illness, what we may refer to as a *psychotic core*; but it is also the very bosom of our being: "The soul is *all-pervasive* . . . it has to be grasped as the truth, the ideality of *all material being*, as the *wholly universal*" (*EG* § 406, *Zusatz*). This is why Hegel assigns all the attributes of character, ethics, disposition, and religiosity to the soul; he also sees conflict there, which is maintained in an unconscious manner and is not entirely accessible to consciousness. Hegel remarkably broaches the issue of amnesia associated with hysterical repression when he says, "[T]here are states in which the soul is aware of a content it has long since *forgotten* [*vergessen*], and which when awake it is no longer able to recall consciously. This occurs in the case of various illnesses" (*EG* § 406, *Zusatz*). He continues to describe this process as the soul's secret unconscious knowledge of itself, distinct from understanding and mediated consciousness, which is deposited into "the abyss [*Schacht*] of our inner being" which we have "no power over" nor are "in possession of. . . . Recollections which have gone to sleep in our inner being, often come forth during illness."[13]

Withdrawal, regression, and fixation to the monadic, symbiotic state of undifferentiated feeling constitutes the psychotic core of unconscious spirit. As a self-enclosed autism, the feeling soul is dissociated from understanding consciousness and objective external reality, which it has forsaken for the self-certainty of its black universe. In fact, Hegel sees derangement as a necessary stage in the development of spirit that the feeling soul must pass over on its ascendance toward ego mastery and control (*EG* § 408, *Zusatz*). The division within the soul that excludes externality constitutes the loss of spiritual freedom and control. When enslaved in the night of the mind—the heart of darkness—spirit is a psychotic organization that knows no negation, no boundaries between inner and outer, only the nothingness of its unitary, empty immediate being. Lost in the pervasive universality of the abyss, the feeling soul lives an isolated and constricted existence. Therefore, the undifferentiated unity of the simple universality of feeling becomes the template that defines the general form of psychopathology in all its manifestations.

THE SICK SOUL

Hegel addresses many forms of derangement (*Verrücktheit*) including (1) imbecility or idiocy (*Blödsinn*), (2) absent-mindedness (*Zerstreutheit*), (3) desipience or the rambling mind (*die Faselei*), (4) folly (*Narrheit*) and its forms of (5) world-weariness (*Lebensüberdruß*) and (6) melancholia (*Melancholie*), and finally (7) madness or insanity proper (*Tollheit oder der Wahnsinn*). In almost all of these categories of mental illness that Hegel addresses, he refers to some form of thought disorder or detachment from objective external reality and the abandonment of the rationally motivated sublation of spirit. This is what constitutes the primary distinction between the neurotic anatomy of spirit and the psychotic disposition that defines madness. In this respect, we are not all mad as

Hyppolite informs us despite the fact that the normal developmental progression of spirit must first pass through a psychotic organization as feeling soul. The neurotic constitution that is inherently present in spirit, such as in the forms of anxiety, despair, and existential suffering, and having the freedom to disclose itself in many malleable forms of expression, is to be distinguished from madness by its constant relation to external reality, even if such relation is transmuted through the intellect or fantasy. In stoicism and skepticism, for example, even though there is a withdrawal into the interior and a denial of reality, the slave still relates to the world and works the land. The deranged mind, however, constricted to the mode of feeling, loses its grip on reason as ego functions erode due to its fixation on inwardness. It is the ego's breach with external reality that constitutes madness.

We may further state that neurosis is the proper form of spiritual maturity. Spirit is an obsessive-compulsive: it is obsessively and addictively engaged in the search for truth, meaning, and completion. It is so committed to achieving wholeness, unity, pure self-actualization—the Absolute—that it pursues this goal with absolute intolerance for failure. An insatiable striving—an *ought*—is intolerable to spirit: it must possess truth, achieve self-satisfaction, and turn the ought into an *is*. Spirit is sated only in absolute knowing. Absolute Spirit, where Logic gains its fullest appreciation of the Idea, is the embodiment of the *Ideal*. The activity of spirit is the obsessional pursuit of perfection, which it achieves only after great suffering and painstaking dialectical labor. Spirit's logical attainment of the Idea signifies such perfection because not only does spirit gain pure understanding of itself and all reality, but the concept of the Idea is the unity of thought and actuality. The IDEA is not merely conceptual abstract thought, but is thought conjoined with the actual. For example, for spirit to have a concept of God is not enough; to conceive of God in absolute knowing is to become aware of God's actuality in pure thinking. Spirit not only seeks the Ideal, it becomes the Ideal.

When spirit suffers from a sick soul, the rational pursuit of the Ideal becomes abandoned for the infantile universe of feeling. Reason no longer obsesses to sublate itself, but rather becomes perverted. While the rational structures of spirit are imbued in all forms of pathology, its motives, aims, and rationale are distracted from its progressive path and distorted in its regressive content and form. It is spirit's disavowal of understanding consciousness that initiates its journey back into the abyss of its undifferentiated universality: this constitutes derangement.

Hegel refers to derangement as a "psychic disease" fixated in its "earthiness," a form of primary narcissism "since the heart in its immediacy is natural and selfish" (*EG* § 408). When the deranged mind retreats from understanding consciousness, it is "in a state of distraction and distress . . . the contradiction of reason." While Hegel states that derangement is a necessary progression of the feeling soul toward reason, he does not mean that every soul has to experience such extreme mental disruptions (*EG* § 408, *Zusatz*). But what is a matter of formal necessity is our self-contradictory nature, which opposes objectivity to a "purely *formal, empty, abstract* subjectivity."

> In this *onesided* state, it assumes itself to be a *true unity of* what is *subjective* and what is *objective*, so that in derangement the unity and separation of the two sides . . . is still *incomplete*. This unity and separation only achieves completeness of form in *rational* consciousness which is *actually objective*. (*EG* § 408, *Zusatz*)

In madness, the sick soul is unable to set itself over against its subjective substantial nature as an objective actuality. Hegel equates mental illness to a "waking dream" "spellbound" to a particular subjective presentation lacking unity with objective consciousness. This is particularly evident in dissociative disorders or dissociative phenomena such as somnambulism where there are "*two personalities* . . . appearing as a *dual state*." But in derangement proper, the dual personalities are converged into one negative state.

In derangement proper, the power of negativity becomes fixated in a retrograde arrested position. Negation no longer serves a positive function in the greater scheme of dialectical progression; any positivity belongs solely to the defensive functions derangement may serve. "The deranged subject is therefore *with itself in the negative* . . . [and] does not overcome this negative" (*EG* § 408, *Zusatz*). This type of negativity is differentiated from the general type of negativity encountered by the soul. The central difference in derangement is the abandonment of "the pursuit of a rational purpose." The deranged mind does not pursue or understand the "great *connectedness*" of subjectivity and objectivity; instead, it remains fastened to subjective presentations and "*unfulfillable*" "wishes" (*Wünsche*) that are at variance with actuality. While this can occur in normal consciousness, the difference lies in the distorted belief that what is subjectively present is objectively actual despite the contradictory evidence that refutes it: this constitutes thought disorder.

Hegel remarkably describes a diagnostic technique that later became a common component to psychiatric evaluation known as the Mental Status Exam, utilized to assess whether an individual meets the criterion for thought disorder. He states:

> [W]hen someone speaks in a deranged manner, one should always begin by reminding him *of his overall situation*, his *concrete actuality*. If, when he is brought to consider and to be aware of this objective context, he still fails to relinquish his false presentation, there can be no doubt that he is in a state of derangement. (*EG* § 408, *Zusatz*)

This constitutes a negation or denial of objective reality for the psychical reality of the interior. In derangement, what is objectively external cannot be recognized as such. Here we can say that reality has been remolded and designed to fit the fantasy organizations that preoccupy one's subjective presentations. Freud also tells us that psychosis is the "*disturbance in the relations between the ego and the external world.*"[14] For Freud, neurosis and psychosis are the result of the ego's inability to function due to the pressures exerted upon it from its "various ruling agencies." For Hegel, the abyss rules the subjective presentations that dominate the mad mind; the ego of consciousness is withdrawn back into the imaginative center of fantasy, which it reconstructs as its concrete reality.

In another paper, Freud reinforces Hegel's point that withdrawal into subjectivity is the mark of a loss of reality: "[P]sychosis . . . [is] in service of the id, [it] withdraws from a piece of reality . . . it actually signifies a flight from real life."[15] Because of the demands placed on the ego by the external world and its own internal self-conflict imposed by the abyss, the sick soul disavows and creates a new reality. Freud also states that once the ego flees from reality, it is succeeded by "an active phase of remodelling . . . psychosis disavows [reality] and tries to replace it" (*SE*, 19, 185). One contemporary psychoanalytic understanding of psychosis is that it is an unconscious projection in response to annihilation panic: the assailed ego attempts to impose some form of organization on a chaotic, persecutory, and disjointed experiential world.[16] Despite the fact that delusions and hallucinations are by definition disordered modes of thought that contradict objective reality, they are at least some form of order superimposed on a frighteningly ominous inner fragmentation that besieges the integrity of the ego. As Hegel says, "[C]onsciousness is therefore not truly with itself, but remains engrossed in the negation of the ego" (*EG* § 408, *Zusatz*). In Hegel's portrait of derangement, as in Freud's notion of psychosis, there is an absolute separation of the subjective from the objective.

In madness, there is a "*fixation* upon a particular feeling" which confines the soul to the stage of its immediate unmediated *being*, developmentally stagnated from the dialectical thrust of becoming. In all forms of derangement, Hegel locates two primary aspects of spirit's self-immersion as being-*in*-self, namely, (1) universality or the indeterminate vacuity of content as an abstract formalism, and (2) the determinate fixated subjective particularity that is given delusional objectivity. When the deranged soul is confined to its self-contradictory nature, we may say that, even in the secluded chambers of its simple unity, the abyss is unhappy.

UNHAPPY UNCONSCIOUSNESS

Absolute Spirit is destined to be the all-encompassing, self-articulated development of pure reason as absolute self-consciousness. It is when spirit achieves its fruition as absolute knowing that its telos is satisfied, the fulfillment of self-actualization. But when spirit is confined to its dark interior and mistakes the simple universal for the absolute universal, we may say that spirit suffers. It suffers from its own ignorance, its isolation, its loneliness; it is bound to unconsciousness not capable of effecting its exalted transition to comprehensive understanding. Imprisoned in night—the pit of its own indeterminateness—spirit is circumscribed by its simple self-certainty. In its fixed universality, spirit only knows its immediacy, not the complex integration of all its moments. Inhabiting the life of feeling, spirit shuts itself off from its arduous labor for truth, where the satisfaction of attaining the Concept is foreclosed, condemned to lack, darkness, and persecutory negation. What does it mean for the abyss to be unhappy? We must assume that happiness is part of the very constitution of spiritual self-satisfaction, the result of overcoming the obstacles inherent in the process of self-consciousness. While Hegel distinguishes between material happiness, which are blank pages in the world's history, and satisfaction as a knowing totality, we may say that satisfaction entails happiness but it is not necessarily the case the other way around. Happiness is often bound to the moment, its duration limited, while satisfaction encompasses a holistic process. Absolute knowing, by definition, includes knowing happiness, and for Hegel, knowing is the unification of the Concept with its actuality, therefore Absolute Spirit not only knows happiness, it is satisfied in its knowing. But unconscious spirit endures another fate. Even if unconscious spirit is able to construct a protective shell that insulates it from the terrors of the external, and even if it is able to temporarily retreat into the bliss of fantasy, we may still say that spirit is unhappy, for it is not complete. When constricted to unconsciousness, spirit is not free, but rather enslaved by corporeality.

Constricted to nature, regressed in feeling, spirit lives in a restless psychotic torment marked by perpetual absence and conflictual aggressivity. The simple form of universality encroaches upon spirit's satisfaction, constricting it to contingent particularity that lacks the potency of objective thought. Here spirit is condemned to one-sided anguish. When a deranged person's purely subjective presentation is forced to confront objective consciousness, there is a fracture in the illusory equilibrium of inwardness. The soul encounters the "sharpness" of the opposition between the inner and the outer, the subjective and the objective, and thus "acquires the uneasy feeling of being self-contradictory" (*EG* § 408, *Zusatz*), which it desperately strives to overcome by restoring its concrete self-identity.

Hegel considers three main forms of derangement with several subcategories characterizing the sick soul: (1) imbecility (*Blödsinn*), (2) folly (*Narrheit*), and (3) madness or insanity proper (*Tollheit oder der Wahnsinn*). In imbecility or idiocy, there is a complete state of self-absorption often accompanied by natural physical deformities; it is what Hegel refers to as "cretinism." Here Hegel speaks of the cretin as having a "closed soul," often the result of a genetic condition that is incurable. From today's account, we may refer to this condition as a pervasive developmental disorder such as mental retardation, organic brain syndrome, or autism such as those associated with Down's syndrome. But Hegel also attributes idiocy to factors possibly brought on by the individual himself, such as the consequence of "frenzy," "epilepsy," or "debauchery." He further points to catatonic conditions where there is a complete suspension of bodily and spiritual activity, such as those found in severe forms of schizophrenia. While Hegel draws on Pinel for support, he is conscientious to qualify that idiocy may be either permanent or a transitory affliction.

Two other conditions that fall within the first form of derangement are absent-mindedness (*Zerstreutheit*) and desipience or the rambling mind (*die Faselei*). It would be fair to say that absent-mindedness and desipience are more often transitory conditions or secondary symptoms of a far more pervasive pathology. The absent-minded soul is simply not aware of its immediate environment or vicinity and is often brought about by "profound mediation." The mind retires or withdraws its attention outwardly and redirects it inwardly to the point that the object world ceases to be significant and is only acknowledged in some unconscious fashion. Hegel sees this symptomatology as the precursor to an "incipient insanity." In this state, objective consciousness is suspended; there is only an abstract self-awareness.

Desipience, on the other hand, manifests itself as a distracted consciousness that cannot focus its attention upon any one thing. It is precisely the inability to affix attention and concentration that gives this set of symptoms a manic, pressured, and chaotic quality. The individual may be flooded with a deluge of excitations, presentations, and/or associations that constitute psychic fracture, splitting, lack of self-cohesion, and decay. It often accompanies florid psychotic symptoms associated with thought disorder, bipolar or manic depressive agitation, and the hyper-emotionality and restlessness of schizoaffective disorder.[17] As Hegel puts it: "It is not uncommon for desipient persons to be already suffering from delirium i.e. not only *non-awareness* but also unconscious *distortion* of what is immediately present to them" (*EG* § 408, *Zusatz*).

Folly, the second main form of derangement, is the condition in which self-absorbed spirit acquires the fixed presentation of a specific content. Spirit centers on a particular content and becomes lost within it as it is within itself, "in the abyss (*Abgrund*) of its *indeterminateness*." Hegel concedes that it is often difficult to determine when folly begins. While he attributes "foolishness" to a general constriction of interests in trivialities, its proper form "involves spirit's being obsessed by a *single* and *merely subjective* presentation, which it regards as *objective*." Hegel continues to tell us that this occurs when the soul is dissatisfied with its actual reality. The soul, in effect, confines itself to its own narcissism whereby "vanity" and "pride" become the main reasons for its withdrawal into self-absorption. Here we may see how Hegel's depiction of spirit's narcissistic self-preoccupation may give rise to unconscious fantasies of grandiosity, omnipotence, specialness, beauty, entitlement, etc. that are generated and maintained within the subjective confines of the abyss. The fool creates and dwells within his own fantasy world whereby the boundaries of objective reality are blurred.

In folly, there is a self-fixation, a return from object relatedness to primary narcissism. But this claim is made with qualifications. In the states of idiocy and desipience, the soul lacks the ability to hold onto anything definite; but the fool, despite his fixed presentation, still remains connected to consciousness and thus can distinguish between the soul and its fixed content. Because the fool is still connected to reality (even though his subjective organizations are poorly constructed and distorted), and possesses understanding consciousness, a quality that differentiates the neurotic from the psychotic, Hegel's classification of derangement needs to be weighed with caution. Here we speculate that what Hegel has in mind is that the soul, while deranged, may still have the capacity to function in its environment even though it possesses delusional propositional beliefs and attitudes. This is to say that the ego of consciousness is not so entirely inverted that it can't perform necessary cognitive operations and actions belonging to understanding consciousness in order to function and survive in its external surroundings. When confronted with the demands of reality, the fool may, in this particular condition, still mobilize and organize his ego functions in order to adapt.[18]

There are countless clinical examples that verify this phenomenon. Even the psychotic can have transient moments of lucidity, where self-conscious ego awareness embraces objective reality. As a psychologist working in an inpatient psychiatric hospital many years ago, I met with an individual diagnosed with paranoid schizophrenia who was requested to undergo psychological testing for treatment planning purposes. Upon my greeting the patient, he informed me that he could read my mind. "Oh really," I replied. "Tell me, if you can read my mind, what am I thinking now?" He looked at me suspiciously then said dryly, "I'm not going to tell you." We both laughed out loud at the same time. Whether his delusional system was active or not, at that moment he was self-consciously aware of the demands placed upon him by an external agent. He in fact was very functional throughout the interview, and performed adequate cognitive tasks and possessed appropriate social skills despite his severely regressed and psychotic profile that emerged from the testing.

Hegel describes that the main difference between fools lies in the multifariousness of their fixed presentations, or in other words, the objects of their fixation. This may take many variegated forms such as the rigid dwelling on a particular experience, fantasy, wish, disappointment, conflict, or emotion. Two particular subcategories Hegel highlights are forms of depression, namely, (1) world-weariness (*Lebensüberdruß*) and (2) melancholia (*Melancholie*). The person who has grown weary of the tribulations of life has a depleted capacity to cope with its continual hardships. As Hegel says, he lacks the ability to "put up with it."

> When life gives rise to *indeterminate* and unfounded disgust, the *capacity* for putting up with it is *lacking*, everything pertaining to actuality elicits a fluctuation between desire and aversion, there is a concentration upon the fixed presentation of the repulsiveness of life and at the same time a drive to overcome it. (*EG* § 408, *Zusatz*)

Hegel specifically refers to melancholia: as the soul fixates on its emotional pain and misfortune, it gives rise to an "uncontrollable impulse to suicide." In *Mourning and Melancholia*, Freud informs us that depressive conditions may be brought on by reaction to the loss of a perceived or actual attachment, such as a love object, emotional detachment or alienation from an object, and the unconscious conflicts and meaning associated with the need for self-punishment, such as guilt, shame, or moral retribution from the critical agency that inverts aggression and turns its on the self.

> The distinguishing mental features of melancholia are a profoundly painful dejection, cessation of interest in the outside world, loss of the capacity to love, inhibition of all activity, and a lowering of the self-regarding feelings to a degree that finds utterance in self-reproaches and self-revilings, and culminates in a delusional expectation of punishment. (*SE*, 14, 244)

Hegel also describes the melancholiac as lacking the ability to initiate "liveliness of thought and action," demonstrating a complete lack of interest in external affairs. Under these circumstances, the soul is in such great distress and pain that its own will toward self-destruction appears through its manifold and divergent symptoms. Here it is important to note that the narcissistic identification with the object world becomes suspended, or rather inverted, for the primary narcissism of a subjective fixed presentation. The unconscious dimensions of depression should not be underestimated in this form of derangement, for as Hegel states, "this aversion to actuality [is] brought on without any rational cause." Freud also tells us that "melancholia is . . . related to an object-loss which is withdrawn from consciousness" (*SE*, 14, 245). Such loss, whether physical, emotional, or merely a wish, remains unconsciously harbored and "unknown" to conscious awareness. Whether the conscious ego understands its loss or not, the unhappy unconsciousness knows that it suffers.

In depression, liveliness is "extinguished," but as Hegel says there are endless varieties of folly in which particular presentations or content stimulate interest and passion. Hegel points to examples of thought disorder, specifically delusions of grandeur when someone professes to be God or a king, as well as gross identity diffusion when someone believes he is a barleycorn or a dog. In these cases, the fool is not able to distinguish between his fixed presentations and objective reality, and thus is unaware of this contradiction.

But in insanity, or madness proper, the third main form of mental disease, the deranged subject *itself* is aware of its contradictory nature and the disruption it experiences. The sick mind knows and intensely feels the contradiction between its subjective content and objectivity—it is painfully aware of its suffering. Cognizant of its discrepancies and the dual fragmentation of consciousness, the mad soul cannot rid itself of its fixed content; subjective presentations haunt its thoughts obsessively, which the subject in turn attempts to actualize by distorting and making its content objective through imaginative delusions and fantasy, or it attempts to demolish what is genuinely actual. As Hegel puts it, if the person continually dwells upon the past, transforming it and keeping it alive, "he becomes incapable of adjusting to the *present*."

Madness may be brought about by extraneous circumstances, social unrest, misfortune, the actual decay of one's individual world, or a "*violent upheaval*" creating world havoc, such as times of war, producing mass hysteria and insanity. "In the insane . . . the feeling of inner disruption can with equal facility be either a *tranquil* pain, or progress into the *frenzy* of *reason raging* against *unreason* and vice versa" (*EG* § 408, *Zusatz*). Hegel continues to describe the "feeling of uneasiness" as a "torment" producing a "*deceitful, jealous, spiteful* and *malicious* attitude" that can give way to a "fury" and "*mania* for *harming* others," even "*murder*." But what is of greater significance is Hegel's consideration of the role of the drives, unbridled desire, unconscious conflict, and irrationality in madness.

> In insanity . . . a *particular presentation* wrests control from the spirit of rationality, and since the *general particularity* of the subject emerges unbridled, so that the *natural impulses* [*Triebe*] of this particularity as well as those developed by reflection throw off the yoke of the *ethical* laws deriving from the *truly universal* will, the dark infernal powers of the heart have free play. (*EG* § 408, *Zusatz*)

In this passage, Hegel foresees the base processes Freud attributes to the dynamic influences of the id, which abolish the rational constraints of the ego and suspend the ethical judgments of the superego. But Hegel further acknowledges the role of what Freud calls the superego and its condemnation and aggressivity in derangement:

> [T]he ill-nature of an insane person does not prevent his having moral and ethical feelings. On the contrary, it can be precisely the misery he suffers, the domination of the *unmediated opposition* within him, which heightens the intensity of such feelings. (*EG* § 408, *Zusatz*)

This is a central doctrine of psychoanalytic thought. Not only are "the activities of the lower passions in the unconscious" (*SE*, 19, 26), but so are our ideals, "what is highest in the human mind" (*SE*, 19, 36). The superego can bring a reign of terror on the subject that is as ruthless as the terror of the id. As Freud puts it, "[T]he ego ideal displays particular severity and often rages against the ego in a cruel fashion" (*SE*, 19, 51). And as Hegel says, this is "precisely the misery he suffers." The cruelty of moral persecution borrows its energies from the death drive that may be said to underlie *all* psychic deterioration. The sick soul, unhappy unconsciousness, is menaced by three central dangers: the reality of the external world, the internal disruption of desire and passion, and the abuse waged against it from its own ego ideal or ethical self-consciousness. It is no wonder that Freud visioned mental life to be a continual battle: "[T]he ego, driven by the id, confined by the super-ego, repulsed by reality, struggles to master its economic task of bringing about harmony among the forces and influences working in and upon it; and we can understand how it is that so often we cannot suppress a cry: 'Life is not easy!'" (*SE*, 22, 78).

In all forms of disease there is what Hegel calls, a "depression of self-conscious life" (*EG* § 392): the logic of madness does not conform to the reason of consciousness. But this is not to say that the ontology of madness lacks reason. For Hegel, all forms of spirit have their basis in a rational foundation even though imperfectly realized. In derangement, reason is perverted by the primal lure of desire, its original form. Indeed, rational spirit is the actualization of desire—reason is the modified and exalted outgrowth of the dialectic. But when life is too cumbersome, and internal forces too debilitating, spirit desires to return to the archaic infancy of the abyss. Like the anxiety, frustration, and despair of unhappy consciousness, there is a corresponding pain within the heart of unconscious spirit. All forms of derangement involve a developmental fixation or regression that slips back into the feeling soul, the home of its original lost unity. From symbiosis to the absolute, unity is the desire and telos of spirit's being.

SYMBIOSIS AND THE ABSOLUTE

For Hegel, the soul is "*all-pervasive*"; it is the common feature of our shared humanity. No matter how individual personality or group identifications form, we are first and foremost soul. In derangement, the soul is immersed in its internality, "*cut off* from its understanding consciousness" where it "intuits its individual world *within itself*, not *outside*" (*EG* § 406, *Zusatz*). Yet this is precisely the condition from which spirit emerges. In its developmental progression, the natural soul evolves from a state of symbiosis or undifferentiation to the standpoint of the Absolute as spiritual liberation and unification. As Hegel tells us, we all have a disposition toward mental disease by virtue of the feeling soul—"flushes of ill-nature occur in all of us" (*EG* § 408, *Zusatz*). But perhaps the drive toward unity and the Absolute is a repetition, a need to recapture the primordial being of unity in a more evolved form. There is a universal tendency of spirit to seek unification, but what merits our attention is how unification is achieved. The striving for unity is fundamentally a progressive dialectical development, but as we have seen in illness, it may also be regressive. Both functions seek to fulfill the same aim, although through different means. We may say that regression serves as a defense while progression is a vicissitude of the drives, each their fate or transformation. This would make the striving for the Absolute both ontologically and psychologically significant for spirit. In symbiosis and the Absolute, spirit achieves unification with the universal.

What is philosophically important for Hegel is to "establish the *principal forms* of the *universal* which in various ways shapes itself within them." The desire for unity is an ontological a priori organization by virtue of spirit's teleology and dialectical process of becoming. But unity is also psychologically motivated: spirit desires a particular content, a particular *result*—*universality*—harmony, the fulfillment of its wish. It is interesting to note that universality is the most *exalted* and the most *depraved* form of spirit. Spirit is degraded in the form of feeling and corporiety and elevated in thought, reason, and action. Spirit as art, religion, and philosophy is the pinnacle of mind on the way to absolute knowing. In fact, it may be argued that Hegel revered religion as the highest spiritual form, even though it lacks full self-understanding.[19] In religiosity and absolute knowing, there is a sense of exaltation, spiritual transcendence. For Hegel, to know God is to unite conceptuality with actuality. But the notion of "spirit" in English also carries another meaning associated with alcohol, celebration, and intoxication. When we consume intoxicants—spirits—the mind withdraws from consciousness to unconsciousness. As Carl Jung tells us: "Alcohol in Latin is *spiritus*, and you use the same word for the highest religious experience as well as for the most depraving poison. The helpful formula therefore is *spiritus contra spiritum*."[20] In the confines of the feeling soul and in the fulfillment of the Absolute, universality is spirit's "principal form."

Universality becomes the goal and form that spirit attempts to achieve throughout its dialectical unfolding. It progresses from a very simple unity as natural soul to a holistic complex universality as Absolute Spirit. The soul is originally enveloped in the undifferentiated natural life of sleep from which it emerges, only to return to it during times of suffering and pain. Ideally, spirit blossoms from its dark universality to the light of reason and complete comprehension, the culmination of universal knowledge. Spirit finds itself as a self-enclosed unity, which it seeks to abandon, transmute, and reconstitute as a complex integrative absolute unity. If the original ontology of spirit is bound to universality, it becomes a logical consequence that spirit would want to hold on to or regain what it knows as its nature, its most elementary essence: this is what it ultimately seeks. But spirit is not content with such a limited form of unity—it wants to become and fulfill its possibilities as absolute essence. It is only in the affliction of pathology that the general dialectical thrust of sublation is overturned for the desire to recover its lost shape.

We must carefully consider the role and structure of the universal in the ontology of spirit. Universality is the principal form in both symbiosis and the Absolute. While each shape of spirit constructs dual means of procuring universality, they both harbor the same aim. This suggests that spirit itself is engaged in an ambivalent dialectic. This is precisely why Hegel insists that the sick soul is self-contradictory and suffers from a "morbid" onesidedness. While spirit is oriented to pursue completion and unity, it recognizes that it has already left its original home of self-certainty and security. Spirit is progressive but it can also operate in reverse in order to reclaim its universality. It is only natural that during times of duress or mental incapacitation spirit would seek to reunite with what it once knew as harmonious. During great stress or conditions that precipitate mental illness, there is a *double pull* of the dialectic—one that presses for the need to surpass and overcome adversity, thus belonging to the tendency toward sublation, and one that seeks to withdraw, regress, and sink back into the interior of the abyss.

Berthold-Bond refers to spiritual withdrawal as a form of "nostalgia" whereby the "second face of desire" orients spirit back toward the pit. I prefer to look at this process by suggesting that spirit has more than a second face, it has a double center. Spirit is ontologically predisposed to seek unification and wholeness, but the way it chooses to perform such activity is radically influenced by its context, environmental demands, internal strengths and limitations, and

the contingencies of the world. The double center of spirit is antithetically constituted as the dialectic serving dual teleological functions motivated by the
identical drive toward unity. Whether in health or in pathology, spirit wants to
merge with the universal. Elsewhere I have argued that subjectivity is constituted by a *double edge* of *centeredness*.[21] The double-centeredness of spirit appears
as a dual tendency toward progression and regression, evolution and devolution,
ascendence and reversal back to archaic structure. While the will-to-spirit is fundamentally oriented toward the acclivity of consciousness, it may be generally
said that spirit is also ontologically disposed toward inversion and withdrawal
due to its negative dialectic. This is why Hegel says we are all inclined to fall ill:
anxiety, despair, and psychic depletion are inevitable features of mental life.

For Freud, character is largely the constellation of wish and defense as psychic structure forms around identifications. This view may be further attributed
to Hegel's notion of spirit. When vital and cohesive, spirit surpasses its earlier
more primitive forms and transfigures its internal structure into a sublimated
achievement, thus fulfilling or completing itself. But when harried and fragmented, it desperately attempts to erect functional defenses that try to reestab-
lish psychic integrity, security, and cohesiveness. In derangement, spirit's
defensive cry for self-protection leads to a regressive path back toward a
preestablished harmony with nature as an earlier form of mastery and control.
While such a defense is ultimately maladaptive, being both ontologically and
psychologically constrictive, it nevertheless provides an illusory haven in the
arms of the abyss. When spirit suffers from psychopathology, the cocoon of its
interiority is all it can bear: reality is just too painful to manage. This is when we
can say that spirit suffers from *ontological insecurity*. The logic of the interior governing unconscious spirit becomes the organization of defense. The inner amal-
gamation of the soul and that of the abyss constitute a defensive fortress that is as
protective as it is besieged. When spirit is harassed by reality to the point that it
can no longer surpass opposition, its natural proclivity is to escape: when tired,
spirit just wants to go to sleep.

It is interesting to note the interconnection of the themes of birth and death
with those of symbiosis and the Absolute. Spirit emerges from an original undifferentiated state or symbiotic universality and achieves union once again with the
collective universality of the Absolute; it is born from unity and returns to unity.
With each sublated shape of spirit comes the destruction of its old form, its death.
But with each death comes rebirth, the death of each shape preserved within a
new form of life. And it is the power of the negative—death—that gives birth to
each new spiritual life. Is it possible that birth and death are merely moments or
polarities of the same unity? Each brings about the other; there could be neither
life nor death without their reciprocal dialectic. The abyss brings life and destroys
it. While the unconscious gives birth to consciousness, it also negates it: each is the
inversion of the other. Life and death, being and nothing, are the same.

In some ways, unconscious spirit signifies the feminine: it bears the child of
consciousness and endures great pains of labor during its delivery. Negativity—

the sensation of death—is imbued in the very process of birth. And for Hegel, it is the feminine that nurtures the development of spirit:

> [T]he divine law has its individualization—or the *unconscious* Spirit of the individual its real existence—in the woman, through whom, as the *middle term*, the unconscious Spirit rises out of its unreality into actual existence, out of a state in which it is unknowing and unconscious into the realm of conscious Spirit. (*PS* § 463)

Recall that the natural soul is first infused within the mother's womb; there is no sense of differentiation between the soul and its natural environment. We may say that the soul in its initial milieu is prone to experience both tranquility and disruption, being at once at peace with its simple universality and at odds with its confinement. The mother's experience of pregnancy, comprising joy, physical discomfort, anxiety, etc., also contributes to the feeling states and experiential conditions the soul will acquire and absorb as its own, predisposing it, as Hegel says, to both adjustment and disease (*EG* § 405, *Zusatz*). The soul in its abyss of universality is the womb of spirit, just as the mother's womb is the original home of the infant.

To what degree is the desire for merger with the Absolute a wish to return to unity? Does spirit seek its original state of symbiosis in the higher form of the Absolute? We cannot deny the psychological correlation between our developmental facticities and the ontological disposition toward the desire for unity. Perhaps the desire for absolute knowing is an extension of spirit's original self-contained universality, albeit actualized in a higher form. If feeling becomes the deposit and basal form of spirit as Hegel insists, then feeling would have to imbue all forms of spirit. In fact, consciousness, thought, reason, and morality are modified outgrowths of spirit's nascent being and thus are imbued with its essence. Because they do not stand ontologically separate from spirit's original essence, only modified, the evolved attributes and properties of spirit must participate in spirit's archaic structure—this is the hallmark of Hegel's monism. While spirit seeks absolute self-consciousness as immersion in the universal, it also seeks that *feeling* of immersion with universality. The feeling of contentment in self-actualization is the evolved return of its symbiotic harmony with its primordial unity. Feeling unity becomes the prototype of the Absolute. Whether in progression or regression, the *need* to experience the *feeling of unity* becomes spirit's primary aim. In absolute knowing, unity is achieved as rational thought, and thus its feeling totality—its genius—is fulfilled through pure reason. This is why reason is the exalted outgrowth of desire, the desire to know.

We have repeatedly seen that for Hegel spirit begins, as does ego development for Freud, in an original undifferentiated unity that emerges from its immediate self-enclosed universality to its mediated determinate singularity.[22] This is initiated through a dialectical process of internal division, self-externalization, and introjection as the reincorporation of the soul's projected qualities back into its interior. Through the complexities of mediation and sublation, spirit achieves higher levels of unification until it arrives at a full integration of itself as a complex whole, uniting earlier finite shapes within its mature universality. For example, the need for social order, unification, and harmony are motivational factors that inform the ideal of global tranquility that pathology threatens to deteriorate, an ideal imbued with the residue of early symbiotic conditions. The ego ensnared in the stage of primary narcissism and spirit asleep in the undifferentiated abyss of its self-absorption constitute the ontological and psychological precursors for differentiation and development. To what degree do these conditions have a role in our wish for higher degrees of unity, concord, and moral self-realization? Are we to understand world spirit as "the universal brotherhood of man"[23] that seeks absolute unity, or is this merely a wish to return to the oceanic feeling of symbiosis, like a fetus in the peaceful sea of its mother's womb? Perhaps these two aims are only differentiated in form.

One would be hard pressed to find someone who would not value the ideal of peace, with communal harmony, accord, and cooperation marshaled in the service of social progression. We may say that this is the pursuit of the ethical that underlies Hegel's *Phenomenology*, despite the fact that he values both domestic peace and international war. But the very nature of the need for progressive unification is also dialectically opposed to destructive and regressive inclinations that derive from the earlier primitive shapes of our psychic constitution, which we seek to act out or recover during conflict precipitated by opposition. If the desire for unification is a derivative of our original psychical ontology, then both progressive and regressive desires may be said to emanate from the same mental (symbiotic) configurations that may further serve the same aim. Both seek unity or peace of a different kind and in a different form: one through the attainment of higher integrated complexities, the other through acting on the wish to return to the warm blanket of its initial undifferentiated beginning.

If the drive toward destruction is responsible for both progress and regress, growth and decay, then how are we to determine which one will prevail and which one will succumb to the tyranny of the other? This is what differentiates spiritual health from madness. In juxtaposition to Freud, this brings into question once again how the nature of negativity and destruction influence the self-preservative drives in their quest for unification and mastery. While the self-preservative drives stand in stark opposition to destructive ones, the two are dialectical complementarities that effect their confluence. Here we may see the structural dynamic of the dialectic with negativity begetting progression—destruction as construction—in the service of achieving higher aims. Just as Being is in opposition to Nothing, so is life and death; two sides of a symmetrical relation constitute their necessary unity.[24]

For subjective spirit, there is universality at birth and universality at death. Universality is the original and final form of spirit. In the *Science of Logic*, Hegel tells us "the I is, *first*, this pure self-related unity. . . . As such it is *universality*; a unity that is unity with itself only through its *negative* attitude." Yet the I as self-related negativity constitutes the nature of the Concept with the Absolute; "[T]he *I* is the pure Concept itself . . . grasped at the same time both in their abstraction and also in their perfect unity" (*SL*, 583). But is there an inherent terror associated with universality? Despite the fact that spirit seeks to free itself from its symbiotic immediacy for the wholeness of absolute knowing, it may desire to return to another form of universality.

We have stated that there is an internal ambitendent drive to spirit directed toward both progression and withdrawal, each functioning in the service of achieving unity. But could there also be a horror associated with each? In both symbiosis and the Absolute, all particularity is nonexistent—individuality is lost even though it is incorporated into the universal. Unconscious spirit ensconced in the natural soul seeks to free itself from its constricting corporeality, yet it seeks to return to this state during times of illness. There are at least two distinct moments when it finds its original unity to be a source of both conflict and comfort. In normal development, the soul evolves into the ego of consciousness and hence surpasses its primitive shape. But despite the fact that the ego sublates the natural soul, spirit remains connected, as Hegel says, to the life of feeling in all its spiritual activities. This occasions spirit to want to recover its lost harmony during times of duress, malaise, or mental illness. This is most prominent during abnormal development when the abyss of symbiosis becomes a welcome haven for spirit lured by the promise of a dulled tranquility, plunging it "back into the universal, veering into the sublime and the monstrous" (*EG* § 389, *Zusatz*).

If the double center of spirit sees symbiosis to be both threatening and peaceful, would it not also harbor such an attitude toward the Absolute? Spirit attains satisfaction in self-consciousness—the Absolute typifies the zenith of spiritual fulfillment; it is the *Ideal*. But for the sick soul, the Absolute is both unattainable and incomprehensible. In pathology, spirit resists its transition toward the Absolute, it fears its loss of self in succumbing to the pull of the dialectic, thus it resists its own process. The Absolute becomes a paranoiac knowledge, the mortal threat of engulfment and incorporation. The same may be said of individuals who fear being absorbed into the fabric of the state. The ego, beleaguered by reality, would rather retreat into its own unity, thus fleeing from the Absolute, rather than to be devoured by the collective. There is a real horror of merging with the collective, for all individuality is annulled. This may truly be the double reality of the unconscious—the abyss is the universal: in the soul and in Absolute Spirit, all particularity is annihilated. The abyss then becomes the face of death—pure negativity, nothingness. But it is precisely death that is the midwife of life.

The process of spirit is tantamount to a sustained trauma: the strife, despair, and anxiety that inform its pathos constitute the crucible that elevates it to salvation. When spirit experiences a nostalgia, it desires the form of union it once had had but lost. Spirit may seek to recover its loss in two opposed ways, viz., through sublation, its normative course, and in regression, its pathological route.

Either way, spirit generates its own fate. The sides of infinite life that subjective spirit alienates itself from in its mortality lead spirit to embrace its infinity in the Absolute—the universal, the reconciliation of its fate. The fate of spirit in abnormality, however, achieves universality via a defensive path.

In spiritual withdrawal, there are two forms of regression that correspond to the stages of the soul in its immediacy. The process of regression may fixate on two points: (1) the feeling soul, approximating the fetus in the womb, and (2) the physical soul, with its simple immediacy of natural determinateness. Strictly speaking, the natural or universal soul is pure undifferentiated, immediate being, while the feeling or individual soul has attained some minor form of mediation by "entering as an individuality into relationship with its immediate being" (*EG* § 390). In fact, the natural soul is the subjective ground of the feeling soul.[25] In the natural soul, spirit is still an "abstract determination," thus it is only implicit. In other words, the natural soul is physically one with nature. Yet despite the slight modification of the soul in feeling, it is still immersed in a dark universality and posits all difference within itself. When it awakens and raises itself to feeling its own life, it moves into its initial mediated immediacy as individuated unconscious spirit, yet still caged in universality. The actual soul, the third movement of unconscious spirit, is the synthesis of the universal soul and the individual soul, its sublated shape.

While Hegel situates madness in the feeling soul—a self-enclosed unity—the natural soul is the pure form of universality, where spirit merely *is*—of pure being, oneness. If we are to consider spiritual motivation as the drive for oneness, then perhaps the inverted and destructive regression to symbiosis is the perversion of this drive, an inverse negation. It is not difficult to see the parallel between Freud's death drive and spiritual disease: if the aim of all life is death, a return to inorganic matter, then perhaps the withdrawal into the abyss of universality is the wish to return to spirit's prenatal condition, its implicitness, its sleeping state. As in Wagner's *Tristan and Isolde*,[26] spirit seeks perfection in death. In symbiosis and the Absolute, we cannot ignore the echo of Freud's thesis: the aim of spirit is to achieve death, the pure negation of all opposition. Whether in its earliest instantiation as sleeping universality, or in the perfect union of all difference with the collective, spirit may seek completion in nullity as identity—nothingness; and it is the circuitous paths toward unity that constitute spiritual freedom.

What would Hegel say of the sick soul in its regressive state of disease? How would he explain the tendency of spirit to revert back to its primitive nature and resist the sublation of the dialectic, hence resist the progress of its own process? How would he address this element of spiritual activity that borders on the excess of Spirit? How can the unconscious be both sublated and not? There are two levels of consideration in Hegel's theory of spirit. The first is the objective account of the historical development of spirit, where spirit is understood as the spirit of the human race. In this development of the universal or collective, the unconscious is superseded—spirit has long ago moved to a level of self-consciousness that drags even the unconscious to the light of self-understanding. In fact, as we have repeatedly said, self-consciousness is the realization or product of unconscious teleology—the unconscious makes consciousness and self-consciousness possible.

The second level of consideration is the subjective account of the development of the individual where the unconscious exists as both a permanent threat and a haven from pain. Madness or mental illness is a problem of individuals, which can further contaminate a collective group of peoples, thus affecting the historical development of societies and cultures. This is why Hegel says that history is a "slaughterbench" (*RH* § 27). Madness is like the slaughterbench, a routine way in which human lives fail to be rational. This may be viewed on one level as a failure of the human mind, though this failure in itself does not negate the very high achievement of the human spirit. Hegel shows that human life as such does not lack reason, and that conceptually, human life is shown to be a self-consistent totality. One cannot entirely separate the two levels because, as history shows us, it is the unruly megalomaniacal desires of individuals that make them into world-historical figures who advance the cause of spirit. But we must distinguish the two levels of the subjective spirit belonging to the individual personality and the collective unification of subject and object belonging to world spirit.

As for Hegel's cure for the deranged mind, he prescribes a brand of dialectical therapy to heal the wounds of spirit:

> There is for example the case of the Englishman who lost interest in everything, first in politics, and then in his affairs and his family. He sat motionless, looking straight in front of him, said nothing for years on end, and exhibited a stupefaction which made it doubtful whether he knew his wife and children or not. He was cured by someone who dressed exactly as he did and sat in front of him copying him in everything. This put the patient into a violent passion, which forced him to pay attention to what was about him, and drove him permanently out of his state of self-absorption. (*EG* § 408, *Zusatz*)

Hegel gives another noteworthy example:

> Another person, who considered himself to be dead, remained motionless and refused to eat, recovered his understanding in the following manner. Someone else, pretending to share in his folly, placed him in a coffin, and took him to a vault where there was another person, also in a coffin, who pretended at first to be dead. After the fool had been there for a while however, the other person sat up and said how pleased he was to have company in death. Then he got up and ate the food he had by him, telling the astonished newcomer that he had been dead for some time and therefore knew how the dead went about things. The fool was taken in by this assurance, followed suit by eating and drinking, and was cured. (*EG* § 408, *Zusatz*)

In these instances, both individuals were brought back to recovery from the self-absorption and destructive pull of the abyss. Even in madness, the dark forces of the unconscious may be superseded.

It may be said that, for Hegel, Absolute Spirit is nonrelative self-conscious life; thus, subjective spirit and objective spirit are incorporated into the more comprehensive perspective of absolute knowing. All other perspectives are in some way relative to other factors or contingencies. But the individual psyche (subjective spirit) is never in fact isolated from the social framework in which it is situated (objective spirit), and societies and states function only because individual minds become self-conscious intelligible beings. Furthermore, the view of the whole that is gained in art, religion, and philosophy is one that takes into account the subjective ways of thinking and the objective reality of cult and social structure. Each domain of spirit presupposes and implies the others. Hegel's philosophy of spirit is therefore the comprehensive examination of the plurality of human life as a complex whole and of the multiple perspectives that inform its diverse yet integrative structure.

For Hegel, spirit is a dynamically self-articulated complex totality where even the irrational mind is understood to be part of the collective. From the *Berlin Phenomenology*, Hegel tells us: "The true standpoint is that of there being no abyss [*Abgrund*] between the object and the knowing subjectivity, and it also occurs in the knowing subject, in man" (*BP* § 362). Thus, spirit advances from the pit to the pyramid as it educates itself to truth, its proper fulfillment. From symbiosis to the Absolute, spirit leaves its universality for another vastly richer universality. In absolute knowing, unconsciousness is brought to full self-awareness, for self-consciousness is the transcendence and fulfillment of the abyss.

SIX

IMPLICATIONS FOR PSYCHOANALYSIS

TOWARD PROCESS PSYCHOLOGY

THROUGHOUT THIS PROJECT, I have attempted to show that Hegel has a surprisingly well articulated theory of the unconscious and the psychodynamic processes that govern the structure, function, and operations of the mind. According to which, the unconscious is the foundation for conscious and self-conscious life and is responsible for the normative and pathological forces that fuel psychic development, thus explaining the breadth, depth, and appearance of both mental health and disease. One point I have emphasized time and again is that although the unconscious undergoes dialectical maturation, it is never fully sublated: the abyss remains a repository or womb in which failed shapes of spirit return. Moreover, what is significant is that Hegel's theory of the unconscious in multiple and remarkable ways parallels several central theses established by Freud almost a century later, a position, I argue, that is of value to psychoanalysis today.

The field of psychoanalysis has gone through many theoretical evolutions since the time of Freud, from drive theory to its current preoccupation with intersubjectivity. As psychoanalysis flirts with the arrival of postmodernism and the Continental tradition, new vistas emerge that bring psychoanalysis into dialogue with philosophy. Largely overlooked for his strong commitment to rationalism, Hegel remains relatively unknown to psychoanalytic discourse. But with greater awareness of Hegel's contributions to psychodynamic thought may come greater appreciation of how he can truly benefit the institution of psychoanalysis.

What is central to Hegel's overall philosophy is the notion of *process*, a thesis that has direct implications for the psychoanalytic understanding of the structure and functional operations of the psyche. In particular, Hegel's logic of the dialectic has promising new appeal for advancing psychoanalytic doctrine. One does not have to espouse Hegel's entire philosophical system, which is neither necessary nor desirable, in order to appreciate the dialectic and its application to psychoanalysis and contemporary modes of thought. The adoption of his dialectical method may complement or augment existing theoretical innovations that enrich our psychoanalytic understanding of mind and human nature. More auspiciously, a proper appreciation of Hegel's dialectic may pave the way toward a new movement within psychoanalysis today: namely, "process psychology," or what we may call "dialectical psychoanalysis." Juxtaposed to current paradigms, Hegel's dialectic has profound significance for the future of psychoanalytic inquiry.

IF FREUD READ HEGEL

We do not know whether Freud actually ever read Hegel. By Jean Hyppolite's account, "Seemingly, Freud had not read Hegel;"[1] but we do know that he was at least acquainted with his philosophy. In a paper titled, "The Importance of Philosophy for the Further Development of Psychoanalysis," delivered at the International Congress for Psychoanalysis at Weimar in 1911, James Putnum advocated the need for philosophical integration within psychoanalytic investigation. From Ernest Jones's biography on Freud, he states:

> [Putnum's] burning plea for the introduction of philosophy—but only his own Hegelian brand—into psychoanalysis did not meet with much success. Most of us did not see the necessity of adopting any particular system. Freud was of course very polite in the matter, but remarked to me afterwards: "Putnum's philosophy reminds me of a decorative centerpiece; everyone admires it but no one touches it."[2]

While Freud's dismissal of Hegel is tacit in his remark, it is well documented that Freud sincerely did admire philosophy.[3] After all, he seriously considered becoming a philosopher. In fact, while attending the University of Vienna, Freud and Husserl were in the same class together under the tutelage of Franz Brentano.

Being a studious and passionate reader of the humanities, it is not only possible but probable that he actually did have formal textual exposure to Hegel.[4] In the footsteps of Kant, whom Freud knew well, Hegel was a monolith of German culture. Just as Freud was exposed to Natural Philosophy, Schopenhauer, and Nietzsche within the same era, it seems very unlikely that Hegel would have eluded his intellectual attention. The question then becomes: If Freud read Hegel, then why didn't he take him seriously? Perhaps this is obvious: Hegel was a rationalist, a theist, and a systematic metaphysician, while Freud was an empiricist and a vociferous atheist who canonized irrationality as the primary force behind the human mind, not to mention the fact that he loathed metaphysics. But perhaps Freud was not exposed to Hegel's concept of madness and the soul, for if he had been, he could not have ignored Hegel's implicit thesis of the primacy of the unconscious. For Hegel, as for Freud, there is a primordial nature to man that precedes reason, namely, the underworld.

OPENINGS TO MUTUAL RECOGNITION

Philosophy and psychoanalysis have historically embraced ambivalent and at times antagonistic attitudes toward one another. Psychoanalysis has been called "mythology" by Wittgenstein,[5] and "unscientific" and "incongruent" by MacIntyre and Grünbaum.[6] James called the notion of the unconscious "unintelligible."[7] In turn, for Freud, any philosophical position that denies the ontology of the unconscious is simply "absurd."[8] We may say there is a great deal of resistance on both sides to broach an amicable conversation on the origins of the self and the psychic processes that govern mental life and human behavior. Philosophers tend to question the epistemic status and scientific verifiability of the concept of the unconscious, while psychoanalysts tend to dismiss much of philosophy as intellectual masturbation, a discipline fixed in a rationalized defense. There is a culture of narcissism that has formed around and entrenched each discipline, each claiming to have acquired a truth that the other lacks. Perhaps it is this rigid identification with one's own group narcissism that keeps both fields from acknowledging and appreciating each other more fully. In the spirit of Hegel, philosophy and psychoanalysis may profit from the recognition that each can understand psychical reality more fully by taking the other seriously, a process which neither discipline could ever achieve alone.

But we may ask: Why does there need to be a compatibility between Hegel and psychoanalysis? They have different agendas, so what value does their convergence serve? I am of the opinion that truth and wisdom are to be found in the realm of process and dialogue, and that the continued independence of philosophy and psychoanalysis does not have to preclude their useful confluence. Recognizing kinship between the ideas of Hegel and Freud leads to a better understanding of both. In general, psychoanalysis is probably more guilty of closing off discourse than is philosophy. But the attitude of practitioners does not imply that psychoanalysis must in principle remain distant from philosophical inquiry, or that philosophy cannot avail itself of the insights of psychoanalysis. In fact, psychology is the child of philosophy; although psychology has grown up and has flown from the nest, philosophy will always remain its Gracious Mother (*alma mater*). Like spirit which emerges from the abyss, as does the ego from the id,[9] psychology is merely a differentiated and modified form of its original philosophical constitution.

There are of course many points of difference between Hegel and Freud. Hegel had a great respect and reverence for religiosity, while Freud saw it as an illusion and as an infantile way of coping with an austere reality.[10] Hegel was an optimist who envisioned spirit as a dynamically self-articulated complex whole, while Freud is often interpreted as a pessimist who was against wholeness and who saw the ego's desire for self-completion as a defensive process fueled by repetition compulsion.[11] Freud's pessimism is reflected in his cultural works primarily represented in *Civilization and its Discontents*, where the degenerative threat of humanity's inability to control its destructive inclinations leads one to envisage a dismal view of human relations.[12] Hegel, on the other hand, sees destruction and negation as the engines that fuel unity, the positive significance of the negative. Freud was also an empiricist who had little use for philosophical speculation,[13] while speculation was the queen of science for Hegel.[14]

There are still other areas of disagreement, but when examined closely, their differences are overshadowed by their common focus. Both share a disdain for reductive materialism; in its proper form, *Geist* is psychical not material. But Freud devalues consciousness while Hegel exalts it.[15] That is to say, Freud sees that unconscious irrational forces exert a powerful influence on the meanings, ideas, beliefs, and desires that affect our conscious lives. Hegel would not disagree with this, in fact he would substantiate it, but he would ultimately say that conscious rational forces exert more priority over our mental lives than do unconscious irrational ones. Both acknowledge the role of irrationality and reason, they just emphasize the significance of one over the other. Yet despite Freud's focus on exploring the irrational mind, he was an ardent champion of reason.[16] The intellect—reason—is what exerts a control over our lives and is mainly responsible for mental health, the ability to work, love, and play.

Both Hegel and Freud place a primacy on self-awareness or self-consciousness, where self-knowledge of one's own unconscious mysteries supersedes the unknown. It is here that both men share a common commitment. Hegel and Freud were fundamental seekers of truth; self-understanding becomes the purpose of spirit and the ultimate goal of psychoanalysis. It is no wonder that psychoanalysis is labeled an "insight-oriented therapy." But beyond the goal of self-consciousness lies an even deeper purpose: the self-actualization of spirit represents the process of the psychoanalytic task, namely, to achieve self-liberating *freedom*. The ultimate purpose of spirit and the human mind is to be free. Ultimately, freedom can be attained only through knowledge.

Purists will groan at any attempt to read Freud into Hegel or Hegel into Freud. But I am under the persuasion that wisdom transcends allegiance to any one mode or system of thinking. If philosophy is to profess to be committed to take into account all possible reality—the *sine qua non* of speculative metaphysics—then it can hardly omit examining the unconscious mind. This was prepared by Hegel and revolutionized by Freud. And psychoanalysis cannot deny its prehistory. Like Hegel's attempt to resurrect and retrace the lost shapes spirit had surpassed in its historical progression toward absolute self-consciousness, psychoanalysis is archeology, an archeology of the soul.

This brings us to address a practical question. Can Hegel's philosophy of spirit be applied to our current understanding of human nature and the mind? How does Hegel's theory of the unconscious stand up to views such as those introduced by Freud and contemporary psychoanalysis? In other words: "Does it bake bread?" Clearly it does, as I have shown throughout this project. Hegel anticipated many key psychoanalytic concepts including the unconscious operations of thought, imagination, fantasy, feelings, conflict, and the very conditions that inform psychopathology.[17] He also recognized that the core of character and one's ethical convictions are preserved and emanate from unconscious processes and values internalized from the family and centrally connected with the community.[18] He further recognized many elements of mental activity that are construed by psychoanalysis as defense mechanisms, including the splitting of the ego, fixation, regression, projection and projective identification, repression as significant "forgetting" that manifests itself as a compromise formation—"disease"—primary narcissism as "subjective universality," the primitive thinking and upheaval of the passions—what Freud called "primary process"—associated with derangement, and the notion of sublation as sublimation; not to mention one of the most important discoveries of all—that the *ego* is also unconscious.[19]

Hegel's notion of the abyss—which corresponds to Freud's id—provides the dynamic force behind the development and evolution of the mind. Unconscious feeling dispositions are informed by the underlying organizations of the natural soul—spirit implicit—and mental illness has its basis in these dynamic-formal characteristics. While Hegel did not anticipate all of psychoanalytic theory nor attend to the phenomenal nuances of symptomatology, sexual etiology, and unconscious conflict and motivation, he did nevertheless advance our understanding of the unconscious workings of the mind, and he did so by means of deduction.[20] By way of dialectical process, there is a logic to the soul.

While Hegel relied on a deductive analysis of the operations of the unconscious that make consciousness possible, Freud relied on empirical observation and experimentation.[21] What Hegel worked out through logic, Freud legitimized through rigorous scientific method. Both approaches confirm the logical and developmental progression of the mind stemming from an unconscious ontology. Hegel and Freud realized that in order to provide an adequate account of consciousness, mental activity and human behavior cannot be explained without evoking the notion of original ground. In mental life, there is a reason or cause for everything, what psychoanalysis calls "psychic determinism." Having its basis in unconscious processes, both Hegel and Freud were able to fashion a paradigm of the human psyche that is perpetually influenced by its primordial past.

When seen for its total worth, it becomes easy to appreciate why each discipline offers something to the other. Hegel anticipated the realm, scope, and range of the abyss while Freud made it more intelligible. While Hegel provided us with a cogent and coherent theory of unconscious subjectivity, Freud greatly advanced our understanding of the powers of the human psyche and the unconscious processes that affect conscious life. In order for Hegel to contribute to the psychoanalytic understanding of the mind, his theories must be able to be applied to contemporary thought. By way of our systematic analysis of Hegel's articulation of the abyss and its dynamic operations in the realm of intelligence, action, and thought corresponding to all human activity including the abnormal processes of mind, psychoanalysis would be hard pressed not to acknowledge Hegel's contribution to the social sciences.

But psychoanalysts may ask: Why should we embrace Hegel? How does he advance our cause? The answer is that he provides a congruous philosophical foundation that fortifies psychoanalytic theory and moves the discipline closer to respectable status. This is why Hegel is good for psychoanalysis: he provides a logic and truth to the unconscious that is internally consistent and coherent, thus capable of withstanding philosophic criticism when empirical limitations are encountered. Hegel can bring philosophical and logical rigor to psychoanalytic theory, and through his dialectical method shows that the unconscious is the foundation of the human psyche.

Through mutual recognition,[22] each discipline moves closer to appreciating the value of the other, and this process is what advances knowledge. Like spirit, which seeks recognition from the other so that it may recover its lost alienated desire, mutual recognition provides mutual validation and acceptance, which opens up further communication and dialogue. There is a wisdom to recognition that even serves a psychological function: it nurtures psyche structure. Heinz Kohut has labeled this phenomenon "mirroring," arguing that the empathic attunement and affirmation of the inherent worth of the other fosters psychic development and internal self-cohesion. If the disciplines of philosophy and psychoanalysis are like the self, each the invention of *Geist*, then both need recognition in order to prosper and grow. Indeed, mutual recognition advances the human spirit, and does so in the interest of advancing its own cause; and in this process it transcends its own narcissism moving toward a mutual, collective identification, the true significance of the universal.

TOWARD PROCESS PSYCHOLOGY

Within this past century, the history of the psychoanalytic movement has proven to be both diverse and adversarial. Since Freud's advent of the classical approach to theory and technique, the field has shifted away from an emphasis on the drives, to ego psychology, object relations theory, self psychology, and is currently preoccupied with postmodern perspectives and those focusing on relationality and intersubjectivity. Each movement offers a central theme informing theory and method, namely (1) drive, (2) ego, (3) object, (4) self, and (5) intersubjectivity. It is often the case that each camp holds allegiance to its preferred theoretical discourse and has little tolerance for mutations in conceptualization or technique. This is especially the case for classically trained psychoanalysts who are forced to combat the radicalization of theoretical and technical change. Contemporary psychoanalysis focuses primarily on relational, interpersonal, and intersubjective approaches, and Freud's metapsychology has been largely subsumed (but in some cases rejected) under the umbrella of these widening perspectives.

Lacanian theory has remained on the fringe of mainstream psychoanalysis mainly due to his unorthodox and perverted technique, his fragmented and unorganized theoretical writing style—corresponding to his theory of desire—and his denunciation of the self and subjectivity. For these reasons, he has been mainly of interest to academe. There have been minimal attempts to offer a comparative-integrative approach combining and synthesizing the main psychoanalytic theories,[23] presumably because of group loyalties, but also because certain theoretical advances clash with orthodoxy. This is especially the case with Kohut who has in implicit ways tacked on the "self" as a fourth agency to Freud's tripartite model, and even more radically with Lacan who has denied the self altogether. Because Lacan decenters the subject—the very heart of psychoanalytic thought—he is not likely to find a proper home in mainstream psychoanalysis.

Yet many psychoanalytic contemporaries are jumping on the postmodern bandwagon advocating nominalism, deconstruction, feminist, and social constructive approaches to theory, and poststructural, linguistic accounts of psychic development, subjectivity, and psychotherapeutic treatment. To those familiar with the Modern philosophical tradition up through German Idealism and twentieth-century Continental philosophy, contemporary psychoanalysis seems to be behind the times. Committed to neither theoretical orthodoxy nor unification, the governing plurality of psychoanalytic discourse informing conceptual and therapeutic practices appears to be fraying around the edges. Theoretically, there is little creativity left; psychoanalysis is at the limit. Camps are divided: many depart from Freud, holding onto relational concepts, and where there is theoretical novelty, it is found in rediscovering past philosophical paradigms. This may be said for Lacan's so-called return to Freud, linguistic and social constructivist approaches borrowed from postmodernism, and the emphasis on phenomenology and intersubjectivity, which unequivocally dates back to Hegel.[24] While still tied to an empirical framework, theoretical revision relies more on observation and practice and less on conceptual improvements. But with a few noteworthy exceptions,[25] psychoanalysis today largely lacks philosophical rigor.

Psychoanalysis not only benefits from Hegel's philosophy, but recognizing that Hegel himself recognized the significance of the unconscious improves our understanding of Hegel. This poses a challenge to those Hegelians who insist that Hegel's rationalism leaves little room for irrational processes that suffuse the very essence of spirit. On the other hand, psychoanalysis today faces a potential danger of remaining either uncreative or stagnant, thus becoming ossified in dogma. If psychoanalysis is to truly profit from Hegelian thought, then it must first embrace the notion of process.

Whether we accept Heraclitus's dictum: "Everything flows" (*panta hrei*), Hegel's dialectic of spirit, or Whitehead's process philosophy, the notion of process, transmutation, and metamorphosis underlie all reality. This is especially applicable to psychic structure. While the notion of the "self-as-process" has been discussed among some contemporary psychoanalytic thinkers,[26] the significance of a process psychology has not been realized. As we have seen, the self-as-process has its full significance acknowledged in Hegel's philosophy of spirit.

Process psychology is an *essentialist* position—not as fixed or stagnant attributes and properties that inhere in the structure of a substance or thing—but rather as a dynamic flux of transposing and self-generative, creative processes having their form and instantiability within the dialectic of becoming. Process as pure activity is the essence of intrapsychic and intersubjective life insofar that if it were removed, psychic reality would perish.

With increasing tolerance for philosophical inquiry, process psychology could open up new directions in psychoanalysis. While the possible range and potential of process thinking for the field of psychoanalysis is beyond the scope of this book, we must repeatedly emphasize the value of the dialectical approach. Because the appropriation of process psychology within psychoanalytic theory rests on a proper appreciation of the Hegelian dialectic, I wish for a moment to briefly return to Hegel's dialectical logic. Understanding the dynamics and nuances of Hegel's dialectical method may lead to advances in theoretical, clinical, and applied psychoanalysis, a proper understanding of which I hope will spark future interest in research and psychoanalytic scholarship.

HEGEL'S DIALECTIC AND PROCESS PSYCHOANALYTIC THOUGHT

Although Hegel is one of the most prodigious and influential thinkers in the history of philosophy, his dialectical method remains one of his least well understood philosophical contributions. While philosophers have made scores of commentaries and interpretations of Hegel's dialectic,[27] some interpreters have gone so far as to deny Hegel's method,[28] or else they have rendered it opaque, simplistic, and imprecise.[29] Hegel's dialectical method naturally governs all three dimensions of his overall philosophical system, namely, the *Logic*, the *Philosophy of Nature*, and the *Philosophy of Spirit*, as well as the *Phenomenology*. The dialectic serves as the quintessential method not only for explicating the fundamental operations of mind, but also for expounding the nature and ontological force behind the unfolding of reality itself, a force that originally has its source outside of consciousness.

Hegel's philosophy of spirit and its specific application to the psychoanalytic mind rests on a proper understanding of the ontology of the dialectic. Hegel refers to the unrest of *Aufhebung*—what we have already said is customarily translated as "sublation," a dialectical process entering into opposition within its own determinations and thus raising this opposition to a higher unity which is continuously being annulled, preserved, and elevated. Hegel's use of *Aufhebung*, a term he borrowed from Schiller but also an ordinary German word, is to be distinguished from its purely negative function whereby there is a complete canceling or drowning of the lower relation in the higher, to also encompass a preservative element. Therefore, the term *aufheben* has a threefold meaning: (1) to suspend or cancel, (2) to surpass or transcend, and (3) to preserve. In the *Encyclopaedia Logic*, Hegel makes this clear: "On the one hand, we understand it to mean 'clear away' or 'cancel,' and in that sense we say that a law or regulation is canceled [*aufgehoben*]. But the word also means 'to preserve' " (*EL* § 96, *Zusatz*).

Unlike Fichte's meaning of the verb *aufheben*, defined as: to eliminate, annihilate, abolish, or destroy, Hegel's designation signifies a threefold activity by which mental operations at once cancel or annul opposition, preserve or retain it, and surpass or elevate its previous shape to a higher structure. This process of the dialectic underlies all operations of mind and is seen as the thrust behind world history and culture. As I have argued, the dialectic is the *essence* of psychic life, for if it were to be removed, consciousness and unconscious processes would evaporate.

Aufhebung is itself a contradiction; the word contradicts itself. Thought as a contradiction is constituted in and through bifurcation, a rigid opposition as antithesis. Thus, as a process, reason cancels the rigid opposition, surpasses the opposition by transcending or moving beyond it in a higher unity, and simultaneously preserving the opposition in the higher unity rather than simply dissolving it. The preservation is a validating function under which opposition is subsumed within a new shape of consciousness. Reason does not merely set up over and against these antitheses; it does not only set up a higher unity but also reasons a unity precisely through these opposites. Thus, the dialectic has a negative and a positive side. This is echoed in Hegel's *Science of Logic*:

> "*To sublate*" has a twofold meaning in the language: on the one hand it means to preserve, to maintain, and equally it also means to cause to cease, to put an end to. Even "to preserve" includes a negative element, namely, that something is removed from its immediacy and so from an existence which is open to external influences, in order to preserve it. Thus what is sublated is at the same time preserved; it has only lost its immediacy but is not on that account annihilated. (*SL*, 107)

When psychoanalysis refers to dialectics, it often uses Fichte's threefold movement of thought in the form of thetic, analytic or antithetic, and synthetic judgments giving rise to the popularized (if not bastardized) phrase: thesis-antithesis-synthesis[30]—a process normally and inaccurately attributed to Hegel;[31] or it describes unresolvable contradictions or mutual oppositions that are analogous to Kant's antinomies or paralogisms of the self.[32] It is important to note that Hegel's dialectic is not the same as Kant's, who takes contradiction and conflict as signs of the breakdown of reason, nor is it Fichte's, who does not explicate the preservative function of the lower relation remaining embedded in the higher. Furthermore, when psychoanalysts and social scientists apply something like the Fichtean dialectic to their respective disciplines, the details of this process are omitted. The presumptive conclusion is that a synthesis cancels the previous moments and initiates a new moment that is once again opposed and reorganized. But the synthesis does not mean that all previous elements are preserved, or that psychic structure is elevated. In fact, this form of dialectic may lead to an infinite repetition of contradictions and conflict that meet with no resolve.

As we have emphasized repeatedly, Hegel's dialectic essentially describes the process by which a mediated dynamic begets a new immediate, thus providing the logical basis to account for the role of negativity within a progressive unitary drive. The process by which mediation collapses into a new immediate provides us with the logical model for understanding the dynamics of the mind. Spirit as an architectonic process burgeons as a self-determining generative activity that builds upon its successive developmental phases, which form its appearances. Spirit educates itself as it passes through its various dialectical configurations ascending toward higher shapes of self-awareness. What spirit takes to be truth in its earlier forms is realized to be merely a moment. It is not until the stage of absolute knowing as pure conceiving or comprehensive, conceptual understanding that spirit finally integrates its previous movements into a synthetic unity as a dynamic self-articulated complex whole.

Not only does the dialectic apply to the nature of intrapsychic development, object relations, the intersubjective field, and social and institutional reform, but it has direct implications for the consulting room. The dialectic informs the very nature of intersubjectivity, the therapist-patient dyad, group dynamics, organizational development, and the historical progression of culture. This issue is of particular importance when examining the dialectical polarities, forces, and operations of the mind outlined by various psychoanalytic theories and how the field itself may be shown to participate in this dialectical process. From this vantage point, Hegel's dialectic is especially helpful in understanding the historical development of psychoanalysis. Psychoanalysis, like spirit, is a process of becoming.

DIALECTICAL PSYCHOANALYSIS

Freud's paradigm of the mind is dialectical. He consistently introduces bipolar forces within psychic structure that give rise to a negative dialectic mediated by the synthetic powers of the ego. Consider the dialectical tensions and dynamic interplay between the major constituents of psychic life: There is opposition between consciousness and the unconscious, the ego and the id, the ego and its modified ideal counterpart—the superego, the two major drives, primary process versus secondary process thinking, the pleasure principle and the reality principle, and wish and defense. The ego mediates all forms of conflict, whether internally motivated or externally imposed by the demands of objective reality. For example, libidinal and aggressive strivings institute a whole network of wishes, defenses, and compromises designed to both satiate the id's desire while keeping it checked, perennially facing the moral condemnation and ideal judgments of the superego. Through dream activity, parapraxes, and symptom formation, the ego attempts to both resolve psychic conflict and fulfill primal wishes through circuitous routes and derivative forms. The dialectical maneuvers of defense and symptom substitution are compromise formations that enable the self to function and adapt to psychic and social life.

Throughout the history of the development of psychoanalysis, theorists have slowly shifted away from drive psychology and have instead emphasized the dialectical dynamics inherent in the self's relation to its object-related environment. For those who interpret Freud through a natural science paradigm, drive theory is closely tied to biology, and therefore sexuality is overemphasized. It is important to note that Freud's classical model as a whole is not at odds with contemporary theoretical advances; in fact, his model introduced and initiated ego psychology and the object relations movement. Ego psychologists highlight the dialectical relations between the self as *Ich* and adaptation to drive and environmental demands. Ego psychology, largely advanced by Anna Freud and Heinz Hartmann, among others, addresses the operations of the ego with regard to its defensive, adaptive, and conflict-free functions.[33] The emphasis here is on the mechanisms or processes of the ego and its functional and constructive capacities to ameliorate psychic conflict. This movement interfaced with the object relations perspectives of Melanie Klein, Wilfred Bion, W. R. D. Fairbairn, D. W. Winnicott, and Harry Guntrip who attempted to bridge both classical psychoanalysis with theories of object or people-relatedness and the development of the self.[34] What is commonly known as the "British school" of object relations emphasized early childhood development, the nature of attachments to parental figures, the role of the maternal environment, responsiveness, and the overall attunement of the object milieu that fostered the development of psychic structure. Because the role of the ego figures prominently within relational theories—many of which were prepared and advanced by other distinguished analytic thinkers such as Ian Suttie, Harry Stack Sullivan, Michael Balint, Margaret Mahler, John Bowlby, and Otto Kernberg, just to name a few[35]—it is often difficult to distinguish the philosophical importance of the ego from its object and aim. While ego psychology primarily emphasized the intrapsychic, object relations psychology emphasized the interpersonal. Here we may not only see the dichotomy of subject and object and the priority claims attributed to one over the other, but we can also observe how the field itself constructed its own oppositions as a result of theoretical preferences. Psychoanalysis became divided over assigning greater significance to the self versus the other, to the inner over the outer, a division that also materialized within many schools of thought over the history of philosophy.

As the dialectic of subject and object continues to preoccupy psychoanalytic revision, attempts at synthetic integration have been broached via relational theories that emphasize subjectivity once again: here enters "self psychology." Somewhat prepared by Winnicott and Guntrip, Heinz Kohut launched the fourth wave in psychoanalytic theory known as self psychology.[36] In an attempt to highlight both dimensions of subject and object, he argued that the human psyche was comprised of "selfobjects," that is, real, perceived, or imagined objects—usually people—that are imbued with psychological significance and seen as a part of the self. More precisely, it is largely the *functions* that selfobjects serve that are important to psychic structure and development.

Kohut's attempt to collapse the self and the object into a unity may be seen as an attempt at resolving their dichotomy; but critics can claim that Kohut still emphasizes intrapsychic processes over interpersonal ones and thus does not truly achieve an appropriate synthesis. In practice, this theoretical determination is not salient, because therapeutic conditions must take into account the multiple dynamics and processes that constitute mental life and intersubjective relations, therefore interpersonal processes cannot be segregated from intrapsychic ones. Kohut's movement, while initially attempting to integrate classical psychoanalytic doctrine into a new paradigm, later became more independently constructed, especially with reference to variation in technique and the broadening of the analysis of the transference. It may be generally said that Freud purists stand opposed to many contemporary perspectives because they depart from orthodoxy in theory and method. And the proliferation of psychoanalytic institutes that emphasize relational, interpersonal, and self psychological approaches to theory and practice is largely a response to the elitist, dogmatic, and medical domination of psychoanalytic training programs that offer little deviation from the classical approach.

In its maturity, self psychology offered radical new advances in theory and practice. Kohut introduced his own set of dialectical relations and structures that inform mental processes and envisioned the self as constituting the dynamic interaction between two poles of psychic development.

> A firm self, resulting from optimal interactions between the child and his selfobjects, is made up of three major constituents: 1) one pole from which emanates the basic strivings for power and success; 2) another pole that harbors the basic idealized goals; and 3) an intermediate area of basic talents and skills that are activated by the tension arc that establishes itself between ambitions and ideals.[37]

While Kohut reinterpreted Freud's views on narcissism, identification, and superego functions such as the need for idealization, empathy, and validation of self-worth, it may be said that selfobject theory (as well as much of intersubjectivity theory) describes psychological configurations that are practically transparent to consciousness. Although self psychology portrays the "self" as a fourth agency alongside Freud's tripartite-structural model, self psychology finds little room for the unconscious.[38] It may be argued, with qualifications, that in contemporary psychoanalytic theory, the emphasis on the unconscious has virtually disappeared.[39]

Contiguous with the work of Stephen Mitchell, Daniel Stern, Jessica Benjamin,[40] and Thomas Ogden,[41] the fifth movement in psychoanalysis that captures our current attention in the field is what is labeled "intersubjectivity theory," mainly initiated by George Atwood, Robert Stolorow, Donna Orange, and others,[42] but also stipulated as a "relational,"[43] dynamic, or "dyadic systems"[44] paradigm. With the exception of a few scholars, most notably Benjamin,[45] psychoanalysis seems to be oblivious to the fact that intersubjectivity was thoroughly addressed by Hegel in his treatment of self-consciousness in the *Phenomenology*. With the emphasis now on intersubjectivity theory, phenomenological, postmodern, and poststructural accounts of human psychology are beginning to take shape within the psychoanalytic domain.

Intersubjectivity theory bridges object relations approaches and self psychology and thus constitutes a sublated achievement in psychoanalytic theory building. Beginning with drive as alienated desire, *das Es* was an object opposed to a subject—*das Ich*. Soon the dichotomy between the Ego and the Other formed rigid group identifications, each emphasizing the significance of one realm over the other. With the centrality of the Self, the subject and the object were collapsed into a unity, however, privileging intrapsychic subjectivity. With the introduction of intersubjectivity theory—itself a modified extension of self psychology, psychoanalysis can now treat subject and object as equiprimordial constructs: subject-object, self-other—are mutually recognized and reciprocally determinant organizations of experience. While there are many different conceptions of intersubjectivity, we may generally say that intersubjective approaches prioritize the phenomenological field that is generated by the mutual presence and influence of two (or more) experiential subjective worlds converging and interpenetrating one another as an interdependent system of reciprocal dialectical relations. In other words, intersubjectivity is process.

As each psychoanalytic movement emerged in dialectical response to its previous shapes, each opposition was canceled, surpassed, yet preserved within its new paradigm. But this process may be said to be a return to what Hegel had stipulated almost two centuries earlier: the self-development of the subject is dependent upon recognition by other subjects; subject and object merge into unity, each side being merely a moment of its totality. Here we may see the value of Hegel's logic of the dialectic. Not only does Hegel contribute to the development of psychoanalysis, but his dialectic gains descriptive power in explaining that development.

Within psychoanalysis, it was Freud himself who paved the way for the consideration of intersubjectivity, for psychic development rests upon the internalization of others and their functional relations through the process of identification. As Freud tells us, identification is the earliest attachment to an object through an emotional bond (*SE*, 18, 105–110; 19, 28–34; 22, 63–68). The process of identification becomes a core feature in building psychic structure which is at once both an ego (intrapsychic) operation and an object (interpersonal) relation, hence an intersubjective dynamic. Together with Freud's mature theory of eros as a relational principle (*SE*, 19, 40–47, 218; 22, 103–107, 209–212; 23, 148–151),[46] Stolorow and his colleagues' misattribution to Freud the notion of an isolated, solipsistic mind becomes an ideology uncritically accepted by many intersubjective theorists.[47] The self is to some degree the internalization of the other (e.g., parental imagos, social values and customs, linguistic acquisitions) which is reappropriated, transformed, and integrated into intrapsychic configurations conforming to intrinsic subjective organizations, pressures, wishes, conflicts, external demands, etc. Combined with the self's own innate propensities—whether this be the influence of the drives, the striving for attachments, relatedness, and object love, the dialectic between ambitions and ideals, or the need for mutual recognition—psychic organization is an intersubjective process of becoming.

Process psychology is an intersubjective theory, but not one that necessarily subordinates or supercedes individual intrapsychic experience: it merely incorporates it within the larger parameters of unfolding dialectical relations. Process psychology must account for all possible conditions of psychic reality, from the moment of the inception of individual unconscious subjectivity (thus prior to intersubjective dynamics), to the cultivated, collective-identificatory aspects of rational, aesthetic, ethical, and social self-conscious life. Process psychology observes the primacy of the dialectic, and that means that opposition is contextual, hence potentially and radically operative within any domain of lived phenomenal experience and the intersubjective matrix affecting such experience. A process approach to psychoanalysis is concerned with both the universals that govern human subjectivity, namely, the *subjective universality* of our shared anthropology as a human race, as well as the particulars that uniquely define each subjective mind within its own personal, experiential, idiosyncratic, embodied, gendered, linguistic, and/or cultural-political contexts. This ensures that process psychoanalytic thought must take into account contingency within universality. When examined in its totality, it is the whole process under consideration that yields greater insights into the ontological, epistemological, and phenomenological configurations governing human dynamics.

Both Hegel and psychoanalysis observe the significance of the family and its peremptory impact on psychic structure. But the value of Hegel for psychoanalysis transcends merely the introduction of process thinking. Hegel stresses the continuity of the private and the public, and thus the importance of community life for mental health. While psychoanalysis is giving increased attention to social, linguistic, feminist, and cultural forces that operate on individual and collective mental organizations, the internalization process, and normal and abnormal development, Hegel adds to our understanding of the role of social structures and institutions that impact on the evolution of the human race. It is from this standpoint that he contributes not only to our conceptualization of mind and individual personality, but also to our appreciation of the multiple, complex overdeterminations and interactions between mankind and society that inform our collective anthropology.

Hegel's dialectic adds to the substantiality of psychoanalytic thought. Nowhere is this application more explicit than in Freud's paradigm of the mind and human nature. Although perhaps unintended by him, Freud's theoretical advances are dialectically informed. The ego grows out of the id as a modified maturation of its original nature and becomes the central agency of mental life (*SE*, 20, 97; 22, 75). The ego, in its tendency toward splitting, division, and synthesis, generates and mediates opposition, and raises itself to the standpoint of self-conscious reason and ethical awareness, thus sublating unconscious structure. Therefore, reason and ethical self-consciousness are the realization of unconscious *Geist*—"Where it was, there I shall become."[48]

The preservative elements of the dialectic are most notably clear in the function of repression: the past is incorporated into present structure which resurfaces in future shapes. The significance of the past informs both the historical progression of spirit and the psychical development of the individual. Just as images and feelings are preserved within the abyss, coming to presence in imagination and in times of illness, the repressed material constituting wish and defense resides in the reservoir of the id. Like the evolution of spirit, primary process mentation, belonging to primitive unconscious organizations, is superceded by secondary process thinking belonging to the mature ego. In times of mental disease, however, the primitive draws the mature back to its original form in the regressed, fixated, and undifferentiated form of feeling. According to Hegel and Freud, the deranged mind is saturated by primitive primary processes and is unable to hold onto its objective ego functions.

For Hegel, tracing the ontology of the unconscious is more than just an empirical inquiry: it rises to the level of a grand metaphysical question. Hegel shows, as does Freud, that the unconscious is the ground of consciousness and the primal being of psychic structure. He shows that unconscious ground gives rise to conscious self-reflective life and is responsible for both mental health and pathology. There is a logic to the interior that generates the manifestations of mind. For Hegel, "appearance is essence" (*PS* § 147); "essence must *appear*" (*EL* § 131), for nothing can exist unless it is made actual. The unconscious appears as consciousness, its modified and evolved form. In this sense, spirit is analogous to a symptom; revealing the hidden dynamics of the soul, consciousness is the disclosure of unconscious concealment. Whether perverted or pristine, spirit is the realization of unconscious being.

The dialectic becomes the logical model by which each mediation collapses into a new immediate thus begetting new shapes of psychic life, preserving the old within its burgeoning structure. The dialectic becomes the ontological and logical force behind the organization of the self and society. Freud's great insight was to show how the unconscious necessarily informs the normative and abnormal functioning of the human mind, without which mental life could not be made intelligible. Likewise, the abyss makes Hegel's system more intelligible, because it accounts for original ground that gives richer meaning and substance to his phenomenology and the logical operations of thought. Taking the unconscious seriously improves our understanding of Hegel.

Hegel's and Freud's models of the psyche are imbued with a negative dialectic:[49] negativity is responsible for both growth and decay. Negativity and chaos underlie the ontology of mind; the ego is constantly under siege by oppressive and combative forces that it must mediate and conquer in order to successfully adapt, thus spirit is the outgrowth of progressive negation. The question of death and destruction is central to our understanding of the human mind. In sickness and in

health, in progression and stagnation, the drive toward unity and mastery constitutes the double center of desire: negativity is our inner being. The tendency toward sublation over withdrawal in Hegel, or sublimation and regression in Freud,
speaks to the tremendous power of the negative.

> But the life of spirit is not the life that shrinks from death and keeps itself un-
> touched by devastation, but rather the life that endures it and maintains itself in
> it. It wins its truth only when, in utter dismemberment, it finds itself. (*PS* § 32)

Negation—Conflict! This is what defines our existence. Whether in spiritual
order or in the abstract unity of the soul, there is nothing in the external world
that can draw us away from the reality of the life within.

At this point I wish to raise the question one last time: To what degree does
the unconscious resist being exalted or surpassed by the dialectic? Does the abyss
resist being integrated into Spirit? This would imply that the abyss would seemingly appear to have a will and a purpose all to its own. Is the urge for unity as
the drive toward the Absolute simultaneously in opposition to a competing urge
to withdraw in the face of nostalgia within the abyss of spirit's unconscious beginning? As the soul passes through its various configurations on the ladder toward truth, does it draw itself back toward the pit of its feeling life? Such
tendency toward withdrawal, back toward the pit, "could perhaps broach a wonder that one could never aspire to surpass."[50] And if the abyss resists the call of
spirit, to what degree does the unconscious inform reason yet remain behind the
back of consciousness? Or is there simply a duality of purpose that spirit fights
in itself? Does desire have a double edge, that of moving forward and backward,
of evolution and devolution, transcendence and descendence? Does spirit struggle between competing inclinations toward reason and feeling, sublimation and
regression, elevation and withdrawal? Is the duality of desire spirit's nature; does
it belong to spirit as such, or is spirit its slave?

Perhaps spirit is merely returning to itself, to the symbiotic abyss of its immediate determinant being. Does spirit merely seek to transform or to go to
sleep once again? In this sense, the yearning for unity is a return to unity, always
its end. Yet for Hegel, this end is always its beginning, the eternal return of the
same. Thus, unconscious spirit remains a "riddle to itself" (*PS* § 365). Perhaps
the greatest conflict occurs when spirit attempts to surpass itself. For spirit resists
itself, it resists the movement of its own becoming. Perhaps subjective spirit resists such integration for fear of losing its sense of self in the collective; it fights
its own process for fear of the loss of its individuality. From this standpoint, spirit
can never rid itself of its desire for the recovery of its lost unity, of the yearning
to return to its primitive existence, its original condition. Perhaps the Absolute
is merely the archetypal image—the call—of spirit's original unity. Perhaps spirit
is even empathic to its own dilemma. I wonder. And with wonder comes wonder, as the abyss redefines itself one more time.

NOTES

INTRODUCTION

1. See Daniel Berthhold-Bond, "Hegel, Nietzsche, and Freud on Madness and the Unconscious," *The Journal of Speculative Philosophy* no. 3 (1991): 193–213; "Intentionality and Madness in Hegel's Psychology of Action," *International Philosophical Quarterly* 32, no. 4 (1992): 427–441; "Hegel on Madness and Tragedy," *History of Philosophy Quarterly* 11, no. 1 (1994): 71–99; *Hegel's Theory of Madness* (Albany: State University of New York Press, 1995); Sean Kelly, *Individuation and the Absolute: Hegel, Jung, and the Path toward Wholeness* (New York: Paulist Press, 1993); Errol E. Harris, "Hegel's Anthropology," *Owl of Minerva* 25, no. 1 (1993): 5–14; and Darrel Christensen, "The Theory of Mental Derangement and the Role and Function of Subjectivity in Hegel," *The Personalist* 49 (1968): 433–453.

2. One of the few accounts that considers the role of the unconscious in Hegel's philosophy that does not focus on the theme of psychopathology is offered by John Russon in *The Self and its Body in Hegel's* Phenomenology of Spirit (Toronto: University of Toronto Press, 1997).

3. Robert C. Solomon provides a nice introduction to the concept of spirit in "Hegel's Concept of *Geist*," in *Hegel: A Collection of Critical Essays*, ed. A. MacIntyre (Garden City, NY: Anchor Doubleday, 1972), 125–149.

4. Cf. *Lectures on the Philosophy of History*, sec. Philosophical Reason in History, 30ff.

5. Sean Kelly provides a comprehensive account of Hegel's theory of complex holism. Cf. *Individuation and the Absolute*, 29–30.

6. Sean Kelly, in *Individuation and the Absolute*, makes this point with reference to Jung's notion of the collective unconscious, p. 62.

7. See *Phenomenology*, § 18. Darrel Christensen, in "The Theory of Mental Derangement and the Role and Function of Subjectivity in Hegel," also discusses in depth the role and function of subjectivity in Hegel's philosophy.

8. Cf. Petry, *Hegel's Philosophy of Subjective Spirit*, Notes to Vol.3, 405.

9. Hegel discusses this in the Introduction of the *Philosophy of Nature*, trans, A. V. Miller (Oxford: Clarendon Press, 1970), Vol.2 of the *Encyclopaedia*.

10. A full account of this argument will be made more explicit in chapters 2 and 3.

11. John Sallis, *Spacings of Reason and Imagination: In Texts of Kant, Fichte, Hegel* (Chicago: University of Chicago Press, 1987), 152.

12. Berthold-Bond demonstrates how Nietzsche and Freud have parallel psychologies of the unconscious that are linked to the body as instinct. See "Hegel, Nietzsche, and Freud on Madness and the Unconscious."

13. Errol E. Harris, "Hegel's Anthropology," 13.

14. Freud is often misunderstood to be a reductive materialist, relying on his unofficial and immature views espoused in the *Project for a Scientific Psychology* (*Standard Edition*, Vol. 1, 1895, 295). Freud realized that he could never offer an adequate theory of mind solely from a neurophysiological account and by 1900 had officially abandoned his earlier materialistic visions for a psychological corpus (Cf. *The Interpretation of Dreams*, Vols. 4–5, 536). I discuss this point more fully in chapter 3.

15. This point has also been discussed by Jerome D. Levin, *Theories of the Self* (Washington, DC: Hemisphere, 1992), 51.

16. In the *Phenomenology*, Hegel tells us: "As Subject . . . the True . . . is the process of its own becoming, the circle that presupposes its end as its goal, having its end also as its beginning; and only by being worked out to its end, is it actual" (*PS* § 18). Later he says, "The realized purpose, or the existent actuality, is movement and unfolded becoming . . . the self is like that immediacy and simplicity of the beginning because it is the result, that which has returned into itself" (*PS* § 22). In the *Science of Logic*, Hegel further extends the development of the self to that of the Concept: "The Concept, when it has developed into a *concrete existence* that is itself free, is none other than the *I* or pure self-consciousness" (*SL*, 583). For Hegel, the self and the Concept are pure becoming: "The Idea is essentially *process*" (*EL* § 215).

17. Daniel Berthold-Bond, in a series of articles culminating in a book, has been the most influential scholar to provide systematic rigor to Hegel's theory of madness. Refer to footnote 1.

18. Berthold-Bond, in "Hegel, Nietzsche, and Freud on Madness and the Unconscious," points out how Hegel's notion of insanity is spirit's self-attempt at healing itself via regression and withdrawal. This notion runs parallel to Freud's theory of repetition compulsion as an expression of the death drive. In contemporary psychoanalysis, the compulsion to unconsciously repeat traumatic past experiences may be generally interpreted as a means of gaining mastery and control over internal conflict or as an attempt to procure object attachments or love.

19. Darrel Christensen, in "The Theory of Mental Derangement," interprets Hegel's central theory of mental derangement as centering on the dialectical opposition between the feeling soul and the physical soul.

20. Freud's conceptualization of the unconscious is organized by the dialectical exchange of psychic forces that seek to maintain homeostasis through drive discharge and

ego adaptation to conflict and environmental demands. Within all psychoanalytic disciplines since Freud, there appears to be a universal dialectical interplay between subject and object. Historically, the postclassical movement in psychoanalysis emphasized the role of the ego as agent of unconscious activity and focused on the ego's motives toward mastery and adaptation of inner forces via defensive construction and cognitive transcendence over instinctual demands. While the classical position emphasized the pleasure-seeking aims of drives, object relations theories have emphasized the primacy of object (people) seeking as the central motive of unconscious and conscious activity oriented toward interpersonal involvement and relational attachment. Self psychology introduced the centrality of the self as agent motivated toward fulfilling "selfobject" needs of empathic attunement and validation from others, mirroring of self-worth from the object world, and the pursuit of idealized relationships all in the narcissistic service of the self. While the field of psychoanalysis has radically departed from Freud's metapsychology and presently focuses on relational theories, intersubjectivity, dyadic systems, and contemporary selfobject theory, Freud's psychoanalytic theory remains subsumed within contemporary thought. However, whether unconscious motivation emanates from the influence of drives, the ego, object relations, the self, or intersubjectivity, all disciplines within the historical development of psychoanalysis observe the phenomenology of the dialectic. For a review see, Howard A. Bacal and Kenneth M. Newman, *Theories of Object Relations: Bridges to Self Psychology* (New York: Columbia University Press, 1990); Steven A. Mitchell, *Relational Concepts in Psychoanalysis: An Integration* (Cambridge: Harvard University Press, 1988); Fred Pine, *Drive, Ego, Object, & Self* (New York: Basic Books, 1990); and Heinz Kohut, *How Does Analysis Cure?*, ed. A. Goldberg and P. Stepansky (Chicago: University of Chicago Press, 1984).

21. See Freud, *Standard Edition*, 19, 24; 20, 97; 22, 75–76.

22. See my article, "Hegel on Projective Identification: Implications for Klein, Bion, and Beyond," *The Psychoanalytic Review* 87, no. 6 (2000): 841–874.

23. Cf. Jürgen Habermas, "The Interpretation of a Case," in *Knowledge and Human Interests* (London: Heinemann, 1972); Adolf Grünbaum, *The Foundations of Psychoanalysis* (Berkeley: University of California Press, 1984). Also see Marilyn Nissim-Sabat, "The Crisis in Psychoanalysis: Resolution Through Husserlian Phenomenology and Feminism," *Human Studies* 14 (1991): 33–66, for a feminist-phenomenological critique; and Paul Ricoeur, *Freud and Philosophy* (New Haven: Yale University Press, 1970), for a hermeneutical analysis.

24. Much ignorance about Freud's theories is due to the fact that many people don't actually read Freud's texts, but rather consult textbook summaries and interpretations offered by incompetent, nonscholarly professionals. This is also an endemic problem in contemporary psychoanalytic training institutes. When Freud's texts are consulted, interpreters often focus on his early work and fail to note the historical transformations of his theories. Frank Sulloway has popularized the notion that Freud was a biologist of the mind, a claim cogently disputed by Richard Wollheim and others. Recently, Donald Levy has impugned Freud's critics by pointing out their limited, selective, and biased arguments under the influence of an ideology. In two influential books, Jonathan Lear also offers a defense of Freud and dispenses with much misconception and disported perceptions of psychoanalysis and its application. See, Frank J. Sulloway, *Freud: Biologist of the Mind* (Cambridge: Harvard University Press, 1979); Richard Wollheim, *Sigmund Freud* (New York: Cambridge University

Press, 1971); Donald Levy, *Freud Among the Philosophers* (New Haven: Yale University Press, 1996); Jonathan Lear, *Love and Its Place in Nature: A Philosophical Interpretation of Freudian Psychoanalysis* (New York: Noonday Press, 1990), and *Open Minded: Working Out the Logic of the Soul* (Cambridge: Harvard University Press, 1998).

CHAPTER ONE. RETRACING THE *UNGRUND*

1. *Science of Logic*, Second Preface, 36–37. Hegel also speaks of the "latent, unconscious" features of all action in *Reason in History*, the Introduction to the *Lectures on the Philosophy of History*, § 35, trans. J. Sibree (New York: Willey Book Co., 1900).

2. See Eric von der Luft's "Comment," in *History and System: Hegel's Philosophy of History*, ed. Robert L. Perkins (Albany: State University of New York Press, 1994), 39.

3. Refer to David Walsh's, "The Historical Dialectic of Spirit: Jacob Boehme's Influence on Hegel," in *History and System*, 16.

4. Cf. Edward Allen Beach, *The Potencies of God(s): Schelling's Philosophy of Mythology* (Albany: State University of New York Press, 1994), 70.

5. There are many different systems of Gnosticism that offer varying accounts on the nature of first principles and the coming into being of God and the universe. However, a cardinal element of Gnostic thought is a radical dualism that governs the relation between God and the world. Gnostics conceive of God as the "Alien" or the "first Life." This appears as a standard introduction of Mandaean compositions: "In the name of the great first alien Life from the worlds of light, the sublime that stands above all," and is reflected throughout gnostic literature such as Marcion's concept of the "alien God," "the Other," "the Nameless," "the Hidden," "the Unknown," and the "unknown Father." Belonging to another (nether) world, the divine Alien is "strange" and "unfamiliar," hence "incomprehensible." Estranged from the comprehensible world, the "great first Life" is conceived of as possessing both positive and negative attributes of superiority and suffering, perfection and tragedy, transcendence and alienation from its original being. Further competing dialectical forces are attributed to the godhead which are understood differently by various gnostic myths and theories on cosmology, cosmogony, and anthropology. The second-century gnostic, Basilides, is said to have postulated a primal "nonexistent god," which was later taken up by Valentinus who claimed that "there is in invisible and ineffable heights a pre-existent perfect aeon (i.e. a supernatural being), whom they also call Pre-beginning, Fore-father and Primal Ground (Bythos), that he is inconceivable and invisible, eternal and uncreated (or: begotten) and that he existed in great peace and stillness in unending spaces (aeons)" (Irenaeus, *Adversus Haereses*, 11). Due to the indescribable nature of the "divine Absolute," the Valentinians were content with using a few alchemical symbols as "Abyss" or "Silence" to represent the ineffable. See Hans Jonas, *The Gnostic Religion*, 2nd Ed. (Boston: Beacon Press, 1958), 42, 49–50, 199; Kurt Rudolph, *Gnosis: The Nature and History of Gnosticism* (San Francisco: Harper & Row, 1977), 62; Irenaeus of Lyons, *Adversus Haereses*, ed. W. W. Harvey, 2 vols. (Cambridge, 1857; reprint Ridgewood, NJ, 1965).

6. Cf. Andrew Weeks, *Boehme: An Intellectual Biography of the Seventeenth-Century Philosopher and Mystic* (Albany: State University of New York Press, 1991), 148.

7. Weeks, 149.

8. Ibid, 148.

9. Most notably in his *Lectures on the History of Modern Philosophy*, Vol.3. Also see David Walsh's essay in *History and System*, ch.2.

10. Cf. Eric von der Luft's "Comment," in *History and System*, 37–39.

11. Cf. Beach, 1994, ch.3.

12. *New Essays on Human Understanding*, trans. and ed. Peter Remnant and Jonathan Bennett (Cambridge: Cambridge University Press, 1981), 133f, 210.

13. *Anthropologie in pragmatischer Hinsicht*, in *Kants Werke*, bd. vii (Berlin: Walter de Gruyter, 1968),136, 138; Also see Beach, 47–48 and footnotes 3 and 4 to ch.3.

14. Hegel, "Jakob Böhme," in *Werke* 20 (*Vorlesungen über die Geschichte der Philosophie* 3) (Frankfurt/M: Suhrkamp, 1971), 91–119.

15. The readily available German editions of Boehme's works are *Die Urschriften*, 2 Vols., ed. Werner Buddecke. (Stuttgart: Frommanns Verlag, 1963 and 1966); and *Sämtliche Schriften*, 11 Vols., ed. Will-Erich Peuckert and August Faust (Stuttgart: Frommanns Verlag, 1955–1961), (originally published in 1730). Hereafter, unless otherwise noted, citations are referenced to the reprinted facsimile 1730 edition of *Sämtliche Schriften* by volume, page, and section number.

16. Boehme, *Forty Questions* (III 11/1.15); Cf. 146–149 in Weeks.

17. Cf. Will-Erich Peuckert, *Das Leben Jakob Böhmes* (Jena: E. Dieterichs, 1924), 101.

18. Cf. Ingrid Merkel, "Aurora; or, The Rising Sun of Allegory: Hermetic Imagery in the Work of Jakob Böhme," in *Hermeticism and the Renaissance: Intellectual History and the Occult in Early Modern Europe*, ed. I. Merkel and A. G. Debus (Washington, DC: Folger Shakespeare Library, 1988), 302–310.

19. See R. H. Hvolbel, "Was Jakob Böhme a Paracelsian?" *Hermetic Journal* 19 (Spring 1983): 6–17.

20. Refer to Beach's review, 69.

21. See Weeks, 147 and footnote 29, 240.

22. Ibid., 148.

23. Alexandre Koyré, *La Philosophie de Jacob Boehme* (New York: Franklin, 1968; originally published in Paris: Vrin, 1929; reissued, 1979), 281.

24. This characterization may be compared to Fichte's "Absolute Self." Cf. J. G. Fichte, *The Science of Knowledge*, trans. and ed. P. Heath and J. Lachs (Cambridge: Cambridge University Press, 1794/1993).

25. In the context of Lacanian psychoanalytic thought, *ungründlich* would be equivalent to desire. For Lacan, desire is always beyond itself, it is the realm of the transcendent. Encased in the domain of the unconscious, the *Ungrund* is that realm of psychic territory we can never know in itself, it is simply the Real (*réel*), or more appropriately, the *unreal*.

26. Koyré, *Galileo Studies* (Brighton: Harvestor, 1977); Cf. Madan Sarup, *Jacques Lacan* (Toronto: University of Toronto Press, 1992), 104 and endnote 3, 187.

27. Weeks, 149.

28. See *Encyclopaedia Logic*, § 44.

29. *The Human Genesis of Christ*, 1620; IV 127/II.3.5.

30. Hegelians are unresolvably divided on the question surrounding the ambiguity of the end of world history due to the self-actualization of Absolute Spirit. I am inclined, however, to interpret the dialectical unfolding of spirit as a continuous, temporal process of becoming. While Hegel saw spirit through to its end, that is, to its pure self-consciousness, this does not mean that spirit no longer permeates world history nor does it imply that spirit completed itself during the time Hegel completed his System of Science. If we are to conceive of Hegel's dialectical system as a never-ending teleological development, then spirit is a temporal process that always seeks to understand its own process of becoming in the moment, (in *this* moment), an activity that never completely vanishes, but rather continually seeks to incorporate history and its evolving experiences in time within its higher forms of self-understanding.

31. *Morgenröte*, ch. 23, par. 17; cf. trans., par. 18, 230.

32. Beach, 71.

33. Weeks, 149.

34. Cf. Beach, 72.

35. Ibid., 70.

36. Especially see sections 721–723 of the *Phenomenology*, 436–438.

37. Beach, 72.

38. Cf. Boehme, *Sämtliche Schriften*, Vol. 3, ch. 1, par. 66; also *Forty Questions*, in Vol. 2 of *The Works*, Law edition, par. 81, 16.

39. This original aggression turned inward may be seen as operative in the psychodynamics of the death drive and depression. Cf. Freud, *Beyond the Pleasure Principle*, 1920, and "Mourning and Melancholia," 1917, *Standard Edition*, Vols. 18 and 14 (London: Hogarth Press).

40. Beach, 73. Cf. *Drey Princ.* ch. 2, par. 9; trans., par. 9, 14.

41. Published posthumously by Karl Ludwig in two different versions and separate redactions of Hegel's *Lectures on the History of Philosophy*. In Vol. 3 of the R. F. Brown, J. M. Stewart, and H. S. Harris translation, ed. Robert F. Brown (Berkeley: University of California Press, 1825–1826/1990), Hegel refers to reading Boehme's works as a "wondrous experience" despite his "extremely confused method." While Boehme's form of expression is "barbaric," his content is the "profoundest idea" (120). "[T]here is here undeniably the greatest profundity, one that grapples with the forceful unification of the most absolute antithesis. Boehme grasps the antithesis in the harshest, crudest fashion, but he does not let their obstinacy deter him from positing their unity" (131).

42. Hegel's note of July 29, 1811, was written to Peter Gabriel van Ghert thanking him for the gift.

43. Walsh, 22–31.

44. Cf. von der Luft, 37 and footnote 2, 42.

45. See the *Phenomenology*, 465–466 and *Lectures on the Philosophy of Religion*, trans. E. B Speirs and J. B. Sanderson (London: Routledge and Kegan Paul, 1962 [1895]), 3: 32.

46. von der Luft, 38.

47. Ibid.; Rufus M. Jones, *The Flowering of Mysticism* (New York: Macmillian, 1939), 67.

48. See Weeks who offers a historical biography.

49. Joannes Scotus Eriugena, *Periphyseon: On the Division of Nature*, ed. and trans. Myra Uhlfelder, summaries by Jean Potter (Indianapolis: Bobbs-Merrill, 1976), 7, 15.

50. von der Luft, 39.

51. *Enneads*, Vol. 5, bk.1, sec. 10, 6.

52. von der Luft, 39.

53. Cf. *Hegel's Theory of Madness* (Albany: State University of New York Press, 1995).

54. In his Introduction to *The Philosophy of Spirit*, Hegel tells us that his project is informed by Aristotle which he seeks to reinterpret: "Aristotle's books on the soul, as well as his discussions on its special aspects and conditions, are still by far the best or even the sole work of speculative interest on this general topic. The essential purpose of philosophy of spirit can be none other than re-introducing the Concept into the cognition of spirit, and so re-interpreting the meaning of these Aristotelian books" (§ 378).

55. See Charles Taylor's discussion in *Hegel* (Cambridge: Cambridge University Press, 1975/1995), 321, 332, 378, 515–516.

56. Günter Zöller, "An Eye for an I: Fichte's Transcendental Experiment," in *Figuring the Self: Subject, Absolute, and Others in Classical German Philosophy*, ed. D. E. Klemm and G. Zöller (Albany: State University of New York Press, 1997), 73.

57. *Versuch einer Kritik aller Offenbarung* (Königsberg: 1792).

58. Daniel N. Robinson, *Toward a Science of Human Nature* (New York: Columbia University Press, 1982), 99.

59. See H. S. Harris, "Introduction to the *Difference* Essay," in *Difference Between Fichte's and Schelling's System of Philosophy*, trans. H. S. Harris and W. Cerf (Albany: State University of New York Press, 1801/1977), 1.

60. Eduard von Hartmann, *Philosophy of the Unconscious*, trans. W. C. Coupland (New York: Harcourt, Brace and Company, 1868/1931), 24.

61. Unless otherwise noted, all references to Fichte's *Wissenschaftslehre* will refer to Peter Heath and John Lachs, eds. and trans., *The Science of Knowledge* (Cambridge: Cambridge University Press, 1970/1982).

62. See Günter Zöller, "Original Duplicity: The Ideal and the Real in Fichte's Transcendental Theory of the Subject," in *The Modern Subject: Conceptions of the Self in Classical German Philosophy*, ed. Karl Ameriks and Dieter Sturma (Albany: State University of New York Press, 1995), 115.

63. Dieter Henrich, "Fichte's Original Insight," trans. D. R. Lachterman, reprinted in *Contemporary German Philosophy*, Vol.1, ed. Darrel E. Christensen et al. (University Park, PA: Penn State Press, 1966/1982), 15–53.

64. See Zöller, "An Eye for an I," 75 for a discussion on the role of freedom in Fichte.

65. From a draft of a letter to Jens Baggesen, April or May 1795, *Early Philosophical Writings*, ed. and trans. D. Breazeale (Ithaca and London: Cornell University Press, 1988), 385; *Gesamtausgabe der Bayerischen Akademie der Wissenschaften*, ed. R. Lauth and H. Gliwitzky (Stuttgart-Bad Cannstatt: Frommann-Holzboog, 1962), III, 2: no. 282a. Also see Zöller, note 13, 90.

66. Harris, "Introduction to the *Difference* Essay," 3.

67. When Hegel discusses "Idealism" at this point in the *Phenomenology*, he takes issue with Fichte's self-positing ego that comes to itself as an immediate present that has no past. In Hegel's words, it "comes on the scene *immediately*" but has "forgotten" its "path," that is, its dialectical progression (§ 233). For Hegel, Fichte's absolute self, as well as his idealism in general, cannot comprehend itself, so it is therefore incomprehensible. He states:

> Thus it [Fichte's self-positing *I*] merely *asserts* that it is all reality, but does not itself comprehend this. . . . The idealism that does not demonstrate that path but starts off with this assertion is therefore, too, a pure *assertion* which does not comprehend its own self, nor can it make itself comprehensible to others. (§§ 233–234)

In Fichte's speculative system of Kant's critical philosophy, the *I* becomes the category for all being. But this singular consciousness, as well as the categories that are said to evolve out of this pure *I*, excludes both the pure category as well as the plurality of all its particular forms. Hegel cannot be satisfied with this account of subjectivity for it does not do justice in reconciling the problem of the one and the many. See H. S. Harris, *Hegel: Phenomenology and System* (Indianapolis: Hackett Publishing Company, Inc., 1995), 47–48 for a review.

68. *Wissenschaftslehre nova methodo-Halle, Gesamtausgabe*, IV, 2: 31.

69. Dieter Henrich, "Fichte's Original Insight," 25.

70. "Chapter One," *Introductions to the Wissenschaftslehre*, 113f; *Versuch einer neuen Darstellung der Wissenschaftslehre, Gesamtausgabe*, I 4, 76f. Cf. *Wissenschaftslehre nova methodo-Krause*, 7, 31.

71. *Johann Gottlieb Fichtes sämmtliche Werke*, 8 vols., ed. I. H. Fichte (Berlin: Veit and Co., 1845–1846), I, 526–527.

72. *Neue Bearbeitung der Wissenschaftslehre, Gesamtausgabe*, II, 5: 335.

73. Günter Zöller summarizes this point, 81.

74. Compare Kant's statement in the first *Critique*:

It must be possible for the "I think" to accompany all my representations . . . I call it *pure apperception*, to distinguish it from empirical apperception . . . because it is that self-consciousness which, while generating the representation "*I think*" (a representation which must be capable of accompanying all other representations, and which in all consciousness is one and the same), cannot itself be accompanied by any further representation. (Sec 2, § 16, B 132)

Here Kant identifies an unconscious "self-consciousness" as a pure unity that "generates" its own self-representation in the form "I think." While Kant does not specify the actual conditions for the possibility of apperception as Fichte does, he nevertheless situates the locus of mental activity within an unconscious agency. *Critique of Pure Reason*, trans. N. K. Smith, (New York: St Martin's Press, 1781/1787–1965). Hereafter, all references to the first *Critique* will refer to *CPR* followed by the section numbers of both the A and B editions.

75. Fichte himself sees his understanding of intellectual intuition to be in agreement with Kant's theory of apperception. Cf. "Second Introduction to *The Science of Knowledge*," *W*, I, 472, 45.

76. Refer to Frederick Neuhouser, *Fichte's Theory of Subjectivity* (Cambridge: Cambridge University Press, 1990) for a detailed account of Fichte's model of self-consciousness.

77. In "Fichte's Original Insight," Dieter Henrich provides an excellent description of Fichte's prereflective model of self-consciousness, as does Günter Zöller (1997) who notes that the prereflective *I* of Fichte's transcendental science of human subjectivity "must be for-itself or with-itself in a manner that excludes all mediation, externality and duplication" (86). For Fichte, "self-consciousness is immediate;" there is a pre-familiarity the *I* has with itself. Fichte explains that immediate self-consciousness is:

nothing else but the *being-with-itself* and *being-for-itself* of the very being that becomes conscious—something that is to be presupposed in all consciousness—the pure reflex of consciousness. (*Neue Bearbeitung der Wissneschaftslehre, Gesamtausgabe*, II, 5: 347)

He also insists that immediate self-consciousness must always remain unconscious:

That immediate self-consciousness is not raised to consciousness nor can it ever be. As soon as one reflects on it, it ceases to be what it is, and it disappears into a higher region. (*Neue Bearbeitung der Wissneschaftslehre, Gesamtausgabe*, II, 5: 335—Also see Zöller, 85–86 and notes 70–71)

78. Cf. Robert B. Pippin, *Hegel's Idealism: The Satisfactions of Self-Consciousness* (Cambridge: Cambridge University Press, 1989), 42; notes, 1.2., 268; also see his discussion in ch. 8, section 1.

79. *The Encyclopaedia Logic*, trans. T. F. Geraets, W. A. Suchting, and H. S. Harris (Indianapolis: Hackett Publishing Company, Inc., 1817/1991), § 31, *Zusatz*, 69. All references to the *Encyclopaedia Logic* refer to this translation unless otherwise noted. Compare to Wallace's translation:

[T]hought is free and enjoys its own privacy—cleared of everything material, and thoroughly at home. The feeling that we are all our own is characteristic of free thought—of that voyage into the open, where nothing is below us or above us, and we stand in solitude with ourselves alone. (*Hegel's Logic*, trans. W. Wallace [London: Oxford University Press, 1975], § 31, 52)

80. See Harris's discussion in his "Introduction," 7, 9.

81. Cf. Hermann Nohl, 356–361, trans. R. Kroner under the title "Fragment of a System." In Hegel's *Early Theological Writings*, trans. T. M. Knox with an introduction, and fragments translated by Richard Kroner (Chicago: University of Chicago Press, 1948), 309–319.

82. Hegel's derision of Fichte is clear from statements such as this:

[A]ll this presupposes an utterly vulgar view of nature and of the relation of the singular person [*Einzelheit*] to nature. This view is one which is denuded of all Reason, for the absolute identity of subject and object is entirely alien to it. (*Faith and Knowledge*, trans. Walter Cerf and H. S. Harris [Albany: State University of New York Press, 1802–1803/1977], 176. Also see Harris, "Introduction," 6)

83. *Lectures on the History of Philosophy: The Lectures of 1825–1826*, Vol. 3, ed. Robert F. Brown, trans. R. F. Brown, J. M. Stewart, and H. S. Harris (Berkeley: University of California Press, 1990), 236.

84. In a recent article titled, "Hegel's Absolutes," *The Owl of Minerva* 29, no. 1 (Fall 1997), John Burbidge provides a compelling case that rejects the traditional view held by many scholars that Hegel's references to the "Absolute" signify an absolute entity or a complete process of knowing. This is further presaged in his *On Hegel's Logic: Fragments of a Commentary* (Atlantic Highlands, NJ: Humanities Press, 1981), and in "Hegel's Conception of Logic," *Cambridge Companion to Hegel* (Cambridge: Cambridge University Press, 1993). Burbidge argues that Hegel's textual occurrences of the Absolute are contextually used to mainly signify references to Schelling, Spinoza, and religion (terminology his audience would be accustomed to hearing) and that Hegel neither intended nor claimed that Absolute Spirit stands for the culmination of all knowledge. Burbidge carefully argues that "the only thing we can know absolutely is that all knowledge will be relative" (27) because the dialectical unfolding of spirit is constantly engaged in the contingencies it encounters within the actual world. This is not only true in Hegel's narrative of the *Phenomenology* where spirit educates itself as it realizes that each shape it initially thinks to be true and certain is merely an appearance, but this contingency claim has a logical tenor in the sense that if Spirit were to complete itself, it would no longer be Spirit because it would no longer desire to surpass itself—the dialectic would vanish entirely, hence spirit would cease to be. This position is at odds with other interpreters who maintain an end to history (since this would imply that the process is over) or that the Absolute is a fixed or static endpoint or terminate realization. One may adopt Robert Solomon's position and equate the Absolute with "the world conceived of as a unity" (*Introducing the German Idealists* [Indianapolis: Hackett, 1981], 68), and perhaps even accept Henry Harris's understanding of the Absolute as "the universal brotherhood of man" (*Hegel's Development: Night Thoughts* [Oxford: Clarendon, 1983], 411) where, in the words of Errol Harris, "all finitude is transcended, although it is still a necessary moment"

(*An Interpretation of Hegel's Logic* [Lanham: University Press of America, 1983], 300). But whether we agree with these positions or can locate their place within Hegel's texts, Burbidge cogently shows that the dynamic interplay of forces that is itself a repetition of the pattern of learning from life experiences which spirit endures is itself a developmental process of becoming that never culminates in absolute fulfillment, only an understanding of how it has evolved and where it has come from. And as G. R. G. Mure puts it, "Becoming" is the "self-definition of the Absolute" (*Introduction to Hegel* [Oxford: Clarendon, 1940], 132). If Burbidge is correct in saying: "The only thing that is genuinely absolute, that is without any condition and any restriction, is not an entity identified by a noun but a living process in which each absolute realization of spirit is overturned in favour of another that is truly more absolute" (33–34), then spirit is an endless, teleological active process of creativity and self-discovery.

85. Compare Kant: "[T]his representation is an act of *spontaneity*, that is, it cannot be regarded as belonging to sensibility. I call it *pure apperception*" (*CPR*, B 132).

86. H. S. Harris, "Introduction to the *Difference* Essay," 2–3; "Introduction to *Faith and Knowledge*," 1.

87. All references to Schelling's *System des transzendentalen Idealismus* (1800) will follow Peter Heath's translation, *System of Transcendental Idealism* (Charlottesville: University Press of Virginia, 1978) and refer to *STI* followed by the page number.

88. See Dale Snow's commentary, "The Role of the Unconscious in Schelling's System of Transcendental Idealism," *Idealistic Studies* 19, no. 3 (1989): 231–250.

89. Textual references will refer to F. W. J. Schelling's, *Sämmtliche Werke*, ed. K. F. A. Schelling, 14 Vols. (Stuttgart and Augsburg: Cotta, 1856–1861), Vol.3, 330.

90. Edward Allen Beach provides an overview in *The Potencies of God(s)*, 48–57.

91. Ibid., 48.

92. The question of intellectual intuition stands in opposition to what Kant advanced earlier in the first *Critique*, claiming that we are epistemologically unable to conceive what an intuitive intellect or understanding would be like because it would have to be given to us as an object of our senses, something very different than having knowledge.

93. See "*The Dominance of the Unconscious*," in the Introduction to Heath's translation of the *System*.

94. *Critique of Judgment*, trans. Werner S. Pluhar (Indianapolis, Hackett, 1770/1987) § 77, 292.

95. Schelling's *Die Weltalter* (second draft, 1813) in English translation by Judith Norman, in Slavoj Žižek and F. W. J. Von Schelling, *The Abyss of Freedom/Ages of the World* (Ann Arbor: University of Michigan Press, 1997), 137.

96. *Ages of the World*, A Fragment, from Writings Left in Manuscript, trans. Frederick de Wolfe Bolman (New York: AMS Press, 1967), 113.

97. By the time Schelling undertook his work *On the Essence of Human Freedom* (1809) leading to the multiple revisions of *Ages of the World* (1811–1815), he had renounced his identity theory and moved toward what Schelling labeled as his "positive

philosophy," of which his lectures *On the History of Modern Philosophy* were largely composed. Positive philosophy was an attempt to respond to the "negative philosophy" Hegel had typified in his *Logic*, the ultimate aim of which was to derive a philosophically justified religion from a reinterpretation of the historical evolution of Christianity.

98. *Ages of the World*, Norman translation, 137.

99. For both Sartre and Lacan, consciousness itself takes the form of lack. While Lacan refers to a "lack of being" throughout his *Écrits*, Sartre is more specific when he tells us that "human reality . . . exists first as lack. . . . In its coming into existence, human reality grasps itself as an incomplete being." Cf. *Being and Nothingness*, trans. H. E. Barnes, (New York: Philosophical Library, 1943/1956), 89.

100. See Beach, chapter 5, especially the section on Baader, 75–82.

101. *Ages of the World*, 137.

102. Slavoj Žižek, *The Abyss of Freedom/Ages of the World*, 14.

103. Ibid., 15.

104. *Ages of the World*, Bolman translation, 132.

105. Ibid., 150.

106. *Ages of the World*, Bolman's translation, 132.

107. *Science of Logic*, Bk Two, Sec. Two, chs. 1–3; *Encyclopaedia Logic* § 131, 199, § 142, 213; Also see the *Phenomenology* § 147, 89.

108. *The Interpretation of Dreams*, 1900, Vols. 4–5, *Standard Edition* (London: Hogarth Press), 613.

109. Preface to the *Phenomenology*, 9. It can further be said that Hegel's real contention with Schelling was Schelling's insistence on beginning philosophy from the standpoint of the Absolute, rather than articulating a process within consciousness that starts with immediacy and through mediation and self-reflection arrives at absolute knowing. For Hegel, the Absolute is the "*result*" as the product of the labor for full self-consciousness. See *Phenomenology*, 24. Andrew Bowie also discusses this point in his Introduction to Schelling's Munich lectures of 1833–1834, *On the History of Modern Philosophy* (Cambridge: Cambridge University Press, 1994), 24.

In addition, Hegel's and Schelling's dialectic is methodologically distinct despite their many shared qualities. Schelling's dialectic is more volitional, linear, and voluntaristic while Hegel's is more conceptually circular, progressive, and internally consistent. Schelling's emphasis on will and productivity as self-constituting generative activity is not necessarily incompatible with Hegel's account, but Schelling's focus on irrationality over rationality and the fundamental demonstrations of logic is attributed to his procreative will, a conceptual move Hegel frowned upon. Hegel's threefold movement of the dialectic as a simultaneous canceling, preserving, and elevating function operating within itself and repeated in successive qua progressive shapes is criticized by Schelling for its annulling feature. For Schelling, nothing is canceled or reconstituted, only supplemented, perhaps even subordinated. Schelling's dialectic emphasizes the act of production and reproduction of successive forms "by a kind of procreative causality which is supposed to reenact the processes by which the outer universe itself has evolved" (Beach, 85). But Schelling ignores the preservative dimension of Hegel's dialectic that retains its previous shapes. Furthermore, Hegel's dialectic surpasses a mere "doubling" function of rote repetition by bringing the rich complexities of experience to bear upon its subsequent encounters. For Schelling, there is a successive (re)production while for Hegel there is a successive sublation. The logic of Hegel's method is that the dialectic turns its own activity upon itself and reconstitutes its own presuppositions while Schelling's method rests on a preconceptual framework that no logic can establish or amend, at least in principle. The dialectic of (re)production thereby disavows the logically autonomous and self-conditioned totality Hegel's system aspires to achieve. Schelling's dialectic may therefore be viewed as a method by which a productive schema is applied over and over again but it isn't purely developmental in a systematic and incorporative way that Hegel's dialectic affords. While you have all these potencies in Schelling's system, form is merely imposed on something rather than appearing from within the structure itself.

CHAPTER TWO. UNCONSCIOUS SPIRIT

1. *Lectures on the History of Philosophy*, Vol. 3, Medieval and Modern Philosophy, 126–128.

2. Cf. *Mysterium Magnum*, ch.1, § 2; *Theosophia Revelata*, 2: 2717–2718.

3. See *Of Divine Contemplation*, Ch.3, § 30; *Theosophia Revelata*, 1: 43.

4. See Petry's discussion, Vol.3, 405, note 153, 33.

5. Refer to the Critical Edition, 1827 and 1830 editions, §§ 453–454, Vols. 19 and 20 of Hegel's *Gesammelte Werke*. The 1817 edition may be found in the *Jubiläums Ausgabe*, §§ 373–375.

6. Cf. Hegel, *Vorlesungen*, Vol. 13 (Hamburg: Meiner, 1994), a new volume of the Lectures devoted the Philosophy of Spirit which reproduces Hegel's lectures of 1827–1828 from the notes of J. E. Erdmann and F. Walter. In the discussion of Recollection, §§ 198–202, the word *Schacht* appears.

7. Hegel had intended to write a full account of Subjective Spirit as he had done for Objective Spirit (*Philosophy of Right*) but died before he had a chance. See F. Nicolin's account of Hegel's plans in "Ein Hegelsches Fragment zur Philosophie des Geistes," *Hegel-Studien* (1961): bd.1, 9–15; and "Hegels Arbeiten zur Theorie des subjektiven Geistes," *Erkenntnis und Verantwortung: Festschrift für Theodor Litt*, ed. J. Derbolav and F. Nicolin (Düsseldorf, 1960), 356–374.

8. Freud comprehensively discusses the realm and function of preconsciousness and the *Pcs.* system originally introduced in chapter VII of *The Interpretation of Dreams*, a theory that incurred many revisions by the time it appeared in "The Unconscious" (1915), 173–176; 186–195, and *The Ego and the Id* (1923), 13–15, 20–27, Vols. 4–5, 14, and 19, *Standard Edition*.

9. Freud distinguishes between the "descriptive" features of the unconscious where preconsciousness is only one of its manifestations, but in the "dynamic" sense there is only one unconscious. *Standard Edition*, Vol. 19, 15.

10. *Nürnberger Schriften, Werke* IV (Suhrkamp).

11. See Hegel's comments in the Introduction to the *Science of Logic*, 48–49.

12. See Tom Rockmore's discussion of Hegel's system as circular in *On Hegel's Epistemology and Contemporary Philosophy* (Atlantic Highlands, NJ: Humanities Press International, 1996), 31–36.

13. Compare with Aristotle's method.

14. *Nürnberger Schriften, Werke* IV (Suhrkamp), 73.

15. Hans-Christian Lucas and Errol Harris both support the view that the emergence of the soul from nature is a struggle for spirit to liberate itself from its corporeality. Cf. Lucas, "The 'Sovereign Ingratitude' of Spirit Toward Nature," *Owl of Minerva* 23, no. 2 (1992): 131–150; Harris, "Hegel's Anthropology."

16. Murray Greene, *Hegel on the Soul: A Speculative Anthropology* (The Hague: Martinus Nijhoff, 1972), 44, fn. 36.

17. Petry, Notes to Vol. 2: Anthropology, 495.

18. In Petry, Vol. 2, 275, see the Kehler manuscript, 125–126 and the Griesheim manuscript, 173–174.

19. Also see Freud's elaboration of fixation as a denial of the "psychical (ideational) representative of an instinct" in the mode of *"primal repression."* This compares to Hegel's emphasis on a "specific content" that has acquired a *"fixed presentation."* Cf. "Repression," 1915, *SE*, 14, 148.

20. See Freud's discussion on the oceanic feeling in relation to religious sentiment and the formation of the ego, *SE*, 21, 64–68.

21. Cf. M. J. Petry, *Hegel's Philosophy of Subjective Spirit* (Dordrecht: D. Reidel, 1979), Vol. 1, cx–ccxv; Theodore Garaets, W. A. Suchting, and H. S. Harris, trans., *Encyclopaedia Logic* (Indianapolis: Hackett, 1991), viii; and J. N. Findlay, trans. *Philosophy of Nature* (Oxford: Clarendon, 1975), vii.

22. Cf. Petry, 37; Kehler Ms., 80; Griesheim Ms.,110–111.

23. Errol E. Harris supports this view in *The Spirit of Hegel* (Atlantic Highlands, NJ: Humanities Press, 1993), 108–110; and "Hegel's Theory of Feeling," 76.

24. See Errol Harris's arguments that despite Hegel's rejection of evolutionary theory, which would surely be recast in light of our current scientific findings, his *Philosophy of Nature* embodies a doctrine of evolution. Cf. "How Final is Hegel's Rejection of Evolution?," in *Hegel and the Philosophy of Nature*, ed. Stephen Houlgate (Albany: State University of New York Press Press, 1998), 189–208; *Nature, Mind, and Modern Science* (London: G.Allen and Unwin, 1954, 1968), 245; *The Spirit of Hegel*; Also see, J. N. Findlay, *Hegel: A Re-examination* (London: G. Allen and Unwin, 1958), 272.

25. We may suspect Hegel's Christian influence from his early theological writings, but in the Introduction to the *Science of Logic*, Hegel gives us a clear metaphysical position:

Accordingly, logic is to be understood as the system of pure reason, as the realm of pure thought. This realm is truth as it is without veil and in its own absolute nature. *It can therefore be said that this content is the exposition of God as he is in his eternal essence before the creation of nature and a finite mind.* (*SL*, 50, italics added)

Apart from how God is to be conceived in Hegel's philosophical system, there are many debates among Hegel scholars about Hegel's own personal views on the nature, defini-tion, and existence of God, from the assumption that he was a devout Christian to the view that he was a closeted atheist (see Jacques D'Hondt, *Hegel in his Time*, trans. John Burbidge with Nelson Roland and Judith Levasseur (Peterborough, Ont.: Broadview Press, 1988); also see Charles Taylor's chapter on Religion in *Hegel*. One way of inter-preting Hegel is that he is a creationist who sees pure reason or thought as identical with God's essence who is responsible for generating the sensible world of nature and mind, mind being the logical extension of pure thinking as the fulfilment of God's subjectivity. From the *Philosophy of Nature*, Hegel asks:

How has God come to create the world? . . . God reveals Himself in two different ways: as Nature and as Spirit. Both manifestations are temples of God which He fills, and in which He is present. God as an abstraction, is not the true God, but only as the living process of positing His Other, the world . . . and it is only in unity with his Other, in Spirit, that God is Subject. (*PN* § 246, *Zusatz*)

26. Hegel's depiction of lack and drive does not merely belong to spirit, but also to animal nature, itself the presupposition of the soul. Outlined in the *Philosophy of Na-ture*, the animal organism feels a lack (*Mangel*) within itself "and the urge [*Trieb*] to get rid of it. . . . Only what is living feels a *lack*; for in Nature it alone is the *Concept*" (*PN* § 359). This is why for Hegel, "[t]he goal of Nature is to destroy itself and to break through its husk of immediate, sensuous existence, to consume itself like the phoenix in order to come forth from its externality rejuvenated as spirit" (*PN* § 376, *Zusatz*).

27. See *The Ego and the Id*, 1923, *SE*, 19, ch.4.

28. Freud's letter to Einstein, "Why War?," 1932, *SE*, 22, 209.

29. The question of whether the dual drives have separate essences should be con-sidered apart from their phenomenal status. Freud, like Hegel, is a monist with respect to the development of the ego: "[T]he ego is identical with the id, and is merely a spe-cially differentiated part of it. . . . The same is true of the relation between the ego and the super-ego. . . .The ego is, indeed, the organized portion of the id." Cf. *Inhibitions, Symptoms and Anxiety*, 1926, *SE*, 20, 97. If the ego is a differentiated and more refined psychic organization of the id, then they both would participate in a mutual essence. Freud's dualism of the drives should therefore be viewed as structural distinctions re-sponsible for the dialectical configurations that constitute psychic life, a position that may stand in complementary relation to Hegel's dialectic.

30. Refer to *The Ego and the Id*, 1923, *SE*, 19, 57; *Inhibitions, Symptoms, and Anx-iety*, 1926, *SE*, 20, 141.

31. For a review see Sulloway, *Freud: Biologist of the Mind*, 393–394.

32. My interpretation of Hegel's thesis of absolute knowing goes against proposed arguments for the end of history in Hegel's *Phenomenology*. This is an ambiguous issue in

the first place, which is also perhaps what Hegel intended, thus accounting for why he treats it so non-directly; but this reading of historical termination furthermore does not account for Hegel's intellectual development that was to occur after his Jena tenure. Hegel was a brilliant young man when he wrote the *Phenomenology*, but we must keep in mind that he had later "intended to delete all references to its being either 'part' of the System or the 'introduction' to it" (H. S. Harris, *Hegel: Phenomenology and System*, 99). His *Logic* on the other hand and his *Encyclopaedia* represent the foundation of his mature system, one that takes the contingencies of phenomena seriously. Even in the last paragraph of the *Phenomenology*, Hegel points this out:

> Their preservation, regarded from the side of their free existence appearing in the form of *contingency*, is History; but regarded from the side of their [philosophically] comprehended organization, it is the Science of Knowing in the sphere of appearance: the two together, comprehended History, form alike the inwardizing and the Calvary of the absolute Spirit, the actuality, truth, and certainty of his throne, without which he would be *lifeless* and alone. (*PS* § 808, italics added)

Hegel shows that spirit comes to know itself as spirit by coming to understand its historical progression of encountering contingencies and this constitutes an absolute position insofar as spirit understands its process, but nowhere does he say that spirit ends, only perhaps that spirit has reached the zenith of the pure form of its understanding which is always open to the introduction of new experiences and novelties. Hegel even ends his *Phenomenology* with an adapted reference to Schiller underscoring the significance of "infinitude." Spirit lives on; it must continue in the lives of individual minds.

33. There are interesting and important similarities between sublating and sublimating, but there are also equally important differences. Sublimation for Freud is a specific process while for Hegel sublation is a general structural dynamic. Furthermore, sublimation is the alteration of drive derivatives that while being generally compatible with Hegel's dialectic, is associated to the pleasure motives of the id, hence the non-rational counterpart of spirit. Hegel's dialectic is also structurally differentiated in that it preforms three distinct yet simultaneous tasks: namely, canceling, annulling, or destroying, retaining or preserving, and surpassing, elevating, or transcending.

34. Freud says, "I am in fact of the opinion that the antithesis of conscious and unconscious is not applicable to drives" (*SE*, 14, 177); drives can only be unconscious and remain unknown in themselves. What is known is how they manifest as phenomena.

35. Harris views the spiritual presence of an individual's genius to direct "subconscious" mental processes. It may be argued, however, that reference to unconscious mentation would be more accurate since subconsciousness implies the existence of content, affect, or other psychic processes that are just below the level of conscious awareness and are thus accessible to the mind if proper attention is paid to such events. Here in Hegel's Anthropology, the soul has not yet achieved consciousness and is still shrouded in unconsciousness. See Harris's essay, "Hegel's Anthropology": 12.

36. Refer to notes 8 and 9.

37. John N. Findlay, "Hegel's Use of Teleology," in *New Studies in Hegel's Philosophy*, ed. Warren E. Steinkraus (New York: Holt, Rinehart and Winston, 1971), 93; Also

see Crawford Elder's discussion of Hegel's teleology in *Appropriating Hegel* (Aberdeen: Aberdeen University Press, 1980).

38. William DeVries, *Hegel's Theory of Mental Activity* (Ithaca: Cornell University Press, 1988), 26.

39. In his *Wissenschaftslehre*, within the context of Spinoza, Fichte equates the pursuit of an ideal unity with an infinite striving that cannot achieve its aim: "We shall encounter his highest unity again in the Science of Knowledge; though not as something that *exists*, but as something that we *ought to*, and yet *cannot*, achieve" (*W* § 1, I, 101).

40. In "Splitting of the Ego in the Process of Defence," a posthumously published unfinished paper, Freud (1940 [1938]) addresses the notion of disavowal and the "alteration of the ego" that goes beyond his earlier treatment of splitting in cases of psychoses (1924, *SE*, 19, 152–153) and fetishism (1927, *SE*, 21, 155–156), which is now to be included within his general theory of neurosis. Freud generally sees the conceptualization of splitting as a defensive process that is usually confined to the domains of conflict, while Hegel's emphasis on the internal divisibility of the soul would make splitting a generic process that may be applied to any mediatory aspects of division and negation within spirit. But in *New Introductory Lectures*, Freud (1933) is clear that splitting is a general ego operation: "[T]he ego can be split; it splits itself during a number of its functions—temporarily at least. Its parts can come together again afterwards" (*SE*, 22, 58). He also alludes to an innate and normative function of splitting as it is applied to the synthetic processes of the ego. He states: "The synthetic function of the ego, though it is of such extraordinary importance, is subject to particular conditions and is liable to a whole number of disturbances" (*SE*, 23, 276). While Freud emphasized the synthetic functions of ego unification in several places before (see *SE*, 22, 76; 20, 97–100, 196), which had always been an implicit part of his theory, it may be said that splitting is a basic psychic operation that may take on more pathological configurations throughout development, as in the cases of pathological narcissism and borderline personality. Cf. Otto Kernberg, *Borderline Conditions and Pathological Narcissism* (New York: Jason Aronson, 1975); James F. Masterson, *The Narcissistic and Borderline Disorders* (New York: Brunner/Mazel, 1981) for a review.

41. Projective identification was coined by Melanie Klein in 1946 in "Notes on some Schizoid Mechanisms," *International Journal of Psycho-analysis* 27: 99–110, where it was conceived as an aggressive forcing of certain parts of the ego into an object in order to dominate it or take over certain aspects of its contents so as to make it part of the ego's own internal structure. For Klein, projective identification was a deposit of the death drive which has further implications for Hegel's emphasis on the negative character of the dialectic. This concept, however, has been advanced by several object relations and self-object theorists to include more normative functions to its operations within consciousness, but it has been given special attention in its manifestation in psychotherapy giving rise to countertransference reactions by therapists. To be sure, projective identification may be viewed in multiple fashions: (1) as an intrinsic organization of the dialectic of mental activity, from unconscious structure to conscious thought, (2) as a defensive maneuver motivated by conflict, and (3) as an intersubjective dynamic that affects the process of therapy. Generally we may say that within the context of therapy, the patient projects onto the therapist certain disavowed and repudiated internal contents which the therapist then unconsciously identifies with, such as the behavioral fantasies, attributions,

or personal qualities that are the objects of projection, which the therapist then introjects as a function of his or her own ego, thus leading to conflicted inner states that the therapist must manage. If the therapist's countertransferential reactions are too strong and/or remain unrecognized as the internalized projected attributions or inner qualities of the patient, he may potentially act out such negative states within the process of therapy, thus potentially leading to further internal disruptions in both parties affecting the success of treatment. See Michael J. Tansey and Walter F. Burke, *Understanding Countertransference: From Projective Identification to Empathy* (Hillsdale, NJ: Analytic Press, 1989); Thomas G. Ogden, *Projective Identification and Psychotherapeutic Technique* (New York: Jason Aronson, 1982).

CHAPTER THREE.
HEGEL'S PHILOSOPHICAL PSYCHOLOGY

1. John Sallis is preoccupied with this issue as well in *Spacings of Reason and Imagination* (Chicago: University of Chicago Press, 1987), 152.

2. This is often attributed to what Hegel asserts in the Preface to his *Philosophy of Right*: "*What is rational is actual and what is actual is rational*" (*PR*, 10); also see *EL* § 6.

3. Charles Taylor, *Hegel* (Cambridge: Cambridge University Press, 1975), 538.

4. Errol E. Harris, *The Spirit of Hegel* (Atlantic Highlands, NJ: Humanities Press, 1993), 17.

5. First sentence to Book I of Aristotle's *Metaphysics*, trans. W. D. Ross, *The Works of Aristotle*, 12 vols. (Oxford: Oxford University Press), italics added.

6. In the *Encyclopaedia*, Hegel tells us that the science of logic is "to arrive at the Concept of its concept and so to arrive at its return [into itself] and contentment" (*EL* § 17).

7. H. S. Harris, "Introduction to the *Difference* Essay," 12

8. See John Burbidge's commentary in *On Hegel's Logic*, 7, fn 2, ch. 2, 234. Derrida also argues that Hegel's psychology and semiology are intimately tied to his Logic. Cf. "The Pit and the Pyramid: Introduction to Hegel's Semiology," in *Margins of Philosophy*, trans. Alan Bass (Chicago: University of Chicago Press, 1972/1982), 73–76.

9. For Hegel, the Delphic injunction does not simply refer to the pursuit of self-knowledge, but rather is a call to comprehend what is "ultimately true and real—of spirit as the true and essential being" (*PM* § 377).

10. *Phänomenologie des Geistes*, ed. W. Bonsiepen and R. Heede, *Gesammelte Werke*, Vol.9 (Hamburg: Felix Meiner Verlag, 1980), 446.

11. Hegel himself saw many conceptual flaws with the *Phenomenology*, which he openly acknowledged. In a May 1807 letter to Schelling, Hegel referred to the "wretched confusion" of the book's composition especially the "major deformity of the later parts." Michael N. Forster provides a detailed account of Hegel's dissatisfaction with the *Phenomenology* (see *Hegel's Idea of a Phenomenology of Spirit* [Chicago: University of Chicago Press, 1998], 547–555, Appendix XII, 612). Petry further tells us: "After the

publication of the *Jena Phenomenology*, Hegel never again had recourse to such a teleological exposition of the 'experience of consciousness' . . . nor did he ever encourage anyone to take it seriously. He concentrated instead upon integrating his doctrine of consciousness into his systematic philosophy" (Introduction, *The Berlin Phenomenology* [Dordrecht, Holland: D. Reidel, 1981], xvii–xviii). However, there is a great deal of debate regarding the role of the *Phenomenology* in his system. In the literature, scholars seem to be preoccupied with Hegel's notion of the Absolute. They largely focus on the section on Absolute Knowing in the *Phenomenology*. But what is puzzling is the degree to which Hegel himself saw his early work to be compatible with his mature system of science. He in fact tried to distance himself from his initial account of his theory of self-consciousness advanced in the *Phenomenology*. While the Jena work is legitimate in its own right, he seems to rely on his latter works as his official position. In the *Encyclopaedia* version, he removed all references to the Absolute, and there are no Additions to his final section on Reason as the final stage of the Phenomenology. In the Berlin *Phenomenology* (based on a summer term course of 1825), he does mention the "absolute substance" of reason (*BP* § 362) but does not mention Absolute Knowing. It appears that he wanted to avoid the pitfalls that incurred from the Jena project. Given this account, we may then ask: Why are scholars so fixated with the Absolute when Hegel displaced this notion in his mature philosophy? This is not easy to reconcile. Michael Petry argues that the Jena *Phenomenology* was left behind. But Hegel had in fact prepared some notes for a revision of the *Phenomenology* just before he died. Note that Hegel does not remove references to the *Phenomenology* in the Preface to the *Science of Logic*, which he revised in 1831. Hegel informs us that he "intended" for the *Phenomenology* to be the first part of his system of science. However, he speaks in past tense, and it is not clear that he viewed the Jena *Phenomenology* as a proper introduction to his system, or whether his new account in the *Encyclopaedia* was sufficient. In his 1831 footnote to the Preface of the *Science of Logic*, he remains ambiguous whether he regards it as part of his system: "In place of the projected second part . . . I have since brought out the *Encyclopaedia of the Philosophical Sciences*" (*SL*, 29). Henry Harris, Robert Pippin, Jay Bernstein, and others are equally vehement that the *Phenomenology* continued to be significant even unto the last days. In the Additions to the *Encyclopaedia Logic*, and even in some of the Remarks, Hegel will say that the Concept he is discussing could be considered a definition of the Absolute. Many have taken this as suggestive, and have built on the discussions in the Preface to the *Phenomenology* (where Hegel is referring to Schelling's use of the term). John Burbidge's argument is that even in the *Phenomenology* one should not talk about the Absolute, but rather absolute knowing, absolute conceiving, or absolute spirit. Jay Bernstein views that the only legitimate use of the word *absolute* is as a qualifier: absolute (unconditioned) knowing, the absolute idea (as the end of the *Logic*), and absolute (as opposed to objective) spirit. But we must be cautious not to entirely dismiss Hegel's references to the Absolute. In the Berlin Introduction (1820) to Hegel's *Introduction to the Lectures on the History of Philosophy*, he specifically equates the medium of religion with "our understanding of the Absolute . . . which constitutes the objective existence of the Absolute, [and] unites the Absolute with our subjective consciousness" (35). He further repeats several references to the "Absolute" in the Introductions of 1823, 1825, and 1827 (see 116, 123, 164 of the *Introduction*, trans. T. M. Knox and A. V. Miller [Oxford: Clarendon Press, 1985]). Since the notion of "absolute" is used in so many complex ways, there is no univocal sense to the term. Therefore, its meaning or significance must be interpreted within the context it appears.

12. See William A. DeVries's discussion, *Hegel's Theory of Mental Activity*, 87–89.

13. Because Hegel begins with the metaphysics of the soul, he is grounding (through his logic) the being of spirit in unconscious processes. This is an ontological account of the very conditions that make psychology possible; thus, Hegel's psychological explanations of subjective spirit are related to his ontological commitments advanced in the Anthropology. Ontological statements give an account of psychic reality broadly construed. Psychological explanations account for both conscious processes and operations as well as events that presumably transpire in the soul, the soul being the very a priori condition for consciousness to occur. Therefore, all psychological explanations presuppose an ontology of the unconscious soul.

14. Recall our discussion in chapter 1. Influenced largely by Jacob Boehme's notion of the *Ungrund*, Hegel looks at the abyss as a ground without a ground, precisely because it is its own self-grounding, pure activity as such. Pure or negative activity is originally unconscious, which becomes the ontological structure and thrust of spirit in its higher stages. Because spirit is a developmental achievement, it matures out of its earlier organizations. Admittedly, the attempt to account for the problem of Beginning or origin runs the danger of engaging in an infinite regress: because earlier stages are presuppositions for higher instantiations of spirit, one can find oneself trying to locate the origin of the origin as an appeal to explain any activity of spirit. Hegel's solution is to originally conceptualize spirit as an active passivity—asleep, implicit, enveloped in a nightlike undifferentiated unity. It rouses itself as the waking soul. This is why Hegel says that spirit in its beginning is nothing but its own being and its own relation to its determinations. This pure activity of spirit is its original being.

15. Self-certainty is not a single stage of spirit, but a feature of every stage. Each development or shape of spirit involves a self-separation or division, a projection into otherness or externality, followed by an incorporation as the reinternalization of itself back into its original structure.

16. *On Hegel's Logic*, 69–70.

17. A. N. Whitehead, *Process and Reality*, Corrected Edition, ed. D. R. Griffin and D. W. Sherburne (New York: Free Press, 1929/1978), 3.

18. For Hegel, the I and the self in its totality are always viewed as processes of becoming. Any discussion of agency, being, or entities should always be viewed in the context of process. Because the terms *agency* and *entity* have been greatly maligned, this qualification is an attempt to displace the sharp historical contrast between substance and process views. When I refer to agency, I am following Hegel in his varied and fluid use of the term. Despite the fact that he says that "substance is subject," subjectivity and spirit are pure process. In this sense, any reference to spirit as agency denotes pure activity, and more specifically, volitional and intelligible self-governing activity. Because Hegel conceives of everything as consisting of processes, it is a mistake to think of agencies as enduring substances that stand behind the events of the world thus providing the source of all activities. Rather, spirit constitutes a fluidity of active processes, which suggests that substance is just a relatively enduring existent or a relationally active phase of leading processes. Therefore, any reference to agency is to be understood as indicating the unfolding of active spiritual processes.

19. William DeVries provides a compelling commentary on the role and function of the ego as a thinking subject in Hegel's *Phenomenology*. While I am generally in agreement with his analysis of the emergence of the *I* from the soul, I do not wish to equate the ego's emergence with consciousness, for this assumes that the ego has no a priori status of its own except as soul. From my account, Hegel is murky with regard to the question of transition; he certainly wants to raise the appearance of the ego over the soul, but this does not mean that the soul is devalued since Hegel himself is committed to the notion that the highest aspirations of spirit resonate in the soul. It is true that the "I is a higher-order organizing principle" (103) and is the sublation of soul, but this does not preclude the ego's prenatal development, which transpires within the soul. DeVries states that the "crucial stages of emergence . . . start with sensation" which are "bodily states," (100–101) and therefore have their origin in the soul's natural corporeality realized in habit. The objects of sensation experienced in sense-certainty, conscious intuition, perception, etc. are merely another (sublated) form of sensation already experienced and prepared in the soul (as "self-certainty," "subjectivity," and "selfhood") to be realized by the conscious ego. Therefore, thinking subjectivity has its epigenesis in the soul gradually modified as the actual ego, which is the prior condition to its proper appearance as the ego of consciousness. Cf., *Hegel's Theory of Mental Activity*, ch. 6.

20. Hegel's theory of consciousness as well as self-consciousness has received overwhelming attention in the Hegel literature. While I do not wish to take up the larger questions and implications that arise from such a critique, a task that is not necessary for the purpose of this current project, the reader should be acquainted with two recent interpretations of Hegel's model of consciousness outlined in the *Phenomenology*. The first is H. S. Harris's magnum opus, *Hegel's Ladder: A Commentary on Hegel's Phenomenology of Spirit*, 2 Vols. (Indianapolis: Hackett, 1997), which provides one of the most comprehensive assessments of that work; and the second is Tom Rockmore's *Cognition: An Introduction to Hegel's Phenomenology of Spirit* (Berkeley: University of California Press, 1997), which is simply one of the best and most accessible guides on the topic.

21. See Petry's discussion, *Berlin Phenomenology*, xviii.

22. M. J. Petry compiled two separate editions of the *Berlin Phenomenology*, the first appearing in the appendix to Vol.3. of *Hegel's Philosophy of Subjective Spirit* while the second appeared as a separate book. Unless otherwise noted, all references to the Berlin lectures are from the appendix to Vol. 3 of Petry's *Hegel's Philosophy of Subjective Spirit* and will refer to *BP* followed by the section number.

23. *BP* § 331, 283; See also Petry's discussion, *Berlin Phenomenology*, xviii–xxiv.

24. See Tom Rockmore, *Cognition* (Berkeley: University of California Press, 1997).

25. See John Burbidge's detailed commentary on Hegel's psychology of theoretical spirit in *On Hegel's Logic*, 7–21.

26. Freud's notion of the "reality principle" nicely corresponds to Hegel's realism. Furthermore, Hegel's philosophical psychology has relevance for Freud's description of the "psychical apparatus" and the development of consciousness, attention, memory, and thinking. Refer to Freud's (1911) essay, "Formulations on the Two Principles of Mental Functioning," *SE*, 12, 219–221.

27. See Dieter Henrich, "Hegels Theorie der Zufall" in *Hegel in Kontext* (Frankfurt: Suhrkamp, 1971), 157–186; (also in *Kant-Studien* 50 (1958–1959): 131–148); Stephen Houlgate, "Necessity and Contingency in Hegel's *Science of Logic*," *The Owl of Minerva* 27, no. 1 (Fall 1995): 37–49; John Burbidge, "The Necessity of Contingency," in *Art and Logic in Hegel's Philosophy*, ed. Schmitz and Steinkraus (Atlantic Highlands, NJ: Humanities Press, 1980), 201–218; (also in *Selected Essays on G. W. F. Hegel*, ed. L. Stepelich (Atlantic Highlands, NJ: Humanities Press, 1993), 60–73; and in J. Burbidge, *Hegel on Logic and Religion* (Albany: State University of New York Press, 1992), 39–51).

28. Burbidge, *On Hegel's Logic*, 12.

29. Ibid., 13.

30. William DeVries interprets reproductive and associative imagination in Hegel's system as one and the same, claiming the distinction was introduced by Boumann; Cf. *Hegel's Theory of Mental Activity*, 135. I do not read that in Hegel at all. In fact, he specifically says, "[T]he content reproduced . . . possesses a general presentation *for* the associative relation of images" (*EG* § 455, italics added). The *Zusatz* also shows that they are two distinct, modified processes. This distinction is crucial and one that Hegel emphasizes. He clearly states that in associative imagination "the *interrelating* of images is a higher activity than merely reproducing them" (*EG* § 455, *Zusatz*).

31. For Hegel, phantasy developmentally and temporally precedes language or linguistic acquisition. In his discussion in the *Encyclopaedia*, §§ 456–457, phantasy occurs before symbolization and signification and "derives from what is furnished by intuition." It is not until § 458 that he introduces language proper.

32. In his seminal essay, "The Pit and the Pyramid: Introduction to Hegel's Semiology," Derrida traces the path that "leads from this night pit, silent as death and resonating with all the powers of the voice which holds it in reserve, to a pyramid . . . there composing the stature and status of the sign. . . .That the pyramid becomes once again the pit that it always will have been—such is the enigma" (77).

33. Ibid., 71.

34. Bruno Bettelheim points this out with precision in *Freud and Man's Soul* (New York: Vintage Books, 1982), 70–78.

35. Compare from Plato's *Republic*: ". . . in the soul whereby it reckons and reasons the rational, and that with which it loves, hungers, thirsts, and feels the flutter and titillation of other desires, the irrational and appetitive—companion of various repletions and pleasures" (4: 439d; also see *Laws*, ib. 9: 863b sq.; ib. 5:727c). Plato also ascribes to the soul the cause of moral qualities (*Laws*, 10: 896d), ends and virtues (*Republic*, ib. I: 353d sq.), and the influence of character (*Laws*, 10: 904c sq.), as well as mental sickness (*Gorgias*, 479b). But perhaps the best allusion to Plato's notion of the soul by Freud is his analogy of the ego and the id as a rider on horseback (*SE*, 19, 25), whereas Plato refers to the soul as a charioteer with a pair of steeds (*Phaedrus*, 246 sq.). Cf. *The Collected Dialogues of Plato*, ed. Edith Hamilton and Huntington Cairns (Princeton: Princeton University Press, 1961).

36. At one stage in his theoretical development, Freud thought that perhaps one day the mind could be explained in quantitative, neurological-physiological terms.

Freud's materialism and scientific realism is reinforced when he addresses the question of "quantity" as the ultimate substance of the world. Freud's quantitative analyses of the mind permeate his early metapsychology which he struggles to differentiate from qualitative accounts. See Freud, "Hysteria" and "Hystero-Epilepsy," *SE*, 1888, 1, 39–59; "Some Points for a Comparative Study of Organic and Hysterical Motor Paralyses," *SE*, 1893, 1, 160–172; *Project for a Scientific Psychology*, *SE*, 1895, 1, 305–306/307–311; and Volney Gay's commentary in *Freud on Sublimation: Reconsiderations* (Albany: State University of New York Press, 1992), 71–74. But Freud abandoned this line of thinking and all attempts to characterize the mind in a reductive manner were aborted. Freud would want to claim that while biology, chemistry, neurology, or physiology is a necessary condition, it could never be a sufficient condition for explaining the mind and human nature.

37. Supported by passages in the early part of the first *Critique*, I am interpreting Kant here as a critical realist, who presumed the existence of objects behind their appearances although they are nevertheless epistemologically inaccessible to the faculties of pure reason. A competing view is that Kant thought reality was knowable and the *Ding-an-sich* was not real, which he calls an empty concept in the section on phenomena and noumena. The problem Kant faces is that he can't commit to a knowledge claim about the thing-in-itself such that it is possible, actual, or necessary because those are categories that would convert it into an object for the understanding. Furthermore, reality claims conform to empirical consciousness and the thing-in-itself cannot be perceived.

38. See Jonathan Lear's discussion, *Love and Its Place in Nature*, 168–169.

39. A "portion [of libido] is directed towards reality. . . . Another portion of the libidinal impulses has been kept away from the conscious personality and from reality, and has either been prevented from further expansion except in phantasy or has remained wholly in the unconscious so that it is unknown to the personality's consciousness." Cf. "The Dynamics of Transference," *SE*, 12, 1912, 100.

CHAPTER FOUR. THE DIALECTIC OF DESIRE

1. The 'Uncanny,' *SE*, 17, 1919, 248, n 1.

2. See Tom Rockmore's discussion in *Cognition*, 64.

3. Russon, *The Self and its Body in Hegel's* Phenomenology of Spirit, ch. 4.

4. Fichte presents his theory of immediate self-consciousness in *Versuch einer neuen Darstellung der Wissenschaftslehre*, ed. Peter Baumanns (Hamburg: Felix Meiner, 1975). This account is further elaborated by Dieter Henrich in "Fichte's Original Insight," and Roger Frie in *Subjectivity and Intersubjectivity in Modern Philosophy and Psychoanalysis* (Lanham, MD: Rowman and Littlefield Publishers, 1997), 8. Refer to my discussion on Fichte in chapter 1.

5. Manfred Frank, *What Is Neo-Structuralism?* trans. S. Wilke and R. Gray (Minneapolis: University of Minnesota Press, 1989), 192–193.

6. Frie, *Subjectivity and Intersubjectivity in Modern Philosophy and Psychoanalysis*, 10.

7. Dieter Henrich, "Fichte's Original Insight," 52.

8. John Russon articulates life as embodiment and shows how the body is the means in which the self fulfills its desires. Cf. *The Self and its Body in Hegel's* Phenomenology of Spirit, 54–61. Drawing on Russon, Peter Simpson also provides an account of "life as desire-in-itself." Cf. *Hegel's Transcendental Induction* (Albany: State University of New York Press, 1998), 41–45.

9. Alexandre Kojève, *Introduction to the Reading of Hegel: Lectures on the Phenomenology of Spirit,* ed. R. Queneau and A. Bloom, trans. J. H. Nichols Jr. (Ithaca: Cornell University Press, 1969), 4.

10. One of the most recent and important works on the question of human embodiment in Hegel's *Phenomenology* is advanced by John Russon in *The Self and its Body in Hegel's* Phenomenology of Spirit. His central argument has three main claims: (1) The body as *phusis* is an unconscious power of fulfilling desire and making sense out of the world which is mainly realized in the natural, organic body principally driven by unconscious processes; (2) The body as *hexis* is a complex system shaped by habits, which is mainly realized in the cultural and social institutions we inhabit; and (3) As *logos,* spiritual embodiment is the practice and cultivation of elaborate self-expression mostly actualized in language, reason, and the higher forms of Absolute Spirit. Because his focus is on the *Phenomenology,* Russon does not directly engage (except for in passing) Hegel's anthropological account of the unconscious soul or the unconscious processes of theoretical spirit. We may presume, however, that since the soul is the locus of habit as well as the inner reservoir of passion, moral sentiment, and cultural ideals—the substance of character, the unconscious becomes a primary force throughout all forms of spirit's embodiment from individual to social, collective, and absolute accounts of self-consciousness.

11. See Henry Harris's discussion, *Phenomenology and System,* 36.

12. Daniel Berthhold-Bond discusses this point as well in *Hegel's Theory of Madness,* 46. Also see Jean Hyppolite's discussion in *Genesis and Structure of Hegel's Phenomenology of Spirit,* trans. Samuel Cherniak and John Heckman (Evanston, IL: Northwestern University Press, 1974), 190.

13. This sentence appeared in the 1827 second edition of the *Encyclopaedia.*

14. Fredrick Neuhouser attempts to elucidate the origin of the need for recognition itself by partially claiming that we seek recognition because our own demands for self-certainty are left unsatisfied without the presence and validation of others. See "Deducing Desire and Recogntion in the *Phenomenology of Spirit.*" This notion is compatible with many psychoanalytic conceptualizations of object relations development and self psychological theory advanced by Kohut and his contemporaries, a point I will further address in the last chapter.

15. Henry S. Harris, "The Concept of Recognition in Hegel's Jena Manuscripts," in *Hegel's Dialectic of Desire and Recognition,* ed. John O'Neill (Albany: State University of New York Press, 1996), 233; *Phenomenology and System,* 37.

16. There are many informative commentaries on the master-slave dialectic. Cf. Alexandre Kojève, *Introduction to the Reading of Hegel,* 41–70; Donald Phillip Verene, *Hegel's Recollection: A Study of Images in the* Phenomenology of Spirit (Albany: State University of New York Press, 1985), 59–69; Terry Pinkard, *Hegel's Phenomenology: The Sociality of Reason* (Cambridge: Cambridge University Press, 1994), 53–63; Allen W. Wood,

Hegel's Ethical Thought (Cambridge: Cambridge University Press, 1990), 85–93; Paul Redding, *Hegel's Hermeneutics* (Ithaca: Cornell University Press, 1996), 123–126; Howard Adelman, "Of Human Bondage: Labor and Freedom in the *Phenomenology*," in *Hegel's Social and Political Thought*, ed. Donald Phillip Verene (Atlantic Highlands, NJ: Humanities Press, 1990), 119–135; H. S. Harris, *Phenomenology and System*, 39–40; Russon, *The Self and its Body in Hegel's* Phenomenology of Spirit, 61–76; Simpson, *Hegel's Transcendental Induction*, 53–74; Leo Rauch and David Sherman, *Hegel's Phenomenology of Self-Consciousness: Text and Commentary* (Albany: State University of New York Press, 1999), 87–101; John O'Neill, ed., *Hegel's Dialectic of Desire and Recognition* (Albany: State University of New York Press, 1996).

17. Jessica Benjamin advances this claim in *The Bonds of Love* (New York: Pantheon Books, 1988), 53–67, a point made famously by Simone de Beauvoir in The *Second Sex* long beforehand.

18. Freud explains this defensive process as a reversal of a drive into its opposite form. This takes two different steps: a change from activity to passivity, and a reversal of its content (*SE*, 13, 126–140).

19. The unhappy consciousness has been interpreted by many to be the central shape of self-consciousness and a fundamental theme of the *Phenomenology*. In my interpretation I try to stay close to Hegel's text but inevitably cover old ground. There are many important commentaries that may be useful to the reader. Cf. Jean Hyppolite, *Genesis and Structure of Hegel's Phenomenology of Spirit*, trans. Samuel Cherniak and John Heckman (Evanston, IL: Northwestern University Press, 1974), 190–215; Taylor, *Hegel*, 57–59/148–170; Joseph Flay, *Hegel's Quest for Certainty* (Albany: State University of New York Press, 1984), 105–112; Verene, *Hegel's Recollection*, 70–79; Pinkard, *Hegel's Phenomenology*, 69–78; Redding, *Hegel's Hermeneutics*, 127–128; H. S. Harris, *Phenomenology and System*, 42–46; Rauch and Sherman, *Hegel's Phenomenology of Self-Consciousness: Text and Commentary*, 103–120.

20. Jean Hyppolite, "Hegel's Phenomenology and Psychoanalysis," 64.

21. See Freud on the "oceanic feeling" in relation to religious sentiment and early ego development, *Civilization and Its Discontents*, 1930, *SE*, 21, 64–68.

CHAPTER FIVE. ABNORMAL SPIRIT

1. *Hegel's Theory of Madness*, 19.

2. On Hegel's depression, see his letter (#158 in the *Briefe*) to Windischmann of May 27, 1810: "For a few years I suffered from this hypochondria to the point of exhaustion. Everyone probably has such a turning point in his life, the nocturnal point of the contraction of his essence in which he is forced through a narrow passage by which his confidence in himself and everyday life grows in strength and assurance—unless he has rendered himself incapable of being fulfilled in everyday life, in which case he is confirmed in an inner, nobler existence" (*Letters*, 561). He also alludes to his hypochondriacal depression in his discussion of insanity in the *Encyclopaedia*: "[T]his feeling of uneasiness combines very easily in an insane person, [and] with a *hypochondriac* mood which torments him with *imaginings* and *crotchets* . . . flushes of ill-nature occur in all of us" (*EG* § 408, *Zusatz*).

3. See M. J. Petry, Vol.2, *Hegel's Philosophy of Subjective Spirit*, 562.

4. Hegel's correspondence to his sister, *Hegel: The Letters*, trans. Clark Butler and Christiane Seiler (Bloomington: Indiana University Press, 1984), 407–408, letter of April 9, 1814.

5. Cf. Berthhold-Bond, *Hegel's Theory of Madness*, 13, 31, 39, 57–59.

6. Ibid., 59; also see Karl Rosenkranz, *G. W. F. Hegels Leben* (Berlin: Duncker und Humbolt Verlag, 1844; reprint, Darmstadt: Wissenschaftliche Buchgesellschaft, 1977).

7. Berthold-Bond gives an extensive bibliography on Hölderlin's illness, 55fn, 230; also see Wilhelm Lange, *Hölderlin: Eine Pathographie* (Stuttgart: Enke, 1909); and Helm Stierlin, "Lyrical Creativity and Schizophrenic Psychosis as Reflected in Friedrich Hölderlin's Fate," in *Friedrich Hölderlin, An Early Modern*, ed. Emery E. George (Ann Arbor: University of Michigan Press, 1972), 192–215.

8. Ibid., 61; *Hölderlin: Sämtliche Werke*, 7 Vols., ed. Friedrich Beissner and Adolf Beck (Stuttgart: Kohlhammer, Cotta, 1943ff) (*Grosse Stuttgarter Hölderlin-Ausgabe*), Vol.7.

9. See Hegel's correspondence to his cousin, the Reverend Göriz, *Letters*, 414.

10. Alan M. Olson, *Hegel and the Spirit: Philosophy as Pneumatology* (Princeton: Princeton University Press, 1992), 96, 104.

11. Berthold-Bond, 60.

12. Under the *DSM-III-R* classification established by the American Psychiatry Association, "the essential feature of this group of disorders is an abnormal event that occurs either during sleep or at the threshold between wakefulness and sleep" (308). See diagnostic criteria for 307.46, Sleepwalking Disorder. The essential diagnostic criteria for Sleepwalking Disorder has remained the same for the revised manuals described in the *DSM-IV* and the *DSM-IV-TR*. Cf. American Psychiatric Association, *Diagnostic and Statistical Manual of Mental Disorders, Fourth Edition-Text Revision (DSM-IV-TR)* (Washington, DC: American Psychiatric Association, 2000).

13. See Kehler Ms., 125–126; Griesheim Ms., 173–174; Petry, Vol.2, 275fn.

14. "Neurosis and Psychosis," *SE*, 1924, 19, 149.

15. "The Loss of Reality in Neurosis and Psychosis," *SE*, 1924, 19, 183.

16. See Ping-Nie Pao, *Schizophrenic Disorders: Theory and Treatment from a Psychodynamic Point of View* (New York: International Universities Press, 1979).

17. According to the diagnostic criteria for 295.70 Schizoaffective Disorder, set forth by the *DSM-III-R*, this disorder displays the prevalent features of both schizophrenia and depressive illnesses. "This diagnostic category should be considered for conditions that do not meet the criteria for either Schizophrenia or a Mood Disorder, but that at one time have presented with both a schizophrenic and a mood disturbance and, at another time, with psychotic symptoms but without mood symptoms" (209).

18. Among post-Freudian ego psychologists, Heinz Hartmann and Harry Guntrip were among the first to posit a "conflict free" sphere of ego development which

accounted for the ego's capacity to function and adapt to its life demands and environ-mental pressures irrespective of the presence of psychopathology.

19. Hegel's lectures on aesthetics and religion were the main focus of his later works. As introduced in the *Phenomenology*, philosophy is the third main shape of Absolute Spirit, a subject he no longer sought to articulate near the end of his life, unlike the philosophy of art and the philosophy of religion. He did not lecture or write on the philosophy of philosophy, only on the history of philosophy. In addition, there is sufficient ambiguity surrounding Hegel's views toward the Jena *Phenomenology*, itself having been dismantled and reintegrated into his mature system. It proves interesting that he never sought to take up the subject of the philosophy of philosophy when it was such an important feature in the *Phenomenology*. Furthermore, Hegel himself was also a religious man, and the meta-physical commitments raised in the *Logic* attributing pure thought to God further suggests that he thought that spirit finds its fulfillment in the realm of religion.

20. C. G. Jung, Letter to Rowland H., founder of Alcoholics Anonymous. From, *The Wisdom of the Dream: Carl Gustav Jung* (A Border Television/Stephen Segallar Films Co-production, 1989).

21. "The False Dasein: From Heidegger to Sartre and Psychoanalysis," *Journal of Phenomenological Psychology* 28, no. 1: 61.

22. For both Hegel and Freud, the inchoate ego is originally encased in a unity and is therefore modally undifferentiated from external forces—the inner and outer are fused in a symbiotic organization. Freud informs us that "originally the ego includes everything, later it separates off an external world from itself. Our present ego-feeling is, therefore, only a shrunken residue of a much more inclusive—indeed, an all embracing—feeling which corresponded to a more intimate bond between the ego and the world about it" (*SE*, 21, 68). As for Hegel, the natural soul moves from an undifferentiated unity to a dif-ferentiated determinate being; so too for Freud, ego boundaries gradually become more contrasted, constructed, and consolidated throughout its burgeoning activity. Freud notes that originally an infant is unable to distinguish between its own ego and the external world as the source of stimulation and sensation. But eventually the organism comes to discern the difference between its own internal sources of excitation, such as its bodily or-gans or somatic processes, and external sources of sensation, (e.g., mother's touch, breast, etc.), that become set apart and integrated within ego organization. It is not until this stage in ego formation that an object is set over against the ego as an existent entity that is outside of itself. Once the ego moves from primary to secondary narcissism, attachments to external cathected (love) objects form the initial dynamics of object-relations and character development.

23. H. S. Harris, *Hegel's Development: Night Thoughts* (Oxford: Clarendon, 1983), 411.

24. From the *Logic*, Hegel states, "that which begins already *is*, but equally, too, *is not* as yet. The opposites, being and non-being are therefore directly united in it, or oth-erwise expressed, it is their *undifferentiated unity*" (*SL*, 74).

25. See Darrel Christensen's discussion in, "The Theory of Mental Derangement and the Role and Function of Subjectivity in Hegel," 441.

26. From Act Two of Wagner's opera, *Tristan and Isolde* (London: English National Opera Guide/John Calder Publishers, 1981), 71–72, Tristan and Isolde sing to one another: "Bright desire of joy Will blind me, And all the world I leave behind me: All that the day Lit with its lie, And all of its madness I can defy, I, myself, Am the world . . . Though I should die, Find the death I long for."

CHAPTER SIX.
IMPLICATIONS FOR PSYCHOANALYSIS

1. Jean Hyppolite, "Hegel's Phenomenology and Psychoanalysis," 57.

2. Ernest Jones, *The Life and Work of Sigmund Freud*, vol.2. (New York: Basic Books, 1955), 85–86.

3. The best account of this is by Patricia Herzog, "The Myth of Freud as Anti-philosopher," in *Freud: Appraisals and Reappraisals* (Hillsdale, NJ: Analytic Press, 1988), 163–189.

4. In the context of Marx, Freud specifically refers to Hegel, but it is unclear whether the dialectics and "obscure Hegelian philosophy" he refers to is not due to Marx's interpretation rather than having direct exposure to Hegel himself. Cf. *New Introductory Lectures, SE*, 22, 177.

5. See Wittgenstein's Blue Book, from *The Blue and Brown Books* (Oxford: Blackwell, 1958), first dictated in 1933–1934; "Conversations on Freud," in *Lectures and Conversations on Aesthetics, Psychology, and Religious Belief*, ed. C. Barrett (Berkeley: University of California Press, 1966).

6. Cf. Alasdair MacIntyre, *The Unconscious: A Conceptual Study* (London: Routledge, 1958); Grünbaum, *The Foundations of Psychoanalysis: A Philosophical Critique*.

7. See William James, *The Principles of Psychology*, 2 Vols. (New York: Dover, 1890/1950). Donald Levy in *Freud Among the Philosophers* has cogently refuted these claims showing that each account harbors selective philosophical biases and misunderstandings and have neglected the broader domain of psychoanalytic doctrine. Also see my review of Levy, in *The Psychoanalytic Quarterly* 4 (1998): 733–737.

8. *The Ego and the Id, SE*, 19, 16, fn.

9. Cf. *Inhibitions, Symptoms, and Anxiety, SE*, 20, 97; *New Introductory Lectures, SE*, 22, 75; *An Outline of Psycho-Analysis, SE*, 23, 145.

10. *Future of an Illusion, SE*, 21, 5–56; *Civilization and its Discontents, SE*, 21, 74.

11. See Volney Gay's discussion in "Against Wholeness: The Ego's Complicity in Religion," *Journal of the American Academy of Religion* 48, no 4 (1979): 539–555. While Freud's views on religion combat spiritual holism, this does not mean that Freud advocates against psychological holism. In fact, Freud insists that with any interpretation of a dream or symptom, for example, one must take into account the whole network of mental configurations, desires, wishes, conflicts, and psychological forces that bear upon the psyche of each unique individual in order to understand its full meaning. See Jonathan Lear's discussion in *Open Minded*, 63.

12. Cf. *Civization and its Discontents*, 1930, *SE*, 21, 111, 145; Freud's reply to Einstein, 1932, *SE*, 22, 211. Also see my, "*Homo Homini Lupus*: Hegel and Freud on the Future of Humanity," in *The Future of Value Inquiry*, ed. Matti Häyry and Tuija Takala (Amsterdam-New York: Rodopi, 2002).

13. In *Introductory Lectures*, Freud states, "you should not for a moment suppose that what I put before you as the psycho-analytic view is a speculative system" (*SE*, 16, 244). Also see *From the History of an Infantile Neurosis*, *SE*, 17, 105–106.

14. "[M]ediative thinking is the thinking that is philosophical in the proper sense, [i.e., it is] *speculative thinking*" (*EL* § 9).

15. At times Hegel devalues the domain of the unconscious, referring to the "impotent natural soul, which is so to speak enclosed in a childlike unity" (*EG* § 413, *Zusatz*). Freud, on the other hand, makes several references of the subordination of consciousness to the unconscious. See *SE*, 5, 611–612; 12, 260; 20, 31–32.

16. Freud tells us, "reason—is among the powers which we may most expect to exercise a unifying influence on men. . . . Our best hope for the future is that intellect—the scientific spirit, reason—may in process of time establish a dictatorship in the mental life of man" (*SE*, 22, 171); Also see Freud's Letter to Einstein, *SE*, 22, 215.

17. See the Philosophy of Spirit (*Die Philosophie des Geistes*), *EG* §§ 388–412; 403–408; 445–465.

18. *Science of Logic*, 36–37, 583; *Phenomenology of Spirit*, § 450, 469, §§ 462–463, § 474.

19. See my articles, "Hegel on the Unconscious Abyss: Implications for Psychoanalysis," *Owl of Minerva* (1996) and "Hegel on Projective Identification: Implications for Klein, Bion, and Beyond."

20. Darrel Christensen, in "The Theory of Mental Derangement and the Role and Function of Subjectivity in Hegel," claims that because Hegel's theory of the unconscious accounts "not only for spurious and mischief-making contents of consciousness but for the normative operations of mind, the breakdown of certain of which play the deleterious role in mental disease, Hegel's concept of the unconscious gains in deductive power over Freud's concept" (448). I interpret Christensen's reference to Hegel's deductive approach as offering valid argumentation whereby the conclusions he draws based on the logic of the dialectic are internally coherent and consistent without contradicting other aspects of his system.

21. In "A Short Account of Psychoanalysis," Freud states: "The 'unconscious' had, it is true, long been under discussion among philosophers as a theoretical concept; but now for the first time, in the phenomena of hypnotism, it became something actual, tangible and subject to experiment" (*SE*, 1924, 19, 192). Of course, Freud would not have been familiar with Hegel's equation of appearance as essence, for nothing could exist unless it is made actual. From the *Encyclopaedia Logic*, Hegel says: "Essence must *appear*. Its inward shining is the sublating of itself into immediacy, which as inward reflection is *subsistence* (matter) as well as *form*, reflection-into-another, subsistence *sublating itself.* . . . Essence therefore is not *behind* or *beyond* appearance, but since the essence is what exists, existence is appearance" (*EL* § 131). Also see the *Phenomenology*, § 147.

22. See my discussion in chapter 4 of Hegel's analysis of desire and recognition advanced in the *Phenomenology*, §§ 178–230.

23. See Brent Willock, "The Comparative-Integrative Perspective in Psychoanalysis," paper presentation at Ontario Psychological Association annual conference, February 22, 2001. Also, Leo Rangell attempts to offer a unitary theory of psychoanalysis advocating theoretical pluralism and synthesis; however, from my viewpoint, he fails to take into serious account how many theoretical positions simply are incompatible with each other, and thus resist integration into a holistic paradigm. This point may also be extended to the notion of pluralism: plurality may oppose particularlity and vice versa, hence making theoretical unification a forced undertaking rather than a logical extension of a synthetic vision. Perhaps psychoanalysis can find points of similarity and even convergence among certain disparate positions, but forcing a unitary theory out of inherently conflicting philosophical models seems like a rather ambitious maneuver at best, perhaps fueled by the wish that psychoanalysts would stop feuding over contentious turf. See Leo Rangell, "Psychoanalysis at the Millennium: A Unitary Theory," *Psychoanalytic Psychology* 17, no. 3 (2000): 451–466, and "Into the Second Psychoanalytic Century. One Psychoanalysis or Many? The Unitary Theory of Leo Rangell, M.D.," *Journal of Clinical Psychoanalysis* 6 (1977): 451–612.

24. Roger Frie and Bruce Reis provide a comprehensive overview of the philosophical foundations of intersubjectivity in "Understanding Intersubjectivity: Psychoanalytic Formulations and their Philosophical Underpinnings," *Contemporary Psychoanalysis* 37, no. 2 (2001): 297–327. They rightfully show how the notion of intersubjectivity has more than a two-hundred-year-old history initiated by early European Continental philosophers such as Jacobi, Fichte, Schelling, and von Hardenberg, but most notably Hegel. Douglas Moggach also argues that even before Hegel drew attention to intersubjectivity in the master-slave dialectic, there are discernable elements of intersubjectivity theory in Fichte; see "Reciprocity, Elicitation, Recognition: The Thematics of Intersubjectivity in the Early Fichte," *Dialogue: Canadian Philosophical Review* 38, no. 2 (1999): 271–296.

25. There are many philosophically minded psychoanalysts and psychologists, however, there are few works on the philosophical justifications of psychoanalysis. For a favorable critique, see Charles Hanly, *The Problem of Truth in Applied Psychoanalysis* (New York: Guilford Press, 1992); Levy, *Freud Among the Philosophers*; Lear, *Love and Its Place in Nature* and *Open Minded*; Ricoeur, *Freud and Philosophy*; and Wollheim, *Sigmund Freud*.

26. Cf. Julia Kristeva, "Woman's Time," in *The Kristeva Reader*, ed. Tori Moi (Oxford: Blackwell, 1986); B. Joseph, *Psychic Equilibrium and Psychic Change* (London: Tavistock Routledge, 1989).

27. There are many useful commentaries on Hegel's dialectical logic. Cf. Frederick C. Beiser, ed., *The Cambridge Companion to Hegel* (New York: Cambridge University Press, 1993); Burbidge, *On Hegel's Logic: Fragments of a Commentary;* John Grier Hibben, *Hegel's Logic: An Essay in Interpretation* (New York: Garland Publishing, Inc., 1984); and John McTaggart, *A Commentary on Hegel's Logic* (New York: Russell and Russell, Inc., 1964).

28. For example, see Robert C. Solomon, *In the Spirit of Hegel* (New York: Oxford University Press, 1983), 21–22.

29. See Michael Forster's recent discussion, "Hegel's Dialectical Method," in *The Cambridge Companion to Hegel.*

30. In his *Wissenschaftslehre* (§§ 1–3), Fichte discerns these three fundamental "principles" (*Grundsät*) or transcendental acts of the mind. Cf. Johann Gottlieb Fichte (1794).

31. For example, see Donald Carveth's (1994) incorrect assessment of Hegel's logic in "Selfobject and Intersubjective Theory: A Dialectical Critique. Part I: Monism, Dualism, Dialectic," *Canadian Journal of Psychoanalysis/Revue Canadienne de Psychanalyse* 2, no. 2: 151–168.

32. Cf. Immanuel Kant (1781/1787), *Critique of Pure Reason*, Second Division: Transcendental Dialectic, Book II, Chapters I–II.

33. For a review see Anna Freud, *The Ego and the Mechanisms of Defense: The Writings of Anna Freud, Vol. II* (Madison: International Universities Press, 1936/1966); Heinz Hartmann, *Ego Psychology and the Problems of Adaptation* (New York: International Universities Press, 1939/1958); *Essays on Ego Psychology* (New York: International Universities Press, 1964).

34. Cf. Melanie Klein, *Envy and Gratitude and Other Works: 1946–1963* (London: Virago Press, 1988); M. Klein and J. Riviere, eds., *Love, Hate, and Reparation* (New York: Norton, 1964); W. R. D. Fairbairn, *Psychoanalytic Studies of the Personality* (London: Tavistock, Routledge and Kegan Paul, 1952); D. W. Winnicott, *D. W. Winnicott, Collected Papers* (London: Tavistock, 1958); *The Maturational Processes and the Facilitating Environment* (London: Hogarth Press, 1965); *Playing and Reality* (London: Tavistock, 1971); Harry Guntrip, *Schizoid Phenomena, Object-Relations, and the Self* (New York: International Universities Press, 1969); *Psychoanalytic Theory, Therapy, and the Self* (New York: Basic Books, 1971).

35. For a more detailed account of how these early pioneers attempted to reconcile classical psychoanalysis with theories of object relations, see Bacal and Newman, *Theories of Object Relations: Bridges to Self Psychology.*

36. Cf. Heinz Kohut, *The Analysis of the Self* (New York: International Universities Press, 1971); *The Restoration of the Self* (New York: International Universities Press, 1977); *How Does Analysis Cure?*

37. *The Restoration of the Self*, 180.

38. Specifically refer to Kohut's (1977) vague definitions of the self as a "center of initiative and a recipient of impressions" (99), which corresponds to the ego of consciousness; but also as "a specific structure in the mental apparatus" (310). This last statement seems to commit Kohut to introducing a new agency to the mind, especially since he uses Freud's terminology of the apparatus of the soul, as though the "self" would be an additional agency to the tripartite division of the mind. While a legitimate case can be made that Kohut's theory of the self is a supraordinate construct that encompasses all aspects of psychic reality, this is unclear from Kohut's actual texts. In a series of articles, W. W. Meissner has been most persuasive in articulating the self as a supraordinate construct. Cf. W. W. Meissner, "The Self as Structural," *Psychoanalysis and Contemporary Thought* 23, no. 3 (2000): 373–416.

39. In *Contexts of Being* (Hillsdale, NJ: Analytic Press, 1992), Stolorow and Atwood address three realms of the unconscious which they call (1) prereflective—largely

culled from Brentano, Sartre, and early phenomenologists, (2), dynamic—a recapitulation of Freud, and (3) the unvalidated—from my account, extrapolated from Binswanger and Sullivan (29–36). But the theory and practice of the intersubjective approach is unquestionably focused on the nature of lived *conscious* experience and affective attunement to emotional resonances within the patient through an empathic-introspective stance (a method, attitude, and/or sensibility derived from Kohut, 1971). For example, Robert Stolorow claims, "In place of the Freudian unconscious . . . we envision a multiply contextualized experimental world, an organized totality of lived personal experience, more or less conscious" (Foreword to Peter Buirski and Pamela Haglund, *Making Sense Together: The Intersubjective Approach to Psychotherapy* [Northvale, NJ: Jason Aronson, 2001], xii). But regardless of current analytic propensities that focus on the understanding and response to conscious rather than unconscious processes, it does not negate the dynamic presence of subjective unconscious activity. Most recently, Timothy J. Zeddies revisits the notion of the unconscious within relational perspectives emphasizing the intersubjective and dialogically constituted processes that comprise the relational matrix particularly in reference to the patient-analyst relationship. Cf. "Within, Outside, and In Between: The Relational Unconscious," *Psychoanalytic Psychology* 17, no. 3 (2000): 467–487.

40. Both Stern and Benjamin rely heavily on intersubjective developmental models. See D. Stern, *The Interpersonal World of the Infant* (New York: Basic Books, 1985); *Unformulated Experience: From Dissociation to Imagination in Psychoanalysis* (Hillsdale, NJ: The Analytic Press, 1997); Benjamin, *The Bonds of Love*; *Like Subjects, Love Objects: Essays on Recognition and Sexual Difference* (New Haven: Yale University Press, 1995); and *Shadow of the Other: Intersubjectivity and Gender in Psychoanalysis* (New York: Routledge, 1999).

41. See T. H. Ogden, *The Matrix of the Mind* (Northvale, NJ: Aronson, 1986); *The Primitive Edge of Experience* (Northvale, NJ: Aronson, 1989); and *Subjects of Analysis* (Northvale, NJ: Aronson, 1994).

42. See G. Atwood and R. Stolorow, *Structures of Subjectivity: Explorations in Psychoanalytic Phenomenology* (Hillsdale, NJ: The Analytic Press, 1984); *Faces in a Cloud: Intersubjectivity in Personality Theory* (Northvale, NJ: Jason Aronson, 1993); Stolorow and Atwood, *Contexts of Being: The Intersubjective Foundations of Psychological Life*; R. Stolorow, B. Brandchaft, and G. Atwood, *Psychoanalytic Treatment: An Intersubjective Approach* (Hillsdale, NJ: The Analytic Press, 1987); Donna Orange, *Emotional Understanding* (New York: Guilford Press, 1995); and Donna Orange, George Atwood, and Robert Stolorow, *Working Intersubjectively: Contextualism in Psychoanalytic Practice* (Hillsdale, NJ: The Analytic Press, 1997).

43. See Mitchell, *Relational Concepts in Psychoanalysis*. Joseph Lichtenberg, in *Psychoanalysis and Motivation* (Hillsdale, NJ: Analytic Press, 1989), and Lewis Aron, in *A Meeting of Minds* (Hillsdale, NJ: Analytic Press, 1996), also offer compatible intersubjective-relational approaches.

44. See B. Beebe, J. Jafee, and F. Lachmann, "A Dyadic Systems View of Communication." In *Relational Perspectives in Psychoanalysis*, ed. N. Skolnick and S. Warchaw (Hillsdale, NJ: The Analytic Press, 1992), 61–81.

45. Benjamin, *The Bonds of Love*; "Recognition and Destruction: An Outline of Intersubjectivity," in *Relational Perspectives in Psychoanalysis*, 43–60.

46. Also see Steven Reisner's critique of the role of Eros in Freud's system in "Eros Reclaimed: Recovering Freud's Relational Theory," in *Relational Perspectives in Psychoanalysis*, 281–312.

47. See Robert Stolorow, Donna Orange, and George Atwood, "World Horizons: A Post-Cartesian Alternative to the Freudian Unconscious," *Contemporary Psychoanalysis* 37, no. 1 (2001): 43–61; Stolorow and Atwood, *Contexts of Being*, 7–28; and Buirski and Haglund, *Making Sense Together*, 6–7, 127.

48. See my discussion in chapter 3 on the appropriate translation of Freud's famous epigram, *Wo Es war, soll Ich werden* (*SE*, 22, 80).

49. As stated many times before, this may be said for the general structure and logical progression of *Aufhebung* (see *Phenomenology*, § 32), but it is also evident in Freud's introduction of the death drive (*Todestrieb*). Cf. *Beyond the Pleasure Principle*, *SE*, 18, particularly 36–46.

50. John Sallis, *Spacings of Reason and Imagination*, 157.

BIBLIOGRAPHY

PRIMARY TEXTS
[LISTED IN ALPHABETICAL ORDER]

GERMAN TEXTS

Hegel, G. W. F. *Briefe von und an Hegel*. 4 Vols. Ed. Johannes Hoffmeister and Rolf Flechsig. Hamburg: Felix Meiner, 1961.

———. *Einleitung in die Geschichte der Philosophie*. Ed. J. Hoffmeister. Hamburg: Felix Meiner, 1940.

———. *Einleitung zur Phänomenologie des Geistes*. Commentary by A. Graeser. Stuttgart: Reclam, 1988.

———. *Enzyklopädie der philosophischen Wissenschaften im Grundrisse*, 3rd Ed. Heidelberg: C. F. Winter, 1830; ed. F. Nicolin and O. Pöggeler, Hamburg, Felix Meiner, 1969.

———. *Erste Druckschriften*. Ed. Georg Lasson. Leipzig: Felix Meiner, 1928.

———. *Gesammelte Werke*. Ed. Rheinisch-Westfaelischen Akademie der Wissenschaften. Hamburg: Felix Meiner, 1968ff.

———. *Grundlinien der Philosophie des Rechts*. Berlin: 1820; reprinted in *Werke*, VII.

———. *Hegels Philosophie des subjektiven Geistes / Hegel's Philosophy of Subjective Spirit*. Vol.1: Introductions, Vol.2: Anthropology, Vol.3: Phenomenology and Psychology. Ed. M. J. Petry. Dordrecht, Holland: D. Reidel Publishing Company, 1978.

———. *Naturphilosophie*, Band 1: Die Vorlesung von 1919/20. Ed. M. Gies. Naples: Bibliopolis, 1982.

———. *Nürnberger Schriften*, *Werke* IV. Ed. E. Moldenhauer and K. M. Michel. Frankfurt-am-Main: Suhrkamp Verlag, 1970–1971.

———. *Phänomenologie des Geiste*. Eds. W. Bonsiepen and R. Heede. Reprinted in *Gesammelte Werke*, Band IX. Hamburg: Felix Meiner Verlag, 1980.

237

————. *Sämtliche Werke. Jubiläumsausgabe.* Ed. H. Glockner. Stuttgart: Fromann, 1927–1940.

————. *Schriften zur Politik und Rechtsphilosophie,* 2nd Ed. Ed. G. Lasson. Leipzig: Felix Meiner, 1923.

————. *System der Wissenschaft: Erster Teil, die Phänomenologie des Geistes.* Bamberg and Würzburg: Goebhardt, 1807.

————. *Theologische Jugendschriften.* Ed. Herman Nohl. Tübingen: Mohr, 1907; reprinted in 1968.

————. *Vorlesungen über die Geschichte der Philosophie.* Ed. P. Garniron and W. Jaeschke. Hamburg: Felix Meiner, 1986–1994.

————. *Vorlesungen über die Geschichte der Philosophie, Einleitung.* Ed. J. Hoffmeister. Leipzig: Felix Meiner, 1940.

————. *Vorlesungen über die Philosophie der Religion,* 3 Vols. Ed. W. Jaeschke. Hamburg: Felix Meiner, 1983–1985.

————. *Werke. Völlstandige Ausgabe durch ein Verein von Freunden der Verweigten.* Berlin: Duncker and Humbolt, 1832–1845.

————. *Wissenschaft der Logik,* Bde I and II. *Gesammelte Werke,* Bde 11 and 12. Ed. Friedrich Hogemann and Walter Jaeschke. Hamburg: Felix Meiner, 1978 (Bd 11) and 1981 (Bd 12).

ENGLISH TRANSLATIONS

————. *Aesthetics,* 2 Vols. Trans. T. M. Knox. Oxford: Clarendon Press, 1975.

————. *The Berlin Phenomenology.* Ed. and trans. M. J. Petry. Dordrecht, Holland: D. Reidel Publishing Co., 1981.

————. *Difference Between Fichte's and Schelling's System of Philosophy.* Trans. H. S. Harris and W. Cerf. Albany: State University of New York Press, 1801/1977.

————. *Early Theological Writings.* Trans. T. M. Knox with intro. and fragments trans. by Richard Kroner. Chicago: Chicago University Press, 1948; reprinted Philadelphia: Philadelphia University Press, 1971.

————. *The Encyclopaedia Logic.* Vol.1 of the *Encyclopaedia of the Philosophical Sciences.* Trans. T. F. Geraets, W. A. Suchting, and H. S. Harris. Indianapolis: Hackett Publishing Company, Inc., 1817/1827/1830/1991.

————. *Faith and Knowledge.* Trans. Walter Cerf and H. S. Harris. Albany: State University of New York Press, 1802–3/1977.

————. *Hegel's Logic.* Trans. W. Wallace. London: Oxford University Press, 1975.

————. *Introduction to the Lectures on the History of Philosophy.* Trans. T. M. Knox and A. V. Miller. Oxford: Clarendon Press, 1833/1985.

————. *Introduction to the Philosophy of History.* Trans. L. Rauch. Indianapolis; Hackett, 1988.

———. *Introductory Lectures on Aesthetics*. Trans. Bernard Bosanquet. Ed. Michael Inwood. London: Penguin Books, 1886/1993.

———. "Jakob Böhme," in *Werke* 20. (*Vorlesungen über die Geschichte der Philosophie* 3). Frankfurt/M: Suhrkamp, 1971.

———. *The Jena System, 1804–5, Logic and Metaphysics*. Trans. and ed. John W. Burbidge and George di Giovanni. Kingston and Montreal: McGill-Queens University Press, 1986.

———. *Lectures on the History of Philosophy*, 3 Vols. Trans. E. S. Haldane ad F. H. Simson. London: Routledge and Kegan Paul, 1892; reprinted 1955.

———. *Lectures on the History of Philosophy: The Lectures of 1825–1826*, Vol. 3. Ed. Robert F. Brown. Trans. R. F. Brown, J. M. Stewart, and H. S. Harris. Berkeley: University of California Press, 1990.

———. *Lectures on the Philosophy of Religion*. Trans. E. B Speirs and J. B. Sanderson. London: Routledge and Kegan Paul, 1962 [1895].

———. *The Letters*. Trans. Clark Butler and Christiane Seiler. Bloomington: Indiana University Press, 1984.

———. *The Philosophy of History*. Trans. J. Sibree. New York: Dover, 1857/1956.

———. *Phenomenology of Spirit*. Trans. A. V. Miller. Oxford: Oxford University Press, 1807/1977.

———. *Philosophy of Mind*. Vol.3 of the *Encyclopaedia of the Philosophical Sciences*. Trans. William Wallace and A. V. Miller. Oxford: Clarendon Press, 1817/1827/1830/1971.

———. *Philosophy of Nature*. Vol.2 of the *Encyclopaedia of the Philosophical Sciences*. Trans. A. V. Miller. Oxford: Clarendon Press, 1817/1827/1830/1970.

———. *Philosophy of Right*. Trans. T. M. Knox. Oxford: Oxford University Press, 1821/1967.

———. *Reason in History*. Introduction to the *Lectures on the Philosophy of History*. Trans. J. Sibree. New York: Willey Book Co., 1900.

———. *Science of Logic*. Trans. A. V. Miller. London: George Allen & Unwin LTD., 1812/1831/1969.

———. *System of Ethical Life and First Philosophy of Spirit*. Eds. and trans. H. S. Harris and T. M. Knox. Albany: State University of New York Press, 1979.

WORKS CONSULTED

Adelman, Howard. "Of Human Bondage: Labor and Freedom in the *Phenomenology*." In *Hegel's Social and Political Thought*, ed. Donald Phillip Verene. Atlantic Highlands, NJ: Humanities Press, 1990.

American Psychiatric Association. *Diagnostic and Statistical Manual of Mental Disorders, Third Edition-Revised (DSM-III-R)*. Washington, DC: American Psychiatric Association, 1987.

———. *Diagnostic and Statistical Manual of Mental Disorders, Fourth Edition (DSM-IV-R)*. Washington, DC: American Psychiatric Association, 1994.

———. *Diagnostic and Statistical Manual of Mental Disorders, Fourth Edition-Text Revision (DSM-IV-TR)*. Washington, DC: American Psychiatric Association, 2000.

Ameriks, Karl, and Dieter Sturma, eds. *The Modern Subject*. Albany: State University of New York Press, 1995.

Archard, D. *Consciousness and the Unconscious*. LaSalle, IL: Open Court Publishing Co., 1984.

Aristotle. *Metaphysics*. Trans. W. D. Ross. *The Works of Aristotle*. 12 Vols. Oxford: Oxford University Press, 1962.

Aron, Lewis. *A Meeting of Minds*. Hillsdale, NJ: Analytic Press, 1996.

Atwood, George, and Robert Stolorow. *Structures of Subjectivity: Explorations in Psychoanalytic Phenomenology*. Hillsdale, NJ: The Analytic Press, 1984.

———. *Faces in a Cloud: Intersubjectivity in Personality Theory*. Northvale, NJ: Jason Aronson, 1993.

Bacal, Howard A., and Kenneth M. Newman. *Theories of Object Relations: Bridges to Self Psychology*. New York: Columbia University Press, 1990.

Beach, Edward Allen. *The Potencies of God(s): Schelling's Philosophy of Mythology*. Albany: State University of New York Press, 1994.

Beebe, B., J. Jafee, and F. Lachmann. "A Dyadic Systems View of Communication." In *Relational Perspectives in Psychoanalysis*, ed. N. Skolnick and S. Warchaw. Hillsdale, NJ: The Analytic Press, 1992.

Beiser, F. C., ed. *The Cambridge Companion to Hegel*. New York: Cambridge University Press, 1993.

Benjamin, Jessica. *The Bonds of Love*. New York: Pantheon Books, 1988.

———. "Recognition and Destruction: An Outline of Intersubjectivity." In *Relational Perspectives in Psychoanalysis*, ed. N. Skolnick and S. Warchaw. Hillsdale, NJ: The Analytic Press, 1992.

———. *Like Subjects, Love Objects: Essays on Recognition and Sexual Difference*. New Haven: Yale University Press, 1995.

———. *Shadow of the Other: Intersubjectivity and Gender in Psychoanalysis*. New York: Routledge, 1999.

Berthhold-Bond, Daniel. "Hegel, Nietzsche, and Freud on Madness and the Unconscious," *The Journal of Speculative Philosophy* V, no.3 (1991): 193–213.

———. "Intentionality and Madness in Hegel's Psychology of Action," *International Philosophical Quarterly* XXXII, no.4 (1992): 427–441.

————. "Hegel on Madness and Tragedy," *History of Philosophy Quarterly* 11, no. 1 (1994): 71–99.

————. *Hegel's Theory of Madness*. Albany: State University of New York Press, 1995.

Bettelheim, Bruno. *Freud and Man's Soul*. New York: Vintage Books, 1982.

Boehme, Jacob. *Die Urschriften*. 2 Vols. Ed. Werner Buddecke. Stuttgart: Frommanns Verlag, 1963/1966.

————. *Sämtliche Schriften*. 11 Vols. Ed. Will-Erich Peuckert and August Faust. Stuttgart: Frommanns Verlag, 1955–1961, originally published in 1730.

————. *Forty Questions (Sämtliche Schriften, III)*.

————. *The Human Genesis of Christ (Sämtliche Schriften, 1620; IV)*.

————. *Of Divine Contemplation (Sämtliche Schriften)*.

————. *Mysterium Magnum (Sämtliche Schriften)*.

————. *Theosophia Revelata (Sämtliche Schriften)*.

Buirski, Peter, and Pamela Haglund. *Making Sense Together: The Intersubjective Approach to Psychotherapy*. Northvale, NJ: Jason Aronson, 2001.

Burbidge, John. "The Necessity of Contingency." In *Art and Logic in Hegel's Philosophy*, ed. Schmitz and Steinkraus. Atlantic Highlands, NJ: Humanities Press, 1980, 201–218.

————. *On Hegel's Logic: Fragments of a Commentary*. Atlantic Highlands, NJ: Humanities Press, 1981.

————. "Hegel's Conception of Logic." In *The Cambridge Companion to Hegel*, ed. F. C. Beiser. New York: Cambridge University Press, 1993.

————. "Hegel's Absolutes," *The Owl of Minerva* 29, no. 1 (Fall, 1997).

Carveth, Donald. "Self object and Intersubjective Theory: A Dialectic Critique. Part I: Monism, Dualism, Dialectic," *Canadian Journal of Psychoanalysis/Revue Canadienne de Psychoanalyze* 2, no. 2 (1994): 151–168.

Casey, E. S., and J. M. Woody. "Hegel, Heidegger, Lacan: The Dialectic of Desire." In *Interpreting Lacan*, ed. J. H. Smith and W. Kerrigan. New Haven: Yale University Press, 1983.

Christensen, Darrel. "The Theory of Mental Derangement and the Role and Function of Subjectivity in Hegel," *The Personalist* 49 (1968): 433–453.

Collins, Ardis B., ed. *Hegel on the Modern World*. Albany: State University of New York Press, 1995.

Cullen, Bernard, ed. *Hegel Today*. Aldershot, UK: Gower Publishing Co. Limited, 1988.

Derrida, Jacques. "The Pit and the Pyramid: Introduction to Hegel's Semiology." In *Margins of Philosophy*. Trans. Alan Bass. Chicago: University of Chicago Press, 1972/1982, 69–108.

Desmond, William, ed. *Hegel and his Critics*. Albany: State University of New York Press, 1989.

D'Hondt, Jacques. *Hegel in his Time*. Trans. John Burbidge with Nelson Roland and Judith Levasseur. Peterborough, Ont: Broadview Press, 1988.

DeVries, William A. *Hegel's Theory of Mental Activity*. Ithaca: Cornell University Press, 1988.

Elder, Crawford. *Appropriating Hegel*. Aberdeen: Aberdeen University Press, 1980.

Ellis, R. *An Ontology of Consciousness*. Dordrecht: Martinus Nijhoff Publishers, 1986.

Eriugena, Joannes Scotus. *Periphyseon: On the Division of Nature*. Ed. and trans. Myra Uhlfelder. Summaries by Jean Potter. Indianapolis: Bobbs-Merrill, 1976.

Fairbairn, W. R. D. *Psychoanalytic Studies of the Personality*. London: Tavistock, Routledge and Kegan Paul, 1952.

Fichte, J. G. *Johann Gottlieb Fichtes sämmtliche Werke*. 8 Vols. Ed. I. H. Fichte. Berlin: Veit and Co., 1845–1846.

———. *Gesamtausgabe der Bayerischen Akademie der Wissenschaften*. Ed. R. Lauth and H. Gliwitzky. Stuttgart-Bad Cannstatt: Frommann-Holzboog, 1962.

———. *Versuch einer neuen Darstellung der Wissenschaftslehre*. Ed. Peter Baumanns. Hamburg: Felix Meiner, 1975.

———. *Neue Bearbeitung der Wissenschaftslehre, Gesamtausgabe*, II.

———. *Wissenschaftslehre nova methodo-Halle, Gesamtausgabe*, IV.

———. *Wissenschaftslehre nova methodo-Krause, Gesamtausgabe*, VII.

———. *Versuch einer neuen Darstellung der Wissenschaftslehre, Gesamtausgabe*, XIV.

———. *Early Philosopjhical Writings*. Ed. and trans. D. Breazeale. Ithaca and London: Cornell University Press, 1988.

———. *Versuch einer Kritik aller Offenbarung*. Königsberg, 1792.

———. *The Science of Knowledge*. Ed. and trans. P. Heath and J. Lachs. Cambridge: Cambridge University Press, 1794/1993.

Findlay, John N. *Hegel: A Re-examination*. London: G. Allen and Unwin, 1958.

———. "Hegel's Use of Teleology." In *New Studies in Hegel's Philosophy*, ed. Warren E. Steinkraus. New York: Holt, Rinehart and Winston, 1971.

Flay, Joseph. *Hegel's Quest for Certainty*. Albany: State University of New York Press, 1984.

Forster, Michael. *Hegel's Ida of a Phenomenology of Spirit*. Chicago: University of Chicago Press, 1998.

Frank, Manfred. *What Is Neo-Structuralism?* Trans. S. Wilke and R. Gray. Minneapolis: University of Minnesota Press, 1989.

Freud, Anna. *The Ego and the Mechanisms of Defense: The Writings of Anna Freud, Vol. II*. Madison: International Universities Press, 1936/1966.

Freud, Sigmund. *Gesammelte Werke, Chronologisch Geordnet.* 18 Vols. Ed. Anna Freud, Edward Bibring, Willi Hoffer, Ernst Kris, and Otto Isakower, in colloboration with Marie Bonaparte. London: 1940–1952; Frankfurt am Main, 1968.

———. *The Standard Edition of the Complete Psychological Works of Sigmund Freud.* 24 Vols. (1886–1940). Ed. and trans. James Strachey in collaboration with Anna Freud, assisted by Alix Strachey and Alan Tyson. London: Hogarth Press, 1966–1995.

———. "Hysteria." (*Standard Edition,* Vol. 1, 1888).

———. "Hystero-Epilepsy." (*Standard Edition,* Vol. 1, 1888).

———. "Some Points for a Comparative Study of Organic and Hysterical Motor Paralyses." (*Standard Edition,* Vol. 1, 1893).

———. *Project for a Scientific Psychology.* (*Standard Edition,* Vol. 1, 1895).

———. *The Interpretation of Dreams.* (*Standard Edition,* Vols. 4–5, 1900).

———. "The Dynamics of Transference." (*Standard Edition,* Vol. 12, 1912).

———. *On the History of the Psycho-Analytic Movement.* (*Standard Edition,* Vol. 14, 1914).

———. "On Narcissism: An Introduction." (*Standard Edition,* Vol. 14, 1914).

———. "Instincts and Their Vicissitudes." (*Standard Edition,* Vol. 14, 1915).

———. "Repression." (*Standard Edition,* Vol. 14, 1915).

———. "The Unconscious." (*Standard Edition,* Vol. 14, 1915).

———. "Mourning and Melancholia." (*Standard Edition,* Vol. 14, 1917 [1915]).

———. *Introductory Lectures on Psycho-Analysis.* (*Standard Edition,* Vols. 15–16, 1916–1917 [1915–1917]).

———. *From the History of an Infantile Neurosis.* (*Standard Edition,* Vol. 17, 1918 [1914]).

———. "The 'Uncanny'." (*Standard Edition,* Vol. 17, 1919).

———. *Beyond the Pleasure Principle.* (*Standard Edition,* Vol. 18, 1920).

———. *Group Psychology and the Analysis of the Ego.* (*Standard Edition,* Vol. 18, 1921).

———. *The Ego and the Id.* (*Standard Edition,* Vol. 19, 1923).

———. "Neurosis and Psychosis." (*Standard Edition,* Vol. 19, 1924 [1923]).

———. "The Loss of Reality in Neurosis and Psychosis." (*Standard Edition,* Vol. 19, 1924).

———. "A Short Account of Psychoanalysis." (*Standard Edition,* Vol. 19, 1924).

———. "Negation." (*Standard Edition,* Vol. 19, 1925).

———. "The Resistances to Psycho-Analysis." (*Standard Edition,* Vol. 19, 1925 [1924]).

———. *Inhibitions, Symptoms, and Anxiety.* (*Standard Edition,* Vol. 20, 1926).

———. *Future of an Illusion.* (*Standard Edition,* Vol. 21, 1927).

———. *Civilization and its Discontents.* (*Standard Edition,* Vol. 21, 1930).

————. *New Introductory Lectures on Psycho-Analysis.* (*Standard Edition*, Vol. 22, 1933 [1932]).

————. "Why War?" Freud's letter to Einstein. (*Standard Edition*, Vol. 22, 1933 [1932]).

————. *An Outline of Psycho-Analysis.* (*Standard Edition*, Vol. 23, 1940 [1938]).

————. "Splitting of the Ego in the Process of Defence." (*Standard Edition*, Vol. 23, 1940 [1938]).

Frie, Roger. *Subjectivity and Intersubjectivity in Modern Philosophy and Psychoanalysis.* Lanham, MD: Rowman & Littlefield Publishers, 1997.

Frie, Roger, and Bruce Reis. "Understanding Intersubjectivity: Psychoanalytic Formulations and their Philosophical Underpinnings," *Contemporary Psychoanalysis* 37, no. 2 (2001): 297–327.

Forster, Michael N. "Hegel's Dialectical Method." In *The Cambridge Companion to Hegel*, ed. F. C. Beiser. New York: Cambridge University Press, 1993.

————. *Hegel's Idea of a Phenomenology of Spirit.* Chicago: University of Chicago Press, 1998.

Gadamer, Hans-Georg. *Hegel's Dialectic.* Trans. P. Christopher Smith. New Haven: Yale University Press, 1971/1976.

Gardner, S. *Irrationality and the Philosophy of Psychoanalysis.* Cambridge: Cambridge University Press, 1993.

Gay, Volney. "Against Wholeness: The Ego's Complicity in Religion," *Journal of the American Academy of Religion* 48, no. 4 (1979): 539–555.

————. *Freud on Sublimation: Reconsiderations.* Albany: State University of New York Press, 1992.

Greene, Murray. *Hegel on the Soul: A Speculative Anthropology.* The Hague: Martinus Nijhoff, 1972.

Grünbaum, Adolf. *The Foundations of Psychoanalysis.* Berkeley: University of California Press, 1984.

Guntrip, Harry. *Schizoid Phenomena, Object-Relations, and the Self.* New York: International Universities Press, 1969.

————. *Psychoanalytic Theory, Therapy, and the Self.* New York: Basic Books, 1971.

Habermas, Jürgen. "The Interpretation of a Case." In *Knowledge and Human Interests.* London: Heinemann, 1972.

Hanly, Charles. *The Problem of Truth in Applied Psychoanalysis.* New York: Guilford Press, 1992.

Harris, Errol E. *Nature, Mind, and Modern Science.* London: G. Allen and Unwin, 1954, 1968.

————. "Hegel's Theory of Feeling." In *New Studies in Hegel's Philosophy*, ed. Warren E. Steinkraus. New York: Holt, Rinehart and Winston, 1971.

————. *An Interpretation of Hegel's Logic.* Lanham: University Press of America, 1983.

————. *The Spirit of Hegel.* Atlantic Highlands, NJ: Humanities Press, 1993.

————. "Hegel's Anthropology," *Owl of Minerva* 25, no. 1 (1993): 5–14.

————. "How Final is Hegel's Rejection of Evolution?" In *Hegel and the Philosophy of Nature*, ed. Stephen Houlgate. Albany: State University of New York Press, 1998, 189–208.

Harris, H. S. "Introduction to the *Difference* Essay." In *Difference Between Fichte's and Schelling's System of Philosophy*, trans. H. S. Harris and W. Cerf. Albany: State University of New York Press, 1801/1977.

————. "Introduction." In *Faith and Knowledge*, trans. Walter Cerf and H. S. Harris. Albany: State University of New York Press, 1802–3/1977.

————. *Hegel's Development: Night Thoughts.* Oxford: Clarendon, 1983.

————. *Hegel: Phenomenology and System.* Indianapolis: Hackett Publishing Co., 1995.

————. "The Concept of Recognition in Hegel's Jena Manuscripts." In *Hegel's Dialectic of Desire and Recognition*, ed. John O'Neill. Albany: State University of New York Press, 1996.

————. *Hegel's Ladder: A Commentary on Hegel's Phenomenology of Spirit.* 2 Vols. Indianapolis: Hackett, 1997.

Hartmann, Heinz. *Ego Psychology and the Problems of Adaptation.* New York: International Universities Press, 1939/1958.

————. *Essays on Ego Psychology.* New York: International Universities Press, 1964.

Henrich, Dieter. "Hegels Theorie der Zufall." In *Hegel in Kontext.* Frankfurt: Suhrkamp, 1971.

————. "Fichte's Original Insight." In *Contemporary German Philosophy, Vol.1*, trans. D. Lachterman, ed. Darrell Christensen. University Park, PA: Penn State Press, 1982, 15–53.

Herzog, Patricia. "The Myth of Freud as Anti-philosopher." In *Freud: Appraisals and Reappraisals.* Hillsdale, NJ: Analytic Press, 1988, 163–189.

Hibben, J. G. *Hegel's Logic: An Essay in Interpretation.* New York: Garland Publishing, Inc., 1984.

Hölderlin, Friedrich. *Sämtliche Werke.* 7 Vols. Ed. Friedrich Beissner and Adolf Beck. Stuttgart: Kohlhammer, Cotta, 1943 (*Grosse Stuttgarter Hölderlin-Ausgabe*), Vol.7.

Houlgate, Stephen. *Freedom, Truth, and History: An Introduction to Hegel's Philosophy.* London: Routledge, 1991.

————. "Necessity and Contingency in Hegel's *Science of Logic*," *The Owl of Minerva* 27, no. 1 (1995): 37–49.

————. *Hegel and the Philosophy of Nature.* Albany: State University of New York Press, 1998, 189–208.

Hvolbel, R. H. "Was Jakob Böhme a Paracelsian?" *Hermetic Journal* 19 (Spring 1983): 6–17.

Hyppolite, Jean. "Hegel's Phenomenology and Psychoanalysis." In *New Studies in Hegel's Philosophy*, ed. W. E. Steinkraus. New York: Holt, Rinehart and Winston, 1971.

———. *Genesis and Structure of Hegel's Phenomenology of Spirit*. Trans. Samuel Cherniak and John Heckman. Evanston, IL: Northwestern University Press, 1974.

Inwood, M. J. *Hegel*. London: Routledge and Kegan Paul, 1983.

Irenaeus of Lyons, *Adversus Haereses*. 2 Vols. Ed. W. W. Harvey. Cambridge, 1857; reprint Ridgewood, NJ, 1965.

James, William. *The Principles of Psychology*. 2 Vols. New York: Dover, 1890/1950.

Jonas, Hans. *The Gnostic Religion*, 2nd Ed. Boston: Beacon Press, 1958.

Jones, Ernest. *The Life and Work of Sigmund Freud*. 3 Vols. New York: Basic Books, 1955.

Jones, Rufus M. *The Flowering of Mysticism*. New York: Macmillan, 1939.

Joseph, B. *Psychic Equilibrium and Psychic Change*. London: Tavistock Routledge, 1989.

Jung, Carl G. Letter to Rowland H., founder of Alcoholics Anonymous. From, *The Wisdom of the Dream: Carl Gustav Jung*. A Border Television/Stephen Segallar Films Co-production, 1989.

Kant, I. *Critique of Pure Reason*. Trans. N. K. Smith. New York: St. Martin's Press, 1781/1965.

———. *Critique of Judgment*. Trans. W. S. Pluhar. Indianapolis: Hacket Publishing Company, 1790/1987.

———. *Anthropologie in pragmatischer Hinsicht*. In *Kants Werke*, bd. vii. Berlin: Walter de Gruyter, 1968.

Kelly, Sean. *Individuation and the Absolute: Hegel, Jung, and the Path toward Wholeness*. New York: Paulist Press, 1993.

Kernberg, Otto. *Borderline Conditions and Pathological Narcissism*. New York: Jason Aronson, 1975.

Klein, Melanie. "Notes on some Schizoid Mechanisms," *International Journal of Psychoanalysis* 27 (1946): 99–110.

———. *Envy and Gratitude and Other Works: 1946–1963*. London: Virago Press, 1988.

Klein, M., and J. Riviere, eds. *Love, Hate, and Reparation*. New York: Norton, 1964.

Klemm, David E., and Günter Zöller, eds. *Figuring the Self*. Albany: State University of New York Press, 1997.

Kohut, Heinz. *The Analysis of the Self*. New York: International Universities Press, 1971.

———. *The Restoration of the Self*. New York: International Universities Press, 1977.

———. *How Does Analysis Cure?* Ed. A. Goldberg and P. Stepansky. Chicago: University of Chicago Press, 1984.

Kojève, Alexandre. *Introduction to the Reading of Hegel: Lectures on the Phenomenology of Spirit*. Assembled by Raymond Queneau. Ed. Allan Bloom. Trans. James H. Nichols Jr. Ithaca: Cornell University Press, 1969/1980.

Koyré, Alexander. *La Philosophie de Jacob Boehme*. New York: Franklin, 1968; originally published in Paris: Vrin, 1929; reissued, 1979.

———. *Galileo Studies*. Brighton: Harvestor, 1977.

Kristeva, Julia. "Woman's Time." In *The Kristeva Reader*, ed. Tori Moi. Oxford: Blackwell, 1986.

Lacan, J. *Écrits: A Selection*. Trans. Alan Sheridan. New York: Norton, 1977.

Lange, Wilhelm. *Hölderlin: Eine Pathographie*. Stuttgart: Enke, 1909.

Lauer, Quentin. *A Reading of Hegel's Phenomenology of Spirit*. New York: Fordham University Press, 1976.

Lear, Jonathan. *Love and Its Place in Nature: A Philosophical Interpretation of Freudian Psychoanalysis*. New York: Noonday Press, 1990.

———. *Open Minded: Working Out the Logic of the Soul*. Cambridge: Harvard University Press, 1998.

Levin, J. D. *Theories of the Self*. Washington, DC: Hemisphere Publishing Corporation, 1992.

Levy, Donald. *Freud Among the Philosophers*. New Haven: Yale University Press, 1996.

Leibniz, G. W. *New Essays on Human Understanding*. Trans. and ed. Peter Remnant and Jonathan Bennett. Cambridge: Cambridge University Press, 1981.

Lichtenberg, Joseph. *Psychoanalysis and Motivation*. Hillsdale, NJ: Analytic Press, 1989.

Lucas, Hans-Christian. "The 'Sovereign Ingratitude' of Spirit Toward Nature," *Owl of Minerva* 23, no. 2 (1992): 131–150.

MacIntyre, Alasdair. *The Unconscious: A Conceptual Study*. London: Routledge, 1958.

MacVannei, John Angus. *Hegel's Doctrine of the Will*. New York: AMS Press, Inc., 1967.

Masterson, James F. *The Narcissistic and Borderline Disorders*. New York: Brunner/Mazel, 1981.

McTaggart, J. *A Commentary on Hegel's Logic*. New York: Russell and Russell, Inc., 1964.

Meissner, W. W. "The Self as Structural," *Psychoanalysis and Contemporary Thought* 23, no. 3 (2000): 373–416.

Merkel, Ingrid. "Aurora; or, The Rising Sun of Allegory: Hermetic Imagery in the Work of Jakob Böhme." In *Hermeticism and the Renaissance: Intellectual History and the Occult in early Modern Europe*, ed. I. Merkel and A. G. Debus. Washington, DC: Folger Shakespeare Library, 1988, 302–310.

Mills, Jon. "Hegel on the Unconscious Abyss: Implications for Psychoanalysis," *The Owl of Minerva* 28, no. 1 (1996): 59–75.

————. "The False Dasein: From Heidegger to Sartre and Psychoanalysis," *Journal of Phenomenological Psychology* 28, no. 1 (1997): 42–65.

————. Review of Donald Levy's *Freud Among the Philosophers, The Psychoanalytic Quarterly* 4 (1998): 733–737.

————. "Theosophic and Neo-Platonic Influences on Hegel's Theory of the Unconscious Abyss," *Colloquia Manilana: Interdisciplinary Journal of the Philippine Dominican Center of Institutional Studies* VI (1998): 25–44.

————. "Hegel on the Unconscious Soul," *Science et Esprit* 52, no. 3 (2000): 321–340.

————. "Hegel and Freud on Psychic Reality," *Journal of the Society for Existential Analysis* 12, no. 1 (2000): 159–183.

————. "Hegel on Projective Identification: Implications for Klein, Bion, and Beyond," *The Psychoanalytic Review* 87, no. 6 (2000): 841–874.

————. "Dialectical Psychoanalysis: Toward Process Psychology," *Psychoanalysis and Contemporary Thought* 23, no. 3 (2000): 20–54.

————. "*Homo Homini Lupus*: Hegel and Freud on the Future of Humanity." In *The Future of Value Inquiry*, ed. Matti Häyry and Tuija Takala. Amsterdam-New York: Rodopi, 2002.

Mitchell, Stephen A. *Relational Concepts in Psychoanalysis: An Integration.* Cambridge: Harvard University Press, 1988.

Moggach, Douglas. "Reciprocity, Elicitation, Recognition: The Thematics of Intersubjectivity in the Early Fichte," *Dialogue: Canadian Philosophical Review* 38, no. 2 (1999): 271–296.

Mure, G. R. G. *Introduction to Hegel.* Oxford: Clarendon, 1940.

Neuhouser, Frederick. "Deducing Desire and Recogntion in the *Phenomenology of Spirit*," *Journal of the History of Philosophy* 24, no. 2 (1986): 243–264.

————. *Fichte's Theory of Subjectivity.* Cambridge: Cambridge University Press, 1990.

Nicolin, F. "Ein Hegelsches Fragment zur Philosophie des Geistes," *Hegel-Studien* (1961): 1, 9–15.

————. "Hegels Arbeiten zur Theorie des subjektiven Geistes." In *Erkenntnis und Verantwortung: Festschrift für Theodor Litt*, ed. J. Derbolav and F. Nicolin. Düsseldorf, 1960, 356–374.

Nissim-Sabat, M. "The Crisis in Psychoanalysis: Resolution through Husserlian Phenomenology and Feminism," *Human Studies* 14 (1991): 33–66.

Noy, P. "Metapsychology as a Multimodal System," *International Review of Psychoanalysis* 4 (1977): 1–12.

O'Connell, David O., ed. *G. W. F. Hegel.* New York: Twayne Publishers, 1996.

Ogden, Thomas G. *Projective Identification and Psychotherapeutic Technique.* New York: Jason Aronson, 1982.

Ogden, Thomas H. *The Matrix of the Mind*. Northvale, NJ: Aronson, 1986.

————. *The Primitive Edge of Experience*. Northvale, NJ: Aronson, 1989.

————. *Subjects of Analysis*. Northvale, NJ: Aronson, 1994.

Olson, Alan M. *Hegel and the Spirit: Philosophy as Pneumatology*. Princeton: Princeton University Press, 1992.

O'Neill, John, ed. *Hegel's Dialectic of Desire and Recognition*. Albany: State University of New York Press, 1996.

Orange, Donna M. *Emotional Understanding*. New York: Guilford Press, 1995.

Orange, Donna M., George Atwood, and Robert D. Stolorow. *Working Intersubjectively: Contextualism in Psychoanalytic Practice*. Hillsdale, NJ: The Analytic Press, 1997.

Pao, Ping-Nie. *Schizophrenic Disorders: Theory and Treatment from a Psychodynamic Point of View*. New York: International Universities Press, 1979.

Peuckert, Will-Erich. *Das Leben Jakob Böhmes*. Jena: E. Dieterichs, 1924.

Pine, Fred. *Drive, Ego, Object, & Self*. New York: Basic Books, 1990.

Pinkard, Terry. *Hegel's Dialectic*. Philadelphia: Temple University Press, 1988.

————. *Hegel's Phenomenology: The Sociality of Reason*. Cambridge: Cambridge University Press, 1994.

Pippin, Robert B. *Hegel's Idealism: The Satisfactions of Self-Consciousness*. Cambridge: Cambridge University Press, 1989.

Plato. *Gorgias*. In *The Collected Dialogues of Plato*, ed. Edith Hamilton and Huntington Cairns. Princeton: Princeton University Press, 1961.

————. *Phaedrus*. In *The Collected Dialogues of Plato*, ed. Edith Hamilton and Huntington Cairns. Princeton: Princeton University Press, 1961.

————. *Republic*. In *The Collected Dialogues of Plato*, ed. Edith Hamilton and Huntington Cairns. Princeton: Princeton University Press, 1961.

————. *Laws*. In *The Collected Dialogues of Plato*, ed. Edith Hamilton and Huntington Cairns. Princeton: Princeton University Press, 1961.

Plotinus. *Enneads*, Vol. 5, bk.1.

Rangell, Leo. "Into the Second Psychoanalytic Century. One psychoanalysis or Many? The Unitary Theory of Leo Rangell, M.D.," *Journal of Clinical Psychoanalysis* 6 (1977): 451–612.

————. "Psychoanalysis at the Millennium: A Unitary Theory," *Psychoanalytic Psychology* 17, no. 3 (2000): 451–466.

Rauch, Leo, and David Sherman. *Hegel's Phenomenology of Self-Consciousness: Text and Commentary*. Albany: State University of New York Press, 1999.

Rapaport, David. *The Structure of Psychoanalytic Theory: A Systematizing Attempt*. Psychological Issues, Monograph 6, Vol. II(2). New York: International Universities Press, 1960.

Redding, Paul. *Hegel's Hermeneutics*. Ithaca: Cornell University Press, 1996.

Reisner, Steven. "Eros Reclaimed: Recovering Freud's Relational Theory." In *Relational Perspectives in Psychoanalysis*, ed. N. J. Skolnick and S. C. Warshaw. Hillsdale, NJ: 1992, 281–312.

Ricoeur, P. *Freud and Philosophy*. New Haven: Yale University Press, 1970.

Robinson, D. N. *Toward a Science of Human Nature*. New York: Columbia University Press, 1982.

Rockmore, Tom. *On Hegel's Epistemology and Contemporary Philosophy*. Atlantic Highlands, NJ: Humanities Press, 1996.

———. *Cognition: An Introduction to Hegel's Phenomenology of Spirit*. Berkeley: University of California Press, 1997.

Rosenkranz, Karl. *G. W. F. Hegels Leben*. Berlin: Duncker und Humbolt Verlag, 1844; reprint, Darmstadt: Wissenschaftliche Buchgesellschaft, 1977.

Rudolph, Kurt. *Gnosis: The Nature and History of Gnosticism*. San Francisco: Harper & Row, 1977.

Russon, John. *The Self and its Body in Hegel's* Phenomenology of Spirit. Toronto: University of Toronto Press, 1997.

Sallis, John. *Spacings of Reason and Imagination: In Texts of Kant, Fichte, Hegel*. Chicago: University of Chicago Press, 1987.

Sartre, J. P. *Being and Nothingness*. Trans. H. E. Barnes. New York: Washington Square Press, 1956.

Sarup, Madan. *Jacques Lacan*. Toronto: University of Toronto Press, 1992.

Schelling, F. W. J. *Sämmtliche Werke*. 14 Vols. Ed. K. F. A. Schelling. Stuttgart and Augsburg: Cotta, 1856–1861.

———. *System des transzendentalen Idealismus*. Trans. Peter Heath. *System of Transcendental Idealism*. Charlottesville: University Press of Virginia, 1800/1978.

———. *Ages of the World*, A Fragment, from Writings Left in Manuscript. Trans. Frederick de Wolfe Bolman. New York: AMS Press, 1967.

———. *Die Weltalter* (second draft, 1813). Trans. Judith Norman. In Slavoj Žižek and F. W. J. Von Schelling, *The Abyss of Freedom/Ages of the World*. Ann Arbor: University of Michigan Press, 1997.

———. *On the History of Modern Philosophy*, Munich lectures of 1833–1834. Trans. Andrew Bowie. Cambridge: Cambridge University Press, 1994.

Simpson, Peter. *Hegel's Transcendental Induction*. Albany: State University of New York Press, 1998.

Snow, Dale. "The Role of the Unconscious in Schelling's System of Transcendental Idealism," *Idealistic Studies* 19, no. 3 (1989): 231–250.

Solomon, Robert C. "Hegel's Concept of *Geist*." In *Hegel: A Collection of Critical Essays*. Ed. A. MacIntyre. Garden City, NY: Anchor Doubleday, 1972, 125–149.

————. *Introducing the German Idealists*. Indianapolis: Hackett, 1981.

————. *In the Spirit of Hegel*. New York: Oxford University Press, 1983.

Stepelevich, Lawrence S., and David Lamb, eds. *Hegel's Philosophy of Action*. Atlantic Highlands, NJ: Humanities Press, 1983.

Stern, Daniel. *The Interpersonal World of the Infant*. New York: Basic Books, 1985.

————. *Unformulated Experience: From Dissociation to Imagination in Psychoanalysis*. Hillsdale, NJ: The Analytic Press, 1997.

Stierlin, Helm. "Lyrical Creativity and Schizophrenic Psychosis as Reflected in Friedrich Hölderlin's Fate." In *Friedrich Hölderlin, An Early Modern*, ed. Emery E. George. Ann Arbor: University of Michigan Press, 1972.

Stolorow, Robert, and George Atwood. *Contexts of Being: The Intersubjective Foundations of Psychological Life*. Hillsdale, NJ: The Analytic Press, 1992.

Stolorow, Robert, B. Brandchaft, and George Atwood. *Psychoanalytic Treatment: An Intersubjective Approach*. Hillsdale, NJ: The Analytic Press, 1987.

Stolorow, Robert, Donna Orange, and George Atwood. "World Horizons: A Post-Cartesian Alternative to the Freudian Unconscious," *Contemporary Psychoanalysis* 37, no. 1 (2001): 43–61.

Sulloway, Frank. *Freud: Biologist of the Mind*. Cambridge: Harvard University Press, 1979.

Tansey, Michael J., and Walter F. Burke. *Understanding Countertransference: From Projective Identification to Empathy*. Hillsdale, NJ: Analytic Press, 1989.

Taylor, C. *Hegel*. Cambridge: Cambridge University Press, 1975/1995.

ver Eecke, Wilfred. "Hegel as Lacan's Source for Necessity in Psychoanalytic Theory." In *Interpreting Lacan*, ed. J. H. Smith and W. Kerrigan. New Haven: Yale University Press, 1983.

Verene, Donald Phillip. *Hegel's Recollection: A Study of Images in the* Phenomenology of Spirit. Albany: State University of New York Press, 1985.

von der Luft, Eric. "Comment." In *History and System: Hegel's Philosophy of History*, ed. Robert L. Perkins. Albany: State University of New York Press, 1994.

von Hartmann, Eduard. *Philosophy of the Unconscious*. Trans. W. C. Coupland. New York: Hartcourt, Brace and Company, 1868/1931.

Wagner, Richard. *Tristan and Isolde*. London: English National Opera Guide/John Calder Publishers, 1981.

Walsh, David. "The Historical Dialectic of Spirit: Jacob Boehme's Influence on Hegel." In *History and System: Hegel's Philosophy of History*, ed. Robert L. Perkins. Albany: State University of New York Press, 1994.

Wartenberg, T. E. "Hegel's Idealism: The Logic of Conceptuality." In *The Cambridge Companion to Hegel*, ed. F. C. Beider. New York: Cambridge University Press, 1993.

Weeks, Andrew. *Boehme: An Intellectual Biography of the Seventeenth-Century Philosopher and Mystic.* Albany, State University of New York Press, 1991.

Whitehead, Alfred North. *Process and Reality.* Corrected Edition. Ed. D. R. Griffin and D. W. Sherburne. New York: Free Press, 1929/1978.

Willock, Brent. "The Comparative-Integrative Perspective in Psychoanalysis." Paper presentation at Ontario Psychological Association annual conference, February 22, 2001.

Winnicott, D. W. *D.W. Winnicott, Collected Papers.* London: Tavistock, 1958.

———. *The Maturational Processes and the Facilitating Environment.* London: Hogarth Press, 1965.

———. *Playing and Reality.* London: Tavistock, 1971.

Wittgenstein, Ludwig. *The Blue and Brown Books.* Oxford: Blackwell, 1958. First dictated in 1933–1934.

———. "Conversations on Freud." In *Lectures and Conversations on Aesthetics, Psychology, and Religious Belief,* ed. C. Barrett. Berkeley: University of California Press, 1966.

Wollheim, Richard. *Sigmund Freud.* New York: Cambridge University Press, 1971.

Wood, Allen W. *Hegel's Ethical Thought.* Cambridge: Cambridge University Press, 1990.

Zeddies, Timothy J. "Within, Outside, and In Between: The Relational Unconscious," *Psychoanalytic Psychology* 17, no. 3 (2000): 467–487.

Žižek, Slavoj. *Tarrying with the Negative.* Durham: Duke University Press, 1993.

———. *The Abyss of Freedom.* In Slavoj Žižek, and F. W. J. Von Schelling, *The Abyss of Freedom/Ages of the World.* Ann Arbor: University of Michigan Press, 1997.

Zöller, Günter. "Original Duplicity: The Ideal and the Real in Fichte's Transcendental Theory of the Subject." In *The Modern Subject: Conceptions of the Self in Classical German Philosophy,* ed. Karl Ameriks and Dieter Sturma. Albany: State University of New York Press, 1995.

———. "An Eye for an I: Fichte's Transcendental Experiment." In *Figuring the Self: Subject, Absolute, and Others in Classical German Philosophy,* ed. D. E. Klemm and G. Zöller. Albany: State University of New York Press, 1997.

SUBJECT INDEX

AUTHOR INDEX